01/03

Comic Book Nation

COMIC BOO

K NATION

The Transformation of Youth Culture
in America

Bradford W. Wright

THE JOHNS HOPKINS UNIVERSITY PRESS   BALTIMORE & LONDON

© 2001 The Johns Hopkins
University Press
All rights reserved. Published 2001
Printed in the United States of America
on acid-free paper
9 8 7 6 5 4 3 2 1

The Johns Hopkins University Press
2715 North Charles Street
Baltimore, Maryland 21218-4363
www.press.jhu.edu

Library of Congress Cataloging-in-
Publication Data

Wright, Bradford W., 1968–
Comic book nation : the transformation
of youth culture in America / Bradford W.
Wright.
    p.   cm.
Includes bibliographical references and
index.
ISBN 0-8018-6514-X (alk. paper)
1. Comic books, strips, etc.—United
States—History—20th century.
2. Comic books and children—United
States. I. Title.
PN6725 .W74 2001
741.5'0973'0904—dc21

00-010277

A catalog record for this book is
available from the British Library.

for my father, Bradford Thomas Wright

Contents

Preface

Few works of historical scholarship can truly claim to represent a lifetime of research as this one does. Long before I became a historian, I read comic books—many comic books. I could not have been more than four years old when my father returned from the corner store with my first handful of comic books. One was *The Mighty Thor*, and several were issues of *The Amazing Spider-Man*—one of which also featured the Incredible Hulk. The Thor comic book had a lot of monsters in it, and they scared me. But the Spider-Man comic books were absolutely amazing. Everything about them fascinated me: the costumes, the superpowers, the characters, and the fantasy. I was hooked. The remainder of my childhood was consumed with superhero comic books, cartoons, action figures, Halloween costumes, coloring books, and anything else I could coax my parents and grandparents into buying for me. After I'd grown old enough to earn an allowance, most of it went directly into comic book purchases. I knew that comic books had led me to enjoy reading and writing at an early age, but I had no idea that I was beginning the initial research for my first book on American cultural history.

I was born in Burlington, Vermont, on 30 May 1968, in-between the assassinations of Martin Luther King Jr. and Robert Kennedy. Growing up, I lived most of the clichés associated with the post–Vietnam/Watergate era and the so-called Generation X: my baby-boom parents divorced when I was four years old, I learned to be cynical about human relationships, government, corporations, and leaders of most kinds, and I indulged myself in the pleasures of mass culture. Most of all, I immersed myself in comic books. Therein I found heroes more "believable" than those in real life, and I discovered a fantasy world that made more sense than the real one. When I grew old enough to contemplate such things, I learned that those comic books had not only afforded me an escape from a confusing reality, they had helped me to perceive reality in terms that I could understand and accept.

Comic books helped me to define myself and my world in a way that made both far less frightening. I honestly cannot imagine how I would have navigated my way through childhood without them.

As a small child I knew how important comic books were to my world, but my first inkling that they had some wider significance came just shy of my ninth birthday. I was traveling with my father on my first trip across Europe, and we were about to cross from West Berlin into the Eastern sector. At the checkpoint, an East German border guard searched our car and confiscated my comic books. He simply thumbed through the issues of *Spider-Man*, *The Incredible Hulk*, and *Captain America* and then tossed them into a bin. That was the last I ever saw of them. I was confused and upset. My father was heartbroken and at least as upset, but he was wise enough not to make much of a fuss about it with the guard. We spent a miserable couple of hours in East Berlin and returned to the West with an anecdote that became a Wright family legend. Traumatic as it all was at the time, I was able to replace most of my lost comic books within a short while. But I still wondered what it was about those comic books that had led the guard to take them. It was not until much later that I realized how they epitomized so much of what was attractive and possible in the advanced consumer culture of the West. Their sheer thrill and accessibility made them subversive in the Communist society of that border guard. Of course, there is a good chance that he was merely taking them to sell on the black market or give to his own children. If the latter was the case, perhaps some of those same children, nurtured on American superheroes and dreams of Western consumption, helped to tear down the Berlin Wall in 1989. I like to think so, at least.

I continued to read comic books throughout my teenage years and into college, although they gradually became a smaller part of my life. I always enjoyed the fantasy world of superheroes but never considered myself a true collector, because I did not have the money or inclination to approach comic books as a serious investment. I simply read them for enjoyment, and, when they became less enjoyable and more expensive, I slowly grew out of them—or so I thought.

I took my traditional undergraduate training in history into graduate school, expecting to pursue research in European diplomatic history. Searching for a paper topic in a seminar on mass culture in post-industrial America, however, opened my eyes to an aspect of the American experience that had been remarkably neglected by scholars. Even more remarkable, I had neglected it in my own historical studies. Comic books had been around since the 1930s, but virtually nothing scholarly had been written about them. The apparent unavailability of sources probably deterred some, but more likely the dearth of serious research simply betrayed a tendency among historians (far more pervasive then than now) to dismiss something as ephemeral and apparently unimportant as comic books. But I knew that comic books were of great importance. I could not imagine my own youth without them, and certainly they had played a large part in other lives as well. Now comic books were about to transform my life once again.

I switched my graduate study emphasis to American history and commenced scholarly research into comic books as cultural history. How have political, cultural, and economic factors intersected to make comic books? What do comic books suggest about the changing world of young people? How does the history of these comic books contribute to our understanding of consumer culture? What is their significance in American culture? The pursuit of these questions has been a challenging but enormously fun and revelatory experience that culminates in this study. And while the years of research and analysis have made it difficult for me to ever simply "enjoy" reading a comic book again, this scholarly inquiry has ultimately confirmed what I first realized as a young boy: comic books are cool!

Researching and writing a book is often a lonely endeavor, and this project was no exception. Nevertheless, I benefited from the assistance, advice, and support of a number of individuals. Randall Scott and Jerry Paulins at Michigan State University in East Lansing were extraordinarily generous and helpful during the research and finishing stages of this work. I wish also to thank Robert J. Brugger at the Johns Hopkins University Press for his early interest in this project and Celestia Ward for her thorough editing and numerous helpful suggestions. This study benefited from supporting grants awarded by the Purdue Research Foundation. I especially thank Randy Roberts, professor of history at Purdue University. He was a wonderful adviser for this project, and his longtime enthusiastic encouragement inspired me to undertake it in the first place.

Also in the Department of History at Purdue, I benefited at various times from the advice and assistance of Michael Morrison, James Farr, Vernon Williams, Jon Teaford, Gunther Rothenberg, Nancy Gabin, John Contreni, and John Larson. William Bettler offered welcome interdisciplinary insight as a scholar in Communications and gave generous support as a close friend. Arthur Leighton, Eric Fisher, and Greg Rose contributed their valuable observations as informed readers of comic books. Angela Firkus lent indispensable emotional support and provided equally crucial lessons in basic computer skills.

I also wish to acknowledge the special contributions of those closest to me. Dylan Wright, Caitlin Wright, and Jeff Manley each offered their unique and valuable perspectives on youth culture. My mother, Lorraine Cota Manley, helped me to acquire many of the original "research materials" cited in this study by paying me a weekly allowance and driving me to the local drug store. I have also benefited tremendously from her love, support, and creativity. And I especially wish to thank my father, Bradford Thomas Wright, to whom this book is dedicated. A poet, teacher, and historian, he has been my greatest inspiration. His love, encouragement, and pride always made me feel like a superhero.

Introduction

Few enduring expressions of American popular culture are so instantly recognizable and still so poorly understood as comic books. They have a lengthy history, approximating that of talking motion pictures. They are sold in thousands of outlets and sit in millions of homes. They have figured into the childhoods of most Americans born since the 1920s. They have produced cultural icons recognized in every corner of the globe. And yet they remain inscrutable to most adults, including scholars. The average thirteen-year-old displays more knowledge about the topic than the average professor of history, even a professor of cultural history.

This is because comic books are ultimately a generational experience. For the most part, they are the domain of young people, who inevitably outgrow them, recall them fondly, and then look at the comic books of their own children and grandchildren with a mixture of bewilderment and, perhaps, concern. Just as each generation writes its own history, each reads its own comic books. The two activities are not unrelated, for comic books are history. Emerging from the shifting interaction of politics, culture, audience tastes, and the economics of publishing, comic books have helped to frame a worldview and define a sense of self for the generations who have grown up with them. They have played a crucial explanatory, therapeutic, and commercial function in young lives. To critically examine the history of comic books is to better understand the changing world of young people as well as the historical forces intersecting to shape it.

Comic books first emerged as a distinct entertainment medium in the 1930s. They communicate narratives through a unique combination of text and sequential illustration that works within its own aesthetic vocabulary. Although they are often grouped together with comic strips, the two mediums are not the same. The key difference lies in marketing. Whereas comic strips are a syndicated feature in newspapers sold to a mass and mostly adult audience, comic books are created, distributed, and sold on their own merits to a paying and over-whelmingly young audience. Although there is some overlap between the two (comic strips have been packaged as comic books, and a few comic book features have been syndicated as comic strips), these differ-ent marketing practices and target audiences have given each medium its own distinctive look and character. The content and themes explored in comic books have diverged drastically from those of comic strips. The term *comic book*, in fact, is one of the great misnomers in entertainment, for they are not books and often are not comical. They have explored virtually every genre of popular entertainment, including adventure, horror, mystery, crime, romance, the western, and humor. But they are most closely associated with superheroes. And it is with fantastic heroes like Superman, Batman, and Spider-Man that comic books have made their most lucrative, influential, and enduring contri-butions to American culture.

Some highly accomplished literary and artistic work has been done in comic books. Laudatory writing by comic book fans and fan-scholars has tended to accentuate these qualities in an effort to make the case for comic books as a mature art form worthy of serious critical evalua-tion. Such an emphasis, however, distracts from the fact that the vast majority of comic books produced over the years has amounted to junk culture cranked out by anonymous creators who had little more than a paycheck on their minds. Comic books epitomize the accessibility, disposability, and appeal to instant gratification that lie at the core of modern consumer culture. To classify comic books as "junk," however, is not to put them down or imply that they have nothing to say. On the contrary, their perennial lowbrow status has allowed them to develop and thrive outside of the critical, aesthetic, and commercial criteria ex-pected of more "mature" media. That development accounts for their wonderful appeal to young people as well as their unique historical sig-nificance. For in these garish comic book images, one glimpses a crude, exaggerated, and absurd caricature of the American experience tailored for young tastes. They offer a revealing fun-house mirror of life, not necessarily as it was or even as it should be but as young people have paid to see it. In this respect, comic books have long predicted the course of consumer culture, a culture so advanced now that it becomes increasingly difficult to discern the reality of our world from the array of images that represent it in our popular culture.

Much of the current scholarship on comic books—and there has not been a great deal—has been produced outside of the historical discipline and without much attention to historical context. This left many avenues open for inquiry in my study. First of all, this is a cultural history that seeks to deepen our understanding of the interaction between politics, social change, and popular culture. Accomplishing this requires a close and critical analysis of comic book formulas. The preeminent factor shaping comic books has been the commercial motive of publishers to craft a product that appeals to paying audiences. Because the cover price and profit potential of individual comic books has historically been very low, publishers have tended to emphasize product quantity over the quality of individual works. This has promoted an incessant search for narrative formulas that can be easily duplicated with minimal variation and expense. Yet for formulas to succeed, they must also speak adequately to the concerns and expectations of their audience.

My working definition of *formulas* is close to that advanced by John G. Cawelti, who summarizes them as "ways in which specific cultural themes and stereotypes become embodied in more universal story archetypes."[1] Audiences turn to formulaic stories for the escape and enjoyment that comes from experiencing the fulfillment of their expectations within a structured imaginary world. While I do not perceive the market as a purely free exchange in which producers simply give the audience "what it wants," there is a certain democratic, or Darwinian, axiom in the entertainment industry that leads popular ideas to prevail over unpopular ones. Put simply, formulas that appeal to audiences tend to proliferate and endure, while those that do not, do neither. As a means through which changing values and assumptions are packaged into mass commodities, formulas are the consequence of determining pressures exerted by producers and consumers, as well as by the historical conditions affecting them both. Formulas, therefore, are essentially historical constructions, and they are central to understanding comic books as history.

Second, by employing comic books as a primary source, I hope to illuminate a revealing but neglected set of documents to reinforce or challenge what we know about historical American perceptions. Mine is not the first work to do something like this. In his pioneering *Comic Books and America, 1945–1954* (Norman: University of Oklahoma Press, 1990), William W. Savage Jr. undertook "an initial effort to employ comic books as primary sources . . . in connection with topics of concern in postwar America."[2] Remarkably, few cultural historians have since incorporated his suggestions and research into their own. By expanding upon Savage's range of consideration and differing with some of his conclusions, I add to the research and insights from which historians can draw, and hopefully my work will encourage them to do so. Any scholar seeking to test how deeply popular assumptions about issues like the New Deal, the Vietnam War, and gender roles penetrated into the American consciousness ought to consider what comic books had to say about those topics.

Third, my study opens a window into the world of young people—a world that the traditional print sources commonly used by historians can do little to illuminate. Comic books have always been the domain of the young: children, adolescents, and young adults. Generally fashioned for an adolescent audience by creators often little older, comic books have spoken to youths' concerns and sensibilities with a consistency and directness that few, if any, other entertainment media can claim. Although aesthetic criticism tends to compare comic books with visual media like film, culturally they have more in common with rock-and-roll music. Like rock-and-roll, comic books responded to the emergence of adolescents as a discrete market with tastes and preoccupations of its own, sometimes in direct conflict with the mores of mainstream adult culture. Comic books, in fact, preceded rock-and-roll by two decades as one of the first entertainment products marketed directly to children and adolescents instead of their parents.

Before television became a fixture in the American home, comic books were the foremost medium of youth entertainment. Indeed, the astonishing proliferation of comic books, especially during the postwar decade, prompted a variety of parents, politicians, civic groups, child-study experts, and other traditional shapers of youth character to link them with a perceived rise in juvenile delinquency. Viewing certain comic books as the harbingers of a degenerate and disturbingly confrontational youth culture, concerned adults launched widespread efforts to control and censor them. While echoes of this mid-twentieth-century controversy resonate into the twenty-first century in debates over the link between violent images in popular culture and a rash of especially horrific juvenile crimes, the youth market has actually grown ever more expansive and influential—to the point where American culture itself has arguably become "juvenilized." The cultural history of comic books thus helps to trace the emergence, challenge, and triumph of adolescence as both a market and a cultural obsession.

Because economic considerations are so crucial to the production of mass culture, I also explore some of the internal workings of the comic book industry. This is not really a "business history," at least not in the traditional sense, but I do devote attention to the key individuals and economics of the industry in order to provide important context and indicate where such discussion has a direct bearing on the emergence, persistence, or disappearance of trends in the comic books. Consideration of comic books as a business is necessary to piece together the broad historical context working to shape the final products.

Finally, there is a rather nonscholarly imperative informing my study: it's fun. Readers should recognize some of the comic books from their own youth in here. Besides sparking some nostalgia, this will hopefully lead people to reflect anew on the popular culture that worked to shape their own worldview during childhood and perhaps beyond. The cultural history of comic books reminds us that historical inquiry need not be defined only by abstract ideas and distant personalities. On the contrary, exploring a topic such as this reveals just how deeply the currents of history run and better locates one's own experiences within the stream.

Mine is not an aesthetic history of comic books. Because I am concerned primarily with comic books as a cultural representation, not as an art form, I emphasize narrative content over graphic qualities. Certainly the two are bound together in this medium, but I hold to the assumption that most comic books succeed or fail on the merits of their storytelling. The marketing of comic books solely on the appeal of style, without regard to the stories, is a relatively recent development that has not served the industry well. I briefly discuss the contributions of important artists who left a mark on the craft of comic book storytelling, but fans and collectors will notice the short shrift given to some of their favorites.

Likewise, I do not consider all types of comic books. While I have researched many thousands of comic books in preparing this work, I confess to having made some compromises in breadth to allow space for greater depth on topics of interest. Because my concern lies with popular commercial comic books, I have not discussed the many underground, "adult," and self-published comic books that have appeared sporadically since the late 1960s. On the other extreme, I chose not to include the many funny animal, cartoon, and teen-humor series in this study. While titles like *Donald Duck*, *Richie Rich*, and *Archie* have enjoyed very large preteen audiences, they all possess a certain timeless and unchanging appeal for young children that makes them relatively unhelpful for the purposes of a cultural history. I do not suggest that these are irrelevant or have nothing to say about their times, only that there is far more fertile ground in exploring those comic books aimed at a slightly older audience—readers who, in other words, have reached a developmental stage at which they are capable of perceiving texts within a broader social and political context. Adolescents have, in fact, been the primary market driving the dynamics of the industry.

The question of exactly what impact entertainment has on an audience emerges inevitably from a study like this. I have not tried to assess precisely how audiences read these comic books or what direct influence the reading may have had on them, because, frankly, I do not know how it can be done in any meaningful way. Consuming entertainment, much like listening to a political speech or reading a newspaper, is ultimately a very personal and idiosyncratic experience. Ten individuals can read a comic book, watch a movie, or listen to a song and come away with ten completely different impressions, interpretations, and influences. While I am familiar with a number of theoretical approaches to "decoding" the meaning of popular texts, I find few of these very compelling, and I confess to finding more than a few bewildering and tedious. My basic theoretical assumption regarding audience is the rather simple but well-grounded contention that audiences consume particular forms of entertainment because they hope to find something pleasurable in the experience. I also assume that there are elements of any narrative that are very difficult for friendly or hostile audiences to miss. One viewer may enjoy the movie *Titanic* for the romance, and another may deplore the violence in it, but both would surely notice the basic class conflict between the poor heroes and the rich villains, and both would agree that the ship does indeed sink. In other words, while popular culture certainly merits close scrutiny, I believe that there are intellectual pitfalls in analyzing something like comic books too deeply. Therefore, I have confined my reading to meanings that were easily perceived by audiences, clearly intended by producers, or suggestive of broad historical developments and cultural assumptions. There are enough of those meanings to easily fill a book like this without one having to "decode" anything.

Readers ought to be familiar with a few preliminary notes on the documentation and citation of comic books. As of this writing, no standard manual of style has provided a form for the citation of comic books. I accept the form established by William W. Savage Jr. in *Comic Books and America, 1945–1954*. Each citation from a comic book includes the title of the story or feature referenced, the title of the comic book in which it appears, the series number of the issue, the publisher, and the issue's cover date. To prolong the shelf life of their comic books, publishers have traditionally postdated their issues by several months.

Thus, a comic book with a cover date of March 1941 likely appeared on newsstands just before the end of 1940. Because pagination in comic books is inconsistent and generally irrelevant, citations include no page numbers. In most cases, the examples cited represent general trends that appeared in dozens, if not hundreds, of other comic books. Where such examples are the exception to trends rather than the rule, I have so noted.

DC Comics and Marvel Comics are the two oldest and most important comic book publishers, and both have gone by different names throughout their long histories. For the first forty years of its existence, DC's company name was National Periodical Publications. Marvel was known as Timely Comics from 1939 to about 1950 and as Atlas Comics during most of the 1950s. Both have also consistently published comic books under their more familiar logos of DC and Marvel. To underscore the continuity of these operations and avoid confusion, I refer to them throughout simply as DC Comics and Marvel Comics.

Comic Book Nation

1
Superheroes
for the Common Man

**The Birth of the
Comic Book Industry,
1933–1941**

It's a simple story, as familiar as any in the English language. A doomed planet explodes. A scientist places his infant son in a rocket ship destined for Earth. An elderly couple, the Kents, adopt the boy and name him Clark. Growing up, the youth demonstrates awesome abilities. He can leap tall buildings, bend steel in his bare hands, and outrun speeding locomotives. Fortunately, he pledges to champion truth, justice, and the American way. To the unsuspecting world, Clark Kent may appear to be just another mild-mannered reporter for a great metropolitan newspaper, but he is no ordinary man. He is, of course, Superman.[1]

Superman may have arrived from a distant planet, but his real origins lay in Cleveland, Ohio. It was there in 1934 that two high-school students and aspiring comic strip writers named Jerry Siegel and Joe Shuster created the character. Lower-middle-class, second-generation Jewish immigrants, Siegel and Shuster believed in the American dream and embraced popular culture. Shy and unpopular in school, unsuccessful with girls, and insecure about their bespectacled appearance and physical abilities, they read body-building magazines, lost themselves in science-fiction magazines, and nurtured fantasies of power and success.[2] If only it could be as easy as removing one's glasses. The epitome of the modern adolescent fantasy, Superman was the ideal that spawned an industry.

The Origins of the Comic Book Industry

The American comic book industry is a twentieth-century phenomenon with origins in the late nineteenth century. While the juxtaposition of words and images is as old as language itself, the nearest precursor to comic books is the newspaper comic strip, which became a familiar daily distraction for Americans as early as the 1890s. Syndicated strips like *The Yellow Kid, Katzenjammer Kids,* and *Mutt and Jeff* satirized the foibles of domestic life, social relations, and ethnicity in the tradition of vaudeville routines. Because of their humorous qualities, they became known as comic strips or "funnies." Even later, when newspaper strips and their offspring in magazine format featured serious narrative content, the term *comic* stuck. The first comic books perpetuated this trend with titles like *Famous Funnies, Funnies on Parade,* and *The Funnies.* However inappropriate it might be, the term *comic* has since referred to the medium of sequential art, regardless of the content.[3]

The earliest comic books derived directly from comic strips, but in many respects they owed more to pulp magazines. Most of the early comic book publishers, in fact, came from the pulp magazine industry. Popularly dubbed "pulp" magazines because of the cheap paper on which they were printed, these publications in turn have antecedents in the sensational dime novels of the Civil War era. Like newspaper comics, pulp magazines enjoyed great popularity during the early decades of the twentieth century, but, unlike the widely appealing comics, pulps often catered to more offbeat tastes. Most featured action, fantasy, adventure, and suspense tales written by low-priced talent. Although some pulp writers, like Edgar Rice Burroughs, Raymond Chandler, and Ray Bradbury, went on to achieve greater literary success and fame, they were the exceptions. Pulps delivered cheap thrills and made few intellectual demands on their authors and their audience. For ten to fifteen cents, readers could purchase one of as many as two hundred fifty pulp titles available at newsstands each month. Titles like *The Shadow, Captain Satan, Amazing Stories,* and *Startling Tales* sometimes went to considerable lengths in their appeal to the sense of the lurid, sadistic, and grotesque. Existing alongside the well-documented 1930s market for best-selling novels like *The Grapes of Wrath* and *Gone with the Wind* was a less-heralded audience for pulp magazine tales like "Volunteer Corpse Brigade," "Cult of the Living Carcass," and "New Girls for Satan's Blood Ballet." The proliferation of such bizarre literature during the interwar years indicates that there existed a lucrative, and mostly young, market with tastes well outside of the mainstream.[4]

In January 1929, pulp fiction met the comics when the pulp heroes
Tarzan and Buck Rogers debuted as newspaper comic strips, soon to be
followed by other adventure strips like *Dick Tracy*, *Flash Gordon*, and *The*
Phantom.[5] Also in that year, the newspaper comic strip appeared for
the first time in something resembling a pulp magazine format. Since
the turn of the century, newspaper syndicates had periodically compiled
hardcover collections of comic strip reprints for sale in bookstores. In
1929 Dell Publishing became the first to experiment with a weekly
comics magazine distributed to newsstands. The tabloid-sized publication, called *The Funnies*, featured original comic strips, puzzles, and
jokes. Dell canceled the series the next year, after thirty-six issues failed
to sell very well. But this experiment inspired other entrepreneurs to
explore the commercial potential of comics magazines.[6]

The Eastern Color Printing Company in Waterbury, Connecticut,
handled the color printing for pulp magazine covers, newspaper syndicates, and Dell's *The Funnies*. In 1933 two sales employees at Eastern
Color, Harry Wildenberg and Max Gaines, discovered that the standard seven-by-nine-inch printing plates, used to print Sunday comic
pages about twice that size, could also print two reduced comic pages
side-by-side on a tabloid-sized page. When folded in half and bound
together, these pages would fit into an economical eight-by-eleven-
inch pulp magazine of color comics. Gaines and Wildenberg proposed
that the company print such magazines for manufacturers who could
use them as advertising premiums and giveaways. Eastern Color agreed
to support the effort and printed 10,000 copies of *Funnies on Parade*
for Proctor and Gamble. After this venture succeeded, Eastern Color
followed with larger print runs of two comic books featuring reprints
of syndicated comic strips like *Mutt and Jeff* and *Joe Palooka* for Canada
Dry, Kinney Shoes, and other youth-oriented manufacturers. In 1934,
Eastern Color printed a half-million copies of *Skippy's Own Book of
Comics* for Phillips Toothpaste, which gave them away to listeners of
the *Skippy* radio show.[7]

Max Gaines suspected that comic books had market potential beyond these limited ventures. Though he was an aggressive and resourceful salesman, he had fallen into financial difficulties during the
early 1930s and saw in the comic magazines an opportunity to lift his
family out of the Depression. He persuaded Dell Publishing to finance
Eastern Color's printing of 35,000 copies of *Famous Funnies, Series 1*, a
sixty-four-page collection of comic strip reprints distributed directly to
chain stores for sale at ten cents an issue. The issue sold out, but Dell
remained cautious. Surveys of potential advertisers revealed skepticism

about the new comic magazines. Dell approached the American News Company, a national distributor based in New York City, about possible newsstand distribution. American News showed little interest, however, so Dell withdrew from the deal with Eastern Color and released its option to the name and concept of *Famous Funnies*.[8] Gaines and Eastern Color continued the project anyway, and the American News Company, encouraged perhaps by recent newspaper stories about the popularity of "the funnies," cautiously agreed to distribute 250,000 copies of *Famous Funnies, Series 2*. The first issue, cover-dated July 1934, lost Eastern Color over $4,000. The sixth issue finally turned a profit, and by the twelfth *Famous Funnies* was netting Eastern Color about $30,000 each month.[9]

Eastern Color's monopoly in the comic book field ended as soon as other publishers noticed its success. By 1938, an embryonic comic book industry comprised half a dozen publishers, most of whom were packaging reprints of newspaper comic strips. Dell Publishing reentered the comic book business in 1936 with titles like *Popular Comics*, *The Funnies*, and *The Comics*. From his new job at a printing company called the McLure Syndicate, Gaines supplied Dell with comics like *Dick Tracy*, *Little Orphan Annie*, and *Terry and the Pirates*. A businessman, not an artist, Gaines seemed to have little interest in the aesthetics of the medium that he was pioneering. His young editor Sheldon Mayer recalled that "it was a schlock operation . . . we bought the [comics] material for practically nothing and slapped it together."[10]

By 1936, newspaper syndicates that had been content to sell the printing rights to their strips for only five to seven dollars per page began to publish their own comic books. William Randolph Hearst's King Features Syndicate put out a line of comic books featuring characters like Popeye and Flash Gordon. The United Features Syndicate entered the field with reprints of its leading humor and adventure strips, *Li'l Abner* and *Tarzan*. Backed up by large capital, enjoying established distribution channels, and using characters with demonstrated market appeal, these publishers initially enjoyed the industry's highest circulation. Yet the field's future belonged not to the syndicates but to those entrepreneurs who suspected that comic books could be more than just repackaged comic strips. The future resided in the imagination and business instincts of individuals determined to somehow make comic books into a distinct entertainment medium.

In 1935, a forty-five-year-old former U.S. Army Major and pulp magazine writer named Malcolm Wheeler-Nicholson started up a small operation called National Allied Publishing. From a tiny office in New York City, Wheeler-Nicholson launched *New Fun* and *New Comics*, featuring original comic material created by freelance cartoonists. The results generally resembled standard newspaper funnies but avoided the increasingly expensive licensing fees charged by the syndicates. Remembered by his associates as an eccentric and something of a charlatan, Wheeler-Nicholson started his publishing venture without having sufficient capital or business acumen. His editor, Vincent Sullivan, recalled that Wheeler-Nicholson "wasn't a very good businessman. . . . We were struggling all the time."[11]

Advertising for freelance contributors willing to work at a rate of five dollars per page, Wheeler-Nicholson attracted young, untried cartoonists hoping to break into the comic strip field as well as experienced but unemployed illustrators needing temporary work. Despite the enthusiastic and occasionally accomplished efforts of these cartoonists, the titles sold poorly. Distributors were still loathe to handle them, vendors did not want to give them valuable newsstand space, and readers seemed wary of gambling their ten cents on a collection of unfamiliar funnies. As bundles of comic books returned to his office unsold, Wheeler-Nicholson fell increasingly into debt to his staff and, more importantly, to his distributor, the Independent News Company. In 1937, Independent's founders, Harry Donenfeld and Jack Liebowitz, entered into partnership with Wheeler-Nicholson and contributed the capital to launch a third title, *Detective Comics*. From this title, the company later took its new name, DC.[12]

As the title promised, *Detective Comics* differed from the "funny" comic books that had come before it. Announcing itself loudly on the newsstands with a sinister Oriental face leering from the cover, *Detective Comics* signaled a new direction for the industry. It featured adventure and mystery series like "Speed Saunders and the River Patrol," "Buck Regan, Spy," and "Claws of the Dragon," derived not from newspaper funnies but from movie serials and pulp fiction. Visibly more adventurous than other comic books, it contained more inventive page lay-outs, larger panels, and heavier shading to create atmosphere. Most importantly, *Detective Comics* signaled a new formula for comic books. Humor was giving way to crime-fighting.[13]

In 1938 Donenfeld and Liebowitz bought out Wheeler-Nicholson's interests in the company. Under their sound management, DC grew into a more viable publishing operation. Liebowitz managed business affairs in their New York office, while editor Vincent Sullivan supervised the work of freelance writers and artists. Their control of the

Independent News Company allowed Donenfeld and Liebowitz to circulate their own comic books and establish connections to build a solid national distribution network. The sales of their comic books, still without a marketable "star," remained unspectacular for the time being, but their investments would soon yield results far beyond anyone's expectations.[14]

To accommodate the fledgling publishers, several comic art studios—or "shops," as they were called within the industry—opened up. Staffed with editors and freelance cartoonists, the shops sold completed comic book stories to publishers who lacked the resources or knowledge to produce their own material. One of these studios was the Universal Phoenix Syndicate, or the Eisner-Iger shop, established by Will Eisner, an accomplished cartoonist in his early twenties, and S. M. Iger, an amateur cartoonist, entrepreneur, and editor of a failed entertainment magazine. Both had been struggling financially, and, according to Eisner, the two men financed the entire operation with fifteen dollars. They promptly attracted a number of clients, including a pulp magazine publisher called Fiction House and Everett M. Arnold, an entrepreneur from the printing business. Shops like this one filled a crucial function in launching the comic book industry, because, as Eisner recalled, "Most of the publishers had no way of knowing whether or not they could even produce the material; they didn't even understand how to produce it."[15]

Comic book production in the shops was a collaborative process, much like a creative assembly line. "We made comic book features pretty much the way Ford made cars," Eisner recalled. "I would write and design the characters, somebody else would pencil them in, somebody else would ink, somebody else would letter." This process contributed to the visual sameness and formulaic stories of many early comic books. After selling the completed stories to publishers and paying the freelance staff, Eisner and Iger split a net profit of $1.50 per page. It made for a small but relatively profitable business during the Depression years. As Eisner later boasted, "I got very rich before I was twenty-two."[16]

The shops attracted young cartoonists fresh out of art school and self-trained enthusiasts with little experience beyond doodling. Also on the shop staffs were older, more experienced illustrators and cartoonists who needed whatever work they could find in lean economic times, even if it meant stooping to draw crude "funny-books." Comic book work for freelancers was neither prestigious nor profitable, and it was for the most part an anonymous affair. Few artists received credits or bylines for their work, and those who did frequently used pseudonyms anyway. Publishers generally preferred their freelancers to remain anonymous so that readers would not easily notice inconsistencies resulting from staff turnover.[17] The work-for-hire system, in which the publisher claimed all rights to the characters created for its titles, further encouraged this anonymity.

Artists often did not want to be publicly associated with their comic book work in any case, fearing it would damage whatever professional reputation they hoped to achieve in other fields. In the artistic profession, comic books ranked just above pornography. Eisner recalled that the comic book industry was "a kind of artistic ghetto in which people with authentic, if offbeat talents had to suffer the disdain of the mainstream." Many of the artists approached the field "as kind of a stepping place . . . dreaming of becoming a syndicated cartoonist for the newspapers, or going into book illustration." While Eisner and his colleagues generally enjoyed their work, they did not suspect that comic books had much of a future.[18] Indeed, they may not have had, were it not for the arrival of a savior from the planet Krypton.

The Industry That Superman Built

Jerry Siegel and Joe Shuster had devised a concept destined to be popular with young readers, but the middle-aged men who ran the newspaper syndicates failed to see the appeal of Superman. The young cartoonists saw one company after another reject their proposed comic strip. To get by in the meantime, they did freelance work for the new comic book publishers. They sold adventure features like "Slam Bradley" to DC but held back Superman, still hoping to launch him as a newspaper strip.[19] In early 1938, a copy of the Superman strip was in Max Gaines's office at the McLure Syndicate, where it was about to be rejected once again and returned to the authors. Gaines's young editor, Sheldon Mayer, liked the strip but could not persuade his employer to accept it. On Mayer's recommendation, though, Gaines sent the strip to his associate Harry Donenfeld, who, with Liebowitz, was about to launch a new DC comic book title called *Action Comics*.[20] Their editor, Vincent Sullivan, proposed they use Superman as the lead feature. DC asked Siegel and Shuster if they would be willing to cut and paste the sample strips into a thirteen-page comic book story and accept payment at the rate of ten dollars per page. Having all but given up hope of ever seeing Superman in newspaper comics, Siegel and Shuster accepted the offer. As part of the deal, they signed a standard release form giving sole copyright ownership of their idea to the company. It was

an unhappy prospect, but as Siegel shrugged, "at least this way [they would] see him in print." So they sold Superman to DC for $130 and went to work on his first comic book adventure.[21]

The first issue of *Action Comics*, cover-dated June 1938, featured Superman on the cover and in the lead story. According to Mayer, Donenfeld grew concerned when he saw the cover image depicting the red-and-blue costumed Superman holding an automobile above his head. "He really got worried," Mayer recalled. "He felt nobody would believe it; that it was ridiculous—crazy." Jack Liebowitz cautiously had 200,000 copies printed but received dealers' requests for more. He kept the print run small until the fourth issue sold out. By the seventh issue, *Action Comics* was selling over half-a-million copies each month. Mayer remembered that "the reader response was immediate," and newsstand surveys revealed Superman to be the most popular feature in the title.[22] So in 1939 DC launched *Superman*, the first comic book title devoted to a single character.

Audiences familiar with the rather stiff and morally upright character that Superman later became would be surprised to discover that Siegel and Shuster's original character was actually a tough and cynical wise guy, similar to the hard-boiled detectives like Sam Spade who also became popular during the Depression years. Superman took to crime-fighting with an adolescent glee, routinely taking the opportunity to mock and humiliate his adversaries as he thrashed them. Shuster's crude artwork evinced a childlike exuberance, giving an added adolescent quality to the stories. It was a distinctly masculine fantasy, too. Superman had little use for women. When in his first adventure an attractive female killer tries to seduce him, he does not waver. Then when she tries to shoot him, he crushes the gun and threatens to do the same to her wrist. Although arguably a protofeminist character of sorts, Superman's romantic interest, Lois Lane, had few admirable qualities from a contemporary male perspective. While physically attractive and spunky, she put her career ahead of romance with the kind but boring Clark Kent and pined after Superman, whom she could never possess. Superman, on the other hand, was too strong and self-assured to succumb to the allure of a beautiful woman. Inevitably, Lois's chief function was to be captured and await rescue by her hero.[23]

Cover of *Action Comics* 1 (DC Comics, June 1938). The most important comic book ever published, DC's *Action Comics* 1 introduced the world to Superman. Art by Joe Shuster.

Siegel and Shuster, however unconsciously, had created a brilliant twentieth-century variation on a classic American hero type. The most pervasive myth in American culture is that of the Western frontier hero, who resolves tensions between the wilderness and civilization while embodying the best virtues of both environments himself. Twentieth-century popular culture has adapted the Western and frontier metaphors to meet contemporary tastes and concerns, but the explicit problems and solutions expressed in the Western myth are historically most relevant to American civilization before the twentieth century.[24] Postindustrial American society raised new tensions. Whereas heroes of the previous centuries, like Daniel Boone, Natty Bumpo, and Wyatt Earp, could conquer and tame the savage American frontier, twentieth-century America demanded a superhero who could resolve the tensions of individuals in an increasingly urban, consumer-driven, and anonymous mass society.

The distance between the American dream and reality seemed particularly large during the Great Depression. Pervasive scarcity and unemployment frustrated consumption and called into question the Victorian middle-class axiom that success follows hard work. The old heroes seemed out of touch with the suffering millions. The self-made men of yesterday, the Herbert Hoovers and Horatio Algers, had become the greedy fat-cats and "economic royalists" of the Depression. Where were the new heroes to be found? They did not emerge—as they did in other nations—from the political extremes, despite the efforts of leftist intellectuals working to forge a radical community vision and right-wing elements enamored with European fascism. Instead, the new heroes in Depression America turned out to be the American people themselves.[25]

From Depression-era popular culture, there came a passionate celebration of the common man. The idea that virtue resided within regular, unassuming Americans found expression in the novels of John Steinbeck, the films of John Ford and Frank Capra, and the compositions of Aaron Copland, as well as in the everyman qualities of Warner Brothers' Bugs Bunny cartoons and integrated big-band swing music. Folk singer Woodie Guthrie wrote new national anthems for the poor and forgotten Americans. Gangster movies of the early 1930s usurped the Victorian myth of the self-made man and perverted it into a gloriously self-destructive revenge narrative for the common man. Even real-life gangsters like John Dillinger and Bonnie and Clyde captured the imagination and vicarious sympathy of dislocated citizens who appreciated the criminals' assault on financial institutions. Despite their subversive implications, all of these cultural narratives and icons actually worked to fashion a new and more inclusive concept of American identity. They served therapeutic, patriotic, and even conservative cultural ends. For why would the common man rise up to take something that he felt was already in his possession? Franklin Roosevelt's most ardent admirers credit him with forestalling a domestic revolution during the Great Depression. But much of the credit must also go to the powerful sense of shared national purpose forged by the creators of popular culture.[26]

Into this cultural exchange entered Superman. Siegel and Shuster's comic book stories affirmed the young, alienated, and dispossessed "Clark Kents" of society in their desire to commit to an inclusive national culture. The young creators cast their superhero as a "champion of the oppressed . . . devoted to helping those in need!" In his initial episode, Superman saves a falsely accused prisoner from a lynch mob, produces evidence that frees an innocent woman on death row, and defends a woman about to be beaten by her husband. In the second issue of *Action Comics*, Superman crushes a conspiracy involving a U.S. senator, a lobbyist, and a munitions manufacturer who wish to embroil the United States in a foreign war. He then ends the fraudulent Latin American war by informing the belligerents that they have been manipulated by greedy American industrialists. Echoing the Nye Committee's conclusion that "merchants of death" had conspired to involve the United States in the Great War, Superman warns that moneyed self-interest remained a menace to the national welfare.[27]

Morality tales attacking the evil of greed dominate the first several years of Superman's adventures. One early story opens with Superman rescuing a miner trapped in a cave-in. The injured miner later tells reporter Clark Kent that the mine tragedy could have been avoided if the owner and foreman had heeded warnings about unsafe working conditions. Kent then interviews the mine owner and asks him if he has arranged compensation for the injured miner. Indignant, the owner answers, "Certainly not!" When Kent inquires about the allegedly faulty safety devices in the mine, the owner retorts, "There are no safety hazards in my mine! But if there were . . . what of it? I'm a businessman, not a humanitarian!" Later, Superman traps the owner in a cave-in and lets him experience the misery that the miners have to endure. The owner discovers that the safety devices he had boasted of fail to operate. In tears, he laments his own callousness and failure to appreciate the plight of his workers. Superman finally extricates the owner and applauds his pledge to make his mines "the safest in the country" and his workers "the best treated" in the land.[28]

Other Superman stories explore the conflict between corporate greed and the public welfare. One finds Superman crushing a plot by wealthy American financiers working for a foreign power to manipulate the stock exchange and plunge the nation into another depression. His mission accomplished, Superman assures readers that "the nation is once again returning to its march toward prosperity!"[29]

In many cautionary tales Superman appeared as a sort of progressive "super-reformer." In a crusade for automobile safety nearly thirty years before anyone heard of Ralph Nader, Superman destroys a car factory after finding that the owner has been using "inferior metals and parts so as to make higher profits at the cost of human lives!" Later, after investigating the collapse of a subway tunnel and the murder of a municipal safety inspector, he discovers that the president of the tunnel construction company has been grafting off of the city by using cheap and unsafe building materials.[30]

In another story, Superman encounters a pair of wealthy and murderous stockbrokers who sell worthless stocks to hundreds of clients, some of whom commit suicide after losing their life savings. Superman, not content to simply turn the crooks over to the police, first devises a complex scheme to swindle them out of all of their cash and investments so that they must endure the humiliating poverty that they had inflicted on others. Once the brokers are themselves broke, Superman delights in their misery and advises them to stop selling stock and start selling shoelaces instead.[31]

Superman also championed social reform and government assistance to the poor. One story opens with an adolescent being arrested and tried for assault and battery. The boy's mother asks the judge for leniency. "He's only like all the other boys in our neighborhood," she pleads. "Hard, resentful, underprivileged . . . he might have been a good boy except for his environment!" Observing the trial, Clark Kent agrees and considers the judge's sentence of two years in reform school too harsh. As Superman, he tells the neighborhood boys, "It's not entirely your fault that you're delinquent—it's these slums—your poor living conditions—if there was only some way I could remedy it!" And remedy it he does, by demolishing the slums himself in defiance of the legal authorities, even fighting off the police and National Guard when they try to stop him. Where the hesitant and inefficient legal process fails, the one-man wrecking crew succeeds. In place of the demolished tenements, the government constructs splendid, shining public housing to give the underprivileged children a healthier and safer neighborhood.[32]

Superman's crusade against greed and injustice sometimes led him into conflict with the legal and political establishment. While he fought rigorously for social justice, traditional authorities appeared slow, inefficient, and occasionally even corrupt. In one episode, Superman cracks down on city authorities for not dealing effectively with the problem of motorist safety: the police are accepting bribes from speeding drivers instead of ticketing them. Even the mayor flaunts the laws by driving recklessly until he receives an angry visit from Superman. In another story, Superman uncovers a gambling racket involving the commissioner of police.[33]

Superman's America was something of a paradox—a land where the virtue of the poor and the weak towered over that of the wealthy and powerful. Yet the common man could not expect to prevail on his own in this America, and neither could the progressive reformers who tried to fight for justice within the system. Only the righteous violence of Superman, it seemed, could relieve deep social problems—a tacit recognition that in American society it took some might to make right after all. Author and cartoonist Jules Feiffer called Superman's world a "fantasy with a cynically realistic base." These stories offered an escape but remained within the reader's frame of reference. For, as Feiffer cynically observed, "once the odds were appraised honestly it was apparent you had to be super to get on in this world."[34]

Superman won a large audience very quickly. At a time when most comic book titles sold between 200,000 and 400,000 copies per issue, each issue of *Action Comics* (featuring one Superman story each) regularly sold about 900,000 copies per month. Each bimonthly issue of the *Superman* title, devoted entirely to the character, sold an average of 1,300,000 copies. The Superman phenomenon transcended comic books. The McLure Syndicate, having earlier turned down the opportunity to be the first to publish Superman, paid DC for the rights to print a Superman newspaper strip, which debuted in January 1939. Siegel and Shuster wrote and drew the strip, thus fulfilling their long-time dream.[35] Beginning in 1939, the adventures of Superman could be heard on a nationally syndicated radio program opening with the memorable lines: "Faster than a speeding bullet! More powerful than a locomotive! Able to leap tall buildings in a single bound! Look! Up in the sky! It's a bird! It's a plane! It's Superman!" Between 1941 and 1943, the Fleischer animation studio also released a series of lavishly produced Superman cartoons for Paramount. And Superman's licensed image sold a myriad of products ranging from toy "Krypto-Rayguns" to, literally, sliced bread.

A later spokesman for DC Comics claimed that "Superman literally created this industry." It is difficult to overstate the importance of the character. Superman established the essential vocabulary of comic books. As Sheldon Mayer later explained, "Jerry [Siegel] was way ahead of us on what was right for comics."[36] Costumed superheroes became the defining fantasy of comic books, largely because it was a fantasy that this medium could indulge better than any other. As William W. Savage Jr. observed,

> Comic books could carry heroes beyond the limits of possibility imposed by radio (sounds without pictures and thus without depth or significant personification) and film (sounds with pictures, but constrained by technology). Radio, short on data, gave the consumer's imagination too much latitude, while film, rife with data, refused to give it enough. Comic books, however accidentally, managed to split the difference. They could show whatever the artist could draw, their lines and colors directing imagination, their balloon-held texts defining time and space. Comic book artists and writers could produce that which could be conceived, which was more than the creators of motion pictures and radio programs could claim.[37]

Superman became the comic book industry's first "star," and DC Comics had him. By 1940 DC enjoyed healthy national distribution for all of its titles and average sales of 800,000 copies per issue, nearly 300,000 more than its closest competitor. According to a 1941 article in the *Saturday Evening Post*, the *Superman* title alone grossed $950,000 for DC in 1940. For the time being, Siegel and Shuster also shared in some of the wealth earned by their creation. The *Post* reported that they each earned thirty-five dollars per page for their comic book work at DC—the highest rate paid in the industry—and five percent of all other revenue earned from Superman. Their position was by no means secure, however, since DC was under no obligation to retain their services in order to keep Superman.[38]

Superman had a strong residual impact on the rest of the industry, which expanded as new publishers entered the field and flooded the market with various imitations of him. Pulp magazine publishers and opportunistic entrepreneurs entered the comic book business looking for quick and easy profits with little financial outlay. Publishers could purchase the stories inexpensively from newspaper syndicates, from

comic art shops, or directly from freelance artists. They needed only a
small office, wherein an editor, or sometimes the publisher himself,
could select and package the features and send them to a printer. The
printed comic books would then be shipped to regional distributors and
wholesalers who sent them on to newsstands, chain stores, and other
outlets selling popular magazines. A publisher usually sold his comic
books to a distributor for 5¼ cents per copy; the distributor would sell
them to wholesalers for 6 cents each. A retailer purchased the issues for
7½ cents each and put them on newsstands with a standard retail price
of 10 cents. Retailers had the option to return any unsold issues to publishers for a refund, but in these booming years refunds averaged less
than 30 percent. Joe Simon, who worked as an editor and writer for
several publishers, recalled that since national distributors were willing
to advance most of the capital to publishers and printers were always
eager to back a line of comic books in order to keep their presses rolling. "It was not unusual for a publisher unfamiliar with the comic book
business to take a fling at the field, fail, and come out with a profit."[39]

One of the first to exploit Superman's appeal was Victor Fox, a Wall
Street businessman and accountant for Harry Donenfeld at DC. When
Fox noticed Superman's rising sales figures, he set up his own publishing operation at an office in the same building as DC's and contracted
with the Eisner-Iger shop for a series of comic book stories. Fox asked
Will Eisner to create a costumed superhero very similar to Superman.
The result, Wonderman, was in fact too similar, and DC filed a lawsuit
for copyright infringement. Fox, who reportedly liked to pace the
floors of his office smoking a cigar and boasting, "I'm the King of Comics," promptly canceled the series but remained in the business and
prospered.[40] As Fox's editor-in-chief, Joe Simon faced, as he put it, "the
bleak prospect of turning out dozens of monthly comic books with
a skeleton crew of novices." He recalled that "the art work was bad
enough, but the best that one could say about the stories was they were
illiterate."[41] Nevertheless, Fox promised readers superhero fantasies,
and that was apparently enough to sell more of his comic books than
their aesthetics merited.

DC itself was also quick to exploit the Superman formula. Vincent
Sullivan asked a young cartoonist named Bob Kane to create a second
costumed superhero for the company. Earning around forty dollars per
week at the time, Kane became very interested in the proposition once
he heard that Siegel and Shuster were each earning eight hundred dollars a week from Superman. Kane and writer Bill Finger designed a
character inspired by pulp fiction heroes like the Shadow and Doc Sav-

age, Hollywood adventure films like *The Mark of Zorro*, and an obscure silent picture called *The Bat*.[42]

Batman was a worthy follow-up to Superman. Like his predecessor, he wore a costume and maintained a secret identity, but Batman possessed no superhuman powers, relying instead upon his own scientific knowledge, detective skills, and athletic prowess.[43] His alter ego, handsome millionaire socialite Bruce Wayne, was not as essential to the character as Clark Kent was to Superman. But the explanation for Wayne's crime-fighting career is particularly intriguing and disturbing. As a child, he sees his parents brutally murdered by a petty burglar. The severely traumatized Bruce inherits his father's fortune, trains his mind and body to the pinnacle of perfection, and devotes himself to a personal war against crime. He dons the frighteningly bizarre Batman costume to strike fear into the hearts of cowardly evildoers everywhere.[44]

The early Batman stories achieved a uniquely surreal quality. Finger's scripts drew heavily from lurid pulp fiction as well as Universal horror films and Warner Brothers gangster movies. Kane's inventive artwork made use of unusual angle shots, distorted perspectives, and heavy shadows to give the series a cinematic and almost expressionistic look. The comparison may be a bit much for some, but the early Batman series had the kind of cutting-edge aesthetic qualities that made it the *Citizen Kane* of comic books.[45] Originally cast as a vigilante, pursued by the police even as he preyed upon criminals, Batman further demonstrated the appeal of a crime-fighter operating free of procedural and institutional restraint. As Batman himself once put it, "If you can't beat them 'inside' the law, you must beat them 'outside' it . . . and that's where I come in!"[46] Set in a claustrophobic netherworld, his adventures benefited from some of the most grotesque and memorable villains ever created for comic books: the Penguin, Two-Face, Catwoman, and, of course, the Joker—a wonderfully deranged homicidal maniac with a white face, green hair, and a ghastly grin who quickly became a favorite of Batman's creators and readers.[47] The brooding series lightened a bit in 1940 with the addition of a teenage sidekick named Robin, a character with whom young readers could supposedly identify.[48]

In the comic book industry, imitation was not only a high form

From "Batman," *Batman* 1 (DC Comics, spring 1940). Batman was the first superhero to follow successfully in the wake of Superman. Here is one of his earliest encounters with his most popular nemesis, the Joker. Script by Bill Finger, art by Bob Kane and Jerry Robinson.

of flattery, it was company policy. Most publishers took the successful examples of Superman and Batman literally and flooded the nation's newsstands with stories of outrageous, brightly colored costumed heroes. A few succeeded without such characters: Dell Publishing scored a licensing coup by securing the comic book rights to the Walt Disney and Warner Brothers cartoon properties. With the likes of Mickey Mouse, Donald Duck, Bugs Bunny, and Porky Pig in their stable, Dell secured a solid market for decades. Fiction House contracted material from the Iger studio and thrived without the benefit of costumed heroes, opting instead for scantily-clad females like Sheena, a shapely blonde heroine who patrolled the African jungles in her leopard-skin bathing suit. In an industry flooded with costumed superheroes, though, Dell and Fiction House were the exceptions.

More common was the approach taken by a young pulp magazine publisher named Martin Goodman, who in 1939 launched an enduring enterprise called Marvel Comics. Goodman purchased comic book stories from the Funnies, Inc. shop before setting up his own staff. He put the project under the editorial direction of his teenage nephew, Stanley Lieberman, who wrote comic books under the pseudonym of Stan Lee. Marvel's chief entries into the burgeoning superhero market were the Human Torch and the Sub-Mariner. The former, created by Carl Burgos, was actually not a human but an android with the rather terrifying ability to burst into flames and set objects ablaze. The Sub-Mariner, created by Bill Everett, was the son of an American sea captain and a princess from the lost underwater kingdom of Atlantis. He possessed superhuman strength, the ability to breathe both air and water, and, unlike his superhero peers, harbored a fierce antipathy towards the human race, thereby demonstrating that superheroes could, despite obvious genre similarities, maintain some discrete character traits.[49]

Fawcett Publications entered the comic book business in 1939 and one year later launched a superhero whose popularity came to rival that of Superman himself. The ingeniously simple premise behind Captain Marvel, conceived by writer Bill Parker and artist C. C. Beck, was a boy named Billy Batson who became a superpowerful adult merely by speaking the magic word, "SHAZAM!" (the letters stood for Solomon, Hercules, Atlas, Zeus, Achilles, and Mercury). Captain Marvel, who looked like a husky Fred MacMurray in a red-and-gold costume, became the best-selling character of the early 1940s, outdoing even Superman for a time. DC responded to Captain Marvel's popularity by suing Fawcett for alleged copyright infringement of Superman. While they may have shared some apparent similarities, Captain Marvel was, in fact, very different from Superman. Whereas Superman evinced self-assuredness and control, Captain Marvel seemed more like a bumbling overgrown child, and his adventures had a distinctively whimsical quality about them.[50] Despite its dubious merits, the legal battle between Superman and Captain Marvel dragged on into the 1950s, and, inevitably, DC's Man of Steel won, as he always did.

Everett M. Arnold's Quality Comics put out some of the most aesthetically accomplished comic books of the time, thanks largely to the publisher's reputation as a fair employer who paid good rates for good work. Among Quality's successful characters were Doll Man (a hero who could shrink to the size of his namesake), Plastic Man (a comical hero who could mold his body into any kind of shape that his artist could imagine), and the Spirit (a masked avenger dressed in a blue suit, hat, and mask, wearing shoes with no socks, created by Will Eisner). Eisner seemed to take his comic book work more seriously than many of his peers, placing the Spirit in a gritty noir setting and developing unusually sophisticated characters and innovative sequential art techniques. Eisner's path-breaking work on the Spirit proved to be a far greater influence on future comic book artists than on most of his own contemporaries, who continued to grind out formulaic superhero stories.[51]

Despite increasing competition from these and other smaller publishers, DC remained the top-selling and most influential publisher in the industry. Superman and Batman were the cornerstones of the company's success, but joining them were many other cleverly conceived superheroes. Billed as "the fastest man alive," the Flash debuted in early 1940, as did the winged Hawkman and the mystical Dr. Fate. All three sprang from the imagination of Gardner Fox, a lawyer who took up comic book writing because, as he put it, "the law, back in those Depression days, was not something at which to get rich."[52] Jerry Siegel created the grim Spectre, the ghost of a slain policeman who is given nearly omnipotent powers by a mysterious deity so that he can avenge his own death and wage a ruthless war against crime and injustice. The Green Lantern, developed by writer Bill Finger and artist Mart Nodell, derived his power from a mystical green ring. Other, less popular DC heroes included Dr. Mid-Nite (who had superpowers only at night), Hourman (who had superpowers for only one hour per day), and the Atom (a short tough guy who had no superpowers but could fight well).[53]

In 1941 DC launched another groundbreaking superhero, Wonder Woman. Perhaps the unlikeliest of comic book writers, William Moul-

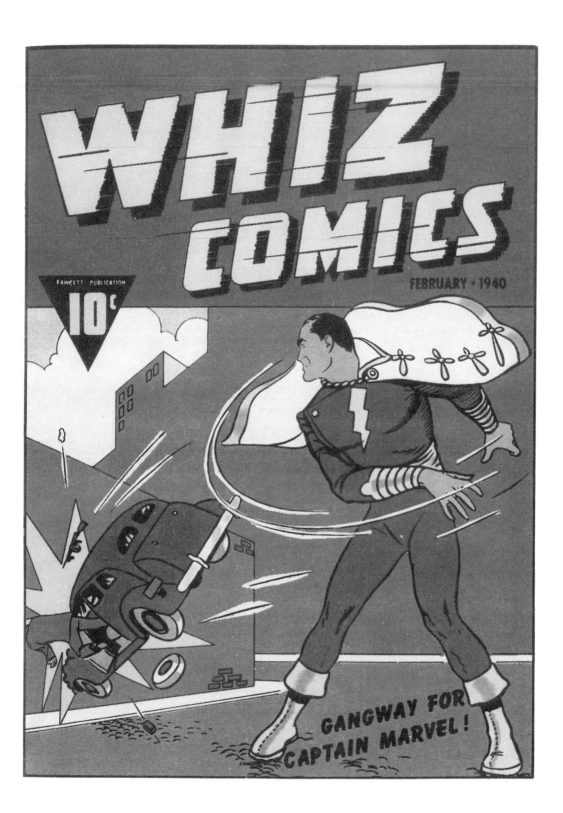

ton Marston was a middle-aged psychologist and author with a Ph.D.
degree from Harvard and connections in the advertising industry. He
became interested in comic books through his association with Max
Gaines. Marston conceived a female superhero who, he believed, would
appeal to both girls and boys. The results were—and remain—controversial. Later feminists have praised Wonder Woman as a progressive
gender image for young girls. Yet, while the character was indeed powerful and the series featured more prominent female characters than
any other, Marston's stories often underscored the Victorian assumption that superior female virtues like compassion and empathy were
best applied as a restraining influence on aggressive men, not as a
means to female self-sufficiency. Billed as a heroine "fighting fearlessly
for down-trodden women and children, in a man-made world," Wonder Woman was rooted more in the gendered tradition of progressive
social work than in modern notions of feminist self-fulfillment.[54]

Of course, that characterization in itself set her apart and made her
far more interesting than most of the otherwise irrelevant female characters in comic books, and it did offer a compelling image of a strong
woman playing a positive role beyond the domestic sphere. But there
was little in Wonder Woman's stories to suggest that women could or
should compete equally with men in the working world. As Wonder
Woman she was an Amazonian superhero, but in her common identity
as Diana Prince, she was a secretary. One typically whimsical storyline
did postulate that the world would be a better place if it were ruled by
compassionate women instead of aggressive men, but it also suggested
that it would take a thousand years before that would ever happen.[55]

On the other hand, there was a lot in these stories to suggest that
Wonder Woman was not so much a pitch to ambitious girls as an object
for male sexual fantasies and fetishes. The stories were rife with suggestive sadomasochistic images like bondage, masters and slaves, and men
groveling at the feet of women. Wonder Woman herself had a tendency
to become enslaved by other women and forced to endure gratuitous
humiliations. Revealing, perhaps, was her chief weapon: a magic lasso
that compelled those it ensnared to obey her every command. Marston

Cover of *Whiz Comics* 2 (Fawcett   Marvel. For several years in the
Publications, February 1940). DC   early 1940s, Captain Marvel
Comics sued Fawcett Publications   eclipsed Superman as the best-
for allegedly infringing on DC's   selling superhero in the comic book
copyright to Superman with Captain   industry. Art by C. C. Beck.

himself explained the appeal of his character by asserting that men secretly longed to submit to women. Writing in the *American Scholar*, he commented, "Give . . . [males] an alluring woman stronger than themselves to submit to, and they'll be *proud* to become her willing slaves!"[56]

During these early years, the sheer novelty of comic books and costumed superheroes was sufficient to generate strong sales. Writers and artists had little motivation to get very sophisticated in their storytelling, and they had compelling reasons not to. They assumed, probably correctly, that a superhero's appeal to juvenile readers depended, most simply, on how interesting his costume and powers were. This market consideration, along with low pay, the absence of royalties, incessant deadlines, and an assembly-line production process, meant that comic books became highly formulaic. Publishers valued comic book writers and artists more as producers than as creators. As one publisher reportedly liked to tell his staff, "Don't give me Rembrandt, give me production."[57] It followed then that comic books most often featured interchangeable heroes fighting against mad scientists, bank robbers, and other generic villains motivated by a simple imperative to be nasty. Yet comic book creators also incorporated real-world concerns into their fantasy tales, even though the limitations of the medium, the market, and the industry reduced these to exaggeration and formulaic predictability. The result was a distinctly "comic book" caricature of Depression-era America, sometimes absurd, always simplistic, yet often revealing.

Superheroes for the Common Man

The Roosevelt administration responded to the Great Depression with a series of initiatives broadly grouped under a reforming ethos called the New Deal. More than just a bewildering alphabet-soup of acts and administrations, the New Deal was a potent cultural idea that worked to knit together an inclusive and enduring liberal coalition for collective action and government intervention. Proponents of New Deal legislation made skillful use of symbols like the NRA Blue Eagle and President Franklin Roosevelt's "fireside chats" to appeal to the sensibilities of common people.[58]

Comic books implicitly, and sometimes explicitly, underscored key New Deal assumptions. Most often they did so by targeting the forces of corporate greed in stories that echoed Roosevelt's rhetoric against "economic royalists." In "The Tycoon's Legacy," the Green Lantern investigates the Jeffers Mortgage and Loan Company, which has been seizing the property of borrowers who meet with mysterious "accidents" that leave them unable to repay their loans. Suspecting foul play, the hero meets with these victims and urges them to sue the company, but they cannot match the corporation's expensive and powerful legal team. The Green Lantern sympathizes and agrees that "most lawyers would be afraid to tackle a big corporation like Jeffers' outfit." So, in a typical Rooseveltian move, the hero intervenes and leads the citizens in collective action. He helps to organize a low-cost law clinic for the poor, funded by contributions from neighborhood citizens, to help otherwise powerless individuals against wealthy malefactors like Jeffers. The corporation retaliates by dispatching thugs to intimidate the community, but the Green Lantern redresses this imbalance of power with his fists, demonstrating that legal protection works best when backed by a healthy dose of righteous violence. In the end, the corporate criminals are brought to justice and convicted, and the Green Lantern takes satisfaction in another victory for the public welfare over corporate self-interest.[59]

In another Green Lantern adventure, the hero comes to the aid of a working man abused by a shipping tycoon who has been luring unemployed men to a Caribbean island to perform slave labor. The worker appeals to the legal authorities and the corporate-owned press, but they refuse to believe that "one of the most successful businessmen in the country" could have committed such crimes. One radio executive, though sympathetic, refuses to air the charges against the tycoon because he fears being sued for libel. The Green Lantern listens and acts. His benevolent intervention finally brings the elusive corporate criminal to justice.[60]

Superheroes repeatedly sounded the warning that business dealings free of public scrutiny and government regulation inevitably led to corruption and crime. Dr. Mid-Nite protected coal miners from an abusive mining company and ensured access for government safety inspectors. Adventurer Barry O'Neill prevented crooks in the urban transportation industry from sabotaging the city's plan to place the subway system under public ownership. Hourman ended an abusive child-labor racket and lobbied for closer government supervision of private reform schools.[61]

Will Eisner's "Smashing the Enemies of Free Speech" carries a particularly strong endorsement for government regulation. This tale, featuring the distinctly American superhero called Uncle Sam, opens with a U.S. senator introducing a bill to "protect the American public from unscrupulous manufacturers." The senator characterizes the progressive law as one that "would force food makers to use only tested materials and print truthful advertising about their products." Uncle Sam applauds the bill because "a lot of candy factories use cheap unhealthy ingredients so they can earn bigger profits," and he praises activist government as "the real frontier of America . . . it is here where the real meaning of freedom and democracy is tested." A corrupt candy manufacturer illustrates the point by kidnapping the senator, trying to kill the consumer protection bill, and working to censor a newspaper exposé of his company's abuses.[62]

Comic books rarely, if ever, questioned the integrity of the federal government or national political leaders. Local politics was a different matter, however. The young writers and artists who created comic books worked in New York City, and many had grown up there. Thoroughly familiar with stories of grafting politicians and organized criminals who ran urban neighborhoods as private fiefdoms, creators often spoke to these concerns in comic book stories that projected a more cynical perspective on the condition of American democracy. Even as comic books celebrated the common man, they evinced a more conservative warning about the perils of political corruption and populist demagoguery. For all of the common man's virtues, he still seemed woefully susceptible to deception and coercion by false benefactors. Yet this apparent critique of the egalitarian spirit embedded in New Deal culture still worked to underscore New Deal principles. By pointing out the failings of local government and the dangers of provincial demagogues, these comic books endorsed the need for outside intervention and tacitly stressed a common interest between public welfare and a strong federal government. In this context, superheroes assumed the role of super–New Dealers.

The Green Lantern reserved some of his greatest moral outrage not for the straightforward crooks that he routinely nabbed but for those self-styled local reformers and public servants who had only their own selfish interests at heart. In one adventure, he exposes the city's Commissioner of Public Works as a corrupt racketeer who accepts kickbacks from his pals in the construction industry. In another story, the Green Lantern exposes "Honest" John Logan, who claims to be a progressive reformer and sponsor of a municipal orphanage when, in fact, he is a crook who has conspired with the superintendent of the orphanage to pocket the public funds while the orphans starve.[63] Political corruption might even reach as high as the mayor's office. After a city bridge nearly collapses, the Green Lantern suspects that inferior construction materials may have been at fault. He confronts the building contractor, who confesses (after receiving a beating) that the mayor gave him contracts in exchange for kickbacks and allowed him to save money by using cheap and unsafe building materials.[64]

Although the political boss system was actually in decline in many American cities, this perennial villain still loomed large in comic books, personifying the conspicuous failure of local politics. His very existence begged outside intervention on behalf of the public interest. On one occasion, Hourman comes to the aid of citizens in a crime-infested city run by a political boss called "Big Benny." No local authority will confront him, because the mayor is also a crook and the police serve as the boss's personal bodyguard. Big Benny also employs thugs as storm troopers to harass and silence anyone daring to speak out against him. Hourman frees the people from the boss's tyranny, much as America itself was about to liberate Europeans from Nazi oppression.[65]

When comic books explored why political corruption and organized crime continued to plague American cities, they sometimes faulted the citizens themselves. In "Suicide Beat," Batman and Robin investigate a crime-ridden neighborhood run by a mobster and a political boss whose goons routinely gun down police with impunity. The murderers cannot be apprehended because the neighborhood people shelter them. The police tell Batman that "a crooked politician runs that street . . . and he's a smart politician! He lends the poor people money, buys them food on Christmas, finds men jobs, etc. . . . and asks in return that they vote for him and protect his jackals!" Only after Batman and Robin have caught the political boss in the act of stealing from the neighborhood people do the citizens recognize him for the criminal that he is. In the end, they reject the patronage of corrupt political leaders and accept the police and Batman as their true benefactors.[66]

Some comic book heroes went to unusual lengths to combat political corruption. During his brief run in comic books, the radio hero Green Hornet (alias muckraking newspaper publisher Britt Reid) exposed a crooked state senator, apprehended politicians stealing from the Veterans Relief Bureau, broke up a crooked political machine, and even appealed directly to the civic responsibility of his readers in order to combat crime and political corruption. A full-page public service message narrated by the Green Hornet urged young people to fight the "racketeers and criminals who work within the law" by telling their parents to vote carefully for only honest politicians.[67]

Real political machines, however corrupt they might have been, historically had met the needs of immigrants and the urban poor. Comic books served the New Deal by portraying local politicians as self-serving tyrants and the federal government as the common man's chief benefactor. They took a similar approach with regard to labor unions, often presenting them as elaborate extortion rackets feigning support on behalf of misguided working men. At first glance, this unfavorable portrayal of unions seems at odds with the Roosevelt administration, which legalized the right to collective bargaining and passed the Fair Labor Standards Act. But comic book writers took their stories from the widely reported cases in which organized crime had, in fact, infiltrated labor unions. By emphasizing this particular failing of unionism, comic books lent further cause for workers to look beyond local means to the federal government for redress of grievances. President Roosevelt may have won admiration as the friend of labor, but he really preferred to improve the lot of workers through social reform legislation and always remained cool towards rising labor militancy.[68] Comic books echoed the president's own trepidation and still championed the cause of the common man.

Typical of this approach was a Green Lantern tale that opens with city taxi-drivers meeting to discuss proposed unionization. Suddenly three thugs force their way onto the platform. One of them is Plug Deagan, the notorious gangster. He urges the cabbies to join his union so that he can "help" them like he has "helped" workers in other cities. One driver retorts, "Sure . . . you got [the workers] higher wages. But you made them pay such high dues that they were worse off than before! You and your organization are nothing but racketeers! . . . Now get out!" The drivers resist Deagan, but he pressures them with a campaign of sabotage and violence. The honest drivers appeal to the Green Lantern for help, assuring him that they want to work with the cab companies and bargain in good faith. As the hero goes after Deagan, he discovers a still more sinister twist behind Degan's scheme. The owner of the cab company turns out to be the gangster's silent partner in the labor racket. Together they have devised a clever scam, whereby the owner would pretend to pay the drivers higher wages, supposedly because of Deagan's bargaining prowess, when in fact the gangster and the company head would be splitting the high "union dues" extorted from the drivers. In the end, encouraged by the Green Lantern, the drivers form an honest union and win higher wages from the new, enlightened company president.[69]

The Comic Book Menace

Comic books emerged at a critical moment in the evolution of youth culture. Progressive education reforms combined with Depression-era

unemployment kept an increasing percentage of adolescents in high
school during the 1930s. As young people spent more time in the company of their peers, they acquired new personal independence and a
generational consciousness that struck some alarmed adults as evidence
of diminishing respect for authority and declining traditional values.
Critics attributed adolescents' irreverent and undesirable behavior to
a variety of causes, including misguided "scientific education," family
financial difficulties, intrusive New Deal policies, movies, swing music,
and comic books.[70]

Comic book publishers bypassed parents and aimed their products
directly at the tastes of children and adolescents. This new trend in
youth entertainment emerged from a growing sense among producers
and some parents, probably furthered by parental guilt over deprived
Depression-era childhoods, that young people deserved greater latitude to pursue their own happiness and means for self-expression. Toy
manufacturers in the 1930s also began to appeal directly to children
with fantasy toys that indulged the child's imagination with no claim to
educational value. While toys generally escaped harsh critique, comic
books reaped some remarkable condemnation.[71]

In his widely reprinted 8 May 1940 article in the *Chicago Daily
News*, Sterling North branded comic books a "national disgrace," warning that "virtually every child in America is reading color 'comic' magazines—a poisonous mushroom growth." North accused the comic book
industry of looting the piggy banks of children and offering in return
an incessant barrage of "graphic insanity." He continued,

> The bulk of these lurid publications depend for their appeal upon may-
> hem, murder, torture, and abduction . . . Superman heroics, voluptuous
> females in scanty attire, blazing machine guns, hooded "justice" and cheap
> political propaganda were to be found on almost every page . . . sadistic
> drivel . . . badly written and badly printed—a strain on young eyes and
> young nervous systems—the effect of these pulp-paper nightmares is that
> of a violent stimulant. . . . Unless we want a coming generation even more
> ferocious than the present one, parents and teachers throughout America
> must band together to break the "comic" magazine.[72]

Publications like the *Wilson Library Bulletin* and *Parents' Magazine*
echoed these concerns, albeit less hysterically. Taking a pragmatic approach, the publishers of *Parents' Magazine* issued their own comic
book, *True Comics*, as an educational alternative parents could purchase
for their children. Featuring "exciting" descriptions of "true-life" heroes like Winston Churchill, Simon Bolivar, and George Rogers Clark,

True Comics was a concept destined to be popular with parents and teachers at least, if not with kids.[73]

Writing for the *American Mercury*, Frank Vlamos charged that comic books represented "the most dismaying mass of undiluted horror and prodigious impossibility ever visited on the sanity of a nation's youth." He saw disturbing cultural implications in the superhero comic books, noting, "You can't go through an issue of a 'comic' magazine without realizing that the lawful processes of police and courts have disappeared and that only the heroism of superheroes keeps us from being annihilated by . . . disasters and crimes." He observed that while the vigilante superhero's "methods may be those of a bully . . . his alleged motives make him a hero." By willfully defying the police, politicians, and other figures of authority, superheroes gave "all the arguments a child ever needs for an omnipotent and infallible 'strong man' beyond all law, the nihilistic man of the totalitarian ideology" to restore order in an "America tottering and overrun by criminals."[74]

Vlamos identified essentially what other intellectual critics would find most threatening about the new medium. Comic books had the power to indulge fantasies and create myths for a young audience hungry for empathy and easy explanations. Here was an entertainment industry catering exclusively to the tastes of the young and impressionable, controlled by urban young men with worldviews far removed from Victorian middle-class ideals and guided, above all, by the pursuit of quick profits. It was a combination that heralded a cultural and market revolution.

The emergence of the comic book industry marked a new stage in the twentieth-century advance of American consumer culture. In earlier decades, Hollywood movie makers also had come under attack from critics repelled by an industry controlled by immigrant men and patronized especially by working-class audiences. Implicit in this critique was a grudging awareness that movies had assumed an enormously powerful role in reshaping the nation's culture and eroding the influence of traditional Victorian mores. By the late 1930s, however, Hollywood had itself become an entrenched American institution, and its lavish productions epitomized the triumph of consumer culture.[75] As Hollywood movies became synonymous with mainstream America, comic books filled a lucrative void at the bottom of the cultural hierarchy. To most of the public, they were a silly diversion for the kids at best and a cultural menace at worst. The characteristics of comic books that critics most deplored were the very qualities accounting for their unique appeal. In a national culture forged by adults for adults, how

refreshing it must have been for young people to discover a source of
entertainment that spoke directly to them as independent consumers.
The fact that this cultural exchange was conducted in a language of
violence, crudeness, and absurdity understandably unsettled more than
a few adult observers. Children are the future, after all, and the youthful
irreverence, vulgarity, and spectacular commercial success of comic
books pointed to an American future that perceptive critics glimpsed
with horror.

Few took the argument to its logical conclusion, but critics who
bemoaned the readily available products appealing to base human desires implicitly warned of the long-term threat that consumer culture
posed to moral authority. To comprehend the currently fragile state
of morality in the world, they cautioned, one merely had to look at
developments overseas. Writing in the *New Republic*, Slater Brown
warned that if the boys and girls of America were drawn to "saviors"
like Superman as part of a "symptomatic desire for a primitive religion,"
then the nation might be on a self-destructive course much like the
Europeans who had already embraced a "vulgarized myth of [Nietz-
sche's] 'Superman.'"[76]

As if in answer, comic book makers were already mobilizing their
cultural resources against the fascists. By 1941 New Deal rhetoric
had given way to talk of war and foreign enemies gradually displaced
the home-grown villains of corporate greed and political corruption.
Whereas the Depression had demanded superheroes for common
Americans, the war years needed patriotic defenders of national interests. On that score, comic books would not let the nation down.

2
Race, Politics, and Propaganda

Comic Books Go to War, 1939–1945

It is the spring of 1941. "The ruthless war-mongers of Europe" have cast their sights on "a peace-loving America," and "the youth of our country" heed "the call to arm for defense." As foreign agents carry out "a wave of sabotage and treason" against the United States, the president authorizes a top-secret defense plan. A patriotic young American named Steve Rogers, too sickly and weak to qualify for standard enlistment, volunteers for a dangerous scientific experiment conducted by the nation's top scientist, Professor Reinstein. Injected with a strange, seething liquid, Rogers undergoes a startling transformation. Growing in height and mass, Rogers's muscles expand and tighten to the peak of human perfection. No longer a frail patriot, he now has a massive physique, a proud new name, and a bold mission. The nation's newest "super-soldier," Captain America, is born.[1]

He was not the first, and he was far from the last superhero to take up the fight against the Axis. But with his instantly recognizable red, white, and blue costume, his shield of stars and stripes, and his partiotic bravado, Captain America became the definitive comic book entry into the culture of World War II. The brash and unforgettable cover of *Captain America Comics* number 1 depicted the ultra-American hero slugging Adolf Hitler in the face almost a full year before the United States declared war on the Axis. As international crises loomed ever larger in

the American consciousness, comic book makers looked outward and
applied their particular brand of conflict resolution to world events.
Captain America's dramatic debut was a call to arms, urging the nation
to unite against foreign aggression. By the spring of 1941, as the U.S.
mobilization was well underway, comic books had already gone to war.

World War II and the Comic Book Industry

The war years were a boom time for most American industries, and the
comic book industry was no exception. As defense spending finally
pulled the nation out of the Great Depression, millions found work
and brought home larger paychecks. Many workers had never had it
so good, and neither had their children. More disposable income for
Mom and Dad meant more nickels and dimes for kids to spend on
comic books. In early 1942 *Publishers Weekly* and *Business Week* both reported that some 15 million comic books were sold each month. Moreover, publishers assumed a generous "pass-along value" of five readers
per comic book. By December 1943, monthly comic book sales had
climbed to 25 million copies. As many as 125 different titles could be
found at newsstands every month. Retail sales of comic books in 1943
added up to nearly $30 million.[2]

Newsweek attributed the robust sales to "the well-filled pockets of
the nation's school children" and "the war-developed market of American servicemen." The *New York Times* reported that one of every four
magazines shipped to troops overseas was a comic book. At least 35,000
copies of *Superman* alone went to servicemen each month. Comic
books became a part of G. I. culture and struck many European observers as further evidence of American immaturity and unsophistication.
Some Americans were evidently concerned as well. A letter to the *New
York Times* charged that "furnishing these lurid pulp papers is certainly
no way to produce an intelligent military." Cheap, disposable, and entertaining, comic books nevertheless won a place in barracks and PXs
for the duration of the war and beyond.[3]

The comic book industry had to sacrifice some production for the
war effort. Government rationing programs after 1943 compelled publishers to reduce their paper usage by 15 to 20 percent. The War Production Board rationed paper allotments for all magazine publishers
and strongly discouraged new publishers from entering the field. Comic
book companies absorbed the cuts by reducing the number of copies
printed per issue, the number of pages in each comic book, or both.
Some had to suspend publication of dozens of titles in order to meet

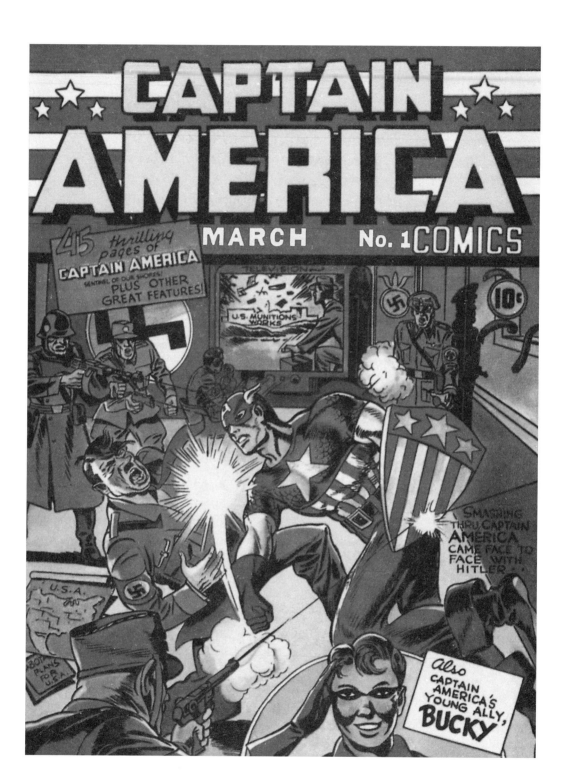

the board's restrictions. Fawcett Publications implored fans of Captain Marvel to reserve a copy of their favorite title at the newsstands, as the publisher complied with wartime rationing.[4]

World War II also drained away much of the talent in the comic book field. Most of the experienced and reliable creators in the business were eligible for service, and leading talents like Jerry Siegel, Will Eisner, and Jack Kirby temporarily left their drawing tables to enlist. Those who remained or returned to the home front after military service benefited from the higher pay rates brought on by the wartime labor shortage. An especially prolific comic book writer, Otto Binder, saw his page rates for scripts jump from a prewar standard of three dollars to a wartime high of ten dollars. William Woolfolk recalled earning a very respectable $15,000 annual income writing for most of the leading publishers during the war. A few comic book shops hired women to fill jobs vacated by male writers and artists. In 1942 the number of women working in the comic book field tripled, and the Iger shop alone employed as many as twenty women at one time. In most cases, however—with the exception of the Iger shop—that proved to be a short-lived hiring policy. The war's end generally saw women replaced by returning men.[5]

World War II gave publishers a valuable opportunity to improve their public image. Having secured an enthusiastic audience of young people, leading companies like DC Comics and Fawcett Publications now made an appeal to parents. In the summer of 1941 DC announced the formation of an Editorial Advisory Board to independently advise and approve the content of all DC comic books so that they met "wholesome" moral standards. In a message to children and parents, DC claimed that the recent proliferation of comic books made it "more important than ever to discriminate between them." Citing "a deep respect for [their] obligation to the young people of America and their parents and [their] responsibility as parents [them]selves," the editors at DC enlisted the assistance of "professional men and women who have made a life work of child psychology, education, and welfare" to serve on the board. These included English professors, child-study experts,

Cover of *Captain America Comics* 1 (Marvel Comics, March 1941). Like many patriotic superheroes of World War II, Captain America declared war on the Axis months before the rest of the nation did. Images like this dramatically illustrated the Nazi menace. Art by Jack Kirby.

Boy Scout leaders, and even retired boxers Jack Dempsey and Gene Tunney.[6] At least some of these advisers received payment for their services to DC, but the publisher never disclosed this in the comic books. The advisory board may indeed have emerged in part from DC's sense of social responsibility, but it was also a calculated move to improve the publisher's image, counter the charges of anti–comic book critics, and distinguish DC's comic books from less scrupulous competitors.

DC's Editorial Advisory Board did not exactly spark an industry-wide trend. Initially only its chief rival, Fawcett Publications, followed suit—by bringing in the director of the Child Study Association of America as a "consulting editor." For a time, Fawcett advertised its own Editorial Advisory Board, which counted First Lady Eleanor Roosevelt among its members. Few other publishers, however, made more than a cursory claim to wholesomeness. And those who did often did so disingenuously, like the publisher of one especially violent comic book that advertised on the cover: "Parents! You'll Say These Comics are the Best!"[7]

Publishers also sought to boost their image by linking their products to patriotism and the war effort. Superman urged readers to give to the American Red Cross. Batman and Robin asked boys and girls to "keep the American eagle flying" by purchasing war bonds and stamps. Captain America and his sidekick Bucky showed readers how to collect paper and scrap metal. Publishers throughout the industry printed an open letter from Treasury Secretary Henry Morgenthau Jr. asking boys and girls to buy savings stamps.[8]

Franklin D. Roosevelt well understood the power of modern media to influence public attitudes. Having made skillful use of the media to further his policies during the Depression, he did so again in wartime. Government agencies like the Office of Facts and Figures and the Office of War Information disseminated the administration's primary war objectives and worked to generate public support. The OWI urged entertainment producers to voluntarily conform to administration guidelines and ask themselves of all their products, "Will this help win the war?" But administration officials were also sensitive to the ineffectiveness of and potential backlash against messages that reeked too heavily of sheer propaganda, and they wished to avoid the sort of ugly intolerance and hatred generated by U.S. propaganda during World War I. So the OWI asked the entertainment industry to raise American morale, encourage public cooperation and participation in the war effort, identify the menace of the Axis powers, and inform audiences about the progressive war aims pursued by the United States and its allies, all in ways that cloaked propaganda within the context of good entertainment as much as possible.[9]

The demands of World War II reoriented New Deal liberalism from domestic political reform to internationalism and the mobilization of national resources. New Dealers still asked Americans to commit to collective action for the sake of reform, but now such action was for patriotic unity behind the war effort and reform on a global scale. Vice President Henry Wallace spoke of the war as an opportunity to usher in the "Century of the Common Man," when New Deal principles would be extended to suffering peoples throughout the world. The enemies of reform now took the shape of profiteers, subversives, and foreign dictators. The "common man" of the Depression era was now America itself, a repository of virtue and morality charged with extending justice and freedom to the oppressed in Europe and Asia. This called for a dramatic reorientation in American culture. Government manuals encouraged the producers of entertainment to present American society as a great melting pot free of racial, ethnic, and class conflict—in other words, an image of American society that was far more united and integrated than American society really was.[10] And, by their nature, comic books seemed well suited to perpetuate this desirable national fantasy.

Comic books actually had launched their own propaganda effort long before the federal government. Many of the young artists creating comic books were Jewish and liberal. Morally repelled by the Nazis, they expressed their politics in their work. Two of these creators, Joe Simon and Jack Kirby, produced Captain America. Kirby was born Jacob Kurtzberg in 1917 in New York City's Lower East Side. The son of working-class Austrian immigrants, he had changed his name to Jack Kirby because he "wanted to be an American." He later cited his experiences growing up in a tough neighborhood where good boys learned to survive by acting tough and standing up to bullies as a primary inspiration for his comic book work and his politics. His art, simple and direct, action-oriented and imaginative, was perfect for comic books. Although the aesthetic virtues of Kirby's work would have been lost on most "serious" art critics and professional illustrators of the time, his innate grasp of the medium and the superhero genre in particular made him one of the most prolific, imitated, and influential artists in the field's history. Kirby later recalled that he had been drawn to comic art because of its simplicity and directness, which he equated with the

American way. "I thought comics were a common form of art and strictly American," he said. "America was the home of the common man, and show me the common man that can't do a comic."[11]

Joe Simon conceived the idea for Captain America, and Kirby's art brought it to life. Simon explained that Captain America's origins were consciously political, because "the opponents to the war were all quite well organized. We wanted to have our say too." Simon and Kirby used Captain America to wage a metaphorical war against Nazi oppression, anticipating the real American war that they believed was inevitable. Most readers responded favorably, but some isolationists and Nazi sympathizers reacted angrily to Captain America's politics. Simon recalled that "when the first issue came out we got a lot of . . . threatening letters and hate mail. Some people really opposed what Cap stood for." Nevertheless, Simon insisted that he and Kirby "felt very good about making a political statement . . . and taking a stand" against Nazism.[12]

Captain America quickly became Marvel's best-selling title and most popular character, selling close to a million copies monthly throughout the war.[13] He spawned his own fan club, the "Sentinels of Liberty," and inspired waves of red-white-and-blue imitators. He came to epitomize not only the values and fighting spirit of the national war effort but also the fortunes that comic book publishers would reap from their enlistment into patriotic wartime culture.

Comic Books Confront a Hostile World

The initial comic book ventures into overseas affairs were not so high-minded. These were the imperial or "jungle" comic books. Usually set in Africa, Asia, or sometimes Latin America, these jungle adventures centered on a hero—either male or female, but always white—who championed Western interests and sensibilities in savage lands plagued by internal chaos and external threats. Most often the hero was a jungle "lord," "queen," or even "goddess" strongly derivative of Edgar Rice Burroughs's Tarzan. Sometimes the hero was a modern imperial adventurer with direct links to the British or French Empires. In all cases the hero, though Western in outlook, understood the ways of the savage land better than the native people. Their intervention was needed because the childlike nonwhite peoples—whether well-meaning or malicious—inevitably proved woefully incapable of self-government. Left to themselves, they fell prey to manipulation and domination by false prophets, evil chieftains, and hostile foreign agents.

Paternalistic, imperialistic, and racist, the jungle comics showed the reductionist comic book style at its ugliest. They posed justification for

Western colonial domination and white supremacy enforced through violence. Africans appeared as either brute savages or minstrel-show stereotypes with huge white eyes and white-rimmed lips, often speaking an imbecilic hybrid of pidgin English and exaggerated African American slang. Above all, they were stupid. In one story, an African American murderer named Broot escapes from a chain gang in the United States to the jungles of West Africa. There he constructs a phony idol and dupes the superstitious natives into worshiping him as a god. The simple Africans obey Broot (who sports a black top-hat and a necklace of ivory teeth) and call him "Massah" as he orders them to brutalize neighboring tribespeople and white colonists. The hero, Kaanga in this case (a blonde version of Tarzan), defeats Broot and exposes the false "god" to the natives, who stop fighting and humbly promise the white jungle lord that they will behave in the future.[14]

The powerful racial anxieties underlying such material are hardly more evident than in one particular episode of Sheena, Queen of the Jungle. The story, set in French West Africa, opens with an African nationalist king uniting scattered tribes into "a single ferocious unit, sworn to drive the white man from the country!" One of the savage tribesmen attacks Sheena and her male companion, crying, "Me now kill them! Show all chiefs, me big ruler. . . . Kill all white people!" Sheena and her contingent of loyalist natives defeat the rebellion and preserve white colonial rule. For this, she is awarded a medal of valor from the French government.[15]

Comic books consistently portrayed anticolonial rebellions as misguided threats to the peace and security enforced by Western imperialism. DC's Zatara, Master Magician, uses his powers in the service of South Africa, helping to put down a Zulu rebellion. Adventurer Lance Larkin defeats an Arab uprising against white imperial troops. The pilot-adventurer Captain Desmo rescues a group of British miners besieged by bloodthirsty Indian rebels. Zara, another contender for the "Jungle Queen" title, pacifies an African uprising by awing the childlike savages with her mere presence. Another story finds a modern-day Genghis Khan leading his "yellow horde" out of Asia to conquer "the white race."[16]

The outbreak of war in Europe added a new imperative to the perpetuation of Western imperialism. For, as comic books explained, native uprisings played into the hands of the Nazis, who incited and exploited them to suit their own hostile interests. The curious linking of American interests with the integrity of the British Empire found expression in the adventures of Captain Desmo. A minor though mem-

orable character, if only because of his ridiculous name and costume (he wears a pilot's uniform, leather flying helmet, and goggles at all times, even indoors), Captain Desmo is an American aviator who volunteers his services to the British Empire and specializes in counterinsurgency. With his aid, the British crush a series of native rebellions, many of which are masterminded by Axis agents. In one tale, a foreign agent named von Stern foments a rebellion among Indians against their British masters. A British officer tries to reason with the Indian rebel leader, reminding him that His Majesty's Government has always treated the Indian people fairly and justly. The rebels, however, are more persuaded by the promises of von Stern, until Desmo reveals to them the agent's hidden motives.[17]

While jungle comics implied that the Allied empires were America's first line of defense in territory overseas, others soon began to warn that the Axis menace was moving closer to America. Reference to the war appeared very early in comic books. Will Eisner's "Espionage," published in *Smash Comics*, was the first comic book series to focus on the war in Europe, doing so even before there was a war. Beginning in the summer of 1939, "Espionage" evinced a rapidly changing American perception of the conflict in Europe. One story tells how a mad dictator, bearing a strong resemblance to Adolf Hitler, seizes control of Argentina and conquers all of South America before turning his forces unsuccessfully against the United States. This story, which appeared in a comic book dated August 1939, indicates that global war was on some comic book makers' minds even before the German invasion of Poland.[18]

After several episodes, the references to World War II became explicit. One story opens with the narrator recounting the aggressive steps taken by Germany and Japan in their movement towards war, beginning with their withdrawal from the League of Nations. Yet the story also endorses American neutrality and distances the interests of the nation from events in Europe and Asia. For in America, "peace reigns . . . prosperity has returned . . . unemployment is a thing of the past . . . while Europeans slay each other, Americans live in peace and

From "Plague of Spotted Killers," *Jumbo Comics* 42 (Fiction House, August 1942). Racism, imperialism, and anti-Nazi sentiment combined in the tales of jungle queens like Sheena, who dethroned evil chiefs and Nazi tribal surrogates like the savage "Leopard Men." Art by Robert Webb.

plenty!" Because the United States is rightfully determined to avoid being entangled in another foreign war, the president orders all Americans abroad to return home. But hostile foreign agents plot to drag the United States into the war by sinking American ships on the high seas, apparently trying to reprise the kind of submarine warfare that had provoked U.S. entry into the last world war. The aggressive foreign power plans to lure America into declaring war so that it can seize Alaska from the United States. A far-fetched premise, perhaps, but not so implausible to Americans bound by the Neutrality Acts and determined to stay out of war.[19]

Already by the end of 1939, however, "Espionage" was suggesting a deeper U.S. commitment. One story opens with Europe once again poised on the brink of war, but this time, the United States rearms in response. The aggressive European dictator then calls off his military plans, admitting that "the United States could wipe Europe off the map in a year! We must sign the peace pacts offered by their president and disarm at once!" Implied is the fanciful hope that armed American neutrality and the mere threat of U.S. intervention might forestall any wars of conquest.[20]

Such optimism belied the course of events, however. The reality of war in Europe soon led some comic books to attack the Nazis more directly. Martin Goodman's Marvel Comics took the lead. The cover of *Marvel Mystery Comics* dated February 1940 depicts the Sub-Mariner fighting the crew of a submarine flying a swastika flag.[21] The Sub-Mariner initially had taken a noncommittal stance in the conflict, as befitted his fiercely independent nature. But by early 1940 he was regularly battling Nazis and keeping the Atlantic shipping lanes open for British and American vessels. In one story, he rescues a crew of American sailors menaced by the German fleet for transporting food and medicine to war-ravaged nations. In the next issue, he pledges to aid the Allies in their struggle against the Germans in the Atlantic—a remarkable declaration, coming a full year before the United States had even commenced lend-lease aid.[22]

As the war in Europe intensified in 1940–41, so did the war in comic books. The United States itself became a battleground, where Nazi spies and saboteurs conspired against the American defense build-up. Marvel's Human Torch defended U.S. munitions plants from foreign saboteurs. Captain America fought German agents and fifth columnists in nearly every issue, and the Destroyer battled the Nazis from within occupied Europe. In early 1941 Will Eisner and Charles Cuidera created a series called "Blackhawk" for Quality Comics. Featuring a multinational paramilitary aviation group led by a Polish pilot dedicated to overthrowing the Nazis, "Blackhawk" struck a serious mood when, in the first issue, the leader of the group vows revenge on the Germans for killing his brother and sister in a bombing raid. Some efforts to bring the war to comic book readers, however, got a bit out of hand. In the ludicrous "Blitzkrieg of the Living Dead," Nazi agents disguised as zombies land on a Caribbean island and try to scare the superstitious natives away so that the Germans can use the island as a base for attacks against the United States.[23]

Other comic books, like Leverett Gleason's *Daredevil Battles Hitler*, took a stronger interventionist position. Described by one of his former associates as a "liberal, almost left-wing, politically committed kind of guy, who lived by his philosophy," Gleason published in the spring of 1941 what amounted to a 64-page comic book declaration of war against the Axis. The issue opens with the superhero Daredevil sneaking into Hitler's citadel at Berchtesgaden so that he can punch the Fuhrer himself. After that, the hero travels to London to discuss war strategy with Winston Churchill. The British are eager for the Americans' assistance, although they appear to be doing fairly well on their own—against the Italians, at least. Daredevil travels to the Mediterranean in time to witness the Royal Navy sinking the Italian fleet, which brings a clownish Mussolini to tears. The hero then goes to the Far East, where he helps the British and Chinese repel an Axis assault on Singapore, and finally to central Africa, where troops of the British Empire turn back an assault by "Hitler and his jungle hordes!"[24]

Following this nonsense was a more serious effort to present the face of Nazi cruelty. A brief biographical sketch entitled "The Man of Hate: Adolf Hitler—Dictator of Germany" explained how Hitler, a "frustrated artist," developed a "demoniacal hatred for the English" and "inferior races" during the First World War. After rising to power, he used the Gestapo to crush political dissidents and domestic opponents. He sent out fifth columns to sabotage the defense industries of neighboring countries before sending in his ruthless armies. Only embattled Great Britain stood defiant against his scheme of world conquest. Although the feature stopped just short of calling for U.S. entry into the war, it clearly justified the need for some type of American intervention and appeared immediately relevant to the contemporary extension of lend-lease aid to the Allies.[25]

Not surprising given the ethnic heritage of comic book makers and the transatlantic culture of New York City, comic books that appeared before Pearl Harbor was attacked featured Nazi villains far more frequently than they did Japanese villains. Yet the Japanese, or their meta-phorical equivalent, could be seen menacing the United States as early as 1939. One comic book plot from December of that year found some agents of the Far Eastern nation of "Japonia" attempting to destroy the U.S. submarine base at Pearl Harbor. Another comic book issued that same month showed the U.S. Navy intervening to stop smugglers from running weapons to the Japanese in their war against China. Early in 1941 the short-lived American superhero called "Captain Battle, Savior of Chungking," assists the beleaguered Chinese against the Japanese invaders. The hero receives thanks from Generalissimo Mao Tung (a contraction of Generalissimo Chiang Kai-shek and Mao Tse-tung, per-haps?). A few comic book scenarios proved remarkably prophetic, such as the coincidentally dated December 1941 issue of Quality's *National Comics*, which shows "Oriental" military forces attacking the U.S. Naval bases at Guam and Pearl Harbor.[26]

Virtually every publisher of action and adventure comic books fol-lowed the same trends in the months leading up to Pearl Harbor, satu-rating newsstands with patriotic superheroes costumed in the American flag and bearing names like "Uncle Sam," "Minute-Man," "The Star-Spangled Kid," and even "Miss America."[27] They championed a loosely defined Americanism synonymous with lofty ideals like democracy, lib-erty, and freedom from oppression. During the Great Depression, the antitheses of these ideals had been manifest in the forces of greed and selfishness personified by "economic royalists," corrupt politicians, and racketeers. Now the anti-American forces took the form of militarism, oppression, and intolerance perpetrated by the Axis powers and their agents operating in America. Comic books presented the victories over new villains and shifting national priorities as a seamless crusade to-wards the inevitable triumph of the common man. Will Eisner's Uncle Sam could not have laid out the stakes for common Americans any more clearly:

> Wherever Americans struggle, their Uncle Sam joins them . . . never rest-ing! Uncle Sam led our boys to victory in the Great War! When people struck for better [working] conditions, he was there too! He was their champion against the forces of oppression! [The accompanying panel shows workers confronting a uniformed man wielding a club.] And now he decides to come to life again, as civil rights of Americans are threatened . . . by evil forces guided by distant powers, prying from within. . . . Our country is nearing a crisis and it needs a champion to steer it clear of its internal and external foes![28]

The patriotic wartime superheroes marked a logical evolution in the genre. Superheroes of the Depression had, through their efforts on behalf of common citizens, consistently pointed to the need for outside intervention to resolve local problems. Now they linked the concerns of the common man to an active, interventionist foreign policy. In this way, comic books looked to unite the American people behind their government for the purpose of waging war.

Comic Books Go to War

The bombing of Pearl Harbor galvanized American public opinion behind the U.S. declaration of war. Isolationist resistance melted in the face of widespread outrage and resolve to avenge Japan's surprise attack on American territory. Having already betrayed interventionist leanings, comic books now escalated their own war effort. Some superheroes enlisted in the armed services. Private Steve Rogers went overseas to battle the "Japanazis" both as a U.S. Army soldier and as Captain America. DC's Justice Society temporarily disbanded so that the individual superhero members could join the armed service branch of their choice. Captain Marvel briefly enlisted in the Marine Corps. Wonder Woman served as a nurse. Most of these formal enlistments were temporary. Comic book makers found creative means to avoid upstaging America's real-life heroes fighting overseas, having superheroes dutifully volunteer for military service only to be honorably discharged to safeguard the American home front from spies and saboteurs.[29]

Some superhero deferments proved more awkward than others. Jerry Siegel and Joe Shuster felt strongly that Superman should participate in the war, but realizing that he could fly to Berlin and Tokyo and promptly bring the war to an end on his own, they did not wish to minimize the daunting task faced by the nation and its fighting forces. Yet for the patriotic superhero not to enlist, when so many millions of young American men were doing so, would have been equally unacceptable. To resolve this dilemma, Siegel and Shuster had Clark Kent declared 4-F. In his enthusiasm to serve his country, Kent mistakenly uses his X-ray vision during the eye examination and inadvertently reads the eye chart in the next room. Concluding that Clark is blind as a bat, the doctor finds him unfit for military service, much to poor Clark's dismay and Lois Lane's continuing disgust. Superman shrugs off the disappointment, resolving to serve the American war effort by policing America's home front and declaring that "the United States Army, Navy, and Marines are capable of smashing their foes without the aid of a Superman!"[30]

Comic books urged all Americans, including children, to participate in the war effort. Those who remained aloof or pursued selfish interests appeared as misguided fools at best, traitors at worst. The comic book war effort, much like the real one, left no room for ambiguity or debate on most issues. Direct, emotional, and naive, comic books contributed to the widespread popular impression, which still persists, that World War II was truly a "good war."

Pre–Pearl Harbor stories saw Superman exposing prominent isolationists and pacifists as spies working for a hostile foreign power. Other comic books portrayed isolationists as paranoid old hermits. In one, an ignorant old man, driven to insanity by the death of his son in the First World War, vows that America must never again wage any war. He insists that it is "far better that we submit to the dictators!" The misguided old fool helps Nazi agents sabotage U.S. Army bases until the American Crusader apprehends him.[31]

In another story, by Joe Simon and Jack Kirby, a patriotic group of kids in New York's East Side called the Newsboy Legion discover a house occupied by two old hermits while going door-to-door selling war bonds. The old men refuse to buy any bonds, explaining, "We locked ourselves up to keep from being annoyed by one war and certainly don't intend to be bothered by this one!" They "absolutely disapprove of war . . . both in principle and practice! . . . [and] refuse to even discuss it!" The kids see this antiwar stance as selfish and unreasonable, and they report the hermits to the police. Although the officer deplores the old men's attitude, he refuses to arrest them because it is a free country, after all, and citizens have the right to be wrong. Later, German agents, taking advantage of this "country where individualism is permitted," infiltrate the neighborhood and break into the old men's house. This brings the war "home" to the hermits, and, once rescued, they enthusiastically endorse the war effort, even trying to enlist in the Army themselves.[32]

DC's "The Little Rebel" pitched this message to young people even more directly. Joan, the teenage daughter of a wealthy businessman, is described as a "little lady of leisure." She snubs her poorer classmates and ridicules their involvement in the war effort. When some of the neighborhood girls come to her house selling government bonds, she scoffs, "How annoying! Why did you have to call just when I was getting dressed for my tea dance?" One of the girls scolds Joan for her self-centeredness and retorts that "the Japs didn't ask our Army and Navy when it would be convenient to raid Pearl Harbor!" They contend that even schoolgirls like themselves should get involved and contribute, for instance, by sacrificing some of their personal time to do the housework while their mothers work in the factory. Joan remains aloof, until her father is murdered by German agents. She understands too late that Americans of all ages and classes have a stake in the war effort.[33]

Comic book writers did not abandon their Depression-era themes entirely; some suggested that corporate greed remained a menace during wartime. One story opens with two large meat-packing companies vying for a big government contract to serve the U.S. Army. The losing bidder maliciously plots to contaminate the meat of his competitor, even though this means poisoning U.S. soldiers. The superheroes known as Red, White, and Blue thwart the scheme and vent their wrath on the murderous profiteers: "What a cheap bunch of heels you turned out to be . . . passing yourselves off as Americans, and then risking the lives of American soldiers just so you could make a few filthy dollars!"[34] In another story, corporate leaders plot to assassinate the president of the United States after they have tried unsuccessfully to pressure him to raise the ceiling on defense contracts. Munitions makers in another tale try to reap profits by selling arms to both sides of the war. For making "a business of human blood" and sacrificing the lives of fellow Americans for money, the grim heroine called the Black Widow condemns them, stating, "There is no crime worse than that!" She kills them and uses her terrifying powers to send them straight to hell.[35]

As a nation, Americans may have never hated a foreign population as intensely as they did the Japanese during the months following the stunning attack on Pearl Harbor. The Pacific war was, in John Dower's phrase, a "war without mercy"—a war between races as much as between nations. Reflecting this deep hostility, American media and popular culture abounded with racist caricatures of the Japanese. Perhaps more than any other medium, comic books proved uniquely suited to portray the Asian enemy as many Americans saw him—a sinister, ugly, subhuman creature who asked for and deserved no quarter. Comic books rendered the Japanese using the most vicious caricatures that artists could imagine. Ghastly yellow demons with fangs and claws or bucktoothed little monkeys with oversized spectacles, comic book Japanese appeared subhuman, inhuman, or even superhuman, but never simply human. Stories with titles like "The Terror of the Slimy Japs," "The Slant Eye of Satan," and "Funeral for Yellow Dogs" glorified the American violence righteously unleashed on "yellow apes," "yellow babies," "yellow punks," "dirty yellow devils," and "little yellow doggies."

Assuming the sinister and sadistic characteristics long associated with the "yellow peril," the Japanese characters in comic books evinced cold cruelty, especially when torturing captives. In one typical scene, a Japanese officer prepares to execute a helpless prisoner, saying, "I shall shoot you . . . not in a vital spot, but in many places . . . so that it will take a long time for you to die . . . in agony!" Comic books joined Hollywood films like *The Flying Tigers* (1942) and *Bataan* (1943), dramatizing actual reports of atrocities and thereby contributed to the popular image of the Japanese as a nation of butchers, worthy of nothing less than unconditional defeat, if not outright extermination.[36]

Comic book creators endeavored to explain how a supposedly inferior race like the Japanese could have acquired such formidable military power. One story noted that the Japanese had not invented the weapons of war used so effectively at Pearl Harbor and elsewhere. Instead they had used spies to steal their technology from the United States. As one Japanese spy admits, "My countrymen are great imitators, but they cannot invent. Therefore they shall steal the secret weapons the masterminds of America are building."[37]

Comic book tales also warned that the Japanese, like the Germans, had an active fifth column operating within the United States. By implication, this assumption justified the internment of Japanese Americans. In one story, Japanese Americans are compelled to aid a spy operation. Although they claim loyalty to their adopted home, the citizens agree to work for Japan; as one explains, "I was born in America and I love this country. . . . There are many more Japs like me. . . . Unfortunately Imperial Japan has put pressure on us and we've been forced to work against Uncle Sam!" After a member of the Justice Society defeats the spy operation, he grudgingly lets the Japanese Americans go free so that they can show "other Japs that there are *some* of them who do love the United States that has sheltered them!"[38]

Despite the hostility directed at the Japanese, comic books tacitly endorsed the Allies' "Germany-first" strategy. In comic books, the Nazis remained the more ubiquitous and more dangerous foe. Comic books presented two kinds of Nazis. One was stiff, militaristic, and ruthless. The other was a fat, bumbling buffoon. All officers, it seemed,

From "The Gruesome Secret of the Dragon of Death," *Captain America Comics* 5 (Marvel Comics, August 1941). The Japanese plot to attack the United States in this *Captain America* comic book, published months before Pearl Harbor was bombed. As sinister and subhuman as America's Asian foe appeared here, images of the Japanese became even uglier after Pearl Harbor. Script by Joe Simon, art by Jack Kirby.

sported a monocle and a dueling scar on their cheek, and all were cruel. Much as Hollywood did, some comic books distinguished between Nazis, who were evil incarnate, and decent German citizens, who had been duped or subverted by a mad leader but were otherwise redeemable— a dispensation not granted the Japanese.[39] One of the heroic Black hawks was a German who despised Hitler. In his battle against the Nazis from within Germany, Marvel's Destroyer sometimes encountered freedom-loving Germans who quietly resisted the Nazis. A few Germans seduced by Nazism also made deathbed conversions, renouncing the ideology that had led to their ruin.[40]

Likewise, German Americans fared considerably better in comic books than did their Japanese counterparts. Captain America comments in one issue that he finds "German-American people to be very nice!" In the same story, a German American declares, "I am of German descent . . . but I'm also a good American citizen! I'll have nothing to do with a [spy] organization that aims to destroy the country that protects me and mine!" At least one comic story, however, did show German Americans swearing their allegiance to "the Fatherland" and working against the United States.[41]

In any case, eclipsing the relatively few sympathetic portrayals of the Germans was the overwhelming barrage of anti-German sentiment. Many comic books simply condemned the Germans as an intolerant, warlike, and deplorable people. One particularly strong indictment of the German nation appeared in an issue of DC's *All Star Comics*. The cover depicts the Four Horsemen of the Apocalypse as a Germanic barbarian, Frederick the Great, Kaiser Wilhelm II, and Adolf Hitler. The feature, entitled "This Is Our Enemy," treats readers to a brief and distorted lesson in German history. Germany is called "a degenerate nation whose people throughout the centuries have always been willing to follow their military leaders into endless, bloody but futile warfare!" Tracing a direct line of German militarism, imperialism, and aggression from the conquests of the Teutonic Knights to the wars of Frederick the Great, Otto von Bismarck, Kaiser Wilhelm II, and Adolf Hitler, it explained that the German people deserved a large measure of blame for their shameful legacy because they had "fallen in so willingly with the plans of their leaders." As an accurate sketch of German history, this left much to be desired; but as an implied justification for the Allied pursuit of unconditional surrender, it was effective propaganda.[42]

The United States was not alone in fighting the Axis powers, though comic books tended to give the impression that it was. A reader with no other points of reference would have concluded from wartime comic books that American heroes battled the Axis with only occasional assistance from the subordinate British, Chinese, and Russians. Comic book makers, of course, wrote about American heroes for a predominantly American audience. But in so doing they often slighted the contribution of U.S. allies rather brazenly and further distorted a war about which Americans were already poorly informed. One story, for instance, portrays an American superhero and the U.S. Army driving the Japanese out of Malaya. The British and Commonwealth forces in the story are grateful to the Americans and dutifully perform their inglorious mopping-up assignments. The irony was striking. For as this comic book appeared on newsstands in early 1942, embattled Commonwealth troops, with no U.S. help anywhere present, were suffering a military rout in southeast Asia.[43]

When the Allies do appear, they evince a favorable—that is to say, an "American"—image. In some cases, comic book makers abruptly ceased perpetuating certain stereotypes and fashioned new, more positive, ones in their place. America's Chinese ally, in particular, needed rehabilitation. Prior to Pearl Harbor, comic books had generally portrayed the Chinese as mysterious and sinister villains who schemed to promote racial domination from the opium dens, torture chambers, and laundries of fog-bound American Chinatowns. Once events had made China an American ally, however, in comic books the Chinese became a peace-loving, albeit rather simple, people, and the Japanese became the standard bearers for the ugliest stereotypes of the yellow peril. With references seemingly drawn from whitewashed accounts in Henry Luce's *Time* and *Life*, comic books characterized Chiang Kai-shek's corrupt dictatorship as an American-style democracy.[44]

Even then, however, the Chinese never quite measured up to Western standards. In one story from 1942, Chinese troops guarding the Burma Road appear "slack, slovenly, and unmilitarized." In a reimagining of General Joseph Stilwell's mission, the U.S. government sends Pat Patriot and her team of female military trainers to Burma to whip the Chinese into shape as an effective fighting force. As if this is not humiliating enough for the Chinese, the American women then discover that the Japanese have infiltrated the officer ranks of the Chinese Army. After Pat Patriot drives out the Japanese, the Chinese humbly admit that they are "velly solly" about the whole miserable affair and duly submit to training by the American "gals."[45]

Things had not improved much for China by 1945. A story published that year lamented "a disturbing enmity among fellow coun-

I AM OF GERMAN DESCENT YES! -- BUT I'M ALSO A GOOD AMERICAN CITIZEN!. I'LL HAVE NOTHING TO DO WITH AN ORGANIZATION THAT AIMS TO DESTROY THE COUNTRY THAT PROTECTS ME AND MINE FROM CREEDS LIKE YOURS!!

WH-WHAT ARE YOU GOING TO DU!

YOU DEMOCRATIC SWINE! SHOW HIM, FRITZ!

UGH-H!

HIT HIM HARDER! HARDER! HE'S NOT UNCONSCIOUS YET

LATER, AS BUCKY AND HIS FRIEND BOB SHMIDT WALK UP THE BLOCK, THEY NOTICE A SLEEK, BLACK SEDAN PULL AWAY FROM THE SHMIDT'S HOME...

GOSH, BOB, THAT WAS A SWELL MOVIE!

BUCKY! THAT CAR! IT JUST LEFT MY HOUSE

THAT'S FUNNY! THERE'S NO LIGHTS ON!

IT'S NOTHING TO WORRY ABOUT. MAYBE YOUR FATHER'S GONE TO SLEEP... SO LONG, BOB. I'VE GOT TO GET BACK TO CAMP...

THE NEXT DAY, BUCKY AND STEVE ROGERS HAVE A CHAT IN THEIR TENT...

HONESTLY, STEVE, BOB SHMIDT AND HIS FATHER ARE TWO SWELL GUYS

YES, BUCKY. I'VE FOUND GERMAN-AMERICAN PEOPLE TO BE VERY NICE

WHAT TH--?

WHY, IT'S BOB SHMIDT!

BUCKY! SOMETHING TERRIBLE HAS HAPPENED!

2

trymen" in China. An official representative of the government is described as "a useless man indeed" and turns out to be a traitor as well. He agrees to work with the Japanese because he fears the prospect of democracy and land reform in his country. Another Chinese representative claims rightful leadership because he is "the best educated man in this part of the country . . . and the richest land-owner," but he is opposed by a peasant who accuses him of caring more about his money than about the welfare of China. The United States sends the Boy Commandos to urge the Chinese to unite against the Japanese. It nevertheless is a hopeless situation that remains unsolved, although all representatives belatedly, and rather unconvincingly, agree to put aside their differences in the short term to wage war against Japan.[46]

As America's most problematic ally, the Russians appeared most infrequently in the comic books of World War II. Prior to the bombing of Pearl Harbor, they rarely appeared at all, although at least one comic book from 1940 portrays the Russians as aggressors against Finland.[47] Even after the United States had entered the war, comic book writers rarely referred to Joseph Stalin and never mentioned the Communists. Instead, they focused on the patriotic Russian people and, especially, the soldiers and partisans who fought tenaciously and courageously in defense of their homeland. One comic book tells of a "true-life" Russian guerrilla fighter "whose reckless heroism serves as an inspiration to his fighting countrymen." Another calls Russian troops "the century's most courageous people" and "the fiercest fighters on Earth." On one occasion, in a rare display of American-Soviet cooperation, the Boy Commandos fight alongside Soviet troops against Germans on the Eastern front. As they do so, Russian citizens listen to "the great President Roosevelt" on the radio and cheer his announcement of the opening of a second Allied front against the Germans in Western Europe. The frozen Red Army soldiers also cheer this heartening, albeit inaccurate, news in the fall of 1942.[48]

The United States had smaller allies in the campaign against the Axis as well. Latin America was a region of paramount concern, and expressions of Roosevelt's "Good Neighbor" policy appeared in comic books often, both before and after the attack on Pearl Harbor. Like the

From "Killers of the Bund," *Captain America Comics* 5 (Marvel Comics, August 1941). Comic books tended to portray German Americans as loyal and patriotic, in contrast to their images of Japanese Americans, who usually appeared treasonous. Script by Joe Simon. Art by Jack Kirby.

policy itself, comic books perceived Latin America in benevolent but paternalistic terms. In one Green Lantern comic book from 1941, the hero travels to a fictional South American nation called Landavo, which he informs us is "a republic . . . with a democratic government just like the United States," and a president who is "a fine, honest man much beloved by his people!" Although most of the population appears to be content, a civil war breaks out. The Green Lantern discovers that the insurrection has been masterminded by a foreign dictatorship that hopes to use the region as a base to attack the United States. The rebels realize in the end that they have been duped. "What fools we were," says one. "To think we might have lost our freedom!" Satisfied that democracy and U.S. security interests have been restored, the Green Lantern bids the citizens farewell now that he is "not needed around here any more!"[49]

This scenario recurred throughout the war years. In one story, Captain America exposes a Nazi agent masquerading as a high priest and rebel leader in Mexico. When the Mexicans learn how they have been misled, they apologize to Captain America for having been "blind and stupid" and reaffirm their friendship with the United States. In another episode, the Justice Society of America goes to Latin America to help the governments of Mexico, Venezuela, Brazil, Bolivia, Chile, and Cuba turn back a series of inept German incursions and intrigues aimed at securing a foothold in the Western Hemisphere. The people of Latin America welcome the assistance and leadership of the United States because, as one Venezuelan official explains, his people "hate totalitarianism and wish to see it beaten!" A Mexican official also tells an American that the "men of Mexico are friendly to the United States, because you do not try to tell us how to live and die!"[50]

When, in one comic book, German agents try to incite an uprising against the government of a South American nation, the superhero Black Terror arrives to help the government forces. The leader of the nation thanks him, adding that "without unity with America, we South Americans can never have lasting peace!" The Black Terror, in turn, expresses hope that this country will become "a powerful Good Neighbor . . . to carry on the fight against the Axis!" Comic books clearly impressed upon readers that, as one character puts it, "Our Good Neighbors . . . are *all Americans!* And they have no more use for Hitler and Hirohito than we have!"[51] But comic books nevertheless conveyed the enduring impression that the United States should act not only as a good neighbor but also as a big brother, one who is quick to intervene in Latin American affairs when it suits American interests.

National unity was vital to the American war effort. Virtually every
proponent of the war repeated this principle, and comic books were no
exception. While most comic books simply paid lip service to vague
concepts of patriotism and unity, a few went further, defining what that
unity really implied in terms of racial and ethnic tolerance. DC Comics
took the industry lead in calling for a liberal and inclusive America.
One DC comic book warns that the Nazis had come to power by ex-
ploiting the hatreds and prejudices of the German people, and they now
hoped to "spread their seeds of hatred and intolerance throughout the
United States" as part of their "divide and conquer" strategy. The
comic book Nazis incite and exploit class and ethnic divisions within
the United States. They exacerbate class hatred between steel workers
and industrialists, between mine workers and mine owners, and between farmers and their wholesalers. They also take over a newspaper
and run a series of hateful editorials against Jews, immigrants, and
Catholics, hoping to further perpetuate intolerance and cause "un-
American people" to be herded "into concentration camps." The Justice Society heroes put an end to this manipulation and remind readers
that "the United States is a great melting pot, into which other races
are poured—a pot which converts all of us into one big nation!" The
moral of the story is that "we may be of different nationalities and reli-
gions . . . but together we're all red-blooded, clean, healthy, free Americans!" And as one superhero defiantly exclaims, "You can't beat that
combination Adolf . . . it's too strong!"[52]

A 1944 Green Lantern chapter entitled "A Tale of a City" makes
one of the strongest statements for tolerance found anywhere in wartime comic books. It opens with the Green Lantern sponsoring a multicultural Christmas radio program, which features a chorus made up of
children of different races and ethnic groups. An elderly woman rudely
interrupts the singing and charges that these children have no right to
celebrate Christmas because "they ain't all real white 100% Americans!
Their color is wrong and their religion is wrong and most of them is
foreigners anyway!" Infuriated by this narrow-minded outburst, the
Green Lantern retorts, "How dare you talk like that in America! You're
a fool! And there are many fools in America who think like you!" He
then recounts how he once investigated a hospital that did not employ
doctors of "a certain religion" and a school that had dismissed a teacher
of "a certain color." The man behind these and other discriminatory
acts was Rogue, a right-wing hatemonger and crook who attracted a
large following of bigots claiming to be patriots. They all claim to believe in "100% American government! No foreigners! No queer reli-

gions! No inferior people!" After the Green Lantern had finally captured Rogue, he called him a swine who made a "foul racket of man's
finest instinctive love of country." The hero charged, "You deliberately
confused patriotism with race hatred for one purpose . . . to make
money!" Returning to the present, the Green Lantern once again
scolds the old lady at the Christmas show, telling her and readers,
"When you hate a man for his race, creed, or color, you're just a sucker
for those who hate America!" The woman then sheepishly admits that
she has "been a fool."[53]

In coupling its patriotic messages with appeals for tolerance and
attacks upon prejudice, DC was ahead of most other publishers. Yet,
whatever the comic book industry generally implied about tolerance
in its call for national unity was overwhelmed by its consistently de-
meaning portrayals of nonwhite races. When they appeared at all in
comic books, Africans and African Americans were relegated to the status of bumbling, clownish sidekicks or childlike jungle savages.[54] Even
DC, for all its talk of cultural inclusion, failed to produce any meaningful characters who were not white.

Some comic books even suggested that it was nonwhites who
needed a lesson in tolerance. A recurring theme found superheroes urging American Indians to abandon their traditional hostility towards the
United States for the sake of the national war effort. In one story, a
Japanese agent masquerades as an American Indian and meets with Native Americans (wearing war paint and other trappings of Hollywood
Indians) to rile them up about the past wars with the white man. "They
fought and killed our fathers, and made us younger Indians prisoners
on these barren prairie reservations!" he reminds them. "But that time
is past! The White Man sees danger in other lands! His back turns
upon us! Now we can rise and take vengeance!" The scheme works for
a time, as the Native Americans do indeed take up arms against the
United States. But the hero known as Spy Smasher exposes the foreign
agent and urges the Native Americans to remain loyal and petition the
government peacefully instead. The chief agrees and regrets that he
and his people had been taken in so easily by the foreigner.[55]

World War II was good for the comic book business. It marked a
rare convergence of interests between publishers, creators, readers, and
government policy. Comic book fans and collectors refer to this era as
the "Golden Age of Comics," with a fondness that approximates the
general popular nostalgia for those "simpler" times before the Cold
War made everything more complicated. Comic books never wavered

in their support for the war effort. Relatively few, however, did much to articulate exactly what the war was about. While leading publishers like DC and Fawcett gave attention to the more high-minded principles guiding U.S. war policy, most left the impression that the war was simply about revenge and beating an evil enemy—and that did seem to be enough to motivate Americans. The slew of racist and hate-filled sentiment in many comic books threatened to overwhelm the progressive spirit and hopes found in others. Still, even the most senseless and mean-spirited comic books did much to rally cultural support for government policies. By insisting that the enemy was absolutely evil and deserving of no mercy, comic books tacitly invited support for Allied policies like the demand for unconditional surrender, the strategic bombing of civilian populations, and the use of the atom bomb. Collectively, comic books helped to reinforce the immediacy of the war to a young home-front audience fighting it largely on imagination alone.

High-minded and hateful, the comic book image of World War II betrays some of the contradictions inherent in America's wartime experience—contradictions that came to shape the strange character of American politics and culture in the Cold War as well. The immediate objective shared by comic book makers, however, was to retain and build upon the sizable market acquired during the war years. And superheroes like Captain America would soon discover that adjusting to the complexities of the postwar world was a challenge far greater than punching Adolf Hitler in the nose.

3
Confronting Success

Comic Books
and Postwar America,
1945–1950

Early in 1950 a story appeared in Fawcett's *Captain Marvel Adventures* entitled "Captain Marvel and the American Century." It opens by reminding readers that "during the first half of this century, America has led all civilization in enormous strides forward toward the ideals of freedom, democracy, and peace." As the whimsical tale unfolds, Captain Marvel foils the sinister Dr. Sivana, who plots to replace the "American Century" with the "Sivana Century." The hero preserves the American Century and receives personal congratulations from President Harry Truman, who then tells the boys and girls of America, "the next half of the American Century from 1950–2000 is yours! In your hands rests the fate of America, of democracy, and of freedom! It is a sacred trust!"[1]

A rather silly story, even by comic book standards, it nevertheless nicely captures the triumphalism of postwar America. The comic book industry had its own cause for self-congratulation in these years. The *New York Times* reported that DC Comics alone sold over 26 million comic books in the first quarter of 1946, up almost 30 percent from the year before.[2] Business watchers noted comic books' undeniable popularity not only with children but also with young adults. The war had played a key role in expanding the market by creating a large "captive audience" in uniform. In November 1945 the weekly U.S. Army newspaper *Yank* reported that comic books at PXs across the nation ex-

ceeded the combined sales of the *Saturday Evening Post* and *Readers'*
Digest by ten to one. The article added that "it's no news to anyone who
has ever killed a Sunday sprawled on his sack in a barracks that GIs go
for comic magazines in a big way." *Yank* cited the estimates of the Market Research Company of America, which found that about 70 million
Americans—roughly half of the U.S. population—read comic books.
The report found that the comic book audience comprised approximately 95 percent of all boys and 91 percent of all girls between the
ages of six and eleven, 87 percent of boys and 81 percent of girls between twelve and seventeen, 41 percent of men and 28 percent of
women aged eighteen to thirty, and 16 percent of men and 12 percent
of women over thirty.[3] Comic book advertising gave further evidence
of an audience that spanned genders and generations, encompassing
the market for Keds sneakers, baseball gloves, Daisy rifles, female hair-
care and weight-loss products, hospital insurance, and correspondence
courses in radio technology.[4]

As promising as the comic book business appeared, problems
loomed. Like other American companies that had prospered during
wartime, publishers faced the threat of a glutted postwar market. The
same encouraging conditions that had propelled the industry's growth
now threatened to curtail it. The end of wartime production controls
opened the door for new publishers and a flood of new titles. With
more publishers producing more comic books than ever before, supply
might easily outstrip demand. Postwar demobilization also threatened
to cost the industry much of its adult audience. Would adults who had
passed the time with comic books in the barracks continue to do so
after they had returned to their families and civilian lives? And would
the superheroes who had spoken to Depression and wartime audiences
have anything to say in the postwar era? Or would they prove to be a
fad that had run its course? If the superheroes faltered, would comic
books follow them into oblivion?

Sales indicators suggested that superheroes alone would no longer
be able to carry the industry. No successful superhero characters were
introduced after 1944, and poor sales compelled publishers to cancel
most superhero titles by the end of the decade. The top-selling title of
the war years, *Captain Marvel Adventures*, suffered declining sales every
year after 1945. By 1949 it was selling at only half its wartime rate.
During the war, over 90 percent of the comic books published by DC
had featured superheroes. By the end of the decade, just over half of
them did so. Major characters like Superman and Batman continued to

sell well, but wartime favorites like Captain America, the Sub-Mariner, the Human Torch, Green Lantern, and the Flash slumped to cancellation in the postwar market.[5]

The solution was product diversity. As publishers gained a greater understanding of how to produce their own comic books, most chose to employ and oversee artists and writers directly rather than purchase finished material from the shops. As the assembly-line shops declined, distinctive and diverse house styles emerged among the publishers. DC Comics and Fawcett Publications continued to dominate the market in superhero comic books. Dell enjoyed perennial success with its licensing rights to the Disney and Warner Brothers cartoons, among other properties. Gilberton Publications cornered the market in "classic comics"—comic book adaptations of classic novels—which purported to be educational, were usually sold separately from other comic books, and became popular with students seeking a shortcut to their book reports. MLJ Publications dropped its lackluster superhero titles after the war and devoted most of its line to lighthearted teen humor based around its most popular character, a freckle-faced teenager named Archie. The Iger shop continued its exclusive publishing relationship with Fiction House, specializing in heavily formulaic jungle comics and an inordinate number of leggy heroines in short skirts and leopard-skin bathing suits. Lev Gleason Publications pioneered the controversial genre of crime comic books, featuring lurid and remarkably graphic tales of notorious killers. Each of these publishers found a substantial audience in the highly diverse and expanding postwar market.

Some in the comic book industry perceived what few other entertainment producers seemed to notice: adolescents constituted an emerging consumer group with tastes that ran more to the adult than the juvenile. In his article published in the February 1951 issue of *Writer*, comic book writer Warren Kuhn claimed that there was "good money" to be made in the comic book field, with publishers willing to pay beginning writers generous rates of five to ten dollars per page. And the highest demand, he added, was for stories that dealt with "bizarre offbeat scenarios." He advised prospective comic book writers to remember that today's "youth . . . is a vast jump ahead of an earlier generation. They were weaned on jet-bombers and boo at a western movie that is corny and unreal." Because these young people tended to reject anything that seemed to condescend to them as juveniles, Kuhn urged prospective writers to "write *up* for them."[6]

Comic book makers who underestimated the maturing tastes of

postwar youth denied themselves an increasingly lucrative market.
Those who did "write up" to their audience challenged traditional assumptions about the innocence of children and drew fire from critics
who feared the changes in youth culture that comic books came to represent. Such was the dilemma confronting the industry during its era
of greatest success.

Superheroes and the Postwar Liberal Vision

Superheroes after World War II had far less to say about their world
than ever before. To some extent, they succumbed to the triumphalism
of postwar America. Victory ushered in an era that seemed to fulfill all
that superheroes had fought for: a powerful federal government committed to positive domestic and foreign intervention, a consumer economy of abundance that could alleviate gross social inequalities, and an
internationalist order codified in the United Nations and the Bretton
Woods Conference. A recovered economy, government assistance programs like the G.I. Bill, and the mass construction of affordable suburban homes made a middle-class lifestyle possible for millions. By
appearances at least, the helpless and oppressed who had cried out
for Superman in 1938 now lived comfortably and contentedly in the
suburbs. Superheroes animated by the crusading spirit of the New Deal
and World War II seemed directionless and even irrelevant now that
those victories had been won. In a vague sense, the decline of the superheroes reflected a postwar public mood that had grown conservative
and weary of reform.[7] More specifically, it reflected editorial policies
grown conservative and wary of innovation.

Once the leader in producing comic books relevant to contemporary issues, DC Comics adopted a postwar editorial direction that increasingly de-emphasized social commentary in favor of lighthearted
juvenile fantasy. Formerly a spirited crusader against social ills and political corruption, the Green Lantern now sparred with clownish criminals in half-baked plots that paved the way for his cancellation in 1949.
The impact of DC's editorial retrenchment was dramatically evident in
the changes surrounding Batman. His bleak and menacing world became a bright and colorful fairyland with none of the shadows and disturbing ambiguities that had made the series so daring when it first
debuted. No longer the mysterious vigilante who stalked the gloomy
nights of Gotham City, Batman now worked fully within the law and
took on paternalistic qualities—especially in his relationship with
Robin, an "A" student who respected his elders and mowed the lawn,

like all good boys should. Even the Joker, once a singularly homicidal madman, became just another goofy crook with a predilection for slapstick gags.[8]

No superhero retreated further from his initial premise than Superman. Having launched his career as a crusading champion of social justice and a militant antifascist, by the end of the war Superman had assumed his befitting role as the conservative elder statesman among comic book heroes, above the political and social concerns of the day.[9] In Superman's case the break with the past was made all the more real by the departure of his creators from the series. In 1947 Jerry Siegel and Joe Shuster sued DC Comics, seeking to regain the rights to their character and recover the five million dollars that they claimed Superman should have earned them over the nine-year period. Citing the release form that they had signed in 1938, the court ruled that the two creators had no property rights to the character. Siegel and Shuster ultimately settled with DC, receiving a one-time sum in exchange for their agreement to forego any future claims to Superman and all related characters. Superman would continue to sell a record number of comic books and generate hundreds of millions of dollars for his company but not for his creators.[10]

Under the creative direction of senior DC editor Mort Weisinger, Superman's comic books developed into a fantastic mythos that owed less and less to any standard of reality. Superman's powers, daunting enough to begin with, grew to staggering, godlike dimensions. Siegel and Shuster's original character was a powerful specimen, but he had been content to leap tall buildings, outrun speeding locomotives, and bend steel in his bare hands. Over the years, Superman had picked up more powers: flight, X-ray vision, faster-than-light speed, unlimited physical strength, and invulnerability to nearly anything except kryptonite. The extent of his powers peaked during Weisinger's tenure, by which time it seemed that there was nothing the character could not do. Weisinger's Superman flew through suns at the speed of light, pushed planets through space, and traveled through time. Weisinger added elements to Superman's self-sustaining fantasy world, including a bottled Kryptonian city of Kandor, a Fortress of Solitude in the Arctic where the hero keeps an endless supply of Superman robots to fill in for him in emergencies, and various colors of ubiquitous kryptonite, each of which have a different effect on Superman.[11]

After DC's writers had exhausted ideas for plots to put the invincible hero through, they resorted to "imaginary" stories, wherein Superman could marry, have different powers, or even die. As the series veered ever further into flights of unreality, so too did its ability to work within a social context. Whereas the original series created by Siegel and Shuster had been a modern social fantasy, the Weisinger series amounted to a modern fairy tale. While the stories produced under his editorship are the ones that baby boomers recall so fondly as the definitive Superman, this latter-day Man of Steel really bore little resemblance to his Depression-era predecessor beyond the red cape and the trademark *S*.

While DC's superheroes increasingly functioned in fantasy worlds of their own, the comic books did not completely ignore the world in which their readers lived. The major difference in the postwar era was that DC comic books now tended to speak to contemporary concerns quietly—through educational or "public-service" features instead of in the superhero stories themselves. These messages tended to disseminate the same basic liberal values that DC had extolled since the New Deal era. They further served to promote DC's desired image as a conscientious publisher striving to educate as well as entertain children. For several years DC even published *Real Fact Comics*, an educational comic book modeled on *Parents' Magazine*'s *True Comics*, featuring "fun" lessons in history, science, and civic responsibility taught by DC superheroes. Like most such pedantic efforts, it folded after several years.

Educational features sold poorly to children when marketed on their own merits, but they could still be inserted into more commercial comic books. One of the most intriguing of these series was "Johnny Everyman." Produced between 1944 and 1948 in cooperation with the East and West Association, a liberal organization of educators and authors later targeted by redbaiters as a "Communist front," "Johnny Everyman" educated readers on the virtues of tolerance, inclusion, and "furthering understanding between the peoples of the world."[12]

Perhaps the most daring message of "Johnny Everyman" was in a feature called "Room for Improvement." Published in 1946, the story opens in Russia with a boy named Nikky on trial for the theft of a piece of cloth. Nikky admits to the court that he did indeed steal the item, but only because his family has no money. He dreams of the toys, games, and consumer products that he has seen in an American magazine and complains that in Russia, "life . . . is so hard—with so much hard work! And mostly black bread and cabbage soup to eat!" The judge tells him that consumer luxuries are not bad, but "before there are luxuries in Russia there must first be necessities." Johnny Everyman then arrives and explains to Nikky that "although America is far ahead

CHARLEY, WE... UH... -THAT IS...

WHAT HE MEANS IS THAT WE'RE SORRY FOR THE THINGS WE SAID TO YOU. WE TAKE IT ALL BACK.

THAT'S OKAY... ANYBODY CAN MAKE A MISTAKE. WOULD YOU GUYS LIKE TO SEE MY WORKROOM?

WE SURE WOULD!

YOU BETCHA, CHARLEY!

ONCE A WEEK I TURN IN THE JUNK I COLLECT. BUT THE STUFF THE WAR EFFORT CAN'T USE I KEEP, AND USE TO MAKE TOYS... LIKE THIS SAIL BOAT.

WOW! WHAT A BEAUTY!

I'LL SAY!

YOU AND YOUR FAMILY ARE SWELL PEOPLE! CHARLEY- WOULDJA LIKE TO JOIN OUR CLUB?

WOULD I? GOSH! PUT 'ER THERE!!!

ONE WEEK LATER...

I PROMISED THE BOYS I'D VISIT THEIR CLUBHOUSE... HUH!?!

WHO GOES THERE? FRIEND OR FOE?

KNOCK KNOCK

WHEW! QUITE A TELEPHONE SYSTEM!

CHARLEY MADE IT... ALL BY HIMSELF. HE USED STUFF THEY DON'T NEED FOR THE WAR EFFORT. PRETTY SHARP, HUH?

I'M GLAD TO SEE YOU'RE ALL PALS... STAY THAT WAY.

DON'T WORRY... WE LEARNED OUR LESSON.

CHECK! IT DON'T MATTER WHAT A MAN'S RACE-OR COLOR- IS. IF HE'S A DECENT GUY, THAT'S ENOUGH... LIKE CHARLEY.

8

Another East and West Story in the next issue of Comic Cavalcade

of Russia in production, not everybody in America possesses the things
you saw advertised in that magazine . . . and in the second place, everyone in your country produces necessities now so as to have the nicer
things later." Johnny praises the Russians for working hard and cooper-
ating to improve their nation, telling Nikky that "because your comrades have learned to live together and respect one another, you will be
assured of a fair opportunity to buy your share!"[13]

After having extolled the virtues of Russia's cooperative society,
Johnny turns a critical eye towards American society. He tells the dark-
complexioned Nikky that everyone is treated equally in Russia, but "to
some people in America, the color of your skin would make a great deal
of difference—and if you were black, it would make more!" To make
the point, Johnny takes the Russian boy on a rather depressing tour of
America. White Americans look at Nikky with prejudice and hostility,
and an employer refuses to hire him because of his dark complexion.
Nikky protests, insisting that he is a good worker and reminding the
employer that Russia was America's ally during the war, but Johnny
tells the boy not to bother with such bigots. "Sorry—but those things
often happen in America," he shrugs. Nikky sees that "America is rich
and beautiful," but wonders, "where is the democracy they talk about?"
Johnny answers, "There's a lot of it, Nikky, but not as much as there
should be." Both Russia and America are great in their own ways, but
both have "room for improvement." Johnny concludes that both Russia
and America have much to learn from each other and, "only by learning
and working together can they create a better world for all!"[14] This was
a remarkable position for any mainstream publication to take in 1946,
much less a comic book. Expressing the kind of arguments one would
have expected from ultraliberals like Henry Wallace, "Johnny Everyman" would not survive the emerging Cold War. But for preaching
messages of tolerance and cooperation, the series won some rare praise
from the *New Republic* and the *Wilson Library Bulletin*, publications not
noted for their endorsement of comic books.[15]

DC disseminated similar messages in the low-key but enduring forum of Jack Schiff's public service pages. Although his primary respon-

From "Meet Charley Wing," *Comic
Cavalcade* 12 (DC Comics, fall 1945).
Created in cooperation with the
East and West Association, "devoted
to furthering understanding
between the peoples of the world,"
DC's Johnny Everyman extolled
a liberal vision of tolerance and
inclusion in postwar America.
Script and art by John Daly.

sibility was the editorial direction of the popular and apolitical Batman comic books, Schiff was also a liberal who took pride in writing a series of one-page public service features on behalf of the National Social Welfare Assembly. Schiff served as DC's representative on the organization's advisory committee, which also included representatives from the Child Study Association, the Health Insurance Plan of New York, the Jewish Family Association, the National Committee on Unemployment, the Camp Fire Girls, the Boy Scouts of America, and the National Association of Social Workers. Beginning in 1949, under Schiff's supervision, DC agreed to publish one page per month in all of its comic books on committee-approved topics like tolerance, cooperation, community service, civic responsibility, social welfare, and internationalism. Even at the height of the Red Scare, Schiff never produced a public service page that attacked or even mentioned Communism. Instead, these educational features underscored inclusive and liberal social values.[16]

Not everyone on the DC staff shared Schiff's political views. Alvin Schwartz, a DC staff writer at the time, recalled that Schiff's politics actually led fellow editor Mort Weisinger to accuse him of being a Communist during the McCarthy years. Weisinger reportedly warned DC's editor-in-chief that Schiff's liberalism was going to get the company in trouble.[17] Such conflict behind the scenes helps explain, perhaps, the inconsistent messages in the comic books. For even as DC's superheroes functioned within a benign mythic fairyland free of social concerns, controversies, and fears, the publisher's educational features consistently pointed out the need to improve society through liberal solutions.

One page published in 1951 entitled "Know Your Country" features Superboy urging readers to respect people of different races and ethnic backgrounds because "no single land, race, or nationality can claim this country as its own!" Another page, printed in 1952, opens with an African American youth courageously helping to keep an escaped circus lion at bay until the authorities arrive to recapture it. The circus owner then thanks a nearby white boy, whom he presumed had performed the service. Superman arrives and says, "Wait a minute! How do you know it wasn't the other lad?" gesturing to the black youth. The circus owner can only stammer, so Superman answers for him, "Because of his color? As a matter of fact, he *was* the one! You just jumped to a conclusion because of a common prejudice." The man admits his mistake, thanks the boy, and says, "This should serve as an example to a lot of people like me who have gotten some wrong notions in their heads!" Superman then warns readers not to judge anyone on the basis of their color or beliefs.[18]

As well-meaning as these educational features were, DC failed to heed the spirit of its own messages by including nonwhites in its comic book stories. Superman may have spoken eloquently about the problem of racial prejudice in one-page features, but he remained conspicuously silent on the issue in his own comic books. There were no African Americans anywhere in Metropolis or Gotham City—not as heroes, villains, or even passers-by. As the leading and most respected comic book publisher, DC was uniquely qualified to advance progressive educational messages, and it did so more often than most of its competition. But by failing to integrate racial minorities into its comic books, DC betrayed the limits of its liberal vision, missing an opportunity to do for comic books what Jackie Robinson did for professional sports.

Like DC, Fawcett Publications largely turned away from politics and social relevancy after World War II. At least one Fawcett series had quite a bit to say about the postwar world, however. This was "Radar, the International Policeman," a peculiar series appearing in *Master Comics* that Fawcett writers conceived in consultation with members of the Office of War Information.[19] Appearing towards the end of World War II, Radar worked as an agent for the "four great powers," a premise obviously mirroring Roosevelt's concept of the "four policemen" (the United States, Great Britain, the Soviet Union, and China) who would patrol the postwar world. Even after Roosevelt's death, the end of the war, and the deepening Cold War in Europe and Asia had cast serious doubts on this vision, Radar continued to champion the International Police Force throughout the immediate postwar years.

At a time when fears of spreading Communism became a pervasive concern in the West, Radar warned that right-wing extremism remained the chief threat to world peace. He apprehended fascist war criminals, helped democratic forces overthrow dictatorships, and ensured the safe delivery of United Nations humanitarian aid by foiling right-wing corporate profiteers.[20] During World War II, Radar urged readers to remember that "victories against the fascists on the battlefield are pointless unless we also clean out all home front fascists! And a fascist, as the American Vice-President Henry A. Wallace said, is anyone whose lust for money and power makes him ruthless in his use of deceit or violence to attain his ends!" Radar remained true to this cause after the war. In "The Death-Dealing Playboy," a wealthy American who is also an admitted fascist supplies an international right-wing organization with weapons to aid in the fight against democratic govern-

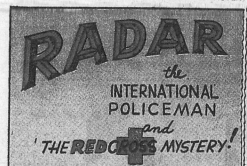

RADAR

the

INTERNATIONAL
POLICEMAN
and
'THE RED CROSS MYSTERY!'

A STRONG BULWARK OF WORLD AMITY IS THE INTERNATIONAL RED CROSS! FOR ITS HELPING HAND GOES INTO ALL COUNTRIES, AND THE NAME OF THE RED CROSS IS BLESSED IN COUNTLESS FOREIGN TONGUES.....
BLESSED? RADAR FINDS THAT THE RED CROSS CAN BE HATED TOO, BY THE VERY PEOPLE IT SEEKS TO AID, AND FOR WHAT, STRANGELY ENOUGH, SEEM TO BE VERY GOOD REASONS! FOLLOW RADAR AS HE SEEKS TO UNRAVEL THE DEADLY SECRET BEHIND THE **RED CROSS MYSTERY!**

AT AN INTERNATIONAL CONFERENCE OF OIL MAGNATES---

I OFFER ONE MILLION BARRELS OF CRUDE OIL FROM CORVATI ISLAND AT TWO DOLLARS A BARREL LOWER THAN THE QUOTED PRICE!

IMPOSSIBLE!

HOW CAN YOU AFFORD TO DO IT? I HAVE HEARD YOU ARE A GENIUS OF PRODUCTION, FRANCISCO PERONO, BUT YOU ARE UNDERSELLING THE WHOLE MARKET!

EFFICIENCY IS THE ANSWER, MY DEAR SIR!

MY PEOPLE WORK GLADLY, BECAUSE I TREAT THEM WELL! AND THE GOVERNMENT OF MY ISLAND IS MOST COOPERATIVE! SO, I PRODUCE MORE, AND SELL FOR LESS....

MR. PERONO! *TERRIBLE NEWS!* **PLAGUE** HAS BROKEN OUT ON CORVATI ISLAND!

WHAT?

MY PEOPLE ARE DYING LIKE FLIES! WHAT CAN I DO?

WE'LL CALL THE INTERNATIONAL RED CROSS!

THEY'LL SEND MEDICAL SUPPLIES, DOCTORS AND NURSES! YOU CAN DEPEND ON THE RED CROSS, PERONO!

YOU ARE RIGHT, MY FRIENDS! I CANNOT TELL YOU HOW GRATEFUL MY PEOPLE WILL BE!

ments, explaining, "The people must learn to accept dictatorships." Radar smashes the plot and encourages cooperation between the United States and its democratic allies to pursue other fascist conspirators.[21]

Radar also underscored the importance of free trade for peace in the postwar world. One story printed near the end of the war opens with a German businessman and Nazi sympathizer named Krug paying a visit to the leader of a peaceful Balkan nation. Krug proposes that they form a chemical industry cartel, in which the Balkan leader would serve as director, "unofficially of course," and Krug would enjoy exclusive trading privileges in his country. The prime minister balks at this outrageous suggestion, exclaiming, "That would ruin the small businessman! You know cartel agreements of this kind are unlawful, Krug! Get out!" Frustrated but determined to pursue his greedy scheme, Krug meets secretly with revolutionary anarchist leaders and proposes to finance their insurrection in exchange for the anarchists' guarantee that his chemical combine will enjoy "sole trading privileges" under the new antidemocratic regime. "You see," says Krug, "the little businessman has to go! The Krug chemical combine already spreads over three European countries . . . soon it will swallow the world!" After the anarchists have launched the revolution, the "Big Four" send Radar to arrest Krug and help restore order. The International Court of Justice sentences Krug to life imprisonment "as an example to other monopolists who with cartels would choke free enterprise—the cornerstone of democracy." A wonderful indictment of fascism, leftist revolution, and corporate monopolism all at once, this Radar story manages to combine these foremost obstacles to American interests into a single sinister conspiracy.[22]

The virtues of free trade reappear in "The Border Incident," in which Radar goes to South America on a mission to heal strained relations between the neighboring countries of "Rolivia" and "Teru." Here, violations of free-trading practices between the nations threaten to provoke war. The crisis began when the president of Rolivia imposed a tariff on imported bricks from Teru, which justifiably upset the Teruvians. Radar meets with the leader of Rolivia, who defends his tariff by claiming, "It ees for the benefit of my people! I must protect our new

From "The Red Cross Mystery," *Master Comics* 72 (Fawcett Publications, September 1946). Radar the International Policeman was the purest expression of the liberal postwar vision to be found in comic books. The embodiment of Roosevelt's internationalism, Radar policed the world, apprehending dictators, monopolists, and extremists of all kinds. Writer and artist unknown.

brick company." Radar appeals to him, "But, Mr. President, Teru can retaliate by putting a tariff on your goods! This will hurt both countries." Unimpressed, the president orders Radar to get out, adding, "Thees whole problem ees none of your business!" As an international policeman, Radar insists that it *is* his business. He investigates the matter further and discovers that the Rolivian president is secretly the owner of the brick company that the tariffs protect, and he stands to profit from the policies that hurt the people of both nations. The crooked president laughs, "What do I care if Rolivians have to pay more than the bricks are worth! In no time I will be a millionaire!" After Radar has exposed the corrupt leader, the new president repeals the tariff and reestablishes peaceful free trade between the two nations.[23]

While Radar clearly represented American interests, those interests were presumed to be synonymous with democracies throughout the world. Radar was consistent enough in his appeal for democracy to call for tolerance and inclusion within America as well. In "Arsenal of Hate," the United Nations instructs Radar to investigate the distribution of hate propaganda in the United States. At the Lincoln Memorial he discovers scattered leaflets propagating race, ethnic, and religious hatred with inflammatory slogans like "The White Race Must Wipe Out the Negroes," "Protestants against Catholics," and "Gentiles against Jews." Radar discovers that this is part of an international plot, aided by a traitor within the U.S. government, to divide and conquer the people of America. The fascist conspirator claims, "When citizen is fighting citizen in the U.S. . . . labor against capitol [*sic*]—Gentile against Jew—White against Negro—great fascist leaders now exiled will step in and seize the government!" Radar puts an end to this scheme and prevails upon others to beware of those who would pit one American against another.[24]

"Radar" was the most political comic book series of the immediate postwar years, but it was not very popular. Too often, the series sacrificed action and adventure for the sake of political education. Far more compelling as a historical document than successful entertainment, "Radar" ceased publication in 1948, joining the long list of postwar superhero casualties.

Fawcett disseminated liberal messages with more subtlety in its popular and whimsical Captain Marvel comic books. A tale called "Captain Marvel and the Imperfect Perfection" portrayed a town called Perfection, where conformity has been "carried to evil extremes." All citizens must conform to community standards for appearance and behavior. "Undesirable" people are not tolerated. When townspeople notice a "disgusting freak with purple hair" walking on the street, they beat him up. The head of the Perfection Civic League explains, "We don't want misfits like that in our wonderful town." Captain Marvel ends this discrimination and advises readers to beware of "snobs and bigots" who hold to unfairly distorted standards of "perfection."[25]

"Captain Marvel: Citizen of the Universe" further illustrates the consequences of intolerance. It opens with an alien from another planet arriving on Earth. Although ugly in appearance, the alien is actually friendly, and he has come to invite the people of Earth to join an interplanetary organization called the "Citizens of the Universe," dedicated to promoting peace and brotherhood among peoples everywhere. The alien explains to a sympathetic Captain Marvel that "if all the people of all worlds sign up as citizens of the universe pledged to eternal peace with each other, then no scheming dictators or munitions makers could ever start a war of worlds!" But when Earth people encounter the alien, the results are sadly predictable. Reacting to the alien's threatening appearance instead of his benign message, a mob attacks him. Then, as if the point was not clear enough, a second alien ship arrives, carrying handsome aliens, whom the citizens greet enthusiastically. These aliens, of course, turn out to be evil and bent on world conquest. Captain Marvel clears up all the confusion and drives the nasty aliens away, but the whole affair reflects poorly on the citizens. Deeply disappointed, the friendly alien departs Earth, having concluded that people here are not sufficiently enlightened to join the community of planets.[26]

Captain Marvel was among a number of postwar superheroes who expressed hope for international cooperation. Making such cooperation all the more imperative was the specter of atomic warfare. During the brief period when the United States enjoyed a monopoly on the bomb, comic books portrayed atomic energy as a force for peace that must not be allowed to fall into the wrong hands. The first comic book to explore the ramifications of the atomic age was an extremely short-lived superhero title called *Atoman*. Published in 1946 by a small company called Spark Publications, the comic book asked metaphorically, "Who is this new man whose body generates atomic power? Whose muscles give him the colossal might of the universe? . . . How will Atoman use his strength? Will it be for good or for evil?" The hero is secretly an atomic scientist who has acquired his powers while working on the Manhattan Project. Upon discovering his new powers, he asks himself, "What am I to do with my power? I can use it for good . . . or selfishly keep it for my own profit." He decides to use the power to help mankind because, as he puts it, "Atomic power cannot belong to one

EPILOGUE

IN THE THUNDEROUS, RESOUNDING CRASH OF THE TWO GREATEST BLOWS EVER DELIVERED, OUR STORY ENDS! WHO WON THE BATTLE?
WELL, MR. ATOM IS TELLING THE STORY....

CAPTAIN MARVEL WAS TOO MUCH FOR ME -- THAT TIME! BUT HE COULD NOT FINALLY DESTROY ME! LIKE THE ATOM THAT GAVE ME BIRTH, I EXIST FOREVER!

BUT CAPTAIN MARVEL WAS CLEVER! HE FORESAW THE DIFFICULTY! ALREADY HE HAD BUILT THIS THICK-WALLED LEAD PRISON WHERE I AM NOW CAGED! EVEN **MY** STRENGTH CANNOT HELP ME TO ESCAPE FROM THIS PLACE!

AFTER THIS BROADCAST, I WILL BE ALLOWED TO SPEAK NO MORE! THIS IS MY LAST MESSAGE TO THE WORLD! YOU, WHO HAVE MADE ME YOUR PRISONER, **BEWARE** LEST I RETURN TO DESTROY MY KEEPERS!...
BEWARE!

THERE YOU ARE, FOLKS! A FINAL MESSAGE FROM MR. ATOM, IN HIS UNDERGROUND LEAD PRISON! I HOPE YOU ALL TAKE HIS WARNING TO YOUR HEARTS! FOR MR. ATOM IS A MENACE THAT THE WORLD CANNOT SAFELY IGNORE!

man . . . or group of men . . . or even one nation! It belongs to the whole world!" Asserting that atomic power "must be used to help all people . . . regardless of race or creed or nationality," Atoman concludes, "I am strong . . . therefore it is my duty to help the weak." Accordingly, he supports the scientists of the Atomic Institute, who agree that "the secret of atomic power must never be permitted to fall into greedy hands!"[27] In his initial adventure, Atoman defeats a corporate executive who tries to steal the secret atomic formula. "Atomic power is too dangerous to be controlled by one man or one corporation," says Atoman. "All the people should benefit from it!" Expressing a remarkably liberal argument for internationalization of the bomb, *Atoman* offered a vision for the atomic age which encompassed the cooperative spirit of the New Deal and the triumphalism of the Allied victory over fascism. Alas, *Atoman* made no impression whatsoever in the comic book marketplace, folding after only two issues, while deepening Cold War tensions quickly doomed the hero's hopes for the bomb.[28]

Other comic books revealed serious anxieties about the dawning atomic age. Captain Marvel encountered the atom bomb on a number of occasions, and he emphasized the peaceful uses of atomic energy. One story predicted that atomic energy would be able to supply power to the entire world by the year 2053. But other cautionary tales illustrated the frightening consequences of atomic energy beyond responsible government control. In the ominously titled "Captain Marvel and the End of the World," a mad Asian scientist builds a proton bomb that is even more powerful than the atomic bomb, and Captain Marvel tries to prevent him from detonating it. He is too late, and the bomb explodes and destroys the world. Only at the end of the story does Captain Marvel reveal to readers that this horrifying event actually occurred on another planet, not on Earth—this time.[29]

It did not necessarily take a madman to unleash the dangers of atomic energy. In "Captain Marvel and the Missing Atom," the hero must capture a "master atom" that has leaked from an atomic reactor. Scientists warn that if the master atom comes into contact with a solid object it would result in a massive atomic explosion. Captain Marvel ultimately does return the atom safely to the power plant but only after

From "Captain Marvel Meets Mr. Atom," *Captain Marvel Adventures* 78 (Fawcett Publications, November 1947). Captain Marvel's encounters with Mr. Atom reflected popular anxiety over the atomic bomb and the fear that its destructive power might be beyond even the ability of superheroes to contain. Script by William Woolfolk. Art by C. C. Beck.

the world narrowly escapes what could have been its first peacetime nuclear disaster.[30]

In the atom bomb, mighty superheroes like Captain Marvel finally met their match. Here they encountered a danger that could not be conquered or adequately explained away. They would continue to try, but the results—much like the falsely reassuring explanations coming from more official sources—proved to be distorted, contradictory, and ultimately unsatisfying. Comic book makers accustomed to dealing in simple solutions frankly did not know how to deal with the reality of the atomic age any better than the rest of the population did. This raised some serious questions about the continuing ability of superheroes to speak to the concerns of their audience. Their shortcomings on this matter were symptomatic of their general failure to reach young readers in the postwar era.

Teen Humor and Jungle Queens

The declining interest in superheroes opened the door for publishers to test the market with other genres. Features put out by Archie Comics represented one avenue open to publishers. Formerly called MLJ Publications, Archie became the leading publisher specializing in light-hearted teenage humor. Producing work in marked contrast to the urban and violent worlds of the superheroes, Archie Comics placed its characters in the placid suburban community of Riverdale. The featured cast drew from familiar high-school character types: freckle-faced Archie himself, billed alternatively as "America's favorite teenager" and "America's typical teenager"; Jughead, the class clown who fears girls; Reggie, the arrogant jock; Betty, the blonde sweetheart; and Veronica, the rich snob. The stories centered on the most benign aspects of middle-class adolescent concerns—dates, cars, school, and parents. The Archie stories struck a commercially sensible middle ground by exploring elements of teen culture while always affirming conformity and respect for authority. Predicting the formula of family-oriented television sitcoms, Archie comic books dealt with problems so trivial and so completely resolvable that they gave an impression of unchanging suburban bliss. Their style, in fact, became so standardized and formulaic that those published in the 1990s look virtually the same as those published forty years earlier.

Archie Comics was the first publisher to tap heavily into the preteen female audience. It offered an idealized, tranquil, and nostalgic vision of high-school life primarily for boys and girls who had not yet experienced it. Although Archie was ostensibly the star of the comic books, many stories revolved around the boy-chasing exploits of Betty and Veronica. While hardly sophisticated characters, they have enough individuality to demand respect from their boyfriends and often seem to be brighter than most of their male classmates. All the characters had enough charm to make the comic books a perennial favorite among young children. Yet the tone of the series betrays the judgmental outlook of adult supervision. America's "typical teenager" never uses teen slang, never fights, never smokes or drinks alcohol, always obeys his parents in the end, and betrays only the vaguest hint of his libido. In other words, he is typical only of the kind of teenager that most adults want to have around. Archie offered young readers a safe glimpse into teen life, while carefully observing the rules of adult society.[31]

Other publishers pushed comic books in more controversial directions. After the sales of superhero titles dropped, some comic book makers tried to seduce male readers with sexy images. Marvel superheroes like the Sub-Mariner and the Human Torch began to share space with shapely blonde characters like Namora and the Asbestos Lady. Captain America's teenage sidekick, Bucky, was shot and hospitalized in one issue, only to be replaced by the Golden Girl in the next—a change apparently to the Captain's liking, since Bucky never returned. Not to be outdone, publisher Victor Fox made sexy women like the Phantom Lady stars of his comic books, featuring them prominently on the covers, often in bondage.[32] No publisher, however, played to male libidos more frequently or effectively than Fiction House. Women with short skirts, long slender legs, and exaggerated breasts adorned the covers of Fiction House's comic books, while the stories prepared for the publisher by the Iger shop (where much of the material, interestingly, was written by women) beckoned randy young males with sexually suggestive and sadomasochistic images. Women in bondage and women placing men in bondage, dominating men with whips, or trampling men with high heels played to common male fetishes.[33]

When this sort of material appeared in Fiction House's ubiquitous jungle comics, the results took on powerful racist and imperialist—as well as sexual and sadomasochistic—overtones. Throughout the postwar era the jungle formula essentially remained what it had been before World War II: white lords, kings, queens, and princesses ruled over jungles populated by childlike, superstitious, and mischievous brown people in need of paternalistic guidance.[34] In one story, a white trader masquerades as a "bird god" in order to frighten the natives into attacking his trading rivals. The scantily clad jungle queen, Camilla in this instance, reveals the false god to the natives, who, like children

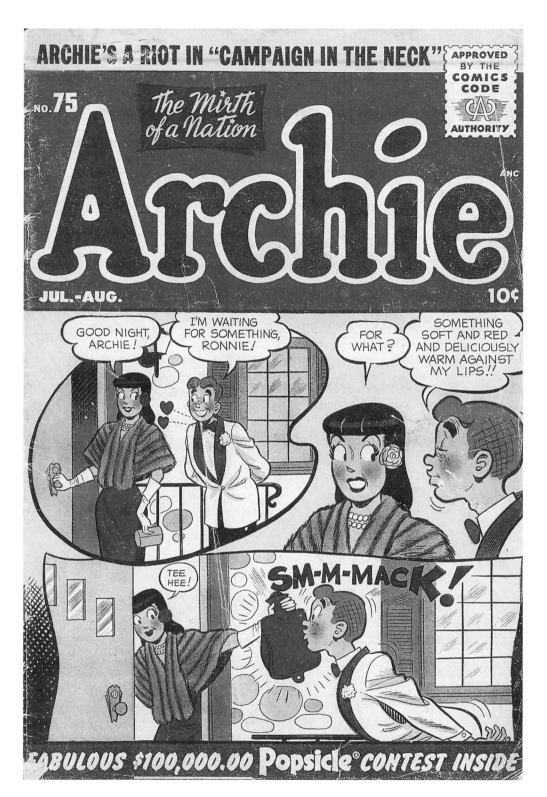

having been scolded by a parent or a teacher, sheepishly apologize to Camilla, "These misguided ones ask thy forgiveness, O Jungle Queen!" Camilla imperiously grants them forgiveness but admonishes the tribe to remember that "traders are their friends."[35] In another story, Sheena, the Queen of the Jungle, orders an African tribe to abolish their "cruel burial customs." The tribal chief responds dutifully, "We hear, O Sheena, we obey!" Jungle queens also commonly installed desirable governments for the natives. When Sheena deposes the evil leader of the "elephant tribe" and chooses a new ruler for the people, the African natives similarly grovel before her and chant, "We hear! We obey, O Sheena!"[36]

The Fiction House comic books sold well throughout the 1940s and spawned a number of imitators who sometimes took the sex and racism to even greater extremes. Collectively, they did little to advance the public image of comic books. Moreover, in the context of the growing civil rights movement and increasing sensitivity to the equality of white and nonwhite peoples, these hideous images seemed anachronistic. Nevertheless, by highlighting the perils of local nationalism, self-government, and hostile foreign exploitation in undeveloped lands, they tacitly underscored the contemporary arguments for U.S. intervention in the affairs of undeveloped countries.

Exploring the Underworld

Despite their obvious genre and political differences, the superhero, teen-humor, and jungle comic books all basically affirmed the triumphalist culture of postwar America. All expressed moral certainty about American virtues, confidence in the nation's institutions, and optimism for a new age of affluence. Such enthusiastic self-congratulation was understandable in a nation that had prevailed so recently and completely in crises of economic depression and war. But undercurrents of profound doubt and anxiety shaped postwar culture as well. Even as Americans regarded themselves as the virtuous leaders of the "Free World" and the vanguard of the "American Century," they persisted, and even indulged, in a much darker self-image. Amidst widespread celebration of the American dream were masochistic expositions of

Cover of *Archie Comics* 75 (Archie Comics, July–August 1955). Billed as "America's typical teenager," Archie and his pals defined the teen-humor genre for young comic book readers, especially preteen girls. With their unchanging benign image of small-town high-school life, Archie's comic books affirmed the values of suburban America. Art by Bob Montana.

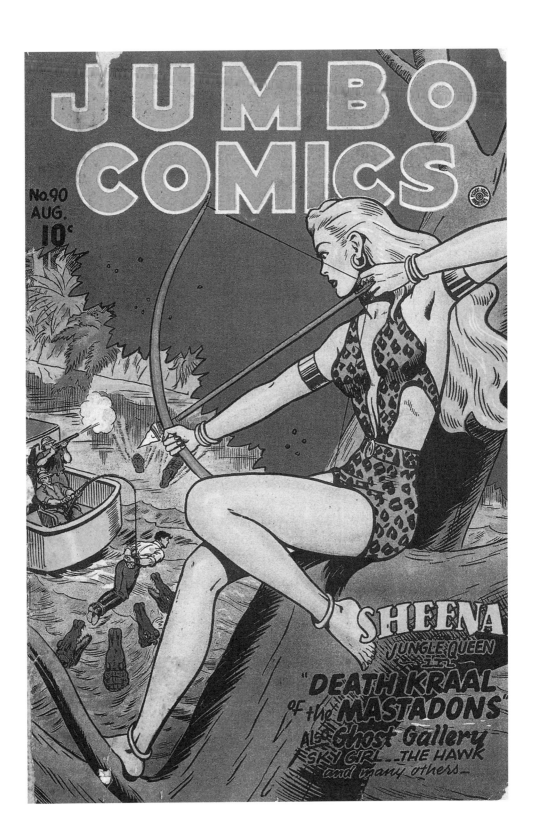

American failures. This was the dark side of America glimpsed in film noir, the novels of Norman Mailer, and even the scholarly writings of Reinhold Niebuhr and Richard Hofstadter. Yet these negative self-images attracted an enthusiastic audience as well. As cultural historian Warren Susman observed, "When men or women saw themselves in the mirror as alienated, weak, and anxious, they cherished that feeling every bit as much as they did while characterizing themselves . . . as heroic and self-sacrificing."[37] American culture, in turn, reflected this willful hypocrisy. And in young people's comic books the morbid fascination with depravity and self-destruction became a lucrative cottage industry.

Crime comic books emerged as one of the most popular and culturally explosive trends in postwar youth entertainment. The genre debuted quietly in comic books in 1942 when publisher Leverett Gleason hired creators Charles Biro and Robert Wood to edit and revitalize two of his lackluster superhero titles. As an added incentive, Gleason promised them a share of the profits earned from their work, an unusually generous proposition in this business. Thus encouraged, Biro and Wood scrapped the superhero series and launched in its place a groundbreaking title called *Crime Does Not Pay*. Inspired by an MGM documentary series of the same name, the comic book featured "true crime" stories about notorious gangsters and killers like "Machine-Gun" Kelly, John Dillinger, and "Pretty Boy" Floyd. Narrated in a documentary, sometimes confessional style, these lurid tales delved into violence, brutality, and sadism to a graphic degree never before seen in comic books—in some instances, never before seen anywhere in mass entertainment.[38]

Beatings, shootings, stabbings, burning bodies, gruesome torture, and sickening varieties of dismemberment were some of the more predictable images found in these comic books. It all appeared within the rather transparent guise of moral cautionary tales about the perils of breaking the law. Yet in actuality these stories offered vicarious guilty pleasure for readers, who followed the criminal protagonist through ten pages of mayhem and murder, only to see it all end in self-destruction on the last page—and often not until the last panel. The fact that the criminals always meet an unhappy end in prison, in the

Cover of *Jumbo Comics* 90 (Fiction House, August 1946). Fiction House was best known for its jungle comics and its leggy heroines. Covers like this vied for the attention of young males in the crowded postwar market. Artist unknown.

THAT WON'T WORK!

OHHH.

I'M GOING TO SHOW YOU UP!

UGHHH.

TELL YOUR PEOPLE THE TRUTH ABOUT BLACK MAGIC OR I'LL SCRATCH YOU WITH THE BRACELET.

NOOO... I'LL TELL...

THE BRACELET IS DIPPED IN A VIPER POISON. WHEN THE WEARER EXERTS HIMSELF, POISON SEEPS INTO HIS PORES, AND KILLS HIM. THE STABBING OF THE CLAY IMAGES WAS ONLY TO IMPRESS MY FOLLOWERS WITH MY POWER!

GO! YOU DON'T DESERVE TO BE QUEEN OF THE WOMAN TRIBE!

AFTER RELEASING BEN, CAMILLA SMASHES THE CLAY FIGURES.

BLACK MAGIC IS FALSE! FEAR IT NO LONGER!

CAMILLA WILL BE OUR QUEEN!

NOW THEY WILL BE FREE OF THE HORROR OF BLACK MAGIC!

UGH- I'M STILL SHIVERING!

CAMILLA APPEARS IN ANOTHER THRILLING, DEATH-DEFYING ADVENTURE IN NEXT MONTH'S COPY OF JUNGLE COMICS!

electric chair, or in a hail of gunfire barely concealed the glorification of their hedonistic and sadistic lifestyles. The message was clear: crime may not pay, but it is highly entertaining.

Crime Does Not Pay sold moderately well during the war years, but not as well as most superhero titles. Retailers may have been unsure of how to display the unusual publication—was it a comic book to be placed alongside the likes of *Superman* and *Donald Duck*, or did it belong with pulp magazines and adult crime fiction? In a deliberate pitch to older teenage and adult readers, Lev Gleason billed the title as "The Magazine with the Widest Range of Appeal." It was not until after the war, however, that Gleason's innovative marketing began to pay off. Postwar changes in the publisher's creative staff improved the look of the comic books and helped them to better fulfill their promise. The underdeveloped cartoon styles of amateur artists hired during the war years had sometimes undermined the deadly serious tone of the series. At times the crude artwork had given the disturbing impression that these tales of graphic brutality were scrawled by a deranged child. But after the war, talented artists like Dan Barry and George Tuska brought to the series more accomplished and illustrative styles better suited to the gritty subject matter. The postwar look and tone of *Crime Does Not Pay* clearly set it apart from the superhero titles, and it avoided their sagging commercial fate. Gleason's sales rose steadily. When it had premiered in 1942 the title had sold 200,000 copies per issue. By 1946 monthly sales figures had risen fourfold. In 1948 it sold over a million copies each month.[39]

Those kind of numbers commanded the attention of the entire industry. Beginning in 1947 the competition saturated the newsstands with flagrant imitations of *Crime Does Not Pay*. Titles with comically derivative names like *Gangsters Can't Win*, *Lawbreakers Always Lose*, *Crime Must Pay the Penalty*, and *Justice Traps the Guilty* closely aped the appearance and formula of Lev Gleason's successful series and threatened to squeeze it off the shelves. In 1948 Gleason himself added a second crime title called *Crime and Punishment*. Even DC bowed to the obvious popularity of this violent genre and published its own relatively

From "Camilla, Jungle Queen," *Jungle Comics* 29 (Fiction House, May 1942). One of many formulaic white jungle queens who proliferated during World War II and the postwar years, Camilla commonly toppled corrupt native leaders and directed the fates of grateful African populations. Writer and artist unknown.

mild *Gang Busters*, a series based on a radio program of the same name and revolving around policemen instead of criminals.[40]

Typical of the crime comic formula was a tale published in the November 1947 issue of *Crime Does Not Pay* called "The Wild Spree of the Laughing Sadist—Herman Duker." It is a graphic biographical sketch of "one of those queers who robbed and killed out of sheer pleasure—experiencing delight in others' terror and agony." The story illustrates how Duker betrays his sadistic tendencies early by torturing canaries and setting cats on fire. When his father tries to discipline his monstrous son, the youth slugs him and runs away to New York City. There, Duker graduates to homicide. At one point, he is arrested and goes to trial, but the judge grants him leniency on account of his youth. After a brief thirty-one month stay in a juvenile reformatory, Duker returns to society and immediately begins to kill again. Finally, after years of senseless brutality and murder, his reign of terror comes to an overdue end in the electric chair. The tale ends, as always, with the solemn warning, "Crime Does Not Pay!"[41]

Other "true crime" stories promised essentially the same: psychopathic personalities, self-destructive lifestyles, killing aplenty, and inevitable, though usually belated, retribution. In the case of "Carlos Barrone, the Murderous Bully," the killer again indulges his terrible passions at an early age. As a schoolboy he hurls a snowball packed with a rock at a little girl's face, blinding her. He pushes a young boy down a flight of stairs, crippling him. He robs his father, beats his girlfriend, and extorts money from his classmates. Somehow, he achieves all of this while evading any kind of prosecution. As an adult, Carlo works as an enforcer for the mob. Several times he is arrested but only serves a few months in jail. Finally, after years of unrestrained brutality, culminating in a vicious killing spree, the authorities catch, convict, and execute him.[42]

Crime comic books could be sickeningly graphic. In "The Woman Who Wouldn't Die," two migrant farm workers return to rob the home of their former employer. The grisly scene that follows could not have appeared in even the most lurid of Hollywood B-movies. The two men kill their employer and his little boy. Then they shoot the mother,

From "The Wild Spree of the Laughing Sadist—Herman Duker," *Crime Does Not Pay* 57 (Lev Gleason Publications, November 1947). In presenting the lurid tales of criminals like Herman Duker, crime comic books like Lev Gleason's *Crime Does Not Pay* offered some of the bloodiest and most sadistic images in visual entertainment. Script by Bob Wood and Charles Biro, art by Fred Guardineer.

CRIME DOES NOT PAY

A TRUE CRIME STORY — MACHINE-GUN KELLY

A BULLY WHO WOULD KILL AT THE DROP OF A HAT— WAS MEEK AS A LAMB WHEN THE SHRILL VOICE OF HIS WIFE GAVE A COMMAND!

HERE WAS A WOMAN, WHO CONCEIVED VICIOUS BANK ROBBERIES AND RUTHLESS, BRUTAL KIDNAPPINGS, WHICH SHE FORCED THROUGH TO A CONCLUSION, LARGELY THROUGH DOMINATION OF HER HUSBAND, WHO, IN SPITE OF HIS TERRORIZING NAME, WOULD ONLY BOW TO HER FURY! IF EVER THERE WAS A HENPECKED MAN, IT WAS GEORGE "MACHINE GUN" KELLY!

ONE NIGHT IN 1927, OUTSIDE THE HOME OF CHARLES AND KATHRYN THORNE, IN FORT WORTH, TEXAS!

OF COURSE I'M DRUNK! WHY SHOULDN'T I GET DRUNK? WHAT'VE I GOT TA LOOK FORWARD TO ALL WEEK-END? NOTHIN' BUT AN EMPTY HOUSE! I SEE YOU'VE GOT YOUR BAGS PACKED, READY TO GO! WELL, GO ON, GO-ONLY THIS TIME DON'T BOTHER TO COME BACK!

STOP SHOUTIN' AT ME, YOU DRUNKEN LOUT! WHAT D'YA WANT ME TO DO, HANG AROUND THIS BURG AND ROT? THIS TOWN IS SO DEAD, IT STINKS!

THERE GO THE THORNES! EVERY NIGHT, DRUNK OR SOBER, IT'S THE SAME THING!

EXCEPT THE WEEK-ENDS! THE WAY THEY FIGHT ALL THE TIME YOU'D THINK CHARLIE WOULD BE GLAD TO LET HIS MISSUS GO AWAY EVERY WEEK-END!

EVENING, KATHRYN, OFF FOR YOUR WEEK-END AGAIN, I SUPPOSE! DO YOU WANT ME TO FILL 'ER UP AS USUAL?

YEAH, AN' JAKE, I WONDER IF YOU'D DO ME A LITTLE FAVOR! WHEN YOU KNOCK OFF HERE, WOULD YOU STOP IN AN' SEE HOW CHARLIE IS? HE WAS AWFUL DRUNK WHEN I LEFT, AN' WE HAD A LITTLE SPAT! I KNOW IT'S FOOLISH OF ME, BUT I'M KINDA WORRIED ABOUT LEAVING HIM THIS TIME!

I CAN'T LIVE WITH HER OR WITHOUT HER, HENCE I AM DEPARTING FROM THIS WORLD! CHARLES THORNE

HMM, I WONDER... WHAT DO YOU MAKE OF IT, DOC?

DEAD ABOUT TWELVE HOURS, SHERIFF! COULD BE SUICIDE OR MURDER! BUT THAT'S UP TO ANY EVIDENCE YOU CAN PRODUCE AT THE INQUEST! I'M ONLY THE CORONER! ALL I CAN SAY IS THE WOUND SHOWS THAT THE BULLET WAS FIRED AT CLOSE RANGE!

douse her and the two bodies in kerosene, and laugh as they set the
family on fire. But the woman does not die. She bites her lip to keep
from screaming, waits for the killers to leave, drags her burning, bullet-
ridden body past the bloody, sizzling corpses of her husband and son,
and crawls to a neighbor's house for help. That the killers are eventually
caught and executed for their heinous crimes hardly suffices as a happy
ending to this gruesome tale.[43]

As the competition among crime comic book publishers intensified, so did the violent imagery in the stories. In one tale appearing in
a 1948 issue of Junior Books' *Crime Must Pay the Penalty*, twenty-three
of the fifty-eight panels depict someone being shot. Victor Fox issued
some of the crudest and most mean-spirited comic books, with shame-
lessly exploitive titles like *Murder Incorporated* and *Crimes by Women*.
Magazine Village's *True Crime Comics* included the notorious "Murder,
Morphine, and Me," which featured within the space of a few pages
images of narcotics sales, drug injections, machine-gunnings, burning
bodies, and a hypodermic needle poised to pierce a woman's eye.[44] With
so many crime titles on the newsstands, it was a buyers' market for
sadism and killing.

Easily the most violent comic books available, the crime titles also
ranked among the most misogynous. Most comic books catered to male
fantasies, but the crime comics were set in an especially macho world
rife with sexual tensions. Women appeared as cheap sex objects, fodder
for male sadistic urges, or scheming murderous gold-diggers who
corrupted men with their sexuality. *Crime Does Not Pay*'s account of
"Machine-Gun Kelly" characterized the notorious killer as "a bully
who would kill at the drop of a hat [but] was meek as a lamb when
the shrill voice of his wife gave a command!" She was "a woman who
conceived vicious bank robberies and ruthless, brutal kidnappings
which she forced through to a conclusion, largely through domination
of her husband who . . . would only bow to her fury." For all of Kelly's
crimes, his most inexcusable seems to have been his submission to the
whims of a domineering woman.[45]

"The Short but Furious Crime Career of Irene Dague and Her Yes-
Man Husband" virtually tells the story with the title. It is the sordid

From "Machine-Gun Kelly," *Crime Does Not Pay* 65 (Lev Gleason Publications, July 1948). A common theme in crime comic books found gold-digging and sadistic women corrupting weak-willed men with their sexuality. According to this story of "Machine-Gun" Kelly, the notorious killer was actually a henpecked weakling who bowed to the fury of his domineering wife. Script by Bob Wood and Charles Biro, artist unknown.

tale of a ruthlessly ambitious woman who pushes her weak-willed husband to commit crimes so that he can afford to buy her the luxuries that she demands. In "Mike Alex," a convicted criminal is released from prison only to be goaded back into crime by his girlfriend, whom he calls a "dirty gold-diggin' louse." Likewise, in the *Crime Does Not Pay* story of Bonnie and Clyde, Bonnie Parker stands revealed as the truly vicious killer, while Clyde Barrow is only a meek fool who slavishly appeases her bloodlust.[46]

There were few positive role models in the crime comic books for males or females. Police rarely figured prominently in the stories, and their dutiful service to the law was almost always overshadowed by the exciting criminals who flouted it. The grinding wheels of justice appeared slow, inefficient, and susceptible to manipulation by criminals with only average intelligence. In one story, an arrested Arkansas serial killer exploits legal technicalities to avoid incarceration, leaving him free to kill again. The story of outlaw Albert Judson relates how this resourceful bank-robber evaded the law for years while leading an arrogant upper-class lifestyle. In each of these cases, the law only caught up with the criminals after they had allowed themselves to be distracted by women.[47]

Whatever might be said about their moral virtues, these crime comic books marked an important stage in the evolution of the industry and youth culture. By demonstrating that successful comic books need not be confined to juvenile adventure stories, fatuous teen humor, and talking animals, they expanded the creative possibilities of the medium considerably. More significantly, they broke from the unwritten code that said comic books had to offer fulfillment, affirmation, and conflict resolution to their young audience on terms established by a supposedly virtuous and progressive society. The crime comic books put forth a remarkably perverse and horrifying image of the affluent society turned upside down. And unlike the superheroes, the freckle-faced teenagers, and the jungle queens, the crime comics offered no way out. Their collective deconstruction of the American dream promised no easy answers, only more of the same. They affronted the triumphalism of postwar America, and young readers bought it up by the millions.

Publishers like Leverett Gleason claimed that a large percentage of their audience were adults—but obviously, the rest were not. The advertising in Gleason's own crime comic books suggested a diverse audience, broad enough to encompass a market for kitchen knives, medical insurance, and "Dick Tracy" toy Tommy guns.[48] This was no small marketing achievement, and it pointed to lucrative possibilities for the comic book industry to reach ever greater audiences. As far as most people were concerned, though, comic books were still strictly for kids. When parents discovered comic books dealing in graphic subject matter often exceeding what was deemed appropriate even for adult entertainment, they were horrified. When they then learned that the industry supplying their children with such material was the least regulated of all mass entertainment, they were outraged. If concerned citizens wanted this industry controlled, they would have to initiate action on their own. And more than a few were prepared to do just that.

4
Youth Crisis

Comic Books
and Controversy,
1947–1950

On December 10, 1948, the students of St. Patrick's Parochial School in Binghamton, New York, achieved brief notoriety. Under the auspices of their proud teachers and parents, the students gathered some two thousand comic books into a pile in the school courtyard and torched them. Community leaders staged the event as part of their movement to boycott comic books that "stressed crime and sex." Elsewhere in New York, the Bishop of the Albany Catholic Diocese urged all Catholics to boycott dealers who sold comic books with "sensational details" of crime and sex. Similar comic book bonfires followed at the Peter and Paul Parochial School in Auburn, New York, and at the St. Cyril's Parish School in Chicago.[1]

Outrage against comic books was not confined to the Catholic Church. These bonfires, disturbingly reminiscent of Nazi book-burnings, signified only the most extreme expressions of an emerging debate on comic books, young people, and the shaping of youth culture in postwar America. Controversy was, of course, nothing new to the comic book industry. Ever since they had first appeared on American newsstands, comic books had been attacked by parents, teachers, librarians, and guardians of traditional culture. Critics charged that comic books caused eyestrain, promoted illiteracy, celebrated bad taste, and encouraged antisocial behavior in children. The patriotic and "educational" comic books of World War II had resulted in part from publishers' efforts to deflect these criticisms. But trends in certain postwar comic books, especially the crime titles, erased whatever progress had been made in that regard. Moreover, the heightened state of Cold War anxiety now raised the pitch of the debate over youth culture to such a hysterical extent that some influential critics began to attack comic books as a threat to the nation's social fabric.

In the broadest sense, the debate over comic books was really about cultural power in postwar America. As Americans looked to define their culture in an age of consumption and cold war, influence over young people became hotly contested terrain. And as the nation mobilized for the war against Communism, questions arose about the children who would one day wage it. Would they have the strength of character to defend the affluent lifestyle now available to them, or would they become complacent and corrupted by the luxuries it offered? Could traditional values and civic virtue be preserved when American youth was seduced daily by consumer culture and its promise of instant self-gratification? Might the very success of the consumer economy be planting the seeds for the ultimate demise of American society? These were profound questions that went to the very core of American culture. Because Americans did not grasp the full implications of these questions, or perhaps because they feared the answers, they debated (and continue to debate) the issues on a microscale, in a series of controversies over certain products of youth entertainment. Comic books would be succeeded by motion pictures, television, rock-and-roll, video games, and the Internet as the disputed agencies of cultural power operating on the nation's youth.

Throughout American history, adults have attributed undesirable changes in youth behavior to some aspect of popular culture. Gilded Age critics attacked dime novels for their sensationalism, violence, and appeal to instant gratification. In the first half of the twentieth century, movies, pulp magazines, and radio programs all came under similar criticism, even as the Victorian culture espoused by the critics became itself overwhelmed by emergent consumerism. Social and cultural concerns arising from the recent experience of World War II set the comic book controversy apart from these precedents, however. One such concern had to do with the newly established power of the media. The war had demonstrated the capacity of the mass media to mold public opinion: when harnessed for sinister purposes, as it had been by Nazi propagandists, it could work to turn citizens against fellow citizens. Another worrying consequence of the war was its social impact on the American home. The war had disrupted families. As fathers went overseas and mothers went to work, a generation of children came of age under re-duced parental supervision, raising alarm about an impending outbreak of juvenile delinquency. As postwar apprehensions about the mass media and juvenile delinquency came together, the comic book industry found itself caught in the crossfire.

Worried observers noted what they viewed as disturbing and un-desirable changes in adolescent behavior. Yet much of what concerned adults termed *juvenile delinquency* was simply adolescents asserting their independence and discovering themselves as individuals within their peer group. These young people and their discrete generational tastes became so pronounced that a new word, *teenager,* came into use to de-scribe them. Statistics did not support the widespread fears about rising juvenile crime, but the press, professional "experts," civic groups, and government agencies all heightened public anxiety about it neverthe-less. In their efforts to explain the appearance of delinquency, many focused on the peculiarities of youth culture. Some charged, in effect, that a commercialized peer culture had intervened between adolescents and sources of traditional values—that is, parents, teachers, and reli-gion. Adults seemed to fear the young generation as the harbingers of a new and frightening social order, one transformed and corrupted by the media and consumer culture.[2]

Comic books were an easy target for those who attributed juvenile delinquency to products of youth culture. The most visible, least cen-sored, and most popular expression of youth entertainment, comic books were also the most bewildering and alien medium to adult sensi-bilities. Crime comic books, in particular, seemed to many the most outrageous evidence of a menacing youth culture that violated and mocked traditional values. The appearance and proliferation of these comic books coincided with the apparent increase in juvenile delin-quency, and many observers viewed this as more than a coincidence. As the controversy escalated, comic books of nearly all varieties came un-der attack for many different reasons. Critics attacked the comic book industry as a subversive agency working to corrupt impressionable minds. As the nation's political leaders planned their strategy of con-tainment in the Cold War, many citizens began to advocate an agenda of cultural containment as well.

The Comic Book Scare

By the end of World War II comic books had assumed an increasingly visible presence in American popular culture. *Publishers Weekly* reported that an estimated 540 million comic books were printed in 1946.

Within a few years that figure nearly doubled. In 1945 the Child Study
Association, anticipating the public concern over this proliferation,
conducted a study of comic books and their audience. The association's
findings, published in the *New York Times Book Review*, explained that
comic books were really just contemporary fairy tales adapted to incorporate elements of current everyday life. Today's children, the author
noted, were "very conscious of living in a 'modern' world," and they
found comic books appealing and relevant to that world. Noting the
concerns of many parents, the experts acknowledged that there was a
lot of violence in some of the comic books, but they also pointed out
that there is "an impulse toward violence in children and that some of
this is worked off vicariously through the medium of the comics." The
Child Study Association, whose members included several paid editorial consultants for DC Comics and Fawcett Publications (a fact that
was not divulged in the article), assured parents that, properly supervised, comic book reading posed no threat to their children.[3]

Columnist Reita Bean offered similar reassurance in the November
1945 issue of *American Home*. As a mother worried about her own son's
fascination with comic books, "especially the lurid ones," she nevertheless permitted them in her home. "If the child was raised in a decent
home and inculcated with proper values," she wrote, "then he will take
as pure fiction the comics that don't follow graphically and truthfully
his own way of life."[4] Even the most influential of child-care experts
assured parents that comic books were not necessarily harmful to the
development of children. Dr. Benjamin Spock wrote in the first edition
of *The Common Sense Book of Baby and Child Care* that children between
the ages of six and ten especially were attracted to comic books. Children of this age group, he noted, felt that they understood the difference between right and wrong, and they delighted in comic book stories where right always triumphed. He added that even violence in
comic books could serve a healthy emotional purpose for children, because it allowed them to indulge their aggressive impulses without acting upon them. Although Dr. Spock appreciated the valid concerns of
parents about excessive comic book reading, he advised them to regulate rather than forbid the activity.[5]

An increasing number of observers, however, branded comic books
a serious menace, especially after 1947, when juvenile delinquency
seemed to be on the rise and the number of crime comic books on
the market had multiplied. In August of that year the Fraternal Order
of Police publicly criticized those comic books that "glorify criminals."
At their convention in Indianapolis, the police condemned such comic

books as "one of the contributing factors to the cause of juvenile delinquency" and urged citizens to fight for the abolition of this "unrestrained, bold, vicious, salacious, and immoral" literature that was "detrimental to the youth of this nation." Law enforcement officials and court judges around the nation echoed this call to civic action.[6]

Even if statistics did not always support the notion of rising juvenile delinquency, knowledgeable observers contended that the brutality of violent crimes committed by young offenders had definitely worsened in recent years. New York's deputy police commissioner in charge of the Juvenile Aid Bureau warned that the crimes committed by today's youth were "in many instances more serious and even of a more violent nature than those committed by youth in the past." To help explain this troubling pattern, the criminal law section of the American Bar Association conducted a survey of comic books and concluded that a large percentage of them emphasized crime and violence. Furthermore, the ABA warned that juvenile violence was not the only problem resulting from these books. A spokesman for the association maintained that even if particular localities did not see an increase in the rate of juvenile crime, these comic books still weakened the "moral codes and ethical concepts" of American youth. He concluded cynically that "with almost every child and adolescent bombarded many times daily with the jargon of the criminal and the horrors and depraved methods of his activity, we should rejoice that we have as much normal and rational child behavior as we do."[7]

Especially troubling to many was the increasing frequency of juvenile crimes allegedly inspired by comic books. In September 1947 a coroner's jury in Pittsburgh blamed comic books in connection with the hanging death of a twelve-year-old boy after the boy's mother told the jury that her son had been an incessant reader of comic books and probably had hanged himself while reenacting a scene depicted in one of them. In May 1948 two boys aged eleven and twelve stole an airplane and flew it 120 miles across Oklahoma. They later told police that they had learned how to fly the aircraft from reading comic books. Three months later, in rural northern Indiana, three small boys aged six to eight strung up another young boy by his neck and tortured him with lit matches. After the boys—all reportedly from "good families"—told authorities that they were avid fans of comic books dealing with crime and torture, official calls arose for a county-wide ban of such publications.[8]

Some critics saw a more profound threat in the comic books than even these apparent copycat episodes suggested. Marya Mannes artic-

ulated the elitist critique of comic books in the February 1947 issue of
the *New Republic.* She noted with concern that comic books had become
"the addiction of three out of four American homes," and in two-thirds
of these homes they were "virtually the only reading matter." Comic
books, she argued, represented "the absence of thought," and a nation
of young people weaned on such trash was on a perilous course towards
cultural bankruptcy. She acknowledged that the superheroes tended to
be "highly patriotic and virtuous" and commended the "sincere" efforts
of DC and Fawcett to "inject material of educational and social value
into the existent adventure stories," but she lamented that high-minded
series like Fawcett's "Radar, the International Policeman" sold relatively poorly. Most of the superhero comic books, she insisted, simply
glorified violence and vigilantism. She found the jungle comics especially repulsive, citing their sexual content as their chief offense—but,
notably, not mentioning their racism or imperialist overtones. And she
deplored crime comic books as the most "lurid and hideous" vignettes
in American entertainment.[9]

Citing an unnamed study that seemed to confirm her assumptions
about a class dimension to the comic book problem, Mannes claimed
that those residing in poorer households were most likely to be regular
readers of comic books while those in wealthier homes read them the
least. Such evidence suggested, at least to the author, that comic books
appealed most to the unsophisticated and poorly educated. If this
"intellectual marijuana" filled "some vacuum in the people who need
them," she warned that America would face the frightening consequences of "a people incapable of reading a page of ordinary text . . . a
society based on the impact of a fist on a jaw . . . [or] a nation that left
[law enforcement] to the man in the costume." Comic books, in Mannes's estimation, were the harbingers of cultural doom.[10]

The most idiosyncratic critique of comic books came from a New
York folklorist named Gershon Legman. In a 100-page polemic titled
Love and Death: A Study in Censorship, published in 1949, Legman contended that current censorship laws were exerting an immoral influence
on American popular literature. Because obscenity laws greatly restricted portrayals and discussions of sex, he argued, writers used violence in their work as a titillating substitute. Moreover, he charged,
Americans relished violence, even as they harbored an irrational fear of
sex. He attacked literature ranging from the novels of Ernest Hem-
mingway to comic books as evidence of the American cult of violence
and advocated the abolition of censorship laws, stating that sex in literature was far more desirable than violence. It was a curious little book

with a strange argument—and, according to a review in the *New Republic*, not a very convincing one. Still, the reviewer found Legman's incidental points about comic books to be the most interesting and important feature of the book.[11]

Legman despised all kinds of comic books, but he targeted superheroes in particular. Echoing the familiar charge that Superman was a fascist figure, he claimed that superheroes had given "every American child a complete course in paranoid megalomania such as no German child ever had, a total conviction of the morality of force such as no Nazi could even aspire to." He pointed to the use of symbols in superhero comic books—Superman's *S* and Captain Marvel's lightning bolt—as "trappings of Nazism." Moreover, he noted, "all the more sinister villains" in comic books "have 'Jewish' noses." The liberal reviewer in the *New Republic* found Legman's arguments on this point especially compelling and compared the implications of vigilante superheroes to the "paranoia of the present loyalty crusade," being waged against suspected Communists in the government.[12]

The *New Republic*'s commentary aside, Legman's book generated little interest. His critique of comic books did not resonate with the American public because it was rooted in a general condemnation of American culture. He even attacked other critics of comic books as hypocrites. Noting that "people want to know what can be done" about comic books, he retorted, "Nothing can be done. Not for children," because "American parents" were "themselves addicted to the same violence." Pointing to evidence throughout American entertainment, Legman argued that "violence in America is a business—big business," and the problem of comic books could only be resolved when parents were ready to confront the degrading implications of their own violent consumer culture.[13] This was not the kind of argument that parents wanted to hear, and it denied Legman a leading voice in the debate over comic books.

Fredric Wertham's Crusade

A far more successful approach was taken by a New York City psychiatrist named Dr. Fredric Wertham. Born in Bavaria in 1895, Wertham had studied medicine in England, Austria, and Germany before earning his medical degree in 1921. The following year he emigrated to the United States and took a position as chief resident at the Phipps Psychiatric Clinic of the Johns Hopkins Hospital. He participated in Baltimore's intellectual community, became a member of H. L. Mencken's Saturday Club, and developed a reputation as a liberal progressive con-

cerned about the poor and disadvantaged. He was also among the few
psychiatrists at the time who would see black patients. In 1932 Wertham moved to New York City to become the senior psychiatrist at
Bellevue and director of the clinic connected with the New York Court
of General Sessions. In 1939 he was appointed director of the Psychiatric Clinic at Queens Hospital Center, where he remained throughout
the next decade. In New York Wertham became more active in social
issues, working (though unsuccessfully) to get the city to establish a
low-cost psychiatric clinic in Harlem. In March 1944 he personally
opened the LaFargue Clinic in the basement of Harlem's St. Philip's
Episcopal Church, where he and his staff offered psychiatric service
to poor clients, most of whom were African Americans, at a cost of
twenty-five cents per visit. *Time* magazine ran a favorable story on the
project and quoted the rector of St. Philip's, who praised the clinic as
"the greatest thing that has happened in Harlem in years."[14]

Wertham's experience treating African American and juvenile patients led him to develop theories about how sociocultural factors acted
on personality development. Unlike most of his Freudian-trained colleagues, Wertham emphasized exterior social conditions to explain the
psychological disorders afflicting the human psyche. He pointed to the
harmful psychological effects of racial segregation in a set of arguments
later used in the Supreme Court's landmark *Brown v. Board of Education*
desegregation ruling. He applied the same social-psychological theories to his analysis of disturbed juveniles. This led him to investigate
their cultural background, their patterns of play, and their choice of
reading material. Consistently, he found that the common cultural influence shared by virtually all of the juvenile cases before him was
comic books.[15]

Wertham's analysis was clinical as well as theoretical. From interviews conducted with juvenile patients, he concluded that certain instances of delinquent and criminal behavior in children were directly
attributable to the comic books they had read. Wertham singled out
comic books because they were the most uncensored, unregulated, and
youth-oriented media products widely available on the market. Comic
books were also—unlike movies, radio, or television—a pastime that
children engaged in completely beyond adult supervision. They purchased them on their own and took them to school, to bed, or to anywhere else they chose. They could share and swap them with friends.
Most importantly, they could secretly enjoy comic books by hiding
them away from parents. The juvenile offenders themselves often
seemed to confirm Wertham's suspicions by identifying comic books,

especially the violent ones, as their favorite entertainment and inspiration.[16]

Like other critics, Wertham objected to comic books for their ideological content. Echoing common elitist critiques and adding some of his own, he criticized crime comic books most of all for their violence, deplored superheroes for their fascist implications, and especially despised the racist, imperialistic, and pornographic images littered throughout the jungle comics. Wertham's private writings reveal that his assault on comic books was, like Legman's, rooted in a general, almost Marxist, critique of American commercial culture. It was this culture, he believed, that subverted the morality of children for the sake of profit. He rarely let the leftist angle of his critique emerge in his public arguments, however.[17] It was a wise tactic. For by understating his broader position on consumer culture, he was able to garner far more popular influence and grassroots support for his attack on comic books.

By 1948 Wertham had become a leading spokesman on the issue of comic books and juvenile delinquency. He presented his theories in March of that year at a Manhattan symposium held by the Association for the Advancement of Psychotherapy titled "The Psychopathology of Comic Books." There, a number of "specialists" on comic books, including Gershon Legman, gave their views on the topic. In its coverage of the symposium, *Time* magazine devoted the most attention to Wertham's testimony and printed a photograph of him to accompany the article. Several representatives from the comic book industry attended, but they had little opportunity to state their defense of comic books. Wertham equated their presence there with distillers attending a symposium on alcoholism.[18]

Judith Crist's March 27, 1948, article in *Collier's* gave Wertham his first opportunity to articulate his theories to a national audience. The substantial piece, titled "Horror in the Nursery," quoted Wertham and his assistants extensively and presented him as the leading muckraker in the crusade against the comic book industry. Wertham charged that comic books "in intent and effect" degraded the morals of youngsters. Contending that comic books were "sexually aggressive in an abnormal way" and made "violence alluring and cruelty heroic," he urged that if those responsible refused to desist, then "the time has come to legislate these books off the newsstands and out of the candy stores."[19]

Wertham tried to clarify his position by noting that comic books did not "automatically" cause delinquency in children, but clinical studies demonstrated that "comic book reading was a distinct influenc-

ing factor in the case of every single delinquent or disturbed child" that
he had studied. He insisted that comic books also contributed to the
particular brutality that juvenile crimes had begun to assume. He referred to some recent examples, such as a Long Island brother and sister, aged eleven and eight, respectively, who had assaulted a seven-year-
old boy simply "to see what it felt like to kill." They had stabbed the boy
with a fountain pen and tried to squirt ink into his wound, mimicking a
hypodermic injection. This horrible act, Wertham insisted, could only
have been inspired by a crime comic book.[20]

Wertham also warned of the sexual threat posed by comic books.
Comic book makers, he claimed, made a "deliberate attempt to emphasize sexual characteristics." Even more sinister, he contended, was the
way in which comic books taught that sexual pleasure went hand in
hand with violence, especially violence directed at women. Recalling
an interview with a twelve-year-old boy who admired the "tough guys"
in comic books, Wertham had asked the youth what made a man tough.
"A tough guy," the boy had explained, "is a man who slaps a girl."[21]
Likewise, Wertham observed that girls exhibited feelings of inferiority
and insecurity as a consequence of reading comic books full of glamorous women with impossibly developed physical attributes. Lamenting
that they did not possess "the full bosom and rounded hips" of comic
book women, girls became withdrawn and depressed. "Even more dangerous," he insisted, was the affected "adolescent girl's fear of sex and
her sometimes resultant frigidity."[22]

Wertham made the case against comic books in his own article,
"The Comics . . . Very Funny!" published in the 29 May 1948 issue
of the *Saturday Review of Literature*. It established the style that Wertham would employ throughout his crusade. Beginning with a sensational account of horrific juvenile crimes, Wertham seemed to be appropriating the lurid style of the very comic books that he condemned:
a group of boys between the ages of three and nine assault a four-year-
old girl by pushing her off a bicycle, stealing her toys, and binding her
with handcuffs purchased from an ad in a comic book; a fifteen-year-
old boy extorts money from a twelve-year-old by threatening to push
him from a fire escape; a twelve-year-old boy kills his younger sister;
another twelve-year-old kills his older sister.[23] In all of these cases,
Wertham pointed out, the young perpetrators had confessed their enthusiasm for violent comic books. He supported the article with a set
of shocking illustrations lifted, out of context, from unidentified jungle
and crime comic books. One of them shows a bikini-clad woman being
carried off by a gorilla. Another, taken from *True Crime Comics*' "Mur-

der, Morphine, and Me," depicts a hand about to plunge a hypodermic needle into a screaming woman's eye.[24]

Pressing his argument further, Wertham called comic books "the greatest book publishing success in history and the greatest mass influence on children." He cautioned parents against heeding the advice of so-called "experts" who defended comic books. These people, he warned, were "apologists" paid by comic book publishers to disseminate favorable "propaganda" about the industry.[25] By singling out comic books as the greatest among many contributing factors to juvenile delinquency, Wertham offered parents a highly visible scapegoat to explain what adults regarded as disturbing changes in youth behavior. His rhetorical arguments resonated with a Cold War audience fearful of corrupting propaganda and subversion.

Wertham's case seemed powerful, but his evidence was highly contentious. The flaws in his arguments were obvious. It was hardly surprising that juvenile delinquents read comic books, since upwards of 90 percent of all children and adolescents read them. Wertham devoted intense clinical study to the worst cases of juvenile behavior, but he could not account for the millions of young people who read comic books and demonstrated perfectly normal behavior and attitudes. Yet even if Wertham's theories about the sweeping influence of comic books were dubious, his contention that particularly violent comic books incited certain disturbed children to commit crimes was more difficult to refute.

Initially the most critical and compelling rejoinder came from David Pace Wigransky, a fourteen-year-old comic book enthusiast who spoke for the most underrepresented party in the debate—the readers. In an articulate letter that belied the age of its author, Wigransky wrote that "capable as Dr. Wertham may be in the psychoanalyzation of adults, I certainly do not believe him able to deal equally well with children, due to his fanatic hatred and prejudice toward comic books." Wigransky argued against adult perceptions about the "innocence" of childhood, insisting that children ought not be kept in "utter and complete ignorance of anything and everything except the innocuous and sterile world that the Dr. Werthams of the world prefer to keep them prisoners within from birth to maturity." Today's young people, he insisted, were more independent and sophisticated than adults realized. They resented the authority wielded over them by adults and worked in various ways to rebel and subvert it. If a child is told not to read comic books, he claimed, that child will "break his neck to do it." Wigransky contended that "comic book publishers know what the kids want and they try to give it to them. This is not only democratic policy but good business sense." Wigransky's was a refreshing perspective on a cultural debate often obscured by confused and judgmental adult perceptions. But most adults were not prepared to grant young people the voice that Wigransky demanded. Some skeptics even suggested that Wigransky's letter itself may have been forged by an adult, perhaps someone working for the comic book industry. After investigating the matter themselves, however, the *Saturday Review* confirmed that the author was indeed a genuine teenager.[26]

Meanwhile, following the publication of his *Saturday Review* article, Wertham became a frequently requested speaker at forums on comic books and juvenile crime. Citing his own clinical studies as evidence of the causal link between comic books and juvenile delinquency, Wertham advocated a legislated solution. He called for a "public health measure" prohibiting the sale and display of crime comic books to children under the age of fifteen. By defining "crime comic books" loosely as those that suggested "criminal or sexually abnormal ideas" or created an "atmosphere of deceit, trickery, and cruelty," Wertham's proposed measure would have restricted the sale of virtually all comic books. Curiously, Wertham also claimed to oppose censorship, maintaining that while adults should have the right to read what they wished, First Amendment rights did not extend to material directed at children.[27] Wertham's proposal was nevertheless a form of censorship, because such onerous restrictions on the medium would have compelled publishers to abide by a code of standards imposed on them or, more likely, it would have simply deprived publishers of their largest audience and forced them out of business.

The politics of the comic book controversy made rather strange bedfellows. Wertham was a liberal who sought and won a leading role in the crusade against comic books, but he remained aloof from conservative organizations like the Catholic National Organization for Decent Literature, which advanced a broad agenda of cultural censorship. His own politics were hostile towards those whose critique of the media was rooted in anti-Semitism, racism, or nativism. And he resisted the temptation to link the comic book problem to a Communist conspiracy. Wertham would have been uncomfortable, for instance, in the company of the Daughters of the American Revolution, which, in a resolution sent to President Truman, listed their crusade against comic books alongside calls for immigration restriction, opposition to compulsory health insurance, and other efforts to "combat the forces of Socialistic planning invading our country." (The DAR apparently saw nothing "Socialistic" about trying to regulate an entertainment industry.)[28] By remaining coy about his own politics, Wertham was able to attract a wide spectrum of support from those concerned about the mass media and juvenile crime. So perhaps the most curious feature of a controversy plagued by peculiarities and contradictions was that a grassroots crusade marked by calls for censorship and book burnings found scientific legitimacy and leadership in an elitist liberal psychiatrist and professed opponent of censorship.

Censoring Comic Books

The year 1948 was not a good one for the embattled comic book industry. In May, officials and civic groups in Indianapolis gained the cooperation of local magazine distributors to effectively ban twenty-five comic book titles from the city's newsstands. Police and community leaders in Detroit banned thirty-six comic book titles. In June, Fredric Wertham proudly reported to the *New York Times* that the most articulate and vigorous attempt yet made to control comic books was gaining wide support in California's San Diego County. Parent and teacher associations, civic organizations, and women's clubs across the nation led efforts to curb the distribution and sale of comic books. The National Congress of Parents and Teachers planned a national publicity campaign against comic books, recommended a code of standards for publishers, and urged city officials to enact controlling measures.[29]

By October 1948 fifty cities had enacted measures to ban or censor comic books, ranging from voluntary community efforts to legal regulations and ordinances. These efforts threatened to deprive comic book publishers of substantial local markets. The Los Angeles County Board of Supervisors lauded an ordinance that made it a misdemeanor, punishable by a $500 fine or up to six months in jail, for anyone to "sell, give or in any way furnish to anyone under eighteen a book, magazine or other publication" that depicted "an account of crime . . . through the use of drawings or photographs." The drafters of the ordinance extolled their "pioneering" act, which eliminated virtually all "objectionable" comic books from Los Angeles newsstands.[30]

The Los Angeles measure served as the model for municipal legislatures in every region of the country. Chicago, Hartford, Topeka, Des Moines, and Birmingham all adopted similar measures. In Philadelphia, the County Council of the American Legion petitioned the city legislature to pass a ban on crime comic books. In New York, the State Pharmaceutical Association called upon its 6,900 member drug stores

to refuse to sell comic books until publishers complied with the standards established by the National Organization for Decent Literature.[31]

In January 1949 the U.S. Army Character Guidance Council advised army purchasing officers at bases across the nation to refuse the
sale of comic books that went "beyond the line of decency." The decision was prompted by concerns raised by an army chaplain who objected to the violent and sexual content of comic books read by U.S.
servicemen. But, perhaps aware of the embarrassing irony in shielding
professional soldiers from comic book violence, the council deferred
the final decision on this matter to the discretion of local officers.[32]

A preliminary study prepared by Charles S. Rhyne for the National
Institute of Municipal Law Officers ranked the control of comic books
among the most serious issues confronting the nation's local governments. Rhyne contended that the harm done by comic books to "the
morals, thinking, and behavior of our youth is becoming more evident
every day." Municipal governments and police departments, who were
being "bombarded with demands by civic groups and newspaper cam-
paigns to bring a halt to this literary menace," had an imperative to take
action. Rhyne cautioned, however, that comic book control was bound
to encounter constitutional difficulties. Lawmakers would have to carefully draft legislation to curb the sale of objectionable comic books
without violating the First Amendment rights of publishers, merchants,
and adult consumers.[33]

The most serious constitutional challenge to comic book legislation was a decision handed down by the U.S. Supreme Court earlier in
1948. In *Winters v. New York* the Court struck down by a vote of six to
three a New York statute that prohibited the distribution of magazines
composed principally of criminal news, bloodshed, or lust. The majority opinion delivered by Justice Reed declared that the law as written
was so "vague and indefinite" that it violated the First Amendment.
Moreover, Reed questioned the defense's dubious claim that massed
written or illustrated accounts of crime and bloodshed incited criminal
tendencies in the people who read them. He was careful to note, however, that the Court's decision respected the right of states to prohibit
the circulation of material that was obscene or otherwise unprotected
by the First Amendment, and he seemed to imply that a more carefully
worded statute might hold up under constitutional scrutiny. Dissenting
Justice Frankfurter gave further hope to the advocates of comic book
legislation. In the minority opinion, he argued that the New York statute should have been upheld because the state had not exceeded its

constitutional right to exercise "police power to minimize all incentives to crime, particularly in the field of sanguinary or salacious publications with their stimulation of juvenile delinquency." His point, of course, stood on the remarkably large assumption that legislation taken against entertainment publications was indeed a measure to control crime.[34]

The specific publication at issue in the *Winters* case had been a pulp magazine, not a comic book, but the Supreme Court's decision held important implications for the war against comic books as well. Chicago was the first battleground. In October 1947 the mayor of Chicago asked the city's police commissioner to act against the circulation of crime comic books. Citing a section of the Municipal Code of Chicago, which declared it "unlawful for any person to exhibit, sell, offer to sell, circulate or distribute any indecent or lewd book, picture or other thing of an immoral or scandalous nature," the commissioner ordered Chicago distributors to discontinue the circulation of Lev Gleason's *Crime Does Not Pay*. The Chicago City Council also introduced a resolution to create a censor board that would screen all comic books before they were distributed for sale to children. When Gleason learned of the *Winters* decision, he successfully filed a suit for injunction in the Illinois Superior Court. The Chicago Law Department then set about the formidable task of trying to prove that crime comic books constituted "obscene" material liable to government control, a case that it ultimately could not make. Crime comic books were violent, but they were clearly not obscene. It appeared that if the comic book industry pursued this legal course in other instances, all of the state and local measures enacted to control crime comic books would be fatally jeopardized.[35]

The controversy over American comic books also assumed international ramifications. Some of America's closest allies dealt with the problem far more swiftly and decisively than the United States had. In January 1949 the French National Assembly approved a measure prohibiting the publication and circulation of all children's periodicals that glorified "banditry, lying, stealing, laziness, cowardice, hatred or any acts of crime." French officials judged American crime comic books to be a contributing factor in the increase of juvenile delinquency in France. The law even banned comic books featuring relatively innocuous superheroes like Superman and Batman because they constituted an "imperialistic" threat to French culture. The measure enjoyed broad political support within France, but the French Communist Party had fought especially hard for it. Linking the comic book issue to their opposition to the Marshall Plan, French Communists accused the United

States of feeding the French people Hollywood movies and "degenerate comics" in an effort to "colonize" the nation through economic and cultural means. Even prior to the Marshall Plan, however, the Communists had supported the French Union of Illustrators when they had lobbied the government to curtail imports of competing American comic books.[36]

In December 1949 Canada became the second major U.S. ally to ban crime comic books. The Canadian Parliament passed into law an astonishingly broad measure that stipulated a maximum sentence of two years in prison for anyone who made, printed, or sold publications that "exclusively or substantially" comprised "matter depicting pictorially the commission of crime, real or fictitious." The law's sponsors claimed that this would combat the spread of juvenile delinquency in Canada. A similar crusade to do away with crime comic books of domestic and American origin was also underway in Great Britain, although it would not come to fruition for a few years yet.[37]

The international controversy over American comic books further fueled the industry's troubles at home. At a time when the United States was locked in an intense propaganda war with the Soviet Union for world opinion, some critics charged that American comic books shipped overseas presented an unfavorably distorted image of American society and culture. In November 1948 the *New York Times* reported that the Economic Cooperative Administration (ECA), an agency of the Marshall Plan, had approved Fawcett Publications' application to ship 10,000 assorted comic books monthly to occupied Germany. The United States and British military governors reportedly agreed to extend $87,000 in funds for the importation of the comic books, stating they could not find the publications objectionable— meaning the comic books were not "Nazi or unsuitable from a security point of view." This news provoked letters of protest to the *New York Times* and the ECA. One argued that sending American comic books overseas handed the Soviets "unlimited material to present further distortions and untruths about our society." Adding that "the worst feature of these so-called 'comics' is the establishment of right over wrong by direct action, usually by killing someone," the writer argued that comic books weakened respect for democratic societies and tacitly endorsed the kind of totalitarianism that the West opposed.[38] The ECA subsequently denied the *New York Times* report, and a spokesman for the U.S. military insisted that these comic books were "exactly the sort of material we have been screening out" of Germany.[39]

Fredric Wertham often made the argument that comic books degraded the image of America abroad. "Taxpayers pay millions to persuade the world's people that we don't consider dark-skinned races inferior human beings," he noted, but "the crime comic book industry does just the opposite." In comic books, he argued, the heroes are always white Aryan types, while the villains are "foreign-born, Jews, Orientals, Slavs, Italians, and dark-skinned races." Wertham claimed that these comic books demonstrated to the world that "the United States is at present the only nation that teaches race hatred to its children."[40]

The Communists had, in fact, made such charges themselves. Soviet spokesmen accused the American "Superman" of serving the same ideological function as the Nazi "Superman" and claimed that violent comic books contributed to the "mass fascisization" of American youth. To counter this perception, the U.S. State Department printed 260,000 copies of its own comic books, featuring "great Americans" like Abraham Lincoln, Thomas Edison, and Andrew Carnegie, and circulated them throughout regions of East Asia susceptible to Communist influence.[41]

Confronted with mounting public criticism, comic book burnings, boycotts, bans, and an avalanche of bad publicity, some of the leading publishers of crime comic books fought back. In 1948 Marvel Comics followed the lead of DC and Fawcett and acquired—briefly, as it turned out—the services of a psychiatrist from the Child Guidance Bureau of the New York City Board of Education to serve as a paid editorial adviser.[42] Lev Gleason, who had pioneered the crime comic book genre and endured the brunt of criticism directed at it, also put up its most determined defense. In a series of editorials printed in his comic books, Gleason and his writers pointed to the ostensible anticrime message of the stories. Arguing that the criminals in these comic books always paid dearly for their crimes and lived a brief, sordid existence that no child in his right mind would wish to emulate, they printed testimonial letters from parents, police officers, and even convicted criminals in their defense. In a letter apparently written by a convict serving time in the Missouri State Penitentiary, the author regretted that he "didn't start reading *Crime Does Not Pay* until too late."[43]

Gleason personally stated his defense of comic books in a lengthy letter published in the *New York Times*. Attacking the outspoken critics of comic books as cultural elitists determined to "set up an intellectual dictatorship over the reading habits of the American people," Gleason passionately defended comic books as a respectable popular entertainment medium. While he acknowledged that their artistic and educational potential remained largely untapped, he added that the audience preferred it this way, as was their right. Moreover, Gleason argued that many of his readers were adults, so any attempt to censor or "control" comic books would violate their First Amendment rights.[44]

Publishers realized, however, that it would take more than a few editorials and endorsements to quell the increasingly serious threat posed by hostile public opinion. Some publishers reluctantly decided that their best opportunity lay in cooperation and self-regulation. On 1 July 1948 a dozen publishers formed the Association of Comics Magazine Publishers (ACMP) and adopted a self-regulating code of standards modeled after Hollywood's Motion Picture Production Code. The ACMP established an office to administer the code and ensure that every comic book published by a member company met these standards. Those comic books that qualified would receive a seal of approval on the cover to assure parents that they met acceptable standards for children. The ACMP code contained six general provisions. The first, and most important, placed restrictions on the presentation of crime, stating that lawbreaking should not be depicted in a manner that would "throw sympathy against law and justice or to inspire others with the desire for imitation." It also declared that policemen, judges, government officials, and "respected institutions should not be portrayed as stupid, ineffective, or represented in such a way as to weaken respect for established authority." The code also prohibited the depiction of "sadistic torture," "sexy, wanton" images, "vulgar and obscene language," and ridicule of religious and racial groups. The ACMP hired an attorney and member of the New York City Board of Higher Education, Henry E. Schultz, to serve as its "comic book czar," charged with enforcing and publicizing the industry's program of self-regulation.[45]

The formation of the ACMP appeared to be a savvy business maneuver, but it was doomed from the start. Initially only twelve out of thirty-four publishers became members, accounting for just 15 million of the 50 million comic books sold each month.[46] Publishers remained aloof for various reasons. Dell Publications claimed, with justification, that since its own wholesome comic books had not come under attack, it should not associate itself with other less scrupulous publishers. Large publishers like DC, Fawcett, Marvel, and Harvey initially joined but left after several months, also claiming that their comic books were already beyond reproach. Cost was a factor for some publishers. The ACMP charged members $100 to screen any publication with a circulation of more than 500,000 copies, and $50 for those with a circulation between 250,000 and 500,000. Dell calculated that this system would cost them $3,000 each month. Other publishers refused to join or subsequently departed simply because they did not wish to subject their comic books to the code.[47]

Lev Gleason was one of the few major publishers who joined and remained in the ACMP. For a time, his crime comic books reflected the changes imposed by the code. The narrative emphasis shifted from the criminals to the police, and tales became noticeably less violent. Within a few years, however, the code's impotence became evident as Gleason's comic books returned to focusing on criminals in all their lurid glory.[48]

Critics generally scoffed at the ACMP and its code. Many saw it as a feeble and deceptive ploy on the part of comic book publishers to deflect deserved criticism. Dr. Wertham ridiculed the effort and accurately predicted its failure. Meanwhile, Henry Schultz struggled to make the ACMP work and implored the public to be patient. But internecine warfare within the comic book industry made his task difficult, if not impossible.[49] After it had become clear that the ACMP code was not going to work, Schultz changed his tactics and launched a media counterattack against the critics of comic books, especially Wertham. In his article, "The Comics as Whipping Boy," published in the magazine *Recreation*, Schultz criticized those who argued "without credible evidence" that a causal relationship existed between comic books and juvenile delinquency. He attacked Wertham's charges, in particular, as "more emotional than scientific or logical." Schultz elaborated on these points more forcefully in an article published in the scholarly *Journal of Educational Sociology*. Echoing Wertham's own indignant rhetorical style as well as his reductionism, Schultz charged that "the recent hysteria" over comic books was a reckless and unfounded assault on American civil liberties "directly attributed to the activity of Dr. Fredric Wertham."[50]

In any case, the ACMP was not the solution. As more publishers left the association, the code became increasingly meaningless. By 1950 it was effectively defunct, and whatever self-regulation remained existed only in the minds of the comic book makers. That still did not stop some publishers from deceitfully affixing the ACMP code to the covers of their comic books, even though there was no longer an office to screen them.[51]

Of all the ordinances and pending legislation to control comic books, the most important was introduced on 13 January 1949 in the New York state legislature. Republican Senator Benjamin Feinberg of Plattsburgh proposed a bill that would require the distribution and sale of comic books to be regulated by the State Department of Education.

The legislation proposed the creation of a comic book division within the department that would be empowered to screen all comic books circulated in the state. Publishers whose comic books were deemed "acceptable" would be issued a permit from the state. The division would refuse a permit to any publication judged to be "indecent" or "of such a character as to encourage breach of law." A publisher who had been denied a permit could still attempt to sell its comic books, but each issue not approved would have to indicate on the cover that a permit had been refused. Additionally, the publisher of unapproved comic books would have to file a copy of each title with the district attorney of the county where they were to be sold at least thirty days prior to the date of sale.[52]

The implications of this bill were huge. Because nearly every comic book publisher operated out of New York, the bill proposed to effectively establish state regulation of the comic book industry. So drastic were the implications of this measure that the proposal garnered the comic book industry some powerful, if reluctant, defenders. The American Civil Liberties Union assailed the bill, characterizing it as "the kind of legislation which a Stalin or a Hitler might have invoked." The president of the American Book Publishers Council, Curtis McGraw, formally protested the legislation in telegrams sent to state senators and in an open letter to Governor Thomas Dewey that asked him to veto what could become "a dangerously repressive precedent." The *New York Times* also came out against the bill. While acknowledging that "comic books have, on the whole, had an injurious effect" on children and adults, the *Times* insisted that existing obscenity laws and public opinion would keep the worst transgressors in check. The pending legislation, the *Times* maintained, was a clear violation of the First Amendment and a rather ludicrous one at that.[53]

The bill passed both Houses of the New York state legislature overwhelmingly. In the Senate it passed by a vote of forty-nine to six. All six opposed were Democratic senators from New York City who expressed concerns about the bill's constitutionality. Opponents of comic books across the nation eagerly anticipated, and publishers dreaded, the signature of Governor Dewey that would give New York the most restrictive comic book legislation in the land.[54] But on 19 April 1949, Dewey vetoed the bill. Citing the Supreme Court's ruling in *Winters v. New York*, he objected to the legislation's vague and sweeping language. His veto on constitutional grounds effectively killed the legislation and carried ramifications beyond New York State. The New York bill had been a crucial test for legislation of its kind, and its failure heralded a series of reverses for the opponents of comic books. Within weeks of Dewey's veto, a similar measure pending in the Massachusetts legislature died before coming to a vote. No other comic book bills made it as far as New York's had that year, and in December the "pioneering" Los Angeles ordinance was struck down in Superior Court.[55]

As the legality of comic book censorship legislation came under increasing attack, so too did the credibility of its leading proponent. In February 1949 the *New York Times* quoted Dr. Paul Tappan, a professor of sociology at New York University, who warned that it was "over-simplification" to blame juvenile delinquency on comic books. Several months later, a New York judge presiding in the criminal case of a young man charged with murder disregarded the testimony of Dr. Wertham, who had contended that the defendant was temporarily insane at the time of the killing. The judge then took the opportunity to blast the theories of those who blamed crime on comic books, arguing that such theories improperly diverted responsibility away from criminals. By the summer of 1949, even the usually sympathetic *Science Digest* cautioned that, although comic books were generally deplorable, Dr. Wertham's charges against them "may be exaggerated."[56]

The most damaging professional critique came in the *Journal of Educational Sociology*, whose December 1949 issue was devoted entirely to defending comic books and attacking Wertham's theories. The *Journal*'s editor, Professor Harvey W. Zorbaugh, who also taught a well-publicized course on the comics medium at New York University, set the tone by stating that "no thoughtful citizen can fail to be disturbed over the emotional excesses generated by the current controversy over the suitability of comics as reading for children." While acknowledging that "the community should concern itself with the developmental experiences of its children," Zorbaugh deplored the "unreasoning condemnation, the setting up of scapegoats, the burning of books and cries for censorship" that had characterized the attacks on comic books.[57] Articles by Zorbaugh, Frederic Thrasher, Josette Frank of the Child Study Association, and Henry Schultz called into question Wertham's theories, research, and even his motivations. Wertham later countered their charges and correctly pointed out that several of the contributors (Thrasher, Frank, and Schultz) were or had been paid consultants and associates of comic book publishers—a fact that the *Journal* had not disclosed.[58] Nevertheless, this sustained assault from a respected scholarly journal raised serious questions about Wertham's findings. At the very least, the comic book industry could now counter Wertham's professional credentials with some of their own.

In 1950 Henry Schultz reported with relief that "sanity is creeping into the entire picture on the comics." Noting the recent trend of constitutional rulings on comic book legislation, Schultz called upon parents to assume responsibility for their own children without relying on "reformers" or the government to do so for them. He added that publishers had begun to demonstrate a greater intention to "put the comic book back on a decent level."[59] Confirming Schultz's latter point was the survey of the Cincinnati Committee on the Evaluation of Comic Books, published in *Parents' Magazine*, which found that of 555 comic book titles surveyed, 57.47 percent were "suitable for children and youth" compared to only 12.43 percent that were "very objectionable." The Cincinnati committee's next survey later that year found only 6 percent to be "very objectionable." The committee concluded that industry self-regulation and public pressure seemed to have resolved the comic book problem.[60]

An editorial in the July 1951 issue of *Harper's* attacked Wertham's theories about comic books and insisted that it was "a dangerous oversimplification to blame the current wave of juvenile delinquency and crime upon comic books or any other reading matter which is available to youth." Wertham replied angrily and accused *Harper's* of misrepresenting his argument, adding that he did not "know anybody in his right mind who says that delinquency as such has increased on account of comic books alone." What could be traced "more or less directly to crime comic books," he insisted, was "the forms of delinquency . . . there being more acts of violence and brutality by children than existed a decade ago." To the critic's charge that he oversimplified and neglected the socioeconomic conditions that caused juvenile delinquency, Wertham retorted that comic books were "one of the clearest and most direct expressions of socio-economic conditions I know of—conditions which permit an immensely rich industry with fantastic profits to reduce children to a market." Equating comic books with slums and broken homes as contributing factors in the degradation of youth, he advocated action against comic books because, as he cynically noted, "it should be easier to clean them up than to abolish the slums."[61]

If, as his personal writings suggested, this was the linchpin of Wertham's argument, then he had underrepresented it himself and wisely so.[62] For if his critiques had located the problem of juvenile delinquency in the consumer economy that made comic books possible, he would have found a popular audience far less receptive to his arguments. Wertham had achieved his greatest influence by understating the broader implications of his cultural argument and focusing instead on the simple remedy of legislation against comic books for the immediate problem of juvenile delinquency. It was a tactic that he would employ with even greater effectiveness several years later. For although the comic book controversy waned slightly as the new decade began, Wertham was not finished with comic books, and concerns about juvenile delinquency persisted. In several years' time, the issue would again surface and plunge the comic book industry into its greatest crisis yet. But before that moment came, publishers would have one last opportunity to demonstrate that comic books could play a positive, as well as a profitable, role in Cold War America.

5

Reds, Romance, and Renegades

**Comic Books
and the Culture
of the Cold War,
1947–1954**

"**Today's headlines** shout of battles with the Communist hordes in Korea—of Red riots in Rome and Paris and Berlin! But there's another secret battle taking place—right here, right now! An unheralded, underground fight between Communism and democracy for the youth of America." That opening, from a 1952 comic book story called "Backyard Battleground," clearly lays out the stakes. The protagonist, a young woman named Ann Booth, narrates the tale and confesses how she came to betray her country and her lover. The story begins when the red-headed Ann is a child, growing up in poverty during the Great Depression. Ann's father is a good man, but he cannot find work, leaving little Ann to endure a childhood of hunger and humiliation. The years pass and somehow Ann's family saves enough money to send her to college. In this exciting new environment she finally has the opportunity to learn and have fun. She dates a handsome athlete named Bart, who introduces her to some new ideas. He takes her to a "club" that he has joined. The club is actually a Communist cell.[1]

Communist speakers deliver oratories on the evils of capitalist oppression, and Ann is impressed. Her boyfriend persuades her that "the Commies are on our side." Sufficiently indoctrinated, Ann enlists in the cause but becomes concerned when her comrades grow increasingly violent. They lead protests chanting "Down with USA!" Her boyfriend beats up a small shop owner to intimidate him into paying higher wages to his workers. After this troubling incident, Ann starts to date another man. She takes her new boyfriend Bill to a Communist party meeting, but he is not so readily converted. Although impressed by talk of help-ing the common people, Bill deplores a speech that denounces the U.S. effort in Korea as "an all-out war on defenseless Koreans." Concluding that this Communist club is just a front for subversives and traitors, he decides to go to the FBI and "expose this whole rotten mess." Ann pan-ics and asks her old boyfriend Bart to talk to Bill. Instead the Commu-nist Bart murders the heroic informer. The police arrive to arrest the Communists, but Ann too is sent to prison for her part in Bill's murder. Returning to the present, Ann laments that her "vile indoctrination in Communism murdered him as surely as if [her] own hands had pulled the trigger." Significantly, this somber tale appeared in a romance comic book called *Daring Confessions*. In these anxious times, even love, it seems, could not escape the Cold War.[2]

Romance and anticommunism were two of the most common and successful themes exploited by comic book makers during the early Cold War years. Although the two rarely meshed as neatly as the tale above would suggest, both served common cultural objectives. They informed young readers about the Cold War and their role in it. The fear of Communism gave the comic book industry an opportunity to reprise its performance in World War II by speaking to the anxieties of its audience and boosting its own patriotic public image. With public controversy linking comic books to juvenile delinquency, the time seemed right for comic book makers to demonstrate anew that they were a socially responsible industry concerned about the values of American youth. The response formed along gender lines. For boys, there were he-man adventure tales of U.S. soldiers and secret agents fighting the Communists in Korea, Europe, and even America. For the girls, there were romance comic books, which were instructional in the virtues of domesticity and offered the means for securing the vital American home front by starting with the American home. Comic books offered up soldiers and housewives as heroic role models for a generation coming of age in a time of both affluence and anxiety. It was a reasonable and promising response to political, cultural, and market demands. But as was often the case with comic books, simple appear-ances belied profound complexities and contradictions.

Comic Books and the Korean War

After a hesitant postwar start, comic books became caught up in the politically charged Cold War culture. Comic books had preceded the

nation into World War II, but they were slow to enlist in the struggle
against Communism. The liberal politics of many in the industry
probably had something to do with this, but so too did the peculiar
nature of the emerging conflict. Unlike World War II, the Cold War
initially defied easy reduction into comic book tales of good versus evil.
There were too many questions. Was the United States at war or not?
Was this an intolerable foe on par with the Nazis or was peaceful coexistence and cooperation still possible? What should the appropriate
U.S. response be? These answers did not crystallize until the events
between the Truman Doctrine and the Korean War forged a national
consensus behind the policy to contain Communism.

The implication of some postwar comic books did point towards
containment. Jungle comics worked from the assumption that Western
forces had the right and obligation to police undeveloped countries.
"Radar, the International Policeman," endorsed American global leadership of the sort called for in the Truman Doctrine. And by 1949 "Blackhawk"'s villains had exchanged most of their Nazi trappings for Soviet
ones.[3] By the early 1950s, when the Cold War pervaded all aspects of
American life, comic book makers in search of relevant material increasingly turned to anticommunist stories. More than any other event
in the Cold War era, the Korean War prompted a vigorous and prolific
comic book response. Here at last was a conventional conflict more
like World War II: featuring a noble cause, a clear enemy, and virtuous
American heroes, it seemed to invite a reprise of patriotic comic book
reductionism. It quickly became clear, however, that Korea was a very
different kind of war, prompting a very different comic book response.

During World War II, every costumed superhero had participated
in the Allied war effort. By the Korean War, though, few of these heroes
were still around. And fewer still enlisted in the American "police action." DC Comics and Fawcett were the only publishers at that time
still producing superhero titles of any commercial significance. The
DC characters remained conspicuously aloof from the war, as they did
from most political concerns during the 1950s. Fawcett's superheroes,
in commercial decline since the end of World War II, had more to gain
and less to lose by going to Korea. In a 1952 adventure, Captain Marvel
Jr. flies to Korea to help the United Nations forces against a comical
villain called the "Mad Mongol Monster." In another story, also from
1952, the hero confronts Vampira, a Communist spy working as a
nightclub performer in Washington who steals U.S. war plans with the
aid of her pet gorilla.[4] But the intervention of Fawcett's superheroes did
nothing to reverse their slide in the marketplace.

Such absurdity had been central to the comic books of World War II, but it seemed unacceptably preposterous in light of the Korean War. Unlike the "good war" against the Axis, the news from Korea defied optimism. After several months of success, by the winter of 1950–51 U.S. troops were in full-scale retreat out of frozen North Korea. Following the stabilization of the front near the 38th parallel, the war settled into a grim and interminable contest of attrition. In this context, the naive scenarios envisioned by Fawcett's writers simply did not work. There were no easy answers and no simple resolution to this war. To

From "Backyard Battleground," *Daring Confessions* 5 (Youthful Magazines, January 1953). Two of the most popular comic book themes of the early 1950s converge wonderfully in this tale of romance and the Communist menace. Red-headed Ann Booth is seduced by both the wrong man and the wrong ideology in this double-edged cautionary tale. Writer and artist unknown.

explain American frustrations at the battlefront, one Captain Marvel Jr. story reveals the existence of a Communist super-weapon developed by the Mad Mongol Monster. After the superhero has destroyed the weapon, the Americans once again resume their march forward—to somewhere. Similarly, a story called "The Regiment That Was Afraid to Fight" explained that U.S. troops had not performed well in recent days because Communist spies had infiltrated their ranks and drugged them with a fear serum. Captain Marvel Jr. gives the troops an antidote, their courage returns, and they eagerly go back to the front. The tale ends with the young superhero cheerfully promising, "We're on the road to victory, folks! And this time there won't be any turning back!"[5] This story appeared in 1953, only a few months prior to the armistice that effectively terminated the Korean War and rendered moot any superhero forecasts for victory.

While the Korean War did not spark renewed interest in costumed superheroes, it did inspire a new comic book variation on an old genre, the war story. War comic books featured the adventures of regular American servicemen, something that the comic books of World War II had rarely done. During the three years of the Korean War, publishers issued more than one hundred different titles based on the conflict. The most optimistic of them featured swaggering John Wayne-type heroes. Some featured Wayne himself. One issue of *John Wayne Adventure Comics* finds the movie star leaving his ranch to enlist in the marines so that he can go to Korea. When he arrives at the front, he promptly leads his men to a big victory over the enemy.[6] This comic book was about as close as the real Wayne would get to the actual fighting in Korea.

Artists rendered North Koreans and Chinese as subhuman caricatures, much as they had portrayed the Japanese in World War II. Sometimes the similarities between America's Asian foes were a little improbable, as when the Red Chinese charged in human waves shouting the Japanese battle cry "Banzai!" Ziff-Davis's *G.I. Joe* was among the first and most chauvinistic Korean War titles. Featuring covers painted in a Norman Rockwell style, but with images of smiling American soldiers gleefully killing ugly yellow Communists, *G.I. Joe* made wartime killing seem grotesquely benign. One cover shows a handsome boyish G. I. grinning broadly as he holds a puppy in one arm and machine-guns some Red soldiers with the other. The stories lived up to the promise of such covers. U.S. forces always won and suffered minimal casualties, generally giving the impression that the Korean War was lots of fun.[7]

Other comic books supported the U.S. effort in a more sophisticated and often more ambivalent manner. One tale in Marvel's *Spy Cases*

opens in Korea with American forces in retreat. Some American con-
gressmen in charge of war appropriations arrive at the battlefront to
survey the situation and report back to Washington. They are not
pleased with what they see. One skeptical congressman voices his disgust to the commanding officer, scoffing, "This is a senseless struggle
at best! Why pour anything into it? A little less coddling and more
performance, and we'll have victories instead of excuses!" The major contends that his troops are doing the best that they can without
the necessary weapons and supplies denied by the war appropriations
committee. The congressman calls that kind of talk "defeatism." Then
comes a surprise Communist attack, and the congressman sees firsthand how the embattled U.S. troops fight valiantly despite being outnumbered and outgunned by the enemy. This experience leads the
politicians to return to Washington and vote for greater war appropriations.[8]

A story that shows U.S. troops outnumbered, outgunned, in retreat,
and hamstrung by clueless Washington politicians was hardly a rosy
assessment of the situation in Korea. But as a picture of frustration it
was consistent with the American experience in the Korean War. The
conflict proved confusing and exasperating for a nation that had triumphed over far more powerful enemies less than a decade earlier. It
raised troubling questions of strategy and purpose. Was the United
States fighting to defend South Korea or to unify the entire peninsula?
Should the nation do more to win the war, even to the point of using
atomic weapons? Or was Korea worth such extremely high risks?
Meanwhile American soldiers died in Korea as peace negotiations
stalled over convoluted issues like the repatriation of North Korean
POWs.

William W. Savage Jr. notes wryly in *Comic Books and America,
1945–1954* that "as a unifying and uplifting cultural experience, the
comic book version of the Korean conflict left much to be desired."[9]
Indeed, compared to the exuberant and sublime comic books of World
War II, those of the Korean War tended to be grim and ironic. Frustration pervaded most of the writing. The Korean landscape appeared
cold and bleak; the enemy, cruel, cunning, and numerous. The war's
principles and objectives often seemed vague or went unstated. And
American soldiers confronted the perils of their own mortality daily. In
a 1952 story called "Do or Die," a truckload of battle-weary U.S. troops
comes under attack from a full division of Communists. Reinforce-
ments arrive but not in time to prevent the entire squad from being
wiped out. The issue containing this story also features an equally dis-

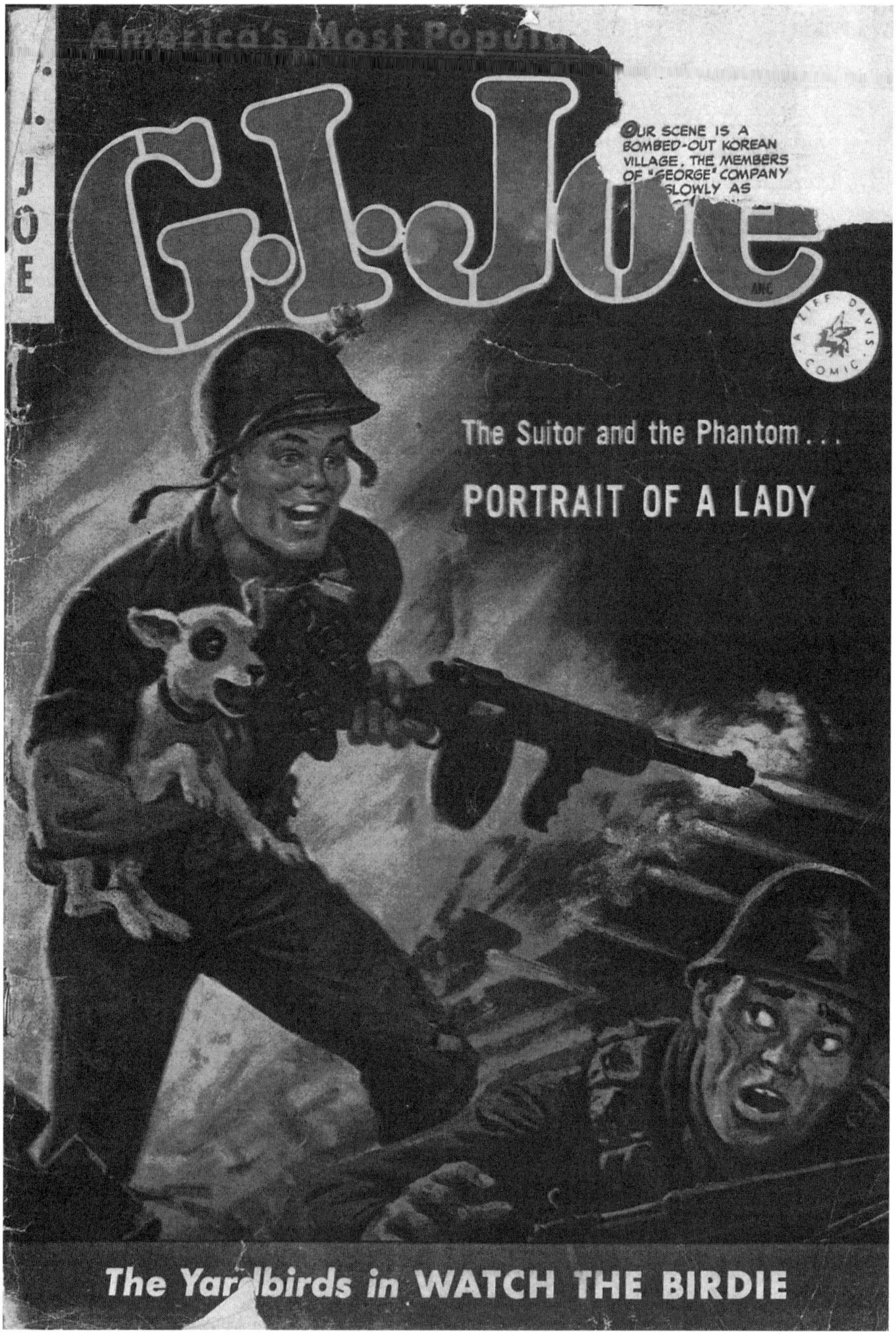

America's Most Popul...
G.I. Joe
OUR SCENE IS A BOMBED-OUT KOREAN VILLAGE. THE MEMBERS OF "GEORGE" COMPANY ... SLOWLY AS
A ZIFF DAVIS COMIC
The Suitor and the Phantom . . .
PORTRAIT OF A LADY
The Yardbirds in WATCH THE BIRDIE

couraging tale about a G.I. photographer who takes one picture too many. He is about to return home and wants to have a photographic record of his war experience to share with his children. When a Communist soldier steals his camera, the G.I. hunts him down and retrieves it. Then when he tries to take one last snapshot, the camera explodes, killing him. A fellow soldier hunches over his friend's corpse and stares blankly at the booby-trapped camera, crying, "He hadda have that camera before he went home . . . and because of it . . . he'll never go home, now."[10]

In World War II comic books American soldiers had only the Axis armies to worry about. In Korea they had to contend not only with the Communists but also with their own terror. Comic book makers, many of whom had served in World War II, were able to conceive stories about G.I.s scarred by battle, both physically and psychologically. Stories abounded of soldiers who struggled to maintain their courage and sanity in a nightmarish environment. In "Fear," a shell-shocked G.I. is ordered to scout for enemy patrols. When, to his horror, he encounters one, he panics and fires uncontrollably into the enemy ranks. After the smoke has cleared, the G.I. is amazed to find that he is still alive and all of the Communist soldiers are dead. In a final touch of irony, the G.I.'s unit commends him for his bravery.[11]

Some comic books presented the war in almost nihilistic terms. Rather than trumpeting lofty principles at issue, they focused on the human drama of life, death, and loyalty. "The Road Back" opens with a group of exhausted, unshaven marines slogging through rain and mud across a desolate Korean landscape. One of the soldiers mutters, "It seems as though there's always been mud . . . always rain . . . always shells and fighting with occasional lulls like this one . . . how much can a man stand?" Morale is obviously low. As they go into battle the hero launches into bitter sarcasm: "Let's go! Happy landings! Here we go again! Over and over again . . . the same thing . . . the same phrases, the same jokes, the same dirty, stinkin' men and mud and fightin'." After emerging alive from one more battle, the soldier learns that his tour of duty is over and he can go home. Yet instead of returning home he reenlists and goes back to the front to rejoin his old unit. As miser-

Cover of *G.I. Joe* 22 (Ziff-Davis, June 1953). Ziff-Davis's *G.I. Joe* glorified the Korean War as few other titles did. Hideously cheerful images like this were vastly outnumbered by comic books with a far bleaker take on the fighting in Korea. Artist unknown.

able as the war is, it has become a way of life for this marine; a self-perpetuating and seemingly meaningless existence.[12]

The enemy in Korea appeared frightening and formidable. It seemed that in bloody, individual confrontations, a well-trained G.I. could usually overcome a Communist soldier.[13] But more often than not, U.S. troops could expect to be vastly outnumbered by a fanatical enemy prepared to sacrifice horrific casualties for the sake of killing a few Americans. As one comic book explained ominously, "The cannon

From "The Road Back," *Battle* 9 (Marvel Comics, June 1952). Many Korean War comic books painted a stark, gloomy, and almost nihilistic image of the conflict. Often the only principles at stake seemed to be survival and the preservation of one's sanity. Writer and artist unknown.

fodder of Communist tyranny is as countless as sands on the beach . . . and as expendable." When U.S. troops retreat in another episode, they acknowledge that the Communist "rats have won this round," but only because "they got twenty men for each of us!" A story from *U.S. Marines in Action* informs readers that American soldiers faced bleak odds of "fifty against five thousand." Communist troops were "cold, ruthless—and extremely efficient! They give no quarter and they are tough fighters." With American skill and intelligence pitted against Communist numbers and ruthlessness, the inevitable result was a stalemate.[14]

The concept of limited war was a new and troubling one for many Americans. Why should the United States suffer defeat and stalemate on the battlefield while withholding the military means needed to ensure victory? And how could American negotiators sit at a table with the enemy while U.S. troops died at the front? Comic books highlighted some of these frustrations. In one story, a North Korean naval base near the Manchurian border menaces U.S. troops, but the United Nations command rejects a proposed aerial bombardment because of the "political repercussions" should any bombs fall on Manchuria.[15]

In comic books, the Communist enemy commonly took advantage of peace talks to launch treacherous surprise attacks on the United Nations forces. A story from 1952 describes how Communist negotiators at Panmunjon "held the olive branch of peace in one hand and the weapon they hoped would destroy the United Nations armies in the other." While the Reds stall at the peace table, they secretly construct a missile base capable of shelling United Nations positions.[16]

In this troubling war, even America's South Korean ally was suspect. In one story, a South Korean guerrilla leader secretly sells his American-supplied weapons to the Communists. The U.S. Marines take great pleasure in killing this traitor and wiping out every one of his guerrilla fighters. After the massacre, one of the Americans surveys the carnage and concludes with smiling satisfaction, "Like our forefathers said of the Injuns—a good Red is a dead Red! Now they're all good and dead!"[17]

The Korean War also raised large questions about the use of the atom bomb. Comic book writers followed the course of action set by U.S. leaders and kept the bomb out of Korea in their stories, but some plotlines did demonstrate changed attitudes about the bomb. The initial comic book response to the bomb in the 1940s, echoing the sentiment of leading atomic scientists and liberal internationalists, had insisted that atomic energy was a force too dangerous to be wielded or monopolized by any one nation.[18] The Cold War broke that consensus, and by the early 1950s some comic books began to suggest that using the atomic bomb might not be a bad idea after all.

One of the most horrifying series issued during the Korean War was Junior Books' *Atomic War!*, which featured the United States and the Soviet Union waging routine atomic warfare. The editors stated up front that the purpose of *Atomic War!* was to illustrate for everyone "the utter devastation that another war will bring to all, the just as well as the unjust." Yet the stories suggested exactly the opposite. Far from bringing about mutual assured destruction, atomic weapons appeared to be a practical means for securing victory over the Soviet Union. In one storyline, when the Soviets invade Western Europe, U.S. forces repel the Red Army with the aid of "atomic artillery." When the Soviets invade Alaska, the American defenders strike back with "atomic anti-personnel grenades" and "atomic shells" fired from howitzers. In both instances the Communists suffer mightily, while the Americans emerge victorious and relatively unscathed.[19]

Similarly, *Atomic War*'s "Operation Vengeance" presented the hypothetical U.S. response to a Soviet atomic strike. As atomic bombs fall on New York, Chicago, and Detroit (the bombings are not illustrated), U.S. heavy bombers set off on a mission of vengeance. One pilot penetrates the Soviet air defenses, drops a hydrogen bomb on Moscow, and admires the resulting holocaust. His mission accomplished, the bomber pilot returns to an Allied base in Turkey and crosses bombed Soviet cities off of the map, smiling and boasting, "We've changed the map of Russia!"[20]

Comic Book Cold Warriors

Comic book makers hoped that the superheroes who had sold so well during World War II could repeat that performance in the Cold War. Between 1953 and 1955 Marvel Comics revived its original superheroes, Captain America, the Sub-Mariner, and the Human Torch, and enlisted them aggressively in the crusade against Communism. As far as these comic books were concerned, peaceful coexistence was not a realistic prospect. In one tale, the United States and the Soviet Union agree to construct a tunnel from Siberia to Alaska. The U.S. government and the Sub-Mariner hope that this joint project will encourage peaceful commerce between the two nations, but the Soviets have other ideas. They conspire to use the tunnel to launch a surprise invasion of Alaska. The Sub-Mariner defeats the "godless Communists" and learns to never again "be conned into anything by a Red."[21]

The quintessential superhero-patriot of World War II was reincar-

nated as "Captain America . . . Commie Smasher." In the last war, Captain America and Bucky had defended the American home front against Nazi and Japanese spies and saboteurs. Now they reprised that role against Communist agents, striking at "the betrayers" who hid behind the privileges of a free society in order to subvert American institutions. The series offered no further discussion of Cold War issues beyond the message that Communists were evil, overweight, and poor dressers.[22]

Marvel's Cold War superhero revival totally failed. During World War II *Captain America* had been Marvel's top-selling title, but the revived series lasted only several issues. Competing anticommunist superhero titles like *Black Cobra, Avenger,* and Jack Kirby and Joe Simon's *Fighting American* fared even worse in the marketplace.[23] All of these series essentially reproduced old superhero formulas, but these no longer proved successful. A major shake-up in the industry after 1954 certainly had something to do with their demise, but these series failed for other reasons as well. Comic book makers overestimated the size of the audience prepared to accept such naive presentations of the Cold War. As the enormous popularity of crime comic books had already demonstrated, the postwar comic book market had not only grown, it had grown up. Even young people understood that the Cold War was not going to be won as quickly and easily as the comic book version of World War II. The existence of the atom bomb alone removed all doubt about that. Times had changed since 1945, but these anticommunist superheroes had not changed with them.[24]

There was a market for anticommunism in comic books, but only for those that approached the subject with the seriousness it demanded. Comic books, of course, were not about to rival *Foreign Affairs* or the *New York Times*, but where the Cold War was concerned they would have to offer less fantasy and more reality. Marvel's *Kent Blake of the Secret Service* was a prototype of sorts for this genre. The editors noted that the name Kent Blake was fictitious because "the real name and identity of this intrepid special agent are not even known to the publisher." Nevertheless, they insisted, all other details and incidents were based on "actual facts." One early story takes place in Greece, where the

Cover of *Atomic War!* 2 (Junior Books, December 1952). Published during the time of U.S. participation in the Korean War, Junior Books' *Atomic War!* speculated on the possibilities of World War III. Despite the series' stated purpose to warn against the horrors of atomic warfare, it did just the opposite. In its stories, U.S. forces employing tactical and strategic nuclear weapons triumphed repeatedly over the Communists. Artist unknown.

KENT BLAKE

All names and places in these true-to-life stories are fictitious.

free government is menaced by Communist rebels. The Communists sabotage the transportation network to disrupt Marshall Plan aid and spread the rumor that greedy capitalists, rather than the common people, are the real beneficiaries of U.S. assistance. The Pentagon sends Kent Blake to investigate. When he arrives in Greece disguised as a tourist, a mob greets him with jeers of "Down with U.S. imperialism" and "Kill the Capitalist!" He quickly surmises that "the fine hand of the Kremlin has been at work here." Later, the Russian Communists capture Blake and boast of their plans to turn Greece into a Red satellite. By fooling the people into believing that the United States is their enemy, the Communists will be able to stage a revolution and make it appear to be the result of popular will. Blake escapes and exposes the Communist conspiracy to the Greek people, who then renounce Communism and cheer the United States as they bid Blake farewell.[25] This story presented a compelling endorsement of the Truman Doctrine— itself announced in response to a Communist insurrection in Greece.

As the Cold War moved into developing countries, comic books championed containment in those regions as well. In a 1953 issue of *John Wayne Adventure Comics*, Wayne travels to the Middle East and visits a friend who runs a U.S. oil field there. Meanwhile, an Arab nationalist movement has launched a terrorist campaign to drive out American oil companies. Wayne gets involved and captures an "Arab terrorist," suspecting that this so-called Arab will "answer to Ivan and pray to Moscow." As expected, Wayne exposes the nationalist leader as a Russian agent sent to stir up trouble for American oil interests. Wayne reveals his identity to a crowd of Arabs and declares, "You see, he was making dupes of you for Moscow! What do you say—shall we produce oil for you?" The people cheer their American friends and enthusiastically pledge to buy the oil that this U.S. company will pump from their country.[26]

Published from 1951 to 1956, Quality Comics' *T-Man* was among the more enduring anticommunist titles and probably the only comic book ever to feature the adventures of a U.S. Treasury agent. A *T-Man* story published in late 1951 opens in Teheran at a meeting between British diplomats and an Iranian official, in which the participants are

From "Condemned to Death," *Kent Blake of the Secret Service* 5 (Marvel Comics, January 1952). One of a number of documentary-style comic books that explicated the Cold War for young readers, this *Kent Blake* story shows how the Russians work to stir up anti-American sentiment and foment Communist revolution in nations like Greece. Writer and artist unknown.

about to conclude a treaty granting Great Britain and the United States exclusive rights to Iranian oil production. The Iranian leader tells the Englishman that he is happy to give away these rights because the British and Americans have demonstrated that they respect Iranian laws and customs. Suddenly he is interrupted by someone who appears to be to be U.S. Treasury agent Pete Trask, who bursts into the room, throws a squealing pig at the Iranian official, and says, "Here rag-head! Take this little fellow home and barbecue him for breakfast!" The agent then flees, having effectively sabotaged the treaty. Outraged by this deliberate (and extraordinarily absurd) insult to Islamic customs, the Iranian leader cancels the treaty. Later it is revealed that this ruse was the work of a Soviet agent disguised as Trask, who is trying to poison relations between Iran and the West. Inevitably, the real Pete Trask sets matters straight and ensures that the treaty is signed. In this tale, obviously inspired by the recent overthrow of the anti-Western Mossadegh government in Iran, Communism is once again contained and the United States and Great Britain win exclusive rights to Iranian oil. What Iran stands to gain from this is unclear and, apparently, unimportant.[27]

Most anticommunist comic books focused on the Cold War overseas, but some responded to the domestic Red Scare as well. In a story from early 1955, Pete Trask infiltrates a Communist cell whose members plot to sabotage a U.S. manufacturing plant. Another episode in the same issue finds Trask in pursuit of a Communist saboteur who has destroyed an experimental Air Force jet in Detroit. In a story appearing in *Kent Blake of the Secret Service*, an American agent arrests an executive at a chemical company who plots to sell secrets about U.S. chemical weapons research to the Communists.[28]

The relative dearth of stories dealing with American Communists suggests that comic book makers were not entirely persuaded by the claims of Joseph McCarthy and other outrageous redbaiters. Some publishers, in fact, did not engage in anticommunist rhetoric at all. Jack Schiff's educational pages for the National Social Welfare Assembly in DC comic books continued to extol moderate liberal values even at the height of the Red Scare, when outspoken liberals found their patriotism questioned and faced persecution. A 1952 page titled "Hop on the Welfare Wagon" defied contemporary political trends by having no less than Superman himself endorse a program of national social welfare. Another telling page called "Be Sure of Your Facts" warned against making premature accusations of people before all the facts were in.[29]

Occasionally DC presented cautionary messages against McCarthyism in its adventure stories. A sci-fi tale from 1951 called "Duel of the Planets" concerned an interplanetary group of heroes called the Knights of the Galaxy, who champion the cause of "Galaxian democracy" against a totalitarian warlord on the planet Mercury. When the knights learn that one of their members, Millo, had once lived on Mercury, some question his loyalty. The leader of the knights comes to the accused man's defense and, chastising the gathering mob, exclaims, "You have never questioned Millo's courage or loyalty before! To condemn him now without cause, is to violate the very principles of democracy we are going to fight Mercury to protect!" Ashamed of their own prejudice, the knights grant Millo the opportunity to demonstrate his loyalty—which he does by sacrificing his life in the war against Mercurian tyranny.[30]

While rarely making explicit reference to the Cold War, DC's comic books consistently emphasized cooperation and understanding over accusation and confrontation. In an episode of *Tomahawk*, a series set in American Colonial times, white settlers and Indians prepare to fight each other over some land. At the end, instead of going to war the two sides agree to share the land, deciding that cooperation is preferable to risking a military confrontation that could destroy them all.[31] With such morals, DC's comic books held out hope for peaceful coexistence.

Romance Comic Books and Domestic Containment

Domesticity was central to the culture of the Cold War. While society had always placed a high value on family life, the integrity of the middle-class family assumed new importance in the Cold War as the preeminent symbol of the affluence, consumption, and spiritual fulfillment that the American way of life promised. Preservation of the traditional family and prescribed gender roles meshed with concerns of national security and resulted in a sort of domestic containment policy. Commentators, "experts," and popular culture underscored the virtues and imperatives of domesticity. Young women were expected to marry early and embrace their role as supportive wife, busy homemaker, and doting mother. Female promiscuity, independence, and career ambitions degraded the domestic ideal, and these perceived threats spawned social crusades as fervent as anticommunist tactics to guard against them.[32]

Into this crusade entered the romance comic books. Joe Simon and Jack Kirby pioneered the genre in 1947 with *Young Romance*. Much as crime comics were derived from true-crime magazines, romance comic books essentially adapted the formula of true-confessions magazines. With *Young Romance*, Simon and Kirby hoped to tap into the largely neglected female market. While surveys suggested that females read comic books only slightly less often than males did, there were few titles aimed principally at girls and young women. Noting that teen-humor titles like *Archie* had demonstrated popularity among young girls, comic book makers reworked the lighthearted explorations of dating found in those comic books into material for more mature female readers. Following the example of Lev Gleason's *Crime Does Not Pay*, the cover of *Young Romance* advertised itself, "For the More Adult Readers of Comics!"[33]

They succeeded all too well. The half-million copies of *Young Romance* number 1 sold out, prompting Feature Publications to double its monthly circulation. The rest of the industry quickly took notice and flooded the market with dozens of slight variations on the *Young Romance* formula. Within a few years, Kirby and Simon's comic book was only one of nearly one hundred romance titles on newsstands each month. By 1949 romance comic books, according to a report in *Time* magazine, outsold all other genres and cut deeply into the market for confessional magazines.[34]

The first issue of *Young Romance* established the basic formula for the genre. Cautionary morality tales told from the perspective of a female protagonist (though generally written by men) illustrated the perils of female independence and celebrated the virtues of domesticity. "The Farmer's Wife" advocated female self-denial for the sake of lasting marriage. It tells the story of a young nurse named Nancy who marries a wounded war veteran named Bill. She is a young woman living in the city, while he is a farmer fifteen years her senior. Foreseeable problems result. At her urging, Bill takes a job with the U.S. Department of Agriculture so that the couple can live in Washington, D.C. But he is miserable in the city. Nancy wants to go to parties and shows, but Bill is always too tired and just wants to stay home. One night Nancy vents her frustration and goes to town on her own. She returns to find a note from Bill explaining that he has returned to his farm because he can see that she is unhappy with him. He agrees to grant her a divorce if she wants one. Nancy breaks out in tears and laments how selfish she has been. She leaves her job in the city and goes to Bill's farm to resume their marriage on his terms.[35]

Romance comic books seldom strayed from the central premise that women were incomplete without a man, even if the same principle did not necessarily apply to men. The twenty-one-year-old narrator in

Lovelorn's "My Perfect Man" feels like an "old maid" because she is still
single. When she finally does meet a handsome prospect named Ted,
she confesses, "I'm not really worthy of a man like Ted, but I'm going
to try to make him love me! I'm going to try so very hard . . . because
my whole happiness . . . my life . . . depends on it!" Wealthy single
women were always unhappier than poor single men.[36]

Some romance comic books offered advice to teenage girls on dating. They urged restraint, self-denial, and accommodation on the part
of the female. An advice page in *Young Romance* counseled that if the
prospect has "shown some definite signs of being a home loving male,
it's up to you to prove to him that domesticity is your true nature." The
same page advised the hopeful female to flatter the male generously and
"be interested in everything that the guy is interested in." It also endorsed what it called the "I'll be waiting whenever you might want me"
approach for those instances "when the guy isn't ready to settle down
yet."[37]

However, romance comic books discouraged the aggressive pursuit
of males and warned against any female behavior that hinted of promiscuity. In *Teen-Age Romances*' "I Tried to Buy Love with Kisses" the protagonist commits the social transgression of taking the initiative to kiss
a boy in public. From that moment forth she is branded as a "man-
chaser," and decent boys avoid her accordingly. An advice page in *Young
Romance* made the same point, explaining that when the wrong sort of
boys seemed interested in a girl, "usually the girl's actions are to blame!
She flirts . . . wears flashy clothes . . . acts conspicuous in public places."
Comic books advised females to maintain passive gender roles, else
they would lose hope for romance, marriage, and happiness.[38]

By suggesting that honesty and stability were more important than
passion and excitement, romance comic books hoped to prepare females for domestic lives. "Back Door Love" concerns a woman who is
attracted to the wrong kind of man. At first "a normal, respectable girl
who thought of love as a beautiful, tender experience," the woman
found herself "lying, cheating, loitering in shadows, descending step by
step into the degrading depths of dishonor" to be with him. Her friends
warn that the man is a "rat," but she is blinded by infatuation that she
believes to be love. Only after she has caught the man cheating on her
does she realize that her irrational passions have led her astray. The
story ends happily when the woman marries an unexciting but nice man
whom she had earlier rejected. The stability and security that he will
provide is what matters most.[39]

Stories abounded of young women who sought excitement but in the end learned to value the quiet life. In "I Ran Away with a Truck Driver" a small-town girl rebels against her parents, who want to send her to a local women's college. She wants to get away from her family and attend a coed school. Most of all, she yearns for independence. One night she runs away to Chicago with a handsome young truck driver who promises her a thrilling time. Instead, he steals her money and abandons her in the city. Disillusioned and chastised by her adventure, she returns home, abides by her parents' wishes, and accepts the courtship of a decent local boy.[40]

Romance comic books encouraged women to marry young and grow up quickly from schoolgirl to devoted housewife. In "Homecoming," published in *Teen-Age Brides*, a pair of newlyweds move into their home in a small town. The wife is from the city and has trouble adjusting to the suburban lifestyle. She also resents her husband's busy work schedule and his declining attention to her. "Things were so different before we were married," she tells him. "You always brought me presents and told me you loved me." Her husband interrupts and scolds her, "Cut it out honey! I still love you . . . but we don't have to play games anymore! You're acting like a kid!" By the end of the story the wife confesses that she has been "a spoiled brat who expected marriage to be a continuous courtship." The secret to achieving a happy marriage, she concludes, is for the wife to give "unselfishly and unfailingly."[41] Of course, when in another story the above situation is reversed (the small-town husband gives in to his wife's wishes to move to the city), it is once again the wife who is being selfish. She regrets having pressured her husband to move away from his home town and agrees to move back there with him. His happiness comes first, and she is all the happier for accommodating his wishes.[42]

Self-denial for the sake of marriage was especially important where the woman's career was concerned. Romance comic books discouraged women from entering the work force. Working women in the comic books remained unfulfilled and unhappy because their careers complicated relationships and jeopardized their prospects for marriage. One story focuses on a young businesswoman who runs a successful advertising firm. Her chief employee is also her former lover. He still has feelings for her, but she rejects his advances because her business is more important to her than romance. When he can no longer tolerate this awkward situation, he calls her an "old maid" and quits to work for a rival firm. Once he leaves, she realizes that she does have feelings for him after all; she misses him terribly and her work suffers in his absence. Eventually her business goes bankrupt, and she has to take a job as a secretary. She soon realizes that marriage is more important to her than a career. Eventually the couple get back together, marry, and have a child. The woman finds her new role as wife and mother to be far happier and more satisfying than her old career in business.[43]

Another reason for women to stay out of the workplace, according to romance comic books, was that men were not attracted to ambitious women. A simple housewife in one story grows jealous of an intelligent career woman who works with her husband. Her fears prove to be groundless, because, as her husband explains, "that sort of woman can very well take care of herself." And "frankly," he adds, her intelligence "was beginning to bore me." The wife is thus reassured that her simplicity and domestic virtues are the very traits that her husband finds most attractive.[44]

Men, on the other hand, needed and deserved their independence. Women were expected to accommodate them, even if things looked fishy. "I Hate Men" features a woman who does indeed hate men. She has left her husband because she believes that he has been unfaithful to her. But by the end of the story she learns that her husband had not cheated on her after all. (She knows this because he tells her so.) It turns out that he had been pursued by another woman but had refused her advances. Thus reassured, the wife blames herself for the misunderstanding and returns to him, promising to be more trusting in the future. The moral of this tale, she concludes, is that "love means faith in the face of any evidence, no matter how overwhelming."[45]

Romance comic books exhorted women to support their men unflinchingly—a moral imperative made all the more necessary by the Korean War. As young men went to Korea, it became the patriotic duty of their sweethearts to wait patiently for their return. Some comic books brought the two gender roles together in the same story. An unusually moving story centers on an engaged couple who love to dance. They enter dance contests and dream of dancing together for the rest of their lives. When the Korean War breaks out, he goes off to do his duty and she pledges to wait for him. In his absence she remains faithful but does dance with other men. When he returns, she is horrified to see that he has lost one of his legs. Embittered and self-pitying, the wounded veteran wonders whether his fiancée will want to marry a "cripple." She does, even though it means they will never dance together again. In its own way, her love and devotion to the man who has sacrificed so much for his country is as patriotic as his military service.[46]

BOB DREW ME OUT TO THE TERRACE... I WAS SHAKING LIKE A LEAF... PHYLLIS, DARLING, OBVIOUSLY YOU DON'T OWE HIM A THING! I THINK I HAVE A RIGHT TO...

OH, NO, BOB! YOU...

MUSTN'T! PLEASE BOB...LET ME GO! AFTER ALL, I'M STILL MARRIED!

YOU HEARD WHAT THE LADY SAID!

PHYLLIS, GET YOUR HAT AND COAT! I SAID *GET YOUR HAT AND COAT!* THERE'S BEEN ENOUGH OF THIS NONSENSE! I'M TAKING YOU HOME, WHERE YOU BELONG!

Y...YES, BOB!

YOU DON'T HAVE TO GO, PHYLLIS! AFTER ALL, IN THIS MODERN DAY AND AGE..

I...I'M SORRY, BOB...I GUESS...I'M STILL A LITTLE OLD-FASHIONED...AT HEART!!

BACK HOME, JAY AND I ALMOST GOT INTO ANOTHER ONE OF OUR QUARRELS...

BUT, DARLING... WHAT ABOUT GLORIA...?

THAT SORT OF WOMAN CAN VERY WELL TAKE CARE OF HERSELF! FRANKLY, PHYLLIS...HER PERFECTION WAS BEGINNING TO BORE ME!

OH, DARLING...IT WAS ALL MY FAULT! I GUESS I WAS SO FOOLISH AND JEALOUS, I THREW YOU INTO HER ARMS!

NO...I WAS TO BLAME! I WAS ILL-TEMPERED... IMPATIENT...

NO, JAY, IF I HADN'T... OH, DARLING...HERE WE GO AGAIN!

HONEY, WE'RE NOT GOING TO QUARREL TONIGHT OF ALL NIGHTS!

NOTHING WRONG WITH A SECOND HONEYMOON, IS THERE?

-END-

In other romance comic books, women played a more direct role in the Korean War. "Lovelife of an Army Nurse" tells how a nurse and a wounded soldier find romance on the Korean battlefield. She had initially gone to Korea not out of patriotism but because she thought it would be a good place to meet men. After falling in love with a soldier who has lost his leg in battle, she gives up this cynical attitude and genuinely devotes herself to both her man and her country. In another tale, a woman misses her man so much when he goes to Korea that she enlists as an Army nurse to be with him at the front—a true Cold War romance.[47]

The culture of the Cold War encouraged the development of romance and war comic books—two very different yet complementary genres. Both purported to be patriotic and educational as well as entertaining. Of the two, romance proved to be far more successful in terms of sales and public image. During the early 1950s romance comic books outsold any other genre. Moreover, parents generally approved. In its annual rating of comic books the Cincinnati Committee on the Evaluation of Comic Books endorsed the overwhelming majority of romance titles. Between 1950 and 1955 the Committee evaluated more than two hundred individual romance titles and gave them an average rating between "A" (no objection) and "B" (some objection). War and spy comic books, on the other hand, did well enough in terms of sales but generally failed to win the committee's approval. More than one hundred such titles evaluated during this period garnered an average grade of "C" (objectionable).[48]

The evaluators objected to the war comic books on the grounds that they contained too much violence and bloodshed and were, by that measure, little better than crime comic books. The committee also disapproved of those war comics that "represented the United Nations soldiers in Korea as being in a hopeless situation." Evidently fearing young people's exposure to imaginary violence more than the real thing, the committee warned that "such comics could be construed as trying to make Americans want to pull out of the war and to discourage young men from enlisting." With typical inconsistency, the evaluators

From "The Honeymoon Is Over," *Romantic Love* 11 (Realistic Comics, May 1952). Romance comic books like this affirmed the virtues of domesticity by showing how desirable men preferred "old-fashioned" housewives to ambitious career women. Writer and artist unknown.

still saw fit to approve of *G.I. Joe*, a series that made the Korean War look like a game of cowboys and Indians that any kid could play.[49]

Such was the irony of comic books and the Cold War. Superheroes who triumphed too easily over Communists failed in the marketplace. U.S. soldiers who agonized in the struggle against the Communists appealed to readers but failed with parents. The closer that comic books came to the troubling realities of the Cold War, the more likely they were to attract readers and repel parents. That was understandable. In frightening times, parents wished to shield their children from a confusing and dangerous world. Yet the comic book market suggested that young people wanted more reality in their entertainment. They bought comic book versions of the world that indulged their anxieties, not ignored them. Comic book makers understood the inquisitive nature of their audience and accommodated it with profitable results. For many concerned parents, that sensible business approach amounted to exploitation and threatened to deprive children of their innocence.

The Cold War presented a curious dilemma for the comic book industry. Anticommunism seemed to be a noble cause for comic book makers to endorse, but when they adapted the subject matter for an audience that demanded less condescension and more realism from their entertainment, the results revealed the inherent contradictions and frustrations of the Cold War itself. Anticommunist though they might be, Korean War comic books could rarely present an encouraging image of the struggle. Instead, the comic book versions of Korea suggested that this new age of limited warfare would be characterized more by hopelessness than heroism. When comic books explored other fronts in the Cold War, the results were less ambivalent but still ambiguous. Secret agents could defeat Communist plots around the world, but they could never vanquish its elusive source. Even as these comic books patriotically endorsed the containment of Communism, they also gave children an early lesson in the exasperation of waging the Cold War. Many of those children would grow up to experience this firsthand in Vietnam.

Still, the war and romance comic books ultimately affirmed young readers in the culture of the Cold War. Whether they dramatized a woman's quest for marriage or a soldier's war against the Communists, these comic books identified the appropriate evils and endorsed the culturally correct course of action. The same could not be said, however, for the comic books pioneered by another publisher from this period, one who discovered the profits and the perils of confronting, not endorsing, Cold War culture.

The EC Challenge

There were comic book publishers, and then there was EC. During the first half of the 1950s EC produced remarkably innovative and distinctive comic books that challenged the creative standards of the industry, attacked the facade of America's Cold War consensus, and considerably raised the stakes for control of youth culture. The origins of EC lay with comic book pioneer Max Gaines. Having helped to launch the comic book industry in 1933, Gaines later entered into a profitable partnership with the publishers of DC Comics, who bought him out in 1945. The following year, Gaines reentered the comic book business and formed his own company, Educational Comics, specializing in decidedly uncommercial titles like *Picture Stories from the Bible*, *Picture Stories from American History*, and *Animal Fables*. They did not perform well in the market. To make matters worse, parting with DC had cost Gaines his national distributor, leaving him to deal with Leader News, one of the weakest distributors on the East Coast. In 1947 Gaines died in a boating accident, leaving his twenty-five-year-old son the struggling comic book company. With no prior experience or interest in comic books or publishing, William M. Gaines hired Al Feldstein as his chief writer, artist, and editor. They canceled the educational series and launched in their place several crime, romance, and western titles that closely aped industry trends. When these too made little impression in the marketplace, the creators decided to launch their own trend in comic books.[50]

In 1950 William Gaines radically changed the direction of his company, phasing out all of the old titles and promoting what he called his "New Trend" line. The first of these was a horror title called *The Crypt of Terror*, but because wholesalers apparently objected to the word *terror* Gaines changed the title shortly thereafter to *Tales from the Crypt*. Two more horror series followed, *The Vault of Horror* (wholesalers apparently had no problem with the word *horror*) and *The Haunt of Fear*. Joining these over the next couple of years were two science-fiction titles called *Weird Fantasy* and *Weird Science*, two crime titles called *Crime Suspen-Stories* and *Shock SuspenStories*, two war series titled *Two-Fisted Tales* and *Frontline Combat*, and a humor comic book called *Mad*. Appropriately, Gaines changed the name of the company from Educational Comics to Entertaining Comics, or simply EC.

It would be difficult to overstate how different the EC comic books were from what came before them. Featuring quality artwork—some of the most innovative and accomplished ever seen in comic books—

and unusually well-crafted stories, the EC comic books easily stood out from the mass of lesser-inspired competition. The stories explored mature themes like murder, lust, psychosis, and political intrigue. And while EC stories could still be as formulaic as other comic books, they rarely seemed tossed off or condescending. Al Feldstein insisted that he and the other EC writers "always wrote to [their own] level." He continued, "If we thought the comics were being read by very young children, we were not particularly concerned with writing to their level." Instead, they wrote for teenagers and adults like themselves, while their striking covers and exciting stories certainly held appeal for younger children as well.[51]

William Gaines later explained that the EC comic books simply reflected his own basic conviction that "people are no damn good."[52] But he was being too modest. Gaines was also, by his own account, "an extreme liberal," and his comic books worked to critique, satire, and subvert entrenched American values and institutions at a time when few other voices in popular culture did so.[53] The EC approach could be devastating, bemused, or absurdist, but rarely was it indifferent. Into a self-satisfied culture of abundance and moral certitudes, EC injected a dose of sober revisionism and liberating anarchy. And for millions of young people, it was a welcome dose indeed.

EC's extraordinary qualities reflected the personality and policies of its publisher. Working with Al Feldstein awakened Gaines's enthusiasm for comic books and inspired his own creativity. At a time when most publishers limited their involvement to the business of comic books, Gaines took an active role in the creative side, plotting or co-writing most of the EC stories himself. In his late twenties, Gaines was among the youngest publishers in the field; he was of the same generation as his staff and little older than most of his audience. And unlike most publishers, who valued quantity over quality, Gaines encouraged his artists to innovate and refine their own individual styles. He paid some of the highest rates in the industry and attracted some of the top talents in the field. Much like Hollywood producers contracted particular movie stars for genre movies, Gaines and Feldstein wrote stories geared to the particular styles of the artists, who always signed their work, and so fostered the comic book industry's first "star system." These workplace conditions promoted an almost familylike environment at the company and helped to give the EC comic books their visionary character.[54]

Young, enthusiastic, and irreverent, William Gaines and the staff at EC had both the inclination to assault the prevailing mores and conventions of mainstream America and the talent to pack a devastating cultural punch. When animated by a sense of moral outrage, EC could deliver some timely and poignant social critiques. As Al Feldstein later explained, "We came out of World War II, and we all had great hopes for the marvelous world of tomorrow." Noting the conspicuous failings of American society, EC produced comic books that carried a "plea to improve our social standards."[55]

Many such messages appeared in *Shock SuspenStories,* and the most remarkable of them confronted issues that few other entertainment producers acknowledged at the time. One of those issues appeared in a story titled "The Guilty." It takes place in a small American town where a murder has been committed and the people lust for revenge. The accused killer is in police captivity, but the case against him is only circumstantial. He is a black man accused of killing a white woman, and that, it seems, is enough to convict him in the eyes of the white population. The sheriff refers to the accused as a "n——r" and would rather see him lynched by the mob than acquitted by the civil rights lawyer who has arrived to defend him. Ultimately, the sheriff takes the law into his own hands and executes the prisoner before he can come to trial. At the end of the story the real killer comes forward to confess and exonerate the black man, but it is too late. The narrator concludes with a solemn warning that "for any American to have so little regard for the life and rights of any other American is a debasement of the principles of the Constitution upon which our country is founded."[56]

Another *Shock SuspenStories* tale, "In Gratitude," pointed to the hypocrisy of a nation that purported to champion freedom and equality in the Cold War while denying the same to its own citizens. It opens with a wounded Korean War veteran returning to a hometown hero's welcome. He learns upon his arrival, however, that his parents had not honored his wishes to bury in their family cemetery plot the G.I. who died while saving his life. The deceased soldier is black, and under community pressure the parents had buried him in a segregated cemetery instead. Outraged, the veteran assails his neighbors at a ceremony held in his honor. "They drafted me into the Army . . . and sent me to Korea," he says. "They said I was fighting for democracy . . . helping to turn back the tide of slavery that threatened to overrun Europe and Asia . . . and the world!" Proud of his mission to defend "freedom and equality," he acidly reminds the silent crowd that the grenade that killed his buddy did not discriminate on the basis of color. That man died defending democracy, and for this he endures discrimination at home, even in death. The veteran shouts at the crowd, "You say you're proud

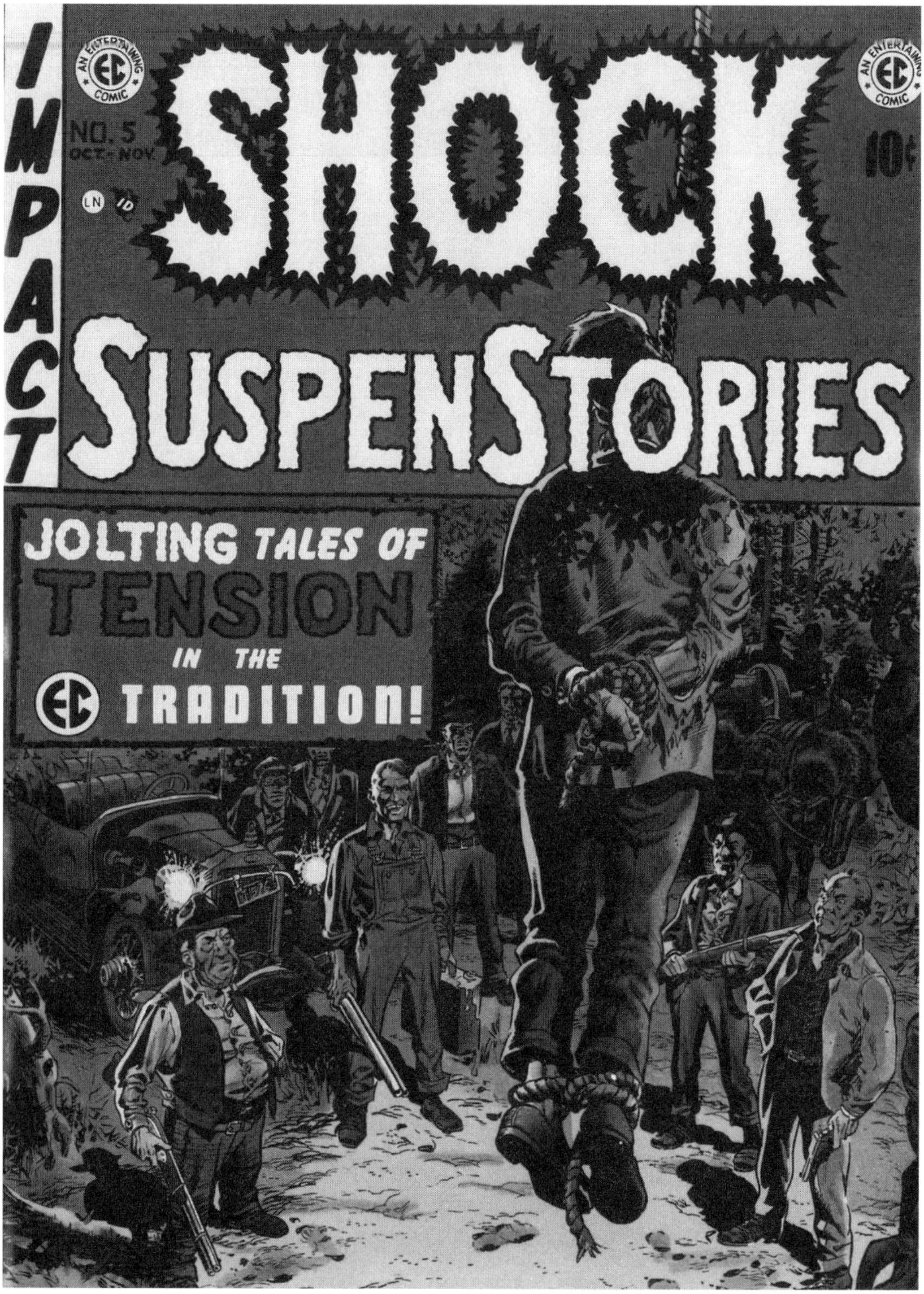
IMPACT
AN ENTERTAINING EC COMIC
NO. 5
OCT.-NOV.
SHOCK
10¢
SUSPENSTORIES
JOLTING TALES OF
TENSION
IN THE
EC TRADITION!

of me! Well, I'm not proud of you! I'm ashamed of you . . . and for
you!" The townspeople file out in silence and leave the veteran alone
on the stage, sobbing.[57]

This story touched a nerve. One critical letter addressed to EC
from a soldier stationed in Biloxi, Mississippi, complained, "This story
stinks." He continued, "I'd like the person who wrote it to sleep, eat,
and live with blacks or niggers" and insisted, "I would not care to have
a nigger eat at the same table with me, or anybody else with self-respect
that I know." Moreover, he added, "the niggers" in his outfit "eat, sleep,
and stay with themselves. And that is the way it will stay without a riot."
EC printed the letter in the next issue and responded simply, "The
above was written by a member of the Armed Forces of the United
States in the year 1953. No further comment."[58]

That letter in turn provoked a critical response from some other
readers. One identified himself as a sergeant stationed at the same
Biloxi base and insisted that the soldier had misrepresented conditions
there. There was, he assured EC, no racial segregation on the base.
Another sergeant wrote a letter insisting that some of the best men
in his platoon were "Negroes."[59] "In Gratitude" accomplished what
Gaines and Feldstein had hoped, as *Shock SuspenStories* became for a
time the only forum in popular entertainment debating the issue of
racial segregation.

In "Judgment Day," Gaines and Feldstein used the vehicle of science fiction to attack prejudice and segregation. Set in the distant future, the story opens as an Earth astronaut named Tarlton arrives on a
planet of robots to see what kind of society these man-made constructions have developed for themselves. Tarlton discovers that although
the robots have made great advances in technology and economy, they
have developed a segregated society, wherein the orange robots receive
all of society's benefits and the blue robots (who live in "Blue Town"
on the south side of the city) labor as second-class citizens. Although
all of the robots are of the same construction, they are each pro-
grammed by an "educator" that instills in them ignorance and prejudice. Saddened, Tarlton leaves the planet, having concluded that the robots have not advanced enough to be admitted into the community of

Cover of *Shock SuspenStories* 5
(EC Comics, October–November
1952). EC's dramatic covers
combined shocking images and
highly polished artwork to command attention on newsstands.
Shock SuspenStories was the most
political of EC's titles, featuring
blunt social commentary on
bigotry, mob violence, and the
dangerous ignorance of small-town
America. Art by Wallace Wood.

planets. In the final panel, Tarlton appears without his helmet, revealing to the reader for the first time that he is black.[60]

EC addressed prejudice against other minorities as well. Often the
stories demonstrated how bigots were destroyed by their own hatred.
"The Whipping" concerns a middle-aged bigot outraged by his daughter's romance with a young Hispanic man, whom he calls a "spick." The
bigot's neighbors share his hostility towards the Hispanics who have
moved into their pleasant suburban town. They form a hooded society modeled after the Ku Klux Klan and undertake a campaign of
hate, harassment, and intimidation to drive them out. In an act of blind

From "Judgment Day," *Weird Fantasy* 18 (EC Comics, March–April 1952). EC was the only comic book publisher of the early 1950s to explicitly attack racial segregation. In the science-fiction story called "Judgment Day," published two years before the *Brown v. Board of Education* ruling, a black astronaut sadly surveys a planet where blue and orange robots are unequally segregated. Script by Al Feldstein, art by Joe Orlando.

hatred and violence, the mob seizes from a darkened room someone they believe to be the daughter's Hispanic lover and beat him to death. Then in the light they discover that the "man" they have killed is actually the daughter herself.[61]

At the height of McCarthyism, EC pointed to the dangers of political hatred and intolerance masquerading as patriotism. Printed in a 1952 issue of *Shock SuspenStories*, "The Patriots" opens with a small-town parade honoring Korean War veterans. As the soldiers march past, some unruly patriots gather around one onlooker who appears indifferent to the proceedings. "Look at his nose," says one of them. "He must be a foreigner," another adds. The mob quickly surmises that the silent observer must be a "lousy Red." When the stranger neglects to remove his hat in the presence of an American flag, the men pounce upon him, shouting "traitor," "subversive," and "Red rat," and they beat him to death. Then they learn that the "commie" whom they have killed was in fact a blind American war veteran. EC later printed a letter from a reader who commended this story for warning against the dangers of anticommunist hysteria—a "dangerous trend . . . choking our democracy."[62]

EC stories also challenged the integrity of established authority. "Confession" opens with a motorist who comes across a woman killed in a hit-and-run accident. Before he can phone for help, the police arrive and arrest the innocent man. The dead woman turns out to be the wife of the police lieutenant, who then supervises the brutal police interrogation himself. After enduring hours of torture at the hands of the police, the man confesses to save his life. Thus satisfied, the lieutenant returns to his home and secretly cleans his wife's blood off his own car, which he had used to kill her. With that, the story ends. Similarly, "A Kind of Justice" relates how an innocent man is beaten by police and lynched by a mob for the rape of a teenage girl. In the end, readers learn that the actual rapist is the town sheriff. He goes unpunished and tells his young victim that he expects her to accommodate him the future.[63]

EC stories like this spoke bluntly to readers' feelings that evil existed in America, without offering the slightest pretense of resolution. It was an image of the affluent society viewed through a penetrating lens indeed. In EC comic books, American society was not a "melting pot" that dissolved racial, religious, ethnic, and political differences into a national consensus. It was a society at war with itself. By turning "traditional values" around and portraying sinister and established heroes as villains, EC turned Cold War America upside down.

The deconstruction of national myths informed EC's war comic
books as well. Most of these were written by Harvey Kurtzman. A reluctant comic book writer and artist, Kurtzman was, in a sense, the
conscience of EC. He began as a cartoonist in the 1930s, working
briefly for the leftist *Daily Worker* before illustrating training guides for
the Army Information Division during World War II. He had come to
work for EC initially because he thought the company was still in the
business of educational comics. Kurtzman combined a careful attention
to historical detail, thoughtful and ironic writing, and a sense of moral
outrage to his war comics. Kurtzman worked to destroy the myth that
war was a glorious endeavor—a myth perpetuated by many rival comic
books. As Kurtzman noted, "Everything that went before . . . had glam-
orized war. Nobody had done anything on the depressing aspects of
war." Kurtzman considered this "a terrible disservice to the children,"
and he especially deplored those comic book writers "feeding this crap
to the children that soldiers spend their time merrily killing little bucktoothed yellow men with the butt of a rifle."[64]

Kurtzman worked to remove war from the context of lofty rhetoric
and crusading zeal and present it in its essence, which, in Kurtzman's
view, amounted to madness and self-destruction. "Kill" commenced
with the narrator cynically inviting readers to "watch the show" and see
the "little people run all over Korea murdering each other." The story
focuses first upon a group of American soldiers—"tired soldiers with
vacant staring eyes . . . eyes that are dumb with sleeplessness and horror." Then the reader meets two individual soldiers on opposite sides
of this drama. One is a "knife-happy" American named Abner, who
busies himself by sharpening his knife in anticipation of killing a Communist. The other is a Communist named Li who devotes similar enthusiastic attention to his rifle in anticipation of shooting an American.
Both characters get their wish when they confront and kill each other.
The narrator then asks rhetorically, "Now that your bodies are growing
cold and your limbs stiffening, how do you like death, Li and Abner?
How do you like death, humanity?"[65]

EC's antiwar message encompassed warnings about the frightening
consequences of war in the atomic age. Al Feldstein later insisted that
he and Gaines believed strongly that any notion of a winnable atomic
war was nonsense. If World War III came, in their estimation, it would
mean "complete annihilation suddenly" for both sides.[66] "The 10th at
Noon" opens with a startling image, drawn in superb detail, of a man
with half of his body burnt away by an atomic blast. The story itself
pursues two subplots: the first concerns scientists who have invented a

THE 10TH AT NOON

HIGH UP OVER NEW YORK'S EAST RIVER, IN THE MODERNISTIC STRUCTURE THAT SERVES AS THE PERMANENT HOME OF THE U.N., THE DOOR TO THE SECURITY COUNCIL'S CHAMBER BURSTS OPEN AND A MELEE OF REPORTERS EXPLODES THROUGH...

ONE SIDE! LEMME AT THAT PHONE!

HOLY COW! *THIS IS IT!*

WHAT *IS* IT? WHAT'S *HAPPENED?*

IT'S THE *EASTERN ALLIANCE!* THEY'VE DELIVERED AN *ULTIMATUM!*

THE PHONE-BOOTHS THAT HUG THE CORRIDOR-WALL ARE FILLED WITH BREATHLESS NEWSMEN...

GIMME THE DESK... PRONTO!

YEAH! THAT'S RIGHT! THEY'VE GIVEN US TILL *DECEMBER 10TH AT 12 NOON!*

...AND IF THEIR DEMANDS *AREN'T MET,* THEY'RE GOING TO USE *THE BOMB!*

YEAH. THE *HYDROGEN BOMB!*

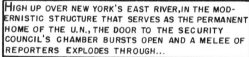

1

camera that can take photographs of the future, and the second, an impending crisis erupting between the United States and the "Eastern Alliance." The tale ends as the scientists develop a picture of how New York City will look exactly twenty-four hours in the future. It is a photograph of a dead city, incinerated by a hydrogen bomb.[67]

In a more perverse commentary typical of EC's black humor, "The Last Man" suggested that nuclear war could bring all kinds of unpleasant surprises. In the tale, an atomic war has killed every human being on Earth except for one man and, as he subsequently learns, one woman. The man searches the world for the lone surviving woman so that they can get together and play Adam and Eve to breed a new civilization. When he finally does meet the woman, he discovers to his horror that she is his own sister. What happens next is left for readers to ponder.[68]

Kurtzman's historical war stories challenged the then-prevailing consensus, a view of history which minimized social conflict and emphasized the "Great Americans" who had forged the proud nation. At a time when General George Armstrong Custer still reigned as a national hero in popular culture, Kurtzman's "Custer's Last Stand" showed the Indian killer as an inept and arrogant villain. The narrator, a U.S. soldier in Custer's Seventh Cavalry, holds the general in contempt: "He don't give a gol durn dang for us! General Custer is just looking out for one fellar . . . General Custer! Going to make us kill Indians so's he can get more glory." The narrator also deplores the war against the Indians. He goes into the Battle of Little Big Horn praying, "God forgive me for the sinning I'll do today! We've got no God given right to kill the poor Redmen!" He continues, "We've broken their treaties again and again! We've chased them out of their hunting grounds and killed their women and children!" When the battle turns into a massacre of white soldiers, the narrator considers it divine retribution for the sins of the United States. The last thing he sees before he dies is General Custer's death, which he cheers, "Custer got us into this! Custer's to blame . . . Custer's hit! He's killed! I'm glad! I'm glad!"[69]

Kurtzman used revisionist history to debunk the myths supporting

---

From "The 10th at Noon," *Weird Fantasy* 11 (EC Comics, January–February 1952). This horrifying and vividly illustrated image shows how EC combined poignant commentary and aesthetic skill to speak to the anxieties of Cold War America. The grim story ends with an image of New York City vaporized by a hydrogen bomb. Script by Al Feldstein, art by Wallace Wood.

what he believed to be a hypocritical triumphalist American culture. In "Caesar," a tale ostensibly about the Roman Empire, Caesar's soldiers return from their brutal conquests over the barbarians and lounge about in the decadent comforts of Rome. They claim to "live the highest form of life possible" and boast of their cultural superiority over all foreigners. As they gorge themselves, drink to excess, and revel in their contempt for others, it is the Romans and not their Germanic adversaries who seem to be the real "barbarians" in this story. Kurtzman later confirmed that it was not really the Romans that he was commenting on in this story but an American nation grown arrogant and distant from the ideals it had espoused.[70]

Much of EC's audience may have missed the implications of Kurtzman's writing. The EC staff recalled that most of the critical mail received from readers simply pointed out inaccuracies in weapons and uniforms, while few commented on the political or antiwar tone of the stories. Kurtzman himself later admitted that some of his stories were too "subtle by comic book standards." It was, he noted, "a little like asking a kid to read the *New York Times*." Although they sold only moderately well compared to the rest of the EC line, Kurtzman's war comic books stand as some of the most nationally self-critical documents in American entertainment at the time.[71]

Kurtzman found greater commercial success by editing and writing EC's humor comic book, *Mad*. Of the title's first several issues, Kurtzman later confessed, "I didn't really know what the hell I was doing." But then he found his satiric voice—at a time when, as Kurtzman recalled, "satire was not very strong" in popular entertainment. Kurtzman initially lampooned the comic books themselves, caustically mocking the trademark characters of rival publishers. Quality Comics' "Blackhawk" became the "Black and Blue Hawks," an international gang of fascists trotting across the globe in search of popular revolutions to crush. "Archie, America's typical teenager," became "Starchie," a more truly "typical" juvenile delinquent who cheats on exams, beats up his teachers, and runs a protection racket at his high school. Instead of clean, suburban Riverdale, Starchie lives in the depressed inner city along with other "typical American teenagers" who are all no good. Kurtzman even lampooned the preeminent comic book icon as "Superduper Man," an idiotic do-gooder who battles "Captain Marbles" in a parody of the lawsuit filed by DC against Fawcett over the rights to be the one and only legal superhero.[72]

The EC staff clearly enjoyed themselves with this material, and within a short time Kurtzman had broadened his range of satire to en-

compass a variety of institutions, conventions, individuals, and events,
including the 1954 Army-McCarthy Hearings.[73] But it was the comic
book lampoons, especially "Superduper Man," that initially built *Mad*'s
reputation and readership. Rival publishers, however, were not amused.
The executives at DC, in particular, objected to EC's unflattering ap-
propriation of Superman and, according to Gaines, threatened to file
suit over the matter. Gaines was prepared to concede, but at Kurtzman's
urging he sought legal counsel and successfully defended EC's right
to parody.[74]

Damage had been done, though. EC had already established itself
as a maverick publisher, and *Mad*'s irreverent assault on its rivals further
isolated the company within the industry. In some instances this led to
distribution troubles. As Gaines explained, EC had taken "cracks at
some of the sanctimonious . . . 'old boy' publishers . . . beloved by the
'old boy' wholesalers," who retaliated by sometimes refusing to handle
EC's comic books.[75] But what most strained relations between EC and
its fragile distribution network was the extremely controversial nature
of the company's most popular comic books.

Crime comic books had been a major presence in the market for
several years prior to EC's "New Trend" line, but Gaines and Feldstein
departed significantly from the proven crime comic formulas. Whereas
most crime comics until that time derived from Lev Gleason's "true"
stories of lower-class criminals inhabiting seedy gangland underworlds,
the closest inspiration for the EC crime stories was the work of novelist
James M. Cain (*Double Indemnity, The Postman Always Rings Twice*). Like
Cain's novels, EC's crime comics featured criminals who were for all
appearances attractive, middle-class, suburban, "normal" people who
happened to possess a disturbing capacity for murder. EC's criminals
could be professionals, mothers, fathers, and even children. Far from
being portrayed as the cornerstone of the affluent society, the middle-
class family now took on a sinister facade which EC worked to deconstruct in gory detail.

Marriage and family may have been central to the American consensus vision, but in EC comic books, failed marriages were the norm
and the common antidote was not divorce but murder. EC's twisted
take on dysfunctional families was like a dark parody of the comic book
romance formula. While romance comic books endorsed suburban values and domesticity, EC's revealed the bitterness, deception, and outright psychosis behind the gilded walls of the American home. In *Crime
SuspenStories*' "Who's Next?" a loving but mousy barber notices that
his glamorous wife no longer seems to care for him. When he discovers

that she has been having an affair with one of his customers, he gives the customer a fatally close shave and bobs his wife's hair—and her head—with an ax.[76]

Shock SuspenStories' "Beauty and the Beach" told two parallel stories of middle-class men married to very attractive women. Both women outrage their husbands by accepting, against the men's wishes, modeling jobs that permit them to flaunt their beauty for all men to see. The husbands, one of whom is also a father, resent having to do the household chores while their wives work. One wife adorns magazine covers and boasts that she enjoys being a spectacle for men. The other models for a suntanning product, despite her husband's professed dislike of the sun. The husbands take revenge on their overly assertive wives in gruesome fashion. One mocks his wife's wish to model for men by boiling her in plastic and preserving her corpse in a display case. The other indulges his wife's love of suntanning by frying her to a blackened crisp with high-intensity sun lamps.[77] Such was divorce in the EC style.

In a grisly tale called "The Neat Job," an attractive young woman marries an older man for his money. A fanatic about neatness, he nags and scolds her for minor transgressions like placing underwear on the wrong side of the drawer and failing to properly organize cans of soup in the cabinet. Inevitably, one of his tirades pushes the neurotic housewife over the edge, and she plants an ax in his skull. When the police arrive they discover that she has finally done a "neat job" for her husband—by carefully removing all of his innards and placing them in labeled jars.[78]

Stories like this were so common that similar examples could be found in virtually every EC crime and horror comic book. The cultural implications of such material in youth entertainment were explosive. These stories were, of course, only fantasy, but that was what made them so provocative. For whose fantasies were they, after all? In "Horror in the School Room," a wicked old schoolteacher punishes a boy for telling lies about an imaginary friend called Magog. As a typically authoritarian adult, the teacher is bent on instilling discipline by crushing the imagination and independent spirit of children. In this case, however, the "imaginary" friend turns out to be quite real and rips the teacher apart.[79] Very similarly, in "Grounds . . . for Horror" a boy's "imaginary" friend comes to life and tosses his cruel father into a meat grinder, pulverizing him into bloody mush.[80] In another tale, adapted from a Ray Bradbury story, an infant murders his own mother as revenge for expelling him from the womb.[81]

Destined to be among EC's most notorious stories was "The Orphan." The narrator is a ten-year-old girl named Lucy, who endures a miserable family life. Lucy's father is an alcoholic who beats her. Lucy's unloving mother tells her that she was a mistake conceived when father was drunk. The little girl tells readers, "I hated them both. I don't know who I hated more . . . Daddy, because he beat me and yelled at me and came home drunk all the time . . . or Mom, because she never wanted me." When Lucy discovers that her mother is having an affair with a man named Steve, she devises a plan to escape from this wretched family, whereby she murders her own father and frames her mother and Steve for the act. The story ends with Dad murdered, Mom and Steve sizzling in the electric chair, and Lucy living happily ever after with her aunt in a nice home where she gets all the love and toys that she wants.[82]

These stories and many others like them invited young readers into a world where parents, teachers, and other adult authority figures were clearly unwelcome. They stood as a challenge to consensus entertainment and marked a major stride towards the autonomy of youth culture. Here was a widely available source of entertainment that sold not despite but *because* of its willfully antagonistic cultural stance. EC comic books appealed to young readers with material that would shock and outrage everybody else. They were tangible evidence of a youth culture slipping out of parental control.

Sales figures bore out the success of EC's controversial approach. With only nine titles and a weak distribution network, EC was a relatively small publisher, but it enjoyed commercial success disproportionate to its size. Moreover, it seemed, the more outrageous the stories, the better they sold. The company's most popular titles were the horror comic books, which sold about 80 percent of their print runs of half a million.[83] It was no coincidence that these best-selling comic books offered the most horrific, grotesque, and gruesome images available anywhere in American mass entertainment.

When it came to grisly imagery, the EC staff seemed determined to consistently outdo themselves. The cover of the April–May 1953 issue of *Vault of Horror* depicts a close-up of a severed arm with blood and bone protruding. The cover of the next issue shows a man whose face has been smashed to a bloody pulp by a man holding a mallet. The next cover displays a corpse with a bloody meat cleaver embedded in its skull. An issue of *Crime SuspenStories* featured an extreme close-up of a man hanging by the neck with eyes rolled up and tongue sticking out. The May 1954 issue depicts a man holding a bloody ax in one hand and a woman's severed head in the other. Corpses in various states of decay and reanimation regularly adorned the covers.

So *NOW* YOU *KNOW*, FIENDS. NOW YOU KNOW *WHY* THERE IS A BALL GAME BEING PLAYED IN THE MOONLIGHT AT MIDNIGHT IN THE DESERTED CENTRAL CITY BALL PARK. LOOK *CLOSELY*. *SEE* THIS *STRANGE BASEBALL GAME!* SEE THE LONG STRINGS OF PULPY INTESTINES THAT MARK THE BASE LINES. SEE THE TWO LUNGS AND THE LIVER THAT INDICATE THE BASES...THE HEART THAT IS HOME PLATE. SEE DOC WHITE BEND AND WHISK THE HEART WITH THE MANGY SCALP, YELLING ...

PLAY BALL... BATTER UP!

LET'S *GO* PHILLY, BOY! *PITCH IT IN...*

SEE THE BATTER COME TO THE PLATE SWINGING THE LEGS, THE ARMS, THEN THROWING ALL BUT ONE AWAY AND STANDING IN THE BOX WAITING FOR THE PITCHER TO HURL THE HEAD IN TO HIM. SEE THE CATCHER WITH THE TORSO STRAPPED ON AS A CHEST-PROTECTOR, THE INFIELDERS WITH THEIR HAND-MITS, THE STOMACH-ROSIN-BAG, AND ALL THE OTHER PIECES OF EQUIPMENT THAT ONCE WAS CENTRAL CITY'S STAR PITCHER, HERBIE SATTEN...

AND IN THE MORNING, WATCH THE FACES OF THE FANS AS THEY PACK THE PARK AND SEE THE GREEN GRASS NOW STAINED RED, AND SEE THE HASTILY SUBSTITUTED PITCHER STEP TO THE RUBBER AND STARE DOWN AT THE STONE PLAQUE EMBEDDED THERE WITH THE ENGRAVED WORDS MEMORIALIZING THE GORY REMAINS BURIED BENEATH THE *PITCHER'S MOUND*...

GOOD LORD!

HERBERT SATTEN
PITCHER
MURDERER
R.I.P.

HEH, HEH! SO THAT'S MY *YELP-YARN* FOR THIS ISSUE, KIDDIES. HERBIE, THE PITCHER, WENT TO *PIECES* THAT NIGHT AND WAS TAKEN *OUT*...OUT OF *EXISTENCE*, THAT IS! THE *PLAQUE* TURNED OUT TO BE HIS *GRAVE STONE*, AND THE *PITCHER'S MOUND* HIS *GRAVE*. OH, BY THE WAY. NEXT TIME YOU GO SEE CENTRAL CITY PLAY, BE CAREFUL WHERE YOU SIT. THAT NIGHT ONE OF BAYVILLE'S BOYS HIT A HOMER, INTO THE STANDS. THEY NEVER FOUND THE ... HEH, HEH... 'BALL'! 'BYE, NOW. WE'LL ALL SEE YOU NEXT IN *MY* MAG, *TALES FROM THE CRYPT!*

This was not false advertising either, as the stories generally lived up to the covers' gruesome promise. "The Living Death" illustrates a horrible death scene with the accompanying description, "His skin shriveled, and turned from pink to blue to a sickening brown! His eyes sunk deep into his head! Then they became hollow black sockets! The flesh . . . rotted and stinking . . . fell from his bones! Soon, the bed was covered with nothing but a seething, oozing mass of putrefied and decayed flesh."[84]

If that and the accompanying artwork leaves precious little to the reader's imagination, "What's Cookin'?" leaves even less, as it concludes with a killer being southern-fried in grease melted down from the fat of his obese accomplice's corpse. In another story, a murderer escapes the haunted visions of his dead victim by stabbing himself in the eyes with an ice pick. In the notorious "Foul Play," a baseball team seeks revenge against a rival ballplayer for the murder of one of their own. They ambush the murderer and kill him, but in EC horror comic books that act alone was rarely sufficient. The team proceeds to disembowel the corpse and then uses his entrails to play a grisly midnight baseball game. His intestines line the base paths, his lungs and liver represent the three bases, and his heart serves as home plate. The batter stands over it swinging a severed leg as a bat, while the pitcher winds up to hurl the corpse's head—with, for good measure, an eyeball dangling from its socket.[85]

Such stories raised obvious questions about taste and restraint. But as titles like "What's Cookin'?" and "Foul Play" suggest, the EC horror comics usually had a tongue-in-cheek quality that gave them the character of a sick joke and diluted somewhat their atrocious implications. They were narrated by ghastly cartoon characters, like the Crypt Keeper, who concluded each tale cackling with a grin, a wink, and ghoulishly bad puns. This further served to lessen the intensity of the stories by letting the readers in on what Gaines and Feldstein regarded as a big joke. At least, that was their intention. Both men contended decades later that they never took themselves seriously when writing the horror comics. Nevertheless, Gaines later acknowledged some lapses in taste, and Feldstein conceded that their lighthearted approach

From "Foul Play," *The Haunt of Fear* 19 (EC Comics, May–June 1953). In perhaps the most notorious panel printed by EC Comics, a murderous baseball team plays a midnight ball game with the limbs and entrails of their victim. Fredric Wertham reproduced this image in *Seduction of the Innocent* and presented it to the Senate Subcommittee to Investigate Juvenile Delinquency in their hearings on the comic book industry. Script by Al Feldstein, art by Jack Davis.

to the subject matter may have had the unintended effect of desensitiz-
ing readers to the violence and sadism in the stories. Of "Foul Play" in
particular, Feldstein recalled thinking at the time that it was simply absurd. Rereading it decades later, however, he called it "an atrocity."[86]

The EC staff was not united in enthusiasm for the horror comics.
Artist Jack Davis (who illustrated "Foul Play" in marvelous detail) felt
uncomfortable illustrating the horror material but did so nevertheless.
Artist Johnny Craig told an interviewer in 1970 that he found many of
the horror stories "too gory, too ugly, simply too gruesome" for his
tastes, and he feared that readers might become dangerously desensi-
tized to such images. Graham Ingels's gothic style probably made him
EC's most effective horror artist, but he developed such intense misgiv-
ings about his own work that he later withdrew entirely from the comic
book field and declined all offers and interviews related to his days with
the company. Harvey Kurtzman especially despised the horror comics,
believing that they had the same kind of harmful residual influence on
children that he deplored in chauvinistic war comics. He also resented
the fact that the exploitive horror titles consistently outsold his own
thoughtful and educational war titles.[87]

As outrageous and deplorable as the EC crime and horror comics
might seem to many, it is easy to understand why they succeeded in the
youth market. They stood apart from virtually every source of information and entertainment available to young Americans in the early
1950s. Mainstream culture at that time exuded conformity and consensus behind Cold War imperatives, established authority, and white
middle-class mores. There were few alternatives to this worldview
available in mass entertainment. Hollywood had not yet exploited the
fertile market for teenage rebellion films, and the first few tentative
initiatives in this genre were colored by a distinctively adult perspective
on teen life. The cultural currents that would soon blossom into rock-
and-roll remained segregated into "race" and "hillbilly" music and still
awaited discovery by the nation's teenagers. Even the majority of comic
books then on the market affirmed the basic principles of Cold War
culture. Few questioned the necessity of aspiring to a middle-class suburban existence and prescribed gender roles. Fewer still raised questions about the national mission to spread American values and virtues
throughout the world. In the culture fashioned by their elders, young
people found only selected "truths" that spoke inadequately to their reality.

EC offered young people a liberating alternative to that culture.
With a calculated editorial strategy that sought to demolish the myths,

triumphalism, and half-truths that informed Cold War America, EC
challenged prevailing assumptions about race, democracy, anticommunism, authority, warfare, the atomic bomb, history, marriage, family,
children, and, ultimately, taste. In the EC comic books, millions of
young Americans saw their own anxieties writ large. A commercial expression of cultural defiance, EC brilliantly perceived the alienated
generation among young people and recognized youth dissatisfaction
as a marketable commodity.

EC's course, however, was also fraught with peril. Well-organized
forces remained aligned and determined to resist the cultural upheaval
that these comic books represented. EC raised the stakes in the battle
to control youth culture, and it quickly found itself on the front lines.
And before the contest was over, William M. Gaines would find himself
in the unenviable position of defending before a committee of U.S.
Senators the virtues of assaulting cultural mores and the finer aesthetic
qualities of a bloody ax and a woman's severed head.

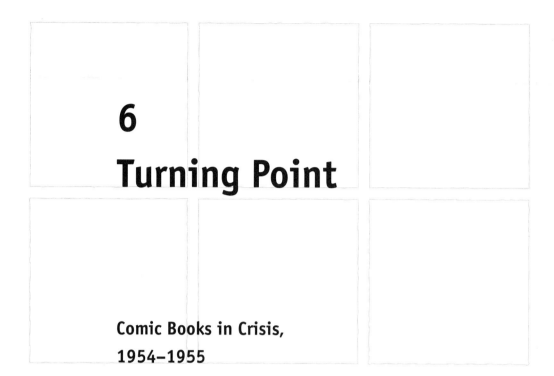

6

Turning Point

**Comic Books in Crisis,
1954–1955**

On 22 April 1954, hearings opened in Washington, D.C., to investigate Senator Joseph McCarthy's charges that Communists had infiltrated the U.S. Army. The televised hearings showcased the senator's boorish tactics and precipitated his dramatic fall from power. Yet by proposing simple solutions to complex problems, McCarthy gave Americans enemies upon whom to focus their anxieties. One day before the Army-McCarthy hearings commenced, the Senate Subcommittee to Investigate Juvenile Delinquency had opened its hearings to investigate the comic book industry. As the anxious public trusted "experts" and government officials to root out the subversive elements "brainwashing" their children into delinquency, the paranoid style of Cold War politics intruded into the debate over the mass media and youth culture.

Comic Book Horrors

The comic book industry seemed to have weathered the storm of criticism that had engulfed it in the late 1940s. The publishers' 1948 code for editorial standards, the constitutional defeat of legislated comic book controls, and the endorsement of experts and civic watchdog groups like the Cincinnati Committee on the Evaluation of Comic Books all helped to reduce the public pressure on the industry. Many of the most flagrantly offensive crime comic books had either been discontinued, toned down, or simply overwhelmed on the newsstands by the proliferation of war and romance comic books. But the industry's troubles were not over. Dr. Fredric Wertham continued to press his indictment of comic books and maintained his core constituency. Parents remained concerned, and influential groups like the General Federation of Women's Clubs, the American Legion, and the Catholic National Organization for Decent Literature still advocated measures against crime comic books and lobbied political leaders to take action. Occasionally, pressure from these groups compelled local wholesalers and dealers to withdraw certain objectionable comic books from the market.[1]

Nevertheless, a robust market had lured the comic book industry into complacency. By conservative estimates, about 300 comic book titles published in 1950 generated an annual industry revenue of $41 million. In 1953 over 650 titles grossed $90 million. Average monthly circulation had grown from 17 million in 1940 to nearly 70 million by 1953. Some estimates put the monthly figure close to 100 million. *Publishers Weekly* reported that the American public in 1953 spent over $1 billion on comic books. Surveys suggested that over 90 percent of boys and girls under eighteen read them, and 25 percent of high school graduates admitted to reading them as well. Comic books also remained the literature of choice for American G.I.s.[2] Between 1950 and 1954 the comic book industry reached its zenith in audience and sales.

The majority of comic books published in the early 1950s were devoted to funny animals, romance, and innocuous adventure stories, but an increasing minority indulged tastes for controversial and provocative subject matter. In October 1950 the Cincinnati committee reported in their annual survey published in *Parents' Magazine* that comic books had improved to the point at which only 30 percent of them remained "slightly objectionable" or "objectionable." One year later, however, the committee noticed a slight increase in the number of objectionable comic books, owing to the recent trend in "mystery and horror" comics. By October 1953, the reviewers noted with alarm that nearly 50 percent of the comic books had become slightly or very objectionable. And virtually every title condemned as "very objectionable" was a horror comic book. The reviewers found every EC title except *Frontline Combat* objectionable.[3]

The rise of horror comic books was the most conspicuous industry trend of this period. EC had launched the genre in 1950 with *Tales from the Crypt*, *Vault of Horror*, and *The Haunt of Fears*. The industry soon took note of EC's success and, as usual, flooded the market with a host of thin imitations. These publications commanded attention on the newsstands with titles like *Chamber of Chills*, *Web of Evil*, *Adventures into Darkness*, *Strange Tales*, *Strange Terrors*, *City of the Living Dead*, and *The Dead Who Walk*. As the editor of Marvel Comics explained simply, "When we found EC's horror books were doing well . . . we published a lot of horror books." From 1950 through 1954 twenty-eight companies published nearly one hundred different horror titles. And this figure would be much larger if the sometimes equally horrific crime comic books were included. The marketability of horror was such that even cautious DC Comics acknowledged the trend with several rather tepid mystery titles. Fawcett tried to revive its ailing Captain Marvel comic books by introducing horror elements into tales like "Captain Marvel and the Death Horror" and "Captain Marvel Battles the Legend Horror." By 1951 the competition within the horror field already had become so intense that EC ran an editorial warning its readers to avoid "inferior" imitations.[4] Although few competitors approached the originality or clever humor of the EC comic books, many equaled and even surpassed them in gruesome shock value. Brutality, sadism, death, and a grisly variety of "living deaths" became lucrative commodities bought and sold in youth culture.

A sudden trend such as this probably would have provoked a public backlash at any historical moment. But with juvenile delinquency already the focus of intense social concern, the horror comic books took on even greater significance. To many, they seemed to be the latest and most outrageous evidence of a youth culture spinning dangerously out of control. Raising further questions about the integrity of young people in the early 1950s was a series of cheating and sports scandals at prominent colleges, including the U.S. Military Academy at West Point. Disturbing reports about the conduct of American POWs in Korea and their supposed susceptibility to Communist "brainwashing" exacerbated concerns that young Americans lacked the strong moral fiber that had been demonstrated by their elders during the Great Depression and World War II.[5] Critics had abundant cause to conclude that something was degrading the character of young people, and many looked for the culprit in youth entertainment. Some had to look no further than the comic books that flaunted defiance of traditional values and common notions of middle-class morality.

Crime and horror comic books epitomized the widening distance between youth culture and traditional adult notions of childhood. Critics of all political inclinations charged that seductive commercial products had intruded between innocent children and proper sources of moral authority. Parents, teachers, church, and government leaders increasingly had to compete with movies, television, and comic books for influence in the shaping of young minds. For many, these were grave developments, especially in the context of the Cold War. Would a generation reared on mass culture of dubious or dangerous moral value possess the strength of character to prevail over Communism? Or had mass entertainment already triumphed too completely by converting, or "brainwashing," young people into consumers of cultural sludge? If traditional morality and market forces did not work together, which would prevail to affect the American character? The superficial and uninformed arguments in the controversy over comic books and juvenile delinquency belied the profound implications of the contest. This was a struggle to determine not only the control of youth culture but also the power of consumer forces to shape American culture itself.

Seduction of the Innocent

Once again, it was Dr. Fredric Wertham who spearheaded the renewed assault on the comic book industry. Even after the controversy had waned somewhat after 1949, Wertham continued to advocate legislation to control comic books. In 1950 he presented his arguments before the U.S. Senate Subcommittee to Investigate Crime in Interstate Commerce. The committee, chaired by Democratic Senator Estes Kefauver of Tennessee, sent out questionnaires soliciting a variety of opinions on comic books and their possible contribution to juvenile delinquency. The responses produced no consensus. Even J. Edgar Hoover concluded indecisively that some crime comic books might contribute to juvenile delinquency while others might actually combat it. The committee reached no conclusions about comic books and moved on to other issues. The national press reported this as a victory for the comic book industry and a defeat for critics like Wertham.[6]

In December 1951 Wertham gave his expert testimony before the New York State Joint Legislative Committee to Study the Comics. Impressed by his arguments, the state legislature passed its second bill to curb the distribution and sale of crime comic books, but Governor Thomas Dewey vetoed the 1952 bill on the same constitutional grounds on which he had done so in 1950.[7]

Frustrated by these legislative failures, Wertham articulated his case against comic books more emphatically in his own writings, culminating in the book *Seduction of the Innocent*. Published in early 1954, *Seduction* was a 400-page indictment of the comic book industry. Pompous, polemical, and sensational, it aimed to impress a popular audience with professional expertise and moral outrage. As he had done in his earlier articles, Wertham supported the angry arguments in his book with evidence culled from his clinical analysis of juvenile patients and his own selective reading of comic books. Probably the most effective section of the book was a damning set of lurid illustrations taken from the comic books themselves. Yet Wertham failed to document any of his evidence, and he provided no footnotes or bibliography to verify his research. He simply expected readers to trust his evidence and conclusions on the basis of his own expert credentials.[8]

Seduction expanded on the general arguments that Wertham had been disseminating since 1948. "Slowly and at first reluctantly," he explained, "I have come to the conclusion that this chronic stimulation, temptation and seduction by comic books . . . are contributing factors to many children's maladjustment" (10). He charged that the comic book industry exploited the innocence and insecurities of children for the sake of profit. They gave children a distorted and unhealthy image of the world and impeded their social adjustment. He insisted that comic books brought out violent tendencies in maladjusted children and even harmed normal children by fostering low self-esteem, sexual deviance, and disrespect for the rules of society. "The cultural back-

From Fredric Wertham, *Seduction of the Innocent* (New York: Holt, Rinehart, and Winston, 1954). These damning illustrations were used with captions that read "A sample of the injury-to-the-eye motif" and "Pity was the keynote when Homer described a dead body dragged behind a war chariot. Dragging living people to death is described without pity in children's comics." Wertham's examples horrified parents and helped to bring public condemnation down on the comic book industry. The infamous "needle and eye" panel comes originally from "Murder, Morphine, and Me," *True Crime Comics* 2 (Magazine Village, May 1947). Writer and artist unknown.

ground of millions of American children," he wrote, "comes from the teaching of the home, the teaching of the school (and church) and from crime comic books." And he warned that "for many children the last is the most exciting" (94). He noted that while adults were protected from obscene material by legislation and conscientious self-censorship in other media, children remained completely vulnerable to the unregulated comic book industry (13). The remedy, he argued, was a progressive "public health" measure to prohibit the sale and display of crime comic books to children under the age of fifteen (336). Wertham's definition of "crime comic books" as those that portrayed any type of crime was broad enough to include most of the titles on the market.

Wertham noted that the harmful effects of crime comic books could most easily be seen in the cases of straightforward emulation: children who hanged themselves after seeing a hanging in a comic book, kids who jumped off of rooftops as if they were Superman, and boys who hit girls because they saw gangsters hit women in the comic books (114–16). Moreover, children often confirmed Wertham's suspicions by citing comic books as educational in the ways of crime. He quoted children who had told him that they learned from comic books how to fight, torture victims, and conceal firearms (170–71). He even claimed that comic books showed children how to take narcotics (25).

Wertham insisted, however, that comic books poisoned the minds of children in a more sinister manner than even these incidents suggested. He argued that comic books amounted to a "distillation of viciousness" that indoctrinated children against the accepted rules of decency, much as propaganda had done in totalitarian nations (94). He echoed some of the arguments of the radical Frankfurt intellectuals who deplored mass culture for creating a homogenized society with false class consciousness and capitalist aspirations. Although he wisely refrained from spelling out the radical implications of his argument, he still insisted that mass culture could impose a false worldview on its audience. Wertham warned that by indoctrinating children into the world of the Superman, comic books paralleled the "blunting of sensibilities in the direction of cruelty that has characterized a whole generation of central European youth fed on the Nietzsche-Nazi myth" (97).

Wertham also charged, more convincingly, that comic books perpetuated racial and ethnic stereotypes. Citing jungle comics as the most flagrant offenders but finding racism, anti-Semitism, and xenophobia in many superhero and war comic books as well, Wertham argued that children learned to identify the bad men in comic books by the color of their skin and their ethnic characteristics. The hero, he pointed out, was always a white-skinned "Nordic" type, while villains were black, brown, or yellow or possessed long noses and foreign accents (32–33). He deplored war comic books that depicted Asians as "cruelly grimacing and toothy creatures, often of an unnatural yellow color." He doubted that this was good for the morale of the American soldiers who consumed such material in vast quantities, and he insisted that it damaged America's image overseas (105–6). "The United States," he pointed out, "is spending millions of dollars to persuade the world . . . that race hatred is not an integral part of American life." Yet at the same time, millions of American comic books exported "the impression that the United States is instilling race hatred in young children" (100).

Wertham argued that comic books harmed girls as well as boys. He contended that female superheroes like Wonder Woman were "always a horror type." Physically powerful, assertive, and cruel, they dominated and tortured men, thus presenting "an undesirable ideal for girls, being the exact opposite of what girls are supposed to be" (34). Even in romance comic books, rarely criticized elsewhere, Wertham found dangers. He deplored these for their "mushiness," "false sentiments," "social hypocrisy," "titillation," and "cheapness." They instilled in female readers feelings of physical inferiority and gave them a false image of love (39).

He attacked not just the content but also the advertising in comic books. Besides the obvious offenders selling knives and guns, he cited ads that exploited insecure adolescents with false promises to help them lose weight, gain strength, erase pimples, or look prettier (198). Many of these nickel-and-dime products—like the "Redoos-U" vinyl weight-loss suit—did, in fact, make dubious claims. Wertham argued that comic book stories presented physical strength and appearance as the measure of an individual's worth, while the ads offered children the supposed means for achieving it. They all functioned as part of a degrading commercial process that preyed upon children's fragile self-esteem (217).

Sexually deviant behavior, too, was attributable to comic books, Wertham charged. "One of the stock mental aphrodisiacs in comic books," he observed, "is to draw girls' breasts in such a way that they are sexually exciting. Wherever possible they protrude and obtrude." He added that "girls are shown . . . with their pubic regions indicated with special care and suggestions" (178). Drawing a direct connection between the sexual images in comic books and adolescent behavior, he recalled a boy who liked to read sexy comic books and then ride his bicycle past girls and hit them on the breasts (179). Another young comic book reader boasted to the author that he wanted "to be a sex maniac" (174). And several boys confessed that they collected sexy images in comic books for masturbation purposes. Some of them evidently used comic book images to indulge their fetish for dominant women with high heels. Abundant masturbatory images also existed for boys with bondage fantasies (181–82).

Wertham contended comic books promoted homosexuality. As evidence for this, he cited his conversation with a twelve-year-old male prostitute who had said that he read as many as fifteen comic books each week (188). Wertham also decoded the homosexual underpinnings of Batman and Robin's relationship, calling it a "wish dream of two homosexuals living together" (190). He observed that Robin was "usually shown in his uniform with bare legs" and often stood "with his legs spread, the genital region discreetly evident" (191). All of this evidently proved that the dynamic duo did more than investigate crime in the Bat Cave. He clinched his argument by recalling that a young homosexual had confessed to him that he fantasized about being either Batman or Robin (192).

The problems inherent in such analyses are obvious, and there is

From Fredric Wertham, *Seduction of the Innocent* (New York: Holt, Rinehart, and Winston, 1954). Wertham reprinted these images to help make his point that comic books led to deviant sexual behavior. On the cropped image of what was ostensibly a man's muscular shoulder, Wertham editorialized, "In ordinary comic books, there are pictures within pictures for children who know how to look." Below the *Phantom Lady* cover, Wertham's caption read, "Sexual stimulation by combining 'headlights' with the sadist's dream of tying up a woman."

really no need to refute the arguments in *Seduction* point by point—a difficult proposition in any case, since Wertham declined to identify the comic books under critique. Nevertheless, in certain instances, Wertham clearly had misread or distorted the evidence. As an example of anti-immigrant messages in comic books, he quoted from a DC story in which a man apparently says to a crowd, "So my fellow Americans, it is time to give America back to Americans! Don't let foreigners take your jobs!" (34). This may indeed have come from a DC comic book, but judging by the many DC stories that preached against intolerance, the speaker was almost certainly characterized as a bigot for effect. Wertham did not note the full context of this or any of the comic books cited in *Seduction*. He similarly attacked many EC comic books (although not by name) while failing to acknowledge any of the publisher's stories that attacked racism, bigotry, and social injustice. Wertham dismissed the notion that comic books could inculcate anything but harmful values, and he simply ignored or misrepresented evidence to the contrary.

Wertham dismissed his own critics with contempt, charging that they were paid apologists for the comic book industry. With typical hyperbole he denounced the defense of comic books by writers in the *Journal of Educational Sociology* as "an all-time low in American science" (220–21). His claim that certain experts and intellectuals were actually a front for the comic book industry sounded very similar to contemporary charges leveled at suspected Communist front organizations.

Conspiracy rhetoric, in fact, pervaded much of *Seduction*. Wertham evoked an image of a large and pervasive industry, cloaked in secrecy, masterminded by a ruthless few, and operating upon young, defenseless minds. It wielded power against helpless newsdealers and forced them to peddle crime and horror comic books. He accused the industry of compelling vendors to purchase comic books or risk losing their rights to carry popular mainstream magazines, a practice much like the "block-booking" long used by the major Hollywood studios to pressure theaters into accepting all of their movies, which had recently been declared illegal by the U.S. Supreme Court (262–63).

Wertham also charged that comic book publishers colluded to force writers and artists into producing crime and horror comics. Most of the individuals who wrote and drew comic books, he insisted, were decent people who had no choice but to create this filth so publishers could sell it to children. These workers were "not free men. They are told what to do and they do it—or else." Like the vendors, Wertham claimed, these writers and artists feared "the ruthless economic power of the comic book industry." As evidence for this, he cited "anonymous" sources from within the industry and cleverly pointed to the "ruthlessness" with which DC had dismissed Superman's creator Jerry Siegel (264–65).

Perhaps the most disturbing theme sounded in *Seduction* was Wertham's contention that the comic book industry made children deceitful, turning them against their own parents. Those who read crime and horror comic books, he observed, usually did so alone or in peer groups away from the company of adults. When parents or teachers were in the room a child might read an innocent funny-animal comic, but when the adults left, the child replaced it with a horror comic book (300). He added that children who genuinely liked the funny comic books were jeered at by their peers and pressured into reading the bad ones (307). Wertham warned of the existence of "clandestine and half-clandestine stores, and backrooms of stores, about which adults know very little." In these dingy settings, a black market of sorts flourished in the trade and sale of second-hand crime and horror comics. Using language that conjured up images of kids skulking around gambling dens and whorehouses, Wertham painted a disturbing picture for parents who wondered what their children did on their way home from school (28).

Wertham concluded *Seduction* with an anecdote about a young mother who came to see him after her teenage son had been arrested and sent to reform school for wielding a switchblade. She sobbed and blamed herself for having been a bad mother. When she asked Wertham where she had gone wrong, he comforted her. She was not a bad mother, he assured her. He had the "charts" to prove it. The influence of the good home that she provided had been "frustrated" by the comic books. Wertham recalled that upon hearing this the woman "seemed to come out from under a cloud." She thanked him profusely and asked, "please—tell me again. . . . Tell me again that it isn't my fault." And so he did (396–97).

"Why, in a democracy," asked Wertham, "should parents feel 'helpless?'" (300). Why indeed? Yet that was exactly how many anxious Americans felt. Bewildered by the complex of economic, social, and cultural factors dividing them from their children, parents wanted an easy answer. For them, Dr. Wertham had diagnosed the problem, identified the malady, and prescribed a remedy. It was a seductive argument.

Seduction of the Innocent became a much talked about book in 1954. *Reader's Digest* and the *Ladies' Home Journal* printed excerpts from it, eliciting uniformly favorable letters which the magazines printed in response. It just missed becoming a Book of the Month Club selection, as the organization was about to select the title but reneged at the last minute. The review that would have accompanied the announcement compared *Seduction* to muckraking classics like Upton Sinclair's *The Jungle*. Wertham later complained that the comic book industry had pressured the Book of the Month Club into withdrawing its announcement.[9]

Seduction garnered generally favorable reviews. Catholic publications like *America* and *Catholic World* praised it and hoped that it would prompt legislation against crime and horror comic books. A review in the *New Yorker* called Wertham's arguments against the comic book industry "altogether . . . a formidable indictment." Writing for the *New York Times Book Review*, noted sociologist and fellow cultural critic C. Wright Mills declared that "all parents should be grateful to Dr. Fredric Wertham" for his work. *Seduction*, Mills wrote, demonstrated a "commendable use of the professional mind in the service of the public." Mysteriously impressed by Wertham's "copious references" to the comic books themselves, he apparently found no fault with the author's failure to document any of his research. Heeding Wertham's call to action, Mills urged immediate legislation to protect children from the harmful effects of comic books.[10]

Not all reviewers agreed however. In a review for the *New Republic*, Reuel Denney criticized *Seduction* as a "tissue of troublesome points." Noting that much of Wertham's "research" was not scientific, Denney contended that the author had evidently tried to impress readers "not with his professional argument, but with his professional status." Denney found no evidence to suggest that many or even some juveniles interpreted comic book stories in the same manner that Wertham did. He concluded that the book proved only that "kids who have trouble with understanding life have trouble understanding fiction too."[11]

Seduction did not generate a consensus for legislative action against the comic book industry or even for the author's central point that crime and horror comic books contributed to juvenile delinquency. But Wertham succeeded in once again focusing public debate on the issue of comic books and articulating the suspicions of concerned parents. Even if comic books were only one factor among the multiple causes of juvenile delinquency, many reasoned, would it not be best to act against them? Surely the matter deserved investigation, at the very least, and what investigative agency was more capable or trusted than the federal government?

The Senate Investigation

While the Senate's first inquiry into comic books in 1950 had yielded only ambiguous findings, Tennessee senator Estes Kefauver continued to suspect a link between the products of mass culture and juvenile delinquency. He also recognized the widespread public concern with juvenile crime and worked to assume a leading political role in the issue. In early 1953 the Senate Subcommittee to Investigate Juvenile Delinquency formed to look into the causes of juvenile crime, with particular attention to the possible contributing factors in mass culture. Kefauver was a powerful voice on the committee and later chaired it, using the resulting publicity to help win himself the Democratic nomination for vice president in 1956. Initially, however, the committee had been chaired by Senator Robert Hendrickson of New Jersey, whose Republican Party had recently assumed control of Congress. Less inclined than Kefauver to focus attention on the entertainment industry, Hendrickson had not wanted to involve the committee in a convoluted debate over censorship and First Amendment issues. Nevertheless, by the beginning of 1954 public pressure compelled the committee to expand its hearings to look into mass culture, starting with comic books.[12]

On 21 April 1954 in New York City, the subcommittee opened its hearings to investigate the comic book industry. Executive director Richard Clendenen opened the proceedings with a horror show: In a slide exhibit of recent horror comic books, Clendenen pointed out a story called "Sanctuary," which featured grotesque drawings of a man with two heads and four arms, a man with a body that extended only to the bottom of his ribs, and a horribly deformed woman killed in a hail of bullets. He then described the plot of "Stick in the Mud," in which a cruel teacher marries the wealthy father of one of her students and then murders her husband to inherit his money. The story ends with the woman drowning in quicksand as her vengeful stepson looks on. Clendenen then held up a copy of *Mysterious Adventures* and described for the senators a featured story that ends with a woman chopping up her alcoholic husband with an ax and stuffing his body parts into liquor bottles.[13]

Clendenen's exhibit of several EC comic books provoked the most interest from the committee. He recounted a story from *The Haunt of Fear* in which an orphan boy comes to live with new foster parents. The evil parents turn out to be vampires and try to kill their foster child. In the end, the youth is revealed to be a werewolf, and he kills them first—then eats them. Clendenen found this story especially disturbing. He pointed out that many foster children who experienced anxieties when moving into a new home might be made even more anxious after reading this story. Then he described the plot of *Shock SuspenStories'* "The Orphan." As the senators listened to the story of sweet little Lucy killing her alcoholic father and rejoicing as her mother fries in the electric chair, they came to understand why so many parents found horror comics so horrible (8–9).

Clendenen assured the committee that his investigation had uncovered no deliberate conspiracy among comic book publishers to corrupt the minds of children. And while he noted scattered allegations of links between the comic book industry and Communists, he dismissed these as nonsense. Instead, he insisted, publishers operated strictly for profit. Democratic Senator Hennings of Missouri remarked that comic book publishers seemed unconcerned what they purveyed to young people "as long as it sells and brings in the money" (58–60).

Fredric Wertham insisted on appearing before the committee. He opened his testimony by presenting a lengthy list of his credentials, then, speaking with authority in his clipped German accent, he indignantly cited comic books as a chief contributing factor to juvenile delinquency. Producing a copy of EC's gruesome "Foul Play," Wertham indignantly pointed out that this was an image of men playing baseball with a corpse's body parts. "They play baseball with a dead man's head," he stated incredulously. "Why do they do that?" Wertham insisted that the measures he advocated to protect children did not amount to censorship, and he leveled the strange counteraccusation that the comic book industry had tried to censor his own findings by curtailing the distribution of *Seduction*. He warned that "as long as the crime comic books industry exists in its present form, there are no secure homes" (79–96).

The committee was impressed by Wertham's passionate testimony. Senator Hennings told Wertham that he had a copy of *Seduction* himself and was "reading it with great interest." Kefauver noted that crime comic books seemed to indoctrinate children in a way similar to Nazi propaganda. Wertham added that "Hitler was a beginner compared to the comic book industry," which taught children race hatred at an early age. As evidence for this, he produced an EC story that used a derogatory term for Hispanics no less than twelve times. He failed to note, however, that in this story, "The Whipping," every character who used the word *spick* was a villain and the story itself carried a statement against intolerance (95–96). William M. Gaines listened angrily as

Wertham misrepresented his comic books. He did not have to wait long to refute the charges, however, because he was the next to testify.

When Gaines had learned that the hearings on comic books would be held, he had asked to testify in defense of his business, figuring that he would have been subpoenaed anyway.[14] Speaking confidently in his thick New York accent, Gaines read his prepared statement. He proudly claimed to be the "first publisher in these United States to publish horror comics. I am responsible. I started them." He acknowledged that while some may not like them, "it would be just as difficult to explain the harmless thrill of a horror story to a Dr. Wertham as it would be to explain the sublimity of love to a frigid old maid." He defended the right of children as consumers, asking, "Are we afraid of our own children? Do we forget that they are citizens too and entitled to select what to read or do?" Rejecting the notion that children were "so evil" and "simple minded that it takes a story of murder to set them to murder, a story of robbery to set them to robbery," Gaines insisted that "delinquency is the product of [the] real environment in which the child lives and not of the fiction he reads" (97–98).

Gaines defended "The Whipping" against Wertham's charges, acknowledging that the words *spick* and *dirty Mexican* did appear in the story but insisting that it was one of "a series of stories designed to show the evils of race prejudice and mob violence." He added that previous stories in the series had attacked anti-Semitism, racism, drug addiction, and even juvenile delinquency. He vigorously contested Wertham's characterization of his comic books and stopped just short of calling him a liar (99).

The committee was taken aback by Gaines's defiant demeanor. They had not expected such a vigorous defense of something they clearly believed was indefensible. The associate chief counsel, Herbert Beaser, took Gaines to task on "The Whipping," pointing out that if the publisher thought it was possible to get across a message against prejudice in one comic book, was it not possible that harmful messages could be communicated to readers through others? Gaines maintained that readers were competent enough to tell when a message was being pitched to them and when a story was sheer entertainment. No horror story, he contended, said to readers, "If you are unhappy with your stepmother, shoot her" (101). The committee remained skeptical as to whether children could make such a distinction.[15]

Then Gaines began to stumble. Beaser asked him to explain the story about the vampire foster parents and the werewolf orphan boy. It was a thankless task. Gaines insisted that it was pure fiction with no bearing on real life, but Beaser pressed him on this. Would not a foster child reading such a story have his own anxieties raised? Gaines did not think so. The foster home in this story, he pointed out, was much worse than any that a real child would likely encounter. At that point, Chief Counsel Herbert Hannoch interrupted Gaines to ask if he believed in vampires. Gaines answered no, and he could not have been encouraged by the turn the questioning had taken (100–101).

Under increasingly hostile questioning, Gaines admitted that the sole limit on what appeared in his comic books was determined by his own standards for good taste. Then came the most heated and famous exchange in the hearings.

Senator Kefauver: (holding up a recent copy of EC's *Crime SuspenStories*) Here is your May 22 issue. This seems to be a man with a bloody ax holding a woman's head up which has been severed from her body. Do you think that is in good taste?

Gaines: Yes, sir; I do, for the cover of a horror comic. A cover in bad taste, for example, might be defined as holding the head a little higher so that the neck could be seen dripping blood from it and moving the body over a little further so that the neck of the body could be seen to be bloody.

Kefauver: You have blood coming out of her mouth.

Gaines: A little.

Kefauver: Here is blood on the ax. I think most adults are shocked by that.

Senator Hendrickson: Here is another one I want to show him.

Kefauver: This is the July one. It seems to be a man with a woman in a boat and he is choking her to death here with a crowbar. Is that in good taste?

Gaines: I think so.

Chief Counsel Hannoch: How could it be worse? (103)

Gaines was in an impossible position, and he knew it. In a later interview, Gaines recalled, "I was so nervous when I was up there that I barely knew what I was doing . . . for the last half hour or so of my testimony, they were batting me around. They were like whacking a corpse."[16] For the remainder of his testimony, he gave terse answers and failed to persuade the committee of anything in support of comic books. Kefauver refuted Gaines's defense of comic books and added evidence of any plea for better race relations (105).

Gaines's testimony concluded with a bizarre exchange over an editorial published in an EC comic book. The one-page feature titled "Are You a Red Dupe?" quoted from an article in the *Daily Worker* that was critical of comic books to suggest that "the group most anxious to destroy comics are the Communists." The tongue-in-cheek cartoon editorial warned readers, "So the next time some joker gets up at a PTA meeting, or starts jabbering about the 'naughty comic books' . . . give him the once over. . . . He may be a dupe. . . . He's swallowed the Red bait . . . hook, line, and sinker!" Gaines, of course, had meant the page as a joke and an insult to critics of comic books. As the EC publisher later admitted, the joke had "backfired." Obviously the senators did not get it, but they were particularly interested in this editorial and asked Gaines if he truly believed what it said. By this time Gaines felt so tired and defeated that he believed any effort to explain his sense of humor to this audience was a lost cause. So he answered yes. With that, the senators had heard all that they needed to from the EC publisher (108).[17]

For Gaines, the hearings were a miserable experience. "It was tough facing those guys," he later recalled. He felt as if he were being cross-examined by a committee of prosecuting attorneys who regarded him as "a freak and a criminal." He realized afterwards that he never had a chance, contending, "That committee was there to hang the comic publishers."[18] And Gaines had unwittingly obliged them by putting his own head into the noose.

The exchange between Kefauver and Gaines over the severed head caught the fancy of the press. The *New York Times* reported the episode in its front-page story on the hearings. *Time* magazine also covered it, and articles critical of comic books made mocking reference to Gaines's explanation of "good taste."[19]

Gaines was the only comic book publisher and writer to appear before the subcommittee, but business representatives of Dell and Marvel also testified on behalf of their respective companies. Yet the comic book industry mounted no unified defense. The vice president of Dell Publications, Helen Meyer, defended her company's wholesome line of comic books and insisted that Dell should not be condemned for the sins of a few unethical publishers (197–98). The business manager for Marvel Comics, Monroe Froehlich, acknowledged that his company did have some "weird" comic books on the market (Marvel, in fact, issued more horror comic books than any other publisher), but he

pointed out that Marvel did not create the demand for these titles and insisted that his company had no choice but to publish at least a few of them if they wished to remain competitive (172–75). The subcommittee was much more sympathetic to this business argument than they were to Gaines's spirited defense of the horror genre. They also agreed with Froehlich's suggestion that concerted industry self-regulation was the best way to rid the market of objectionable comic books (182–83).

The most contentious issue emerging from the second day of testimony concerned the Child Study Association of America. The association's executive director, Gunnar Dybwad, defended the experts who had written about comic books while working for the Child Study Association and serving on DC Comics's editorial advisory board. Dybwad strongly disputed Wertham's charges that these professionals had been "paid off" by the comic book industry, and he blasted *Seduction of the Innocent* as "a mockery of research" (143). Under heated questioning, from Kefauver especially, Dybwad admitted that some members of the association had received money from DC for their work as consultants, but he pointed out that since 1941, DC's comic books had improved markedly as a result. The subcommittee was unmoved. Kefauver repeatedly referred to child study expert Josette Frank as being "in the pay of the comic book industry," and he accused the Child Study Association of deceiving parents by producing favorable studies of comic books without disclosing the relationship between its members and the comic book publishers. Kefauver tacitly accepted the charges and rhetoric of Wertham, adding that the association "might be called a front for the publishers of these crime magazines" (135–36). The Child Study Association stood discredited—and, with it, the foremost expert opinion opposed to Wertham's (120–40).

The subcommittee recessed until June 4 and then heard conflicting testimony on the alleged practice of "tie-in sales." Representatives for newsdealers contended that tie-in sales forced vendors to sell crime and horror comic books or risk losing the rights to sell other magazines. They insisted that because of tie-in sales, newsdealers could not be held responsible for selling objectionable comic books (215). Witnesses representing the publishers and distributors disputed these accusations

Cover of *Crime Suspenstories* 22 (EC Comics, May 1954). The cover of this EC comic book achieved widespread infamy when it became the subject of a debate on horror comics and "good taste" between Senator Estes Kefauver and EC publisher William M. Gaines during the hearings of the Senate Subcommittee to Investigate Juvenile Delinquency. Art by Johnny Craig.

(178, 239). The debate on tie-in sales was as confused and inconclusive as most other aspects of the comic book debate, but it nevertheless prompted New York and several other states to pass laws banning the practice.[20]

The subcommittee adjourned on June 4 to mull over the evidence, announcing that it would issue its conclusions early in 1955. Although the senators did not take an official position immediately after the hearings, they publicly advocated the need for some sort of action to curtail the dissemination of crime and horror comic books. Senator Hendrickson called for united community action against those comic books "packed with every form of vice, sadism, and violence conceivable." He added that "not even the Communist conspiracy could devise a more effective way to demoralize, disrupt, confuse and destroy our future citizens than apathy on the part of adult Americans to the scourge known as juvenile delinquency."[21]

The Comics Code

For months the comic book industry reeled in a state of crisis. Increasing pressure from civic groups, wholesalers, and retailers as well as government officials at all levels compelled publishers to act before they were acted upon. In September 1954 the industry announced the formation of the Comics Magazine Association of America (CMAA) and the appointment of New York City magistrate Charles F. Murphy as the new "comics czar." Murphy's task was to do for the comic book industry what Joseph Breen had done for Hollywood and Kennesaw Landis had done for professional baseball—administer and enforce a code of standards to regain the trust of the public.[22]

On 26 October 1954 the CMAA published its code. Addressing most of the criticisms frequently hurled at comic books, it was far more extensive, precise, and restrictive than the publishers' 1948 code. The standards governing editorial matters forbade the presentation of crime in any manner that created sympathy for criminals and declared that "policemen, judges, government officials, and respected institutions shall never be presented in such a way as to create disrespect for established authority." It effectively prohibited all of the visual elements and subject matter that defined horror comic books and even banned the words *horror* and *terror* from appearing on the cover of a comic book. It strictly forbade insults or attacks on any religious or racial group. The guidelines also placed severe prohibitions on anything that hinted of sex or lust. Women were not to be drawn in "salacious" or "suggestive" dress and postures, and "passion or romantic interest" would "never be treated in such a way to stimulate the lower and baser emotions." Respect for parents, "the moral code," and "honorable behavior" was to be fostered at all times. Romantic stories should always "emphasize the value of the home and the sanctity of marriage." The last section of the code governed advertising in comic books and excluded ads for knives, guns, and other weapons as well as those for liquor, tobacco, and sex products—which had never appeared in comic books anyway.[23]

Even by the conservative standards of the time, the code was extremely restrictive. Indeed, spokesmen for the code boasted that it "imposed restrictions far greater than any in force against competing media." Publicly, the CMAA hailed this as evidence that the industry took seriously its moral obligation to American youth. Privately, the publishers hoped that extreme self-regulation would appease the public and stave off the possibility of regulation imposed by an outside agency. Success depended completely on the ability of the CMAA to convince the public that, this time, the industry was serious about policing itself.[24]

To this end, the hiring of Charles Murphy as comics czar was a wise move. A city magistrate with some credentials as a local crusader against juvenile crime, Murphy had no prior association with the comic book industry, and he had a good Irish-Catholic name. With a staff of reviewers composed mostly of women with backgrounds in education and social work, the code authority had an annual budget of $100,000 and a mandate to scrutinize the proofs of every comic book submitted by a member publisher. Reviewers would note objectionable material, suggest revisions, and return the proofs to the editor, who would implement the recommended changes. When a comic book met the office's standards, it received the seal of the Comics Code Authority. Parents would then know that this comic book had passed the stringent requirements of Murphy's office.[25]

The CMAA approached self-regulation mindful of past failures. The industry's last effort at self-regulation had failed primarily because it had never included more than a minority of publishers. The CMAA, however, included all but three publishers. Most of the major distributors, wholesalers, engravers, and printers also joined, giving the code authority considerable industry-wide enforcement powers. Only Dell, Classics Illustrated, and EC refused to join. Dell and Classics Illustrated remained aloof because they claimed, correctly, that their comic books were not a source of serious controversy, and they did not wish to be associated with the more criticized elements of the industry. William Gaines initially kept EC out of the CMAA because he despised the code and the cynical manner with which it had been devised. Most publishers, however, were in no mood to take a courageous stand for First Amendment rights. They wanted to preserve their business. And if the code would achieve that result, so be it.[26]

The success of self-regulation depended on publicity. CMAA representatives and Charles Murphy stressed the code's effectiveness at a variety of public appearances and through the media. At a December press conference, Murphy boasted that his office had already screened 285 different comic books and rejected 126 stories as well as 5,656 individual drawings. Thanks to the code, all of these had been "cleaned up" into material suitable for children. Mort Weisinger of DC Comics made the same case in an article printed in *Better Homes and Gardens*. He asked parents not to condemn all publishers for the "minority of unethical publishers within their ranks." A series of before-and-after illustrations accompanied the article, showing how the code sanitized dialogue, eradicated bloodshed, and lengthened female hemlines. Like other advocates of the code, Weisinger pointed with pride to its extreme restrictions on content.[27]

Critics had considerable cause for skepticism. The industry's last attempt at self-regulation had been half-hearted and had failed miserably, a fact that came out in the Senate hearings. Why, many asked, should the current endeavor be any more successful than the last? The Catholic weekly *America* cautiously endorsed the CMAA's program and admonished parents to allow only code-approved comic books into their homes. The General Federation of Women's Clubs, on the other hand, resolved to continue their vigilant crusade against objectionable comic books, code-approved or not.[28]

In February 1955 the Senate Subcommittee to Investigate Juvenile Delinquency published its tentative conclusions on the influence of comic books. It stopped short of accepting Wertham's findings, concluding that further research of a broad and controlled nature was needed before the precise influence of comic books could be determined. But the report concluded that crime and horror comic books were at least a potential threat to the mental health of juveniles and to America's image overseas. It stated flatly that "this country cannot afford the calculated risk involved in feeding its children, through comic books, a concentrated diet of crime, horror, and violence." While praising the CMAA's program of self-regulation, the committee resolved to watch its progress closely and report on it at a later date. If this latest effort failed, the committee warned that "other ways and means must—

and will—be found to prevent our nation's young from being harmed by crime and horror comic books."[29]

Fredric Wertham found nothing to praise in comic book industry self-regulation. He dismissed the code as the latest attempt by publishers to whitewash their products and deceive the public. He argued with Charles Murphy before the New York State Joint Legislative Committee to Study Comic Books and, with his usual flair for the dramatic, brandished a bullwhip that he claimed had been purchased through an ad in a code-approved comic book. After this charge had been verified, Murphy ordered the ad discontinued and protested that his hard-working office should not be dismissed as a result of one oversight. The committee, however, concluded that Murphy had been given an "impossible" task and judged the CMAA code a failure.[30]

Impressed by Wertham's arguments, the New York State legislature passed its third anti–crime comic book bill in six years. The bill, sponsored by Plattsburgh Republican James Fitzpatrick, was as poorly written and vague as its predecessors, declaring it a misdemeanor to publish or distribute "any book, pamphlet or magazine consisting of narrative material in pictorial form" that contained the words *crime, sex, horror,* or *terror* in its title or had contents "devoted to or principally made up of pictures or accounts of methods of crime, of illicit sex, horror, terror, physical torture, brutality, or physical violence." Violations would be punishable by a year in jail, a $500 fine, or both. As mentioned earlier, two bills with similar provisions had been vetoed by Republican Governor Thomas Dewey on constitutional grounds, but recently elected Democratic Governor W. Averell Harriman signed this bill into law. The CMAA, ACLU, American Book Publishers Council, and other First Amendment advocates denounced the Fitzpatrick Act as grossly unconstitutional. The U.S. Supreme Court would have no doubt agreed had anyone challenged it.[31] Ironically, though, after six years of legislative struggle and constitutional setbacks, New York had effectively banned comic books that no longer existed.

In 1955, thirteen states enacted laws to curb the distribution and sale of crime and horror comic books, either prohibiting their sale to minors or banning them outright. Several other states had similar legislation pending.[32] But the comic book industry had already accomplished what this legislation aimed to achieve. Although it did not become clear until 1956, the code had indeed "cleaned up" comic books to the satisfaction of virtually all critics but Dr. Wertham. Comic books continued to depict crimes, but they were rarely violent, never bloody, and always punished with swift and sure legal justice. Crime and horror comic books were gone entirely, while those that remained were of the most innocuous sort. Reflecting a bland consensus vision of America, comic books now championed without criticism American institutions, authority figures, and middle-class mores. The alternatives simply disappeared.

EC had once exemplified the alternative vision, but its fortunes declined precipitously in the wake of the Senate hearings. Gaines's unfavorable notoriety made EC a lighting rod for the industry's critics. Nervous retailers and wholesalers returned bundles of issues to the publisher unopened. EC clearly felt the pressure. In the second half of 1954 its comic book covers became noticeably more restrained. Morale at the office fell as the EC staff were shaken and intimidated by the public outrage and government warnings directed at them.[33]

In a final act of desperation, EC ran an editorial in its fall issues appealing for reader action. "Due to the efforts of various 'do-gooders' and 'do-gooder' groups," it read, "a large segment of the public is being led to believe that certain comic magazines cause juvenile delinquency." Blaming the hysteria chiefly on "a psychiatrist who has made a lucrative career of attacking comic magazines," EC stated flatly that "many groups of adults . . . would like to blame their lack of ability as responsible parents on comic magazines instead of on themselves." The publisher asked readers and their parents to write a "nice polite letter" to the Subcommittee to Investigate Juvenile Delinquency in defense of comic books and warned that if the subcommittee did not hear from actual comic book readers and listened instead to only those who wanted to destroy comic books, then the "very existence of the whole comic magazine industry" would be in jeopardy.[34]

Yet it was not the subcommittee that doomed EC, it was the industry itself. Gaines received no support from fellow publishers. As EC's business manager later recalled, "In those days the industry was so competitive that the happiest news for a publisher was that a competitor was dying—and dying painfully." Some of the largest and most conservative publishers blamed EC for bringing condemnation down upon the entire industry, and EC's irreverence toward established publishers over the years had earned it few friends within the industry.[35]

Gaines's resistance was short-lived. In September 1954 he called a press conference to announce that he was canceling all of his crime and horror comic books and substituting for them a "clean, clean line," because this seemed to be "what the American parents want." His explanation in *Tales from the Crypt* was more to the point: "As a result of the hysterical, injudicious, and unfounded charges leveled at crime and horror comics, many retailers and wholesalers throughout the country have been intimidated into refusing to handle this type of magazine." Financially, EC had no choice but to capitulate. Gaines concluded that there was "no point going into a defense of this kind of literature" at that time and added sarcastically that "with comic magazine censorship now a fact, we at EC look forward to an immediate drop in the crime and juvenile delinquency rate of the United States."[36]

Gaines replaced the crime and horror titles with what he called his "New Direction line" of tamer adventure and social-drama titles. He initially refused to submit them to the CMAA code, but distribution and sales of these first issues were so horrendous that he capitulated again and signed onto the code. Even though the next several issues bore the code's seal of approval, sales remained poor. Gaines suspected that wholesalers had conspired to refuse all EC comic books with or without the seal. The final outrage for the EC publisher came when the code authority rejected a reprint of the antidiscrimination story called "Judgment Day" (see chap. 5), apparently because it contained a drawing of a black man perspiring. According to Gaines, the reviewers claimed that the sweat was distasteful. Gaines printed the story anyway, sent the code office a letter telling them "to go screw," withdrew from the CMAA, and canceled all of his comic books except one.[37]

Gaines then introduced what he called "Picto-Fiction" magazines. Experimental text-heavy publications more like illustrated pulp fiction than comic magazines, they sold so dismally that Gaines canceled them after only a few issues. This venture sent EC deep into debt, then its distributor went bankrupt. Though these years were miserable for Gaines and his staff, the future was destined to be considerably brighter. He kept only one EC publication in circulation, converting it from a traditional comic book to a black-and-white magazine format. This, of course, was *Mad*, which went on to become an extraordinarily successful and enduring humor magazine.[38] So William M. Gaines had the last laugh on his critics after all.

In 1956 the controversy over crime and horror comic books effectively came to an end. Charles Murphy resigned his position as comics czar, having won accolades from civic, veteran, and religious groups as well as from the Senate Subcommittee to Investigate Juvenile Delinquency.[39] Those who linked the products of mass culture to juvenile delinquency shifted their attention away from comic books to focus on movies and television. At the same time, rock-and-roll was emerging as the newest and seemingly most threatening expression of youth culture. By the second half of the 1950s, comic books seemed like kid stuff by comparison.

Wertham, meanwhile, never endorsed the comics code. The code did not ban violence from comic books, he insisted, but merely sanitized it into a bloodless and painless exercise with less graphic consequences. The process could be as absurd as asking artists to reduce the puff of smoke leaving a fired pistol in order to make the gunshot appear less violent, which the code did in fact call for on at least one occasion. This was not what Wertham had labored for years to achieve. He continued to speak and write critically about comic books and violence in other media but generated little interest beyond his own shrinking audience.[40] In his later years, he took pains to undo his image as an anti–comic book crusader, granting interviews to comic book fans and even writing a book on fan culture and fanzines. He always regretted deeply that his name had become associated with censorship. To embittered comic book enthusiasts he was an infamous figure—the Joe McCarthy of the hysterical comic book scare. The comparison between the two manipulators of public anxieties is tempting but ultimately unfair and inaccurate. Even William Gaines, with a few decades of perspective, found Wertham's genuine concern for children difficult to fault.[41]

In the final analysis, Fredric Wertham must be seen as the central and most curious figure in the first round of the postwar struggle to control commercial youth culture. Despite his flawed scientific methods, gross misrepresentation of evidence, and outrageous sensationalism, Wertham's basic argument was perceptive and prophetic. His central contention that comic books contributed to juvenile delinquency was problematic, but some of his warnings about the implications of commercial youth culture were on target. If young people were not "indoctrinated" by seductive comic books, they certainly were drawn into a culture defined more by market considerations than by traditional values. That in itself would not have provoked such outrage, had it not been for the irreverent tastes that defined that market. Parents, educators, and government officials found it deeply troubling that their children seemed to be fascinated by images that undermined the serene vision of affluent America. Yet ironically facilitating this development was the affluence itself. With more money in their pockets, America's young people had the consumer power to help shape their own culture, and entertainment industries proved increasingly eager to accommodate them. When America's parents attacked comic books,

they were assaulting the very consequences of the expanding consumer
culture that they otherwise revered. Comic book censorship notwithstanding, the consumer forces transforming youth culture would ultimately prove insuperable.

Comic book publishers bore much of the responsibility for the
industry's crisis. Their unrestrained onslaught of horror and brutality
may have been profitable in the short term, but by providing critics
with a generous amount of bloody ammunition, publishers had effectively cut their own throats in the process. Recriminations within the
industry and the demands of the code authority purged the field of publishers as well as comic books. Between 1954 and 1956, eighteen publishers exited the field, and none entered. The number of comic book
titles published annually fell from about 650 in 1954 to just over 300
in 1956, and only the several largest publishers accounted for most of
those. Never again would the comic book industry enjoy the kind of
mass circulation and readership that it had commanded before the
code.

Considering contemporary developments in youth culture, the
timing of the code for the comic book industry could hardly have been
worse. By 1955 most American homes had a television offering entertainment to compete fiercely for the leisure time of young people. With
The Wild One (1954), *Blackboard Jungle* (1954), and *Rebel without a Cause*
(1955), Hollywood finally discovered the teenage market that it would
exploit with increasing effectiveness in the coming years. And by the
mid-1950s the arrival of rock-and-roll, with its liberating spirit of
rebellion, sexual energy, and brilliant adolescent appeal, supplanted
comic books as the most "dangerous," vital, and lucrative expression
of youth culture. Teenagers had arrived as a major market just as the
comic book industry had effectively forsook its adolescent audience. By
stripping away the freedom of writers and artists to depict the varieties
of their readers' fantasies and concerns, the code confined comic books
to a supervised, puerile level and enforced the very kind of conformity
that millions of young people were beginning to reject. Comic books
now stood to become a strictly preadolescent pastime at best or an out-
moded nostalgic curiosity at worst. The code had saved the industry
from public indignation and perhaps even legislated regulation, but
what would now save the industry from the code?

7

Great Power
and Great Responsibility

Superheroes
in a Superpower,
1956–1967

Awesome power often comes at a high cost and carries tremendous burdens. Young Peter Parker understood this well. The bite of a radioactive spider had transformed the awkward teenager into the extraordinary Spider-Man, but it had also robbed him of his innocence and led him into arrogant complacency, doubt and anxiety, and wrenching tragedy.[1] An adolescent fantasy of power and vulnerability, *Spider-Man* found a vast sympathetic audience that was becoming aware of their country's growing pains as well as their own. Between 1956 and 1967, an American Cold War consensus engulfed American culture, cracked, and then disintegrated amidst the movement for civil rights, dissent over the Vietnam War, and a youthful rebellion against a variety of authorities and cultural norms. As comic book makers negotiated the often conflicting pressures of self-censorship, political culture, and market demands, a compromise emerged in reluctant superheroes who struggled with the confusion and ambivalent consequences of their own power. Heroes like Spider-Man helped keep code-approved comic books relevant and profitable in the age of television and rock-and-roll, a prospect that had seemed quite unlikely only a few years earlier.

The Comic Book Recession
In the years following the Senate investigation and the institution of the comics code, the comic book industry plunged into its worst reces-

sion yet. Several factors contributed to the industry's troubles. One immediate problem was the collapse of the American News Company. In 1955 the company that distributed more than half of the comic books in circulation pulled out of national magazine distribution following the settlement of a lawsuit filed by the U.S. Justice Department for alleged monopolistic practices. The demise of American News left many publishers—already reeling from the controversy of the Senate hearings in 1954—without a national distributor. For some this proved to be the fatal blow that forced them out of business.[2]

Another more serious and long-term problem was television. By 1955 nearly three-quarters of American homes had one. As television became the primary source of family entertainment, all other media, including films, magazines, popular music, and comic books were left to compete for a shrinking remainder of the public's leisure time. As a cheap, accessible, and immediate form of audiovisual entertainment, television was unchallengeable. Yet its very success also made it vulnerable to alternatives. Quickly dominated by large commercial interests, television programs became conservative, bland, and predictable—a "vast wasteland," according to some critics.[3] Hollywood answered the challenge of television with grand epics in Technicolor, grittier subject matter, and greater sex appeal. Edgy to begin with, rock-and-roll used television to reach an ever wider audience of young people, despite adult resistance.[4]

The comic book industry, however, could not find an edge to compete with television. In adopting the code, publishers had given up much of the creative latitude that had made their products so popular with adolescents. By forbidding challenges to established authority and many varieties of conflict, the code ran counter to emerging trends in youth culture at a time when the market for young consumers had never been greater or the competition more intense. Far from marking the end of crime and violence in youth entertainment, the comics code merely gave up the lucrative market to the exploitive juvenile delinquent films and paperback novels that proliferated in the late 1950s.[5]

The code essentially dictated that comic books ought to be produced only for young children. Those established publishers who had rarely looked outside that market anyway remained unaffected by the code, and some, no doubt, welcomed the opportunity to purge the glutted industry. Most of the smaller publishers who had entered the business a few years earlier to exploit the booming market for crime and horror exited with the institution of the code. EC, Lev Gleason, Fawcett Publications, and Quality Comics all left because of distribution problems, poor sales, or both. Artists and writers recently in high demand suddenly found employment scarce. Some drifted into other fields of commercial art like advertising and greeting cards. Others scrambled to find whatever work they could in the contracted comic book industry, often suffering cuts in pay. By 1962 less than a dozen publishers accounted for a total annual industry output of 350 million comic books, a drop of over 50 percent from the previous decade.[6]

Some publishers thrived in the code era, either because they successfully adapted their products to the preteen market or because their comic books had never had much of an edge anyway. Harvey Publications proved especially adaptable. After the code Harvey dropped all of its crime, horror, and war titles and concentrated instead on innocuous fare like *Casper the Friendly Ghost* and *Richie Rich*, both among the most successful and enduring comic book characters of their kind. Archie Comics also entered its most successful period after the code, publishing essentially the same innocuous teen-humor formulas that had made its reputation before the code.[7]

The code could have easily relegated all comic books to the kind of detached, juvenile humor of Archie and Richie Rich. But room remained for other genres that conformed to the code and still tapped into mainstream cultural currents. Four different publishers tried this course with varying styles and commercial results. Their efforts reveal the limits and possibilities of comic books in a time of self-censorship, consensus culture, and an explosive baby boom coming of age.

DC Comics and the New Frontiers

DC Comics survived the recession as well as any publisher. It had abided by its own rigorous editorial code since 1941, and the comics code scarcely affected its comic books. With its own first-rate distribution network, the industry's most popular superheroes, and a solid public reputation, DC stood poised to dominate the field as no publisher had yet. By 1962 it ranked as the industry's undisputed leader in sales and published about 30 percent of all the comic books on the market. Yet even DC's sales dropped significantly after the code, largely due to competition from television. Still, DC weathered the challenge of television better than its competitors, primarily because of the popular *Adventures of Superman* television show (1953–57), which kept DC's flagship character highly visible and caused an entire generation to associate Superman with actor George Reeves. The Superman comic books seemed immune from recession, consistently selling around a million copies per issue.[8]

DC published comic books in a variety of genres, including humor, sci-fi, romance, western, war, mystery, and even adaptations of television shows. Its most important and influential editorial move, though, was a return to its roots. Costumed superheroes had made comic books a viable industry in the first place, and they would restore its vitality in the code era. In 1956 DC editor Julius Schwartz decided to revive one of his favorite characters from the company's past, the Flash. But instead of simply reissuing the old Flash, Schwartz revamped the character for modern times and reinvented him as police scientist Barry Allen. After being simultaneously struck by lightning and bathed in a mysterious combination of chemicals, Allen gains the impressive ability to move at superspeed—up to ten times the speed of light, or approximately 1,860,000,000 miles per second, it is later explained. Without a moment of hesitation, Allen designs a tight-fitting red and gold costume, calls himself the Flash, and pledges to use his powers to fight crime and aid humanity.[9] Apparently untroubled by the staggering physical impossibility of such a being, readers made the Flash a success and asked for more.

In 1959 Schwartz reinvented another popular superhero from the 1940s, the Green Lantern. This new incarnation is a test pilot named Hal Jordan who receives a power ring from a dying extraterrestrial. Jordan then assumes the alien's role in the Green Lantern Corps, an intergalactic police force assigned to patrol Earth's sector.[10]

Schwartz followed the Green Lantern with revamped versions of Hawkman and the Atom. The bizarre-looking Hawkman and his wife, Hawkgirl, are police officers from the planet Thanagar who emigrate to Earth and stay to fight crime both as winged superheroes and in their adopted identities as American police officers. The new Atom is a scientist named Ray Palmer who becomes a superhero after learning how to shrink himself down to a variety of sizes—not the most helpful ability to have in a fight, but he made do.[11]

These characters joined DC's stalwarts Superman, Batman, and Wonder Woman to give the publisher its largest stable of superheroes since the 1940s. By 1960 DC had enough costumed characters to feature a team of them in *The Justice League of America*.[12] Although the company continued to publish comic books in other genres, it became clear by the early 1960s that superheroes would be the key to the industry's survival in the age of television. Costumed superheroes had always been the stuff of comic books, and it really was the genre best suited to the medium. In an era of extremely limited special-effects technology, comic books could present fantastic visual imagery more imaginatively than could a live-action medium. Individuals in tight, colorful costumes and masks performing impossible deeds simply looked ridiculous in live-action, but they seemed perfectly natural in comic books. And as a young male fantasy, superheroes were just as compelling in 1960 as they had been twenty years earlier.

Comic book superheroes remained a fantasy grounded in real-world assumptions and concerns. DC aligned its superheroes squarely on the side of established authority, with which it naturally equated the best interests of American citizens. There was nothing unusual about that. In the pre–Vietnam War era, the general public's confidence in the integrity of American values, leaders, and institutions remained high and—the challenge of rock-and-roll and the Beats notwithstanding—popular culture still tended to reinforce a blandly optimistic consensus vision of America premised on the virtues of anticommunism, corporatism, consumption, domesticity, and middle-class social aspirations.[13] This was the consensus embodied in the spirit and, in some cases, the letter of the comics code, and it was the consensus that DC championed.

DC's comic books were the image of affluent America. Handsome superheroes resided in clean, green suburbs and modern, even futuristic, cities with shimmering glass skyscrapers, no slums, and populations of uniformly well-dressed white people. There was nothing ambiguous about the hero's character, cause, or inevitable triumph. Mindful of past criticism directed at comic books, the editors left little to chance and took pains to avoid the implication—always present—that superheroes were glorified vigilantes and thus harmful role models for children. To this end, all of the DC superheroes held respected positions in society. When not in costume, most of them were members of either the police force or the scientific community. Hawkman and Hawkgirl were police officers. The Green Lantern served in an intergalactic police force. The Atom was a respected scientist. The Flash was a police scientist. Batman and Robin were deputized members of the Gotham City police force with a direct hotline to Commissioner Gordon, and Superman was a citizen of the world who dutifully respected all established authorities. So law-abiding was the Man of Steel, in fact, that one entire story was devoted to the fantastic premise of "The Day Superman Broke the Law."[14]

Like all other publishers of the time, DC tended to reinforce traditional gender and genre expectations by relegating female characters to a subordinate status. The primary function served by women was to resist the romantic advances of the superhero's alter-ego, pine for the superhero, scheme to get close to him, screw things up, get captured by the bad guy, and await rescue by the hero, who usually scolded her for being so bold in the first place. Superman's Lois Lane epitomized this plot device, but most other superheroes had an equivalent. Often the female supporting characters were career women, like Lois, but they remained just as unfulfilled and eager to forsake their work for the love of a man as their counterparts in the romance comics. The exceptions were Hawkgirl (who, despite the implied subordination in her name, served as a fairly equal partner to her husband, Hawkman), Wonder Woman, and Superman's teenage cousin Supergirl. The Supergirl character, in particular, seemed to be a concerted effort to appeal to young girls; her stories were whimsical adventures that also featured Streaky the Supercat and Comet the Superhorse. But the men who created DC comic books were clearly uncomfortable writing stories with female stars, as evidenced by *Wonder Woman*, a series that languished creatively and commercially in a series of incoherent and silly stories.[15]

Of course, the male superheroes were hardly dynamic individuals themselves, but this was inherent in the DC style. DC's comic books emphasized responsibility to the community over individualism, and the creators minimized the importance of the latter, perhaps unintentionally, by giving all of their superheroes essentially the same personality. Superman, Batman, the Flash, and all other DC superheroes "spoke" in the same carefully measured sentences. Each reacted to situations in the same predictable manner. They were always in control, rarely impulsive, and never irrational. Most importantly, all of the DC superheroes were impossibly altruistic. Helping humanity was their only motivation. Individualism and nonconformity were, by the same token, equated with criminal activity. In one Flash story, the hero investigates a "fabulous individualist" who "defies the government" by refusing to pay taxes despite his enormous personal wealth. The villain turns out to be an alien invader posing as a wealthy tax-evader in order to cause mischief. Another Flash story portrays a group of nonconforming "beatniks" as a criminal gang. Common villains included renegade scientists who leave government service in order to pursue personal, and always criminal, ambitions.[16] When Julius Schwartz created the Justice League of America, he consciously chose the word *league* over *society* (as in the Justice Society of America, DC's superhero group of the 1940s), because he felt that *society* only implies a loose association of individuals, whereas *league* implies a team of superheroes contributing their individual abilities to a common purpose.[17]

Meshing with DC's celebration of affluent society was a fascination with the dawning space age and wide-eyed optimism for the world of tomorrow. In the aftermath of *Sputnik*, the U.S. government created the National Aeronautic and Space Administration, passed the National Defense Education Act, and called upon parents, educators, and other authorities to cultivate a vigorous interest in science among the nation's youth. DC did its part by hailing science as a progressive force in the service of humankind. Superheroes often overcame adversity not with their physical powers but with their brains and applied science—albeit in scenarios of dubious plausibility. Julius Schwartz, who edited DC's sci-fi comics as well as the superhero titles, cited Adam Strange, his creation in the style of Buck Rogers, among his favorites. A costumed superhero with no superhuman powers, Strange relied upon his scientific skills and ingenuity to vanquish physically superior villains. Most of DC's heroes in the sci-fi comics were mortal astronauts and scientists. In these stories, even common television engineers and gas company workers had the scientific ingenuity to defeat alien invasions.[18]

DC's sci-fi comic books rarely hinted at any unforeseen or harmful consequences of scientific progress, even in the atomic age. A fanciful story from 1959 predicted that the coming decade would see American scientists devise a nearly perfect defense against enemy missiles so that there would be only a "one in a million" chance that one would get through to the United States. Thus unable to inflict damage on the American continent, the enemy is compelled to sign a treaty to guarantee "peaceful coexistence." A 1963 story speculated that "when we [of Earth] reach Saturn and Jupiter we'll find marvelous inventions waiting for us—that we'll share equally." Moreover, DC predicted that "in the Space Age there will be no rival nations—only peaceful Earthmen." Scientific progress would usher in a utopian age of international cooperation and egalitarianism.[19]

The exception to this vision seemed to be "The Atomic Knights." One of DC's more interesting sci-fi series, it took place in a postapocalyptic future, in which civilization has been virtually wiped out by "the great atomic war." Only isolated and disorganized settlements remain, and they are dominated by strongmen like the Black Baron, who hoards all of the food supplies. Out of the devastation emerge the Atomic Knights—a small group of heroes dedicated to restoring law and order in the service of the people. Comprised of past authority figures, including an army officer, a scientist, and a schoolteacher, the Knights defeat the Black Baron and distribute the food equally among the population. They decide that "humanity needs an organization" like theirs because "there aren't any more police—there isn't any government. . . . There is no authority except evil power." And "someone has to represent law and order and the forces of justice in these terrible times."[20]

That "The Atomic Knights" was set in a dystopian landscape devastated by atomic weapons seemed to violate DC's usual confidence in progress. Yet the stark setting belied the moral thrust of the series. In the stories, people who lash out at the symbols of science and blamed them for the nuclear holocaust always appear ignorant and irrational. After the Atomic Knights have demonstrated the virtues of science and technology, the people abandon their backward rituals and embrace progress wholeheartedly. Lest any ambiguity remain, the Atomic Knights eventually discover that World War III had not been the doing of human governments, as originally believed, but instead had been perpetrated by a subterranean race of mole creatures. Qualifiers like this signified DC's cautious approach to the anxieties of Cold War America. In hailing the consensus behind American progress, DC left little to chance.[21]

Dell, Charlton, and Vietnam

During the late 1950s, Dell Publications was the largest publisher of comic books in the world. In addition to its paperback book business, Dell published comic book adaptations of popular cartoon characters from Walt Disney, Warner Brothers, and newspaper comic strips, as well as adaptations of movie and television characters like Tarzan, Davy Crockett, and the Lone Ranger. Dell's comic books remained steadfastly traditional in their cultural outlook and in their target audience of young children. Walt Disney maintained tight editorial supervision over the comics featuring his characters and ensured that they stayed true to the conservative Disney vision. Gaylord Dubois, a seasoned, prudent writer born in 1899, wrote thousands of adventure stories for Dell. Several generations removed from his audience, he consistently worked to integrate "old-time moral and emotional values" into his stories. He claimed that "as a Bible-believing Christian" he had "prayed for guidance in . . . every comic" that he had ever written.[22] Dell's comic books rarely generated controversy, and they actually gave the company such a conservative reputation that Dell's refusal to participate in the comics code provoked no backlash. Dell's comic books met the expectations of adult supervision and overlooked entirely the more dynamic and rebellious qualities of youth culture.

Dell entered the 1960s in fine shape but promptly made a series of disastrous business decisions that sent its market share plummeting and

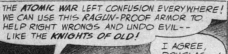

THE *ATOMIC WAR* LEFT CONFUSION EVERYWHERE! WE CAN USE THIS *RAGUN*-PROOF ARMOR TO HELP RIGHT WRONGS AND UNDO EVIL-- LIKE THE *KNIGHTS OF OLD!*

I AGREE, DOUGLAS...!

HUMANITY NEEDS AN ORGANIZATION LIKE OURS! THERE AREN'T ANY MORE POLICE--THERE ISN'T ANY GOVERNMENT, SO FAR AS WE KNOW! THERE IS NO AUTHORITY--EXCEPT *EVIL POWER*--LIKE THE *BLACK BARON* WIELDED!

SOMEONE HAS TO REPRESENT LAW AND ORDER AND THE FORCES OF *JUSTICE* IN THESE TERRIBLE TIMES--AND IT LOOKS LIKE THE JOB IS OURS! WE HAVE TO BE READY TO HELP PEOPLE--

MAY I SAY SOMETHING, GRAYLE?

IT'S ABOUT TIME WE HEARD FROM OUR *SCIENTIST* MEMBER! WHAT IS IT, BRYNDON?

I'VE BEEN TESTING THE METAL OF OUR SUITS! THEY SHIELD AGAINST *RAGUN* FIRE--BUT ONLY FOR A *LIMITED* TIME...

AFTER THAT TIME, THE RAYS GET THROUGH! SO WE'RE NOT *INVULNERABLE*...

THAT'S JUST *ONE MORE DANGER* WE HAVE TO FACE...

BUT THE *WORLD* NEEDS US-- WE *SIX* CAN'T THINK OF OURSELVES ANYMORE...

A STRANGE FEELING HAS COME OVER ME! HAVE I--FALLEN IN LOVE WITH GARDNER GRAYLE?

WATCH FOR THE NEXT EXCITING EPISODE OF THE *Atomic Knights* IN A FORTH-COMING ISSUE OF

STRANGE ADVENTURES

MEANWHILE, IF YOU LIKE THIS NEW FEATURE PLEASE WRITE AND LET US KNOW! STRANGE ADVENTURES, 575 LEXINGTON AVE. NEW YORK 22, N.Y.

The End

eventually led it to exit the comic book business altogether. In 1961 the
company raised the price of its comic books from the longtime industry
standard of ten cents to fifteen cents. Other publishers held their price
at ten cents for several months and then only raised it to twelve cents.
Sales of Dell's leading titles dropped nearly 75 percent over the next
few years. Declining sales and expensive licensing fees led Dell to discontinue its most popular titles and publish its own comic books in-
house. Dell's printer, Western Printing and Lithography, broke away
from the publisher and took its most popular titles with them. Western
continued to publish Disney, Warner Brothers, and Hanna-Barbera
cartoon comics under the Gold Key logo with great success, while Dell
was left to try some new ideas.[23]

Dell's forays into the market with its own new titles found only
mediocre commercial success, but a few proved intriguing nonetheless.
Trying to reach beyond its traditional audience of young children, Dell
launched a series of war comic books aimed at adolescent boys. Among
these was *Jungle War Stories*, the first comic book devoted primarily to
the conflict in Vietnam. Launched in the spring of 1962, *Jungle War
Stories* was, in fact, among the first presentations of the Vietnam War
to appear anywhere in American entertainment.

The early issues of *Jungle War Stories* paralleled the escalation of
American involvement in Vietnam and justified U.S. policy there as
necessary for the containment of Communism. One story, told from
the point of view of a Soviet military adviser to the Viet Cong, illustrates how every step of the Russian's campaign of Communist insur-
gency is frustrated by the intervention of "Yankee weapons." In China
his attack against Nationalist supply ships is foiled by American machine guns. In Greece and Malaya his Communist rebels are van-
quished by government troops wielding American firearms. And then
in South Vietnam the Russian-led Viet Cong troops are turned back

From "The Rise of the Atomic
Knights," *Strange Adventures* 117
(DC Comics, June 1960). Despite
being set in a future America
devastated by an atomic war, DC's
"Atomic Knights" showcased the
publisher's characteristic optimism
during the Cold War and the
Space Age. Even in this dystopia,
the traditional forces of law and
authority reassert themselves in
the form of the Atomic Knights,
who use science to restore order
and progress. Script by John
Broome. Art by Murphy Anderson.

VIET CONG:

THE FACE OF THE ENEMY

THE "VIET CONG"---THE NORTH VIETNAMESE COMMUNIST ARMY---IS REPUTED TO CONSIST OF APPROXIMATELY 23,000 HARD-CORE COMMUNIST REGULARS AND ABOUT 100,000 MEN IN SO-CALLED PARAMILITARY GROUPS. COMMANDER OF THIS GUERRILLA FORCE IS WILY GENERAL VO NGUYEN GIAP, THE LITTLE-KNOWN AUTHOR OF THE MASTER PLAN FOR CONQUEST BY SUBVERSION.

VIET CONG TACTICS, AS OUTLINED BY GENERAL VO NGUYEN GIAP, IS A BRUTAL SUCCESSION OF VILLAGE BURNINGS, ROAD MININGS AND BRIDGE BLOWING... TOGETHER WITH THE CAPTURE OF VITAL RICE BARGES AND INCESSANT EXTORTION OF MONEY AND FOOD FROM VIETNAMESE PEASANTS.

VIET CONG SOLDIERS ARE FREQUENTLY HARD TO DISTINGUISH FROM THE REST OF THE VIETNAMESE POPULATION BECAUSE OF THE TYPICAL BLACK CALICO PEASANT PAJAMAS WHICH THEY WEAR ON ALL OCCASIONS... EVEN WHEN GOING INTO BATTLE!

REMINISCENT OF THE BRUTAL WAR IN NORTH KOREA IS THE "HUMAN WAVE" TECHNIQUE PRACTICED BY THE VIET CONG. ACCOMPANIED BY THE WILD BLOWING OF BUGLES, THE NORTH VIETNAMESE COMMUNISTS ATTACK IN OVERWHELMING NUMBERS!

and the Soviet guerrilla leader is himself killed by U.S. Special Forces and South Vietnamese troops armed with American weapons.[24]

Unlike earlier Communist insurrections, however, the Vietnam War would not be won by proxy. As early as 1962 *Jungle War Stories* suggested that the South Vietnamese military was not up to the task. The Communists usually had their way with the native troops until American Green Beret "advisers" took charge. Observing the dismal state of the South Vietnamese regulars, an American soldier in one story concludes that "these people got no belly for fighting the Viet Cong guerrillas!" Under direct U.S. leadership, however, the troops become an effective fighting force.[25]

The South Vietnamese civilian population also needed close American guidance. In "A Walk in the Sun," Green Berets assigned to relocate some villagers to a strategic hamlet discuss the natives' frustrating ambivalence towards the war effort. One American observes that "half the peasants want no part of [the war] . . . either side!" Another scoffs, "There'll always be folks who figure the world owes them a living." The leader of the village to be relocated denounces the strategic hamlet program and contends that "the sides of this cursed war are like grains of rice . . . no difference." But he changes his mind after seeing the atrocities committed by the Communists and observing the Americans giving medical attention and food to the Vietnamese people. Upon arriving at the strategic hamlet, the converted village leader admits that he and his people "were fools." Thanking the Americans for showing them the truth about Communist treachery, the villagers pledge to do their "part to fight the Red dogs." The Green Berets thus win another important battle for the hearts and minds of the Vietnamese.[26]

Yet even as *Jungle War Stories* endorsed the U.S. presence in Southeast Asia, it also suggested the formidable obstacles to victory. Among the most troubling of these was the ambiguous nature of the enemy and, for that matter, the ally as well. For every South Vietnamese civilian who was friendly, there seemed to be one who turned traitor. The Communists could emerge from anywhere, and it was difficult to tell friend from foe. One feature explained how the Viet Cong's devious tactics include using children as spies. Another story warned that "the

"Viet Cong: The Face of the Enemy," *Jungle War Stories* 4 (Dell Publications, July–September 1963). The first comic book series to regularly feature stories about the conflict in Vietnam, Dell Publications' *Jungle War Stories* championed American intervention on behalf of South Vietnam. In addition to the stories, pages like this "informed" readers about the war against the Communists and why it had to be fought. Writer and artist unknown.

enemy has many faces." Communist troops masqueraded as peaceful villagers, South Vietnamese soldiers, schoolteachers, and even Buddhist monks.[27] Implicitly then, all Vietnamese were suspect in this war.

With an elusive enemy and an unreliable ally, even the formidable Green Berets had huge hurdles to overcome. The frustrations of limited warfare mounted in *Jungle War Stories* even as actual U.S. involvement escalated in the real Vietnam. In one story an American pilot has to abandon his pursuit of retreating Viet Cong troops because they cross into neighboring Laos. The Communists mock the American's predicament, scoffing that "a little thing like a border . . . saps their strength and turns them into cowards!" When the exasperated pilot returns to base, he complains, "If that crazy [border is] . . . gonna stop us every time. . . . Well that's a dang fool way to fight a war!"[28]

The series made it clear early on that if the Communists were going to be defeated in Vietnam, the United States would have to shoulder the burden of fighting. When left in charge, the South Vietnamese bungled everything. In "Frontal Assault" the South Vietnamese Army commanders devise a plan of attack and jealously keep it secret from the Americans because they want to show their arrogant ally that they can work out a clever and successful battle scheme without help. Of course, they accomplish exactly the opposite, as the plan inevitably fails, partly because a spy among their ranks leaks the secrets to the Communists.[29] Stories like this simultaneously made a case for greater U.S. involvement in Vietnam and sounded a cautionary note about the difficulties Americans could expect to face there. Indeed, were it not for the inevitable American triumph that came in every story, *Jungle War Stories* might not have qualified as an endorsement of the war at all. Perhaps, though, the warning signs are more obvious in historical hindsight than they were to most young readers at the time.

Evidence suggests, however, that the creators behind the series (who remain unknown, since Dell did not credit its writers) developed their own reservations about the war in 1965, just as Vietnam was becoming an American war. One comic book from that time included a curious nonillustrated page titled "A Letter from Vietnam," purportedly written by a serviceman in Vietnam to his younger brother in the states. In it, the soldier tells his brother to stay in high school, go to college, and avoid enlisting as he did, because, he writes, "I just don't want my kid brother to waste his life when it isn't necessary." A dramatic reversal from the established editorial slant of *Jungle War Stories*, this "Letter from Vietnam" appeared in the same issue as "Face of the Enemy," a story that gives the reader a previously unseen and sympathetic

glimpse of the humanity of a Communist Vietnamese soldier. The
North Vietnamese regular helps a downed American pilot escape to
the south and explains that he is only doing his best to bring about
peace "for the benefit of all Vietnam."[30]

This bit of hedging in a Vietnam War comic book apparently found
little support among hawks or doves, and even a name change to the
more appropriate *Guerilla War* in 1966 failed to forestall its cancellation. Although a run of fourteen issues had qualified it as a marginal
success, the series demonstrated what other publishers would discover
as well. Although Vietnam dominated the headlines and the nightly
news, this war did not capture the public imagination as World War II
or even the Korean War had. The important exception of rock-and-
roll aside, entertainment industries tended to refer only slightly to the
conflict that would soon tear American society apart.

Vietnam War comic books failed to find a lasting audience, in part,
because they appeared at a time when superheroes reigned as the most
popular genre. As publishers discovered, the grim conflict simply did
not lend itself well to superhero fantasies. Some publishers tried to
market the Green Beret as the superhero of the Vietnam War, but these
ventures met with no success. At the same time, a number of newspapers rejected a syndicated comic strip based on Robin Moore's prowar novel, *Tales of the Green Beret*, apparently because readers complained that it was too propagandistic and an unwelcome subject for
entertainment in any case. Dell's 1967 comic book adaptation of the
novel also failed, lasting only five issues. DC flirted briefly with the war
in 1966, launching a series called "Captain Hunter" about a retired
Green Beret who returns to South Vietnam in search of his missing
brother, anticipating the many Vietnam MIA and POW movies of later
decades. Easily the most absurd of the comic book forays into Vietnam
was the Milson Publishing Company's *Super Green Beret*, featuring a
boy who becomes a super-powered Green Beret not by saying "Shazam" but by donning a magical green beret. This poorly conceived and
badly executed idea failed so miserably that both the series and the publisher folded after only a few months. In a 1966 article regarding the
recent and less-than-successful intrusion of the Vietnam War into
American comic books and strips, *Newsweek* wryly concluded that these
comic book efforts were "having much the same kind of trouble holding reader support for their war that the Administration is having ral-
lying support for the real war."[31]

There was a market for Vietnam War comic books, though, and
it was left for the marginal publishers to exploit. Of these, Charlton

Publications proved the most tireless. An established, family-owned magazine publisher whose presence in the comic book industry dated back to 1946, Charlton had survived the recession of the late 1950s partly because it owned and operated its own distribution system and published other entertainment magazines in addition to comic books. Charlton never won an especially large or lasting audience, but it enjoyed consistent, if modest, sales and carved out a niche for itself in nonsuperhero genres like romance, sci-fi, and, especially, war comics. In fact, Charlton produced more war titles than any other publisher during the 1960s, and, unlike its competitors, it did not shy away from Vietnam.[32]

Charlton's war comic books evoked the muscular anticommunism of the Kennedy years. A series of "educational" pages called "Your Role in the Cold War," which ran in all of Charlton's titles, is illustrative. They trumpet the virtues of "The American Way" as the way of "freedom, peace, and plenty . . . a way of life that is without parallel in the civilized world." But they add that, although "we are a peaceful nation, without greed or the need for conquest, we will fight fiercely for these things that are ours." To that end, a page titled "Are You Physically Fit?" urged young men and boys to exercise and stay in shape so that they will be prepared to heed the nation's call to arms. And "God Is Never Out of Style" called upon boys and girls to attend church with their parents and cultivate the moral fiber needed to prevail over godless Communists.[33]

Charlton's comic books spelled out the need for ceaseless Cold War confrontation. U.S. forces triumphed endlessly over Communists on land, at sea, and in the air on a global battlefield that stretched from Europe and the Middle East to the Caribbean and the Far East. The stories called for a flexible response to meet the Communist threat wherever and however it appeared. They explicitly endorsed increases in defense spending and training for counterinsurgency.[34]

When Charlton portrayed the Vietnam War, it expounded an unqualified endorsement of U.S. intervention that made Dell's seem cautious by comparison. Charlton presented the Vietnam War as many Americans at the time saw it—a battleground between the forces of good and evil, in which the United States would ultimately triumph through the nobility of its motives and the might of its military power.[35] Representing American might and humanitarianism in Vietnam was "the Man in the Green Beret," who, in Charlton's stories, would win the hearts and minds of the Vietnamese people. Charlton aimed to boost support for U.S. escalation in Vietnam. One story from 1963 concerns an American enlisted man who regrets that his airborne unit has been shipped to South Vietnam. Telling an army chaplain of his wish to return to the states as soon as possible, he says, "This ain't for me! We're not doin' any good here." The father disagrees, reminding the young soldier that "Communism is a terrible cancer of the human soul! And it must be stopped by those of us who are not infected. You'll understand that some day and know that any sacrifice we make here is justified." Impressed by this sermon and driven to rage by the Communist atrocities that he witnesses, the young recruit finally concludes happily that he is where he belongs, even adding with a smile, "I might turn out to be a career man after all!"[36]

Appearing in 1967, "A Tough War" exemplified Charlton's tendency to engage in straightforward propaganda. The story opens with two young men who have been notified that they are eligible to serve in the U.S. Army, while the narrator laments that "in their world few boys volunteer. They hang back, drag their feet, do everything they can think of to avoid serving their country." One of these young men, wearing an untucked shirt, sideburns, and a beard, is among the draft-dodgers, but the handsome, blond Tom Smith is not. He volunteers, passes the draft physical, and undergoes intensive military training, "growing into manhood more quickly than he ever could back home." On his way to Vietnam, Tom ponders the war that he will be waging and the narrator voices Tom's concerns. "It's a war no one wants to mention. People resent it . . . they don't think it's worth being fought. Tom isn't so sure it makes sense either." In Vietnam, Tom learns what is truly at stake in this struggle. The Viet Cong "use terror and murder as their most effective weapons." They kill innocent civilians, burn crops, and "maintain this war that nobody wants to fight." As Tom sees the evidence of Communist brutality, his doubts about the war vanish. "The fools back home who burn draft cards or march in peace demonstrations are helping the Viet Cong. They too are his enemies and he knows it now."[37]

Charlton's simplistic presentation of the Vietnam War was squarely within the tradition of anticommunist war comic books, but that tradition was passing. As the conflict came to consume more lives and public attention, these comic books started to seem increasingly at odds with reality and maybe even sanity. A 1966 Charlton story called "Executioners from Hanoi" relates how the Chinese (who are evidently directing the war in Vietnam) send a group of assassins into the jungles of the south to murder "the enemies of Chinese Communism." When the U.S. Marines encounter the Chinese, they gleefully incinerate them

with flame-throwers. The narrator assures the reader that the Communists "screamed in greater terror than any they had ever inspired . . . they died screaming." Another job well done, the marines leave the charred scene with smiles and the chilling remark that "it's only a small war out here but it's the only war we've got!"[38]

For all of the patriotic fervor in Charlton's portrayal of the war, even these comic books unintentionally showed how Vietnam unsettled traditional notions of the American war hero. In order to defeat the

From "A Tough War," *Fightin' Army* 74 (Charlton Publications, June 1967). Charlton urges youth enlistment in the Vietnam War and takes aim at the antiwar movement in this short feature, which could have easily passed as U.S. government propaganda. Writer and artist unknown.

THEY TURNED THE CHINESE ASSASSINS' BASE INTO A MARINE STRONG POINT, USING HEAVY MACHINE GUNS ETC. CAPTURED FROM THE ENEMY! LT. NASEBY RADIOED SAIGON TO GIVE THEM THE SCORE!

THIS IS BUGINHACKER! WE FOUND THE SKIPPER, ALIVE, BUT HE CAN'T BE MOVED UNTIL HE GETS A TRANSFUSION AND ONE OF OUR DOCTORS HAS A LOOK AT HIM! REQUEST A PARAMEDIC JOIN US HERE! ALSO REQUEST SATURATION AIR SUPPORT, AND AN AIRLIFT SOMETIME THIS AFTERNOON!

THE MARINE DOCTOR CHUTED IN LESS THAN AN HOUR LATER... WHILE A BITTER FIREFIGHT WAS TEACHING THE VIET CONG NOT TO MESS AROUND WITH THE MARINE CORPS!

BUDDA
BUDDA

YOU'RE AN OPPORTUNIST, GUS... YOU DIDN'T MISS THE CHANCE TO TURN A SMALL RESCUE INTO A MAJOR MILITARY CAMPAIGN, DID YOU?

NO, SIR... LIKE SGT. SCHWARTZ SAID BACK IN SAN DIEGO BEFORE WE SHIPPED OUT HERE...

...IT'S ONLY A SMALL WAR OUT HERE, BUT IT'S THE ONLY WAR WE'VE GOT!

END

Viet Cong, American soldiers sometimes behaved disturbingly like the enemy. U.S. troops learned to win, not by gallant charges and brave defenses, but by hiding in the underbrush and ambushing unsuspecting enemy soldiers. Against this elusive foe who refused to play by the rules, "an enemy nobody ever sees . . . hidden in the grass, in the trees . . . even lurking underneath the water," American soldiers had to use the Viet Cong's sadistic, sneaky, and unheroic tactics against him.[39] This boded ill for Charlton's Vietnam War, and it certainly held troubling implications for the real thing.

If Charlton's sales were any indication, the youth market for prowar sentiment in the Vietnam era was not a large one. With average sales under 150,000 copies per issue, Charlton's war comic books sold fewer copies than the competition's poorest selling titles. Then again, Charlton's comic books had never sold particularly well anyway. The publisher paid some of the industry's lowest rates to creators and had never adapted successfully to the most popular market trends, namely superheroes. The proliferation and relative longevity of Charlton's war comics, however, testified to the persistence of their brand of youthful entertainment. There was still a market for red-blooded anticommunist heroes in uniform, even at the height of the antiwar movement. Their era was quickly fading, though. Charlton's vigorous endorsement of U.S. actions in Vietnam and bitter condemnation of domestic dissent ran counter to developing trends in youth culture—trends that rival publishers chose to exploit with far more lucrative results.

Despite significant differences in approach, the comic books of DC, Dell, and Charlton all affirmed the basic assumptions of an American Cold War consensus. All conformed nicely with the comics code, and none questioned the state of American society or the meaningful place of individuals within it. Evincing a pedantic, judgmental, and ultimately condescending adult perspective on young people, these comic books seemed determined to assure parents that comic book publishers could act *in loco parentis* to inculcate appropriate values in children. These comic books were, in other words, slipping behind the times.

From "Executioners From Hanoi,"
Fightin' Marines 68 (Charlton
Publications, March–April 1966).
Charlton was the most hawkish
comic book publisher on the
Vietnam War. In Charlton's comic
books, if nowhere else, the issues
in Vietnam were black and white
and the war was good fun. Writer
and artist unknown.

The early 1960s saw a major reevaluation of youth culture as an economic, social, and political force. As the first postwar baby boomers reached teenage years, marketing analysts like Eugene Gilbert, who had sung the praises of youth since the 1940s, now seemed like prophets. Advertisers who had traditionally approached the youth market by appealing to parents became increasingly aware of the adolescent as an independent consumer. Toy companies bypassed adults and appealed directly to children through television advertising and product tie-ins with television shows like *The Mickey Mouse Club* and *Davy Crockett*. Record companies tamed rock-and-roll into a major pop music industry and manufactured "teen idols" for mass adolescent consumption. As the disposable income wielded independently by young people grew, public apprehension about youth culture receded. As James Gilbert has written, "the most important factor underlying the rise and decline of the great debate over delinquency and the media derived from a further extension of the market economy in American life." While still viewed with some trepidation, young consumers now garnered more enthusiasm than fear, especially in Hollywood and on Madison Avenue.[40]

Also, a consensus began to emerge among intellectuals and social scientists that regarded teenage rebellion as a natural and functional process in adolescent development. Multiple editions of J. D. Salinger's best-selling *The Catcher in the Rye* (1951) evoked sympathy for the adolescent struggling to develop authentic self-identity in a conformist and "phony" adult world. In *Growing Up Absurd* Paul Goodman deplored the scarcity of meaningful roles for young people in organized society. Edgar Z. Friedenberg argued in *The Vanishing Adolescent* that adolescent conflict was a necessary means through which individuals learned to differentiate themselves from their environment. According to Friedenberg, conflict between the adolescent and his world did not necessarily amount to juvenile delinquency. Instead, it was a crucial dialectical process that led to the formation of adult personality and the individual's critical participation in society. He urged adults to facilitate this process as much as possible by respecting assertions of adolescent identity and granting young people the cultural means for discovering themselves as individuals. Friedenberg also warned that an increasingly homogenized and conformist mass culture restricted the adolescent's available choices for self-definition through popular culture.[41]

Perhaps the greatest champion of youth was no less than the youthful President of the United States himself. John F. Kennedy exploited his own age, energy, and youthful good looks to great political advantage, and he reserved an essential role for young people in his vision for the nation's "New Frontiers." By the middle of the 1960s, millions of young Americans were taking an increasingly active role in shaping the political culture of their times.

Most comic books, however, had not kept up with these changes in youth culture. In presenting a world that conformed to a restrictive code and a bland consensus vision, DC, Dell, and Charlton failed to speak to the social and emotional disorientation of young people. For an audience that demanded the empathy of peers, these comic books offered only the measured explanations of elders. Lucrative possibilities existed for the publisher that could bridge the widening gap between the consensus of the code and the confusion of adolescence. That publisher turned out to be Marvel Comics.

The Marvel Age

Once among the largest publishers in the field, Marvel Comics fell upon hard times in the late 1950s. Marvel initially survived the aftershocks of 1954 better than most because publisher Martin Goodman distributed his comic books through his own distribution company, but the company's sales plummeted nonetheless. To save expenses, Goodman shut down his distribution operation and signed a contract with DC Comics, which agreed to distribute a monthly total of eight Marvel titles through its Independent News Company. So Marvel entered the 1960s ingloriously with only a handful of titles to its name, distributed by its chief competitor.[42]

Goodman's editor, art director, and chief writer was Stan Lee. Having started work at Marvel in 1940 at the age of seventeen, Lee was one of the few individuals who had spent his entire career in the field. Under his long tenure as editor, Marvel had prospered even without the benefit of much creative innovation. Until the recession of the late 1950s, Goodman's publishing strategy had amounted to mass imitation of trends launched by rivals like DC, Lev Gleason, and EC. Emphasizing quantity of production, Marvel had always had at least several titles in every genre on the newsstands, but the company's decline rendered such an approach unworkable. For a time in 1957, the company's financial situation deteriorated so badly that Lee let go his entire freelance staff and issued only reprints. He had good reason to suspect that his own long career in the comic book business was coming to an end.[43]

By 1958, Marvel's situation had improved enough for Lee to once again offer employment. Two of the new Marvel artists, Jack Kirby and Steve Ditko, would play a major role in the company's resurgence. With over two decades of experience, Jack Kirby was among the most respected and sought-after talents in the field. Although he had worked in all genres, Kirby's formidable creative and commercial talents were best suited to larger-than-life action and adventure comic books. Steve Ditko had worked in the industry since 1953, specializing in horror and sci-fi with a highly distinctive and surrealistic style. As comic book critics Will Jacobs and Gerard Jones accurately observed, Ditko's work combined "a pervasive eeriness" and "a disconcerting sense of unreality" in such a way that "a disturbing undercurrent of madness seemed to flow through all his stories."[44]

Working with Kirby and Ditko seemed to instill Stan Lee with new enthusiasm. After years of derivative genre hackwork, Marvel's comic books finally assumed distinctive qualities. The initial results, while hardly a ringing commercial success, certainly posed a clear alternative to the competition. And they pointed towards the themes that Marvel would eventually develop into a winning formula. Marvel's reduced output at the start of the 1960s consisted mostly of sci-fi comics, an especially popular genre in youth entertainment at the time. Lee recognized more astutely than his peers at DC the particular themes of the genre that seemed to fascinate contemporary young people the most. While DC used sci-fi to exalt the virtues of scientific progress and the certainty of peace through technology, Marvel spoke to the anxieties of the atomic age.

Marvel's sci-fi stories fell into two general categories geared to the individual styles of the principal artists. The first type, conceived to suit Jack Kirby's talents, was clearly inspired by contemporary Saturday-matinee monster movies. They featured colorful and bizarre monsters with ridiculous names like Monsteroso, Grogg, and—Lee's personal favorite—Fin Fang Foom, who came from outer space, underground, or "Dimension X," and generally emerged as a consequence of impudent human activity. Often they were awakened by reckless scientists or atomic testing. In accordance with the comics code, these monsters were more ludicrous than frightening. Their rampages might result in great material destruction, but rarely loss of life—unless the victims happened to be Communists and thus deserving of such a fate.[45] Tossed-off and formulaic as they were, these monster stories still spoke to concerns rarely addressed in other contemporary comic books. The unknown in DC's comic books was something to be conquered through scientific progress. In Marvel's, it was something best left undisturbed. Even though humanity inevitably overcame the destructive consequences of its own actions, the lesson was always the same: tampering with unknown forces beyond man's control invited trouble. Collectively, these stories sounded a cautionary tone about the fragility of civilization in the atomic age.

The stories produced by Stan Lee and Steve Ditko could be even more unsettling. Ditko's characters tended to be alienated and neurotic individuals—small, pathetic men unable to adapt to the national spirit of consensus. A typical Lee-Ditko tale, "The Last Man on Earth" introduced millionaire Sidney Blake, who is terrified about the threat of nuclear war. He cares nothing for his country or his fellow citizens. "They're not important," he scoffs, "but I'm too rich to die!" So he constructs the most elaborate bomb shelter that money can buy and refuses to share it with anyone. When World War III appears imminent, Sidney descends into his shelter to wait out the nuclear holocaust. When he emerges, he discovers that everyone is gone, but there is no destruction. It turns out that as he had withdrawn into isolation, all humanity left in spaceships to inhabit a newly discovered world where life could be prolonged for centuries. So poor Sidney is left on a deserted planet Earth to ponder the consequences of his own selfishness.[46]

While the moral thrust of these comic books ultimately affirms the individual's obligation to society, much like those of DC did, the important difference—and the key to Marvel's developing formula—lay in the grim endings and the tragic qualities of the characters. Marvel presented its cautionary tales not through moral platitudes but in the form of alienated antiheroes. On the surface these characters were not sympathetic, they were hopelessly selfish individuals who planted the seeds of their own destruction.[47] Yet in these pathetic characters, readers recognized familiar human failings and glimpsed their own anxieties. The Marvel sci-fi formula essentially amounted to a less sophisticated variation on television's *Twilight Zone*, which had recently won a large and loyal youth audience for its twisted tales about the moral and emotional fragility of human beings.[48]

Stan Lee suspected that the unique qualities of his work with Steve Ditko might appeal especially to teenagers and young adults. So he changed the title of *Amazing Fantasy* to *Amazing Adult Fantasy* and subtitled it *The Magazine That Respects Your Intelligence*. It was a canny sales pitch to young people looking for an alternative to the triumphalist comic books of the competition. The wisdom of Marvel's approach was not immediately apparent, however. The sci-fi titles managed monthly sales of fewer than 200,000 copies, making them only moderately successful. By 1961 Stan Lee was once again ready to move on to another career, but circumstances soon led him to change his mind.[49]

Noticing that DC's new superhero titles were selling well, Martin

Goodman asked Stan Lee to start a new comic book featuring a team of superheroes modeled after DC's *Justice League of America*. In past years, Marvel's response to popular trends had been as derivative as copyright laws would allow, but Lee had something quite original in mind for this new title. Personally, he had never liked comic book superheroes very much. They were always too perfect and unbelievable, and he felt that most discerning adolescents could not relate to such stiff and silly characters. Lee hoped to recapture the teenage audience with a new kind of superhero comic book—one that played to some of the moral ambivalence that young people recognized and responded to. With only a handful of foundering titles on the market, Marvel had little to lose and everything to gain from such an experiment.[50]

Working with Jack Kirby, Lee created a superhero family of four individuals, all possessing distinct personalities. One was Reed Richards, a father figure, appropriately pragmatic, authoritative, and dull. His fiancée, Sue Storm, was not just a romantic interest but an integral member of the team and a potential draw for female readers. Her teenage brother, Johnny Storm, was no teen sidekick, he was a typical adolescent—brash, rebellious, and affectionately obnoxious. Ben Grimm was an uncle figure, a longtime friend of the family with a gruff Brooklyn manner, short temper, and caustic sense of humor. Together they take off in a rocket ship of Reed's own construction with the aim of beating the Soviets in the space race. However, they fail to anticipate the mysterious cosmic rays that penetrate their ship. After they safely crash land on Earth, they discover that the rays have affected each of them in different and incredible ways. Reed now has the ability to stretch his body into any shape. Sue can make herself invisible. Johnny is able to burst into flames and wield control over fire. And Ben finds himself transformed into an orange rock-skinned monster with enormous physical strength. With little pause, they pledge to use their powers to aid humanity, calling themselves Mr. Fantastic, the Invisible Girl, the Human Torch, and the Thing, respectively. Henceforth, they would be known as the Fantastic Four.[51]

The Fantastic Four's characterization immediately set the series apart from all other superheroes. In a significant departure from superhero conventions, the Fantastic Four make no effort to conceal their identities from the public, who regard them with understandable awe and a certain degree of suspicion. The heroes' idiosyncrasies often impede their work as a team. They frequently argue and even fight with each other. The Thing throws destructive temper tantrums and has to be physically restrained by his teammates. The Human Torch briefly quits the group because he resents the three adults bossing him around. The Invisible Girl lets romance cloud her judgment by taking an interest in the Sub-Mariner, a sworn enemy of the Fantastic Four. And Mr. Fantastic blames himself for the failed space mission and the cosmic ray accident that robbed his friend Ben of his human appearance. It was an often volatile mix of human emotions and personalities. In one issue, after breaking up the latest skirmish between the Thing and the Human Torch, an exasperated Mr. Fantastic asks, "What's the matter with the four of us? Whenever we're not fighting some menace to mankind, we end up fighting among ourselves!" To this the Thing retorts, "Skip the lecture pal! I'm a big boy now!" Despite their bickering and personality clashes, however, the Fantastic Four always prove to be a cohesive and formidable team in times of crisis.[52]

Of the four, the Thing stood as the most compelling and original character. Acerbic to begin with, Ben Grimm's mutation into the Thing left him deeply embittered and hostile. Never before had a comic book suggested that a superhero's power would alienate him from the human race. When society reacts to him with suspicion and fear, the Thing lashes out in rage, "Well, maybe they're right! Maybe I am a monster! I look like one—and sometimes I feel like one! . . . If they say I'm a menace, I'll be a menace! I'll show 'em all!" What adolescent beset by the frustrations of the adult world has not felt like that at one time or another? Although the Thing later softened his animosity towards the human race and actually became rather cuddly, he always betrayed familiar tendencies towards anguish, loneliness, and self-pity. Despite his monstrous appearance and awesome power, the Thing's tragic flaws ironically made him one of the most "human" comic book characters ever created. Young readers empathized immediately with the character, and they consistently ranked him as the Fantastic Four's most popular member.[53]

The Fantastic Four, and the Thing in particular, reworked the formula for comic book superheroes. These were heroes who reconciled the competing imperatives of individualism and communal responsibility. Although the concept was new to comic books, such character types were actually well grounded in American popular culture, since American audiences had historically shown a marked preference for reluctant heroes who defend the community while maintaining a personal distance from society. The classic archetype, of course, is the Western frontier hero, existing on the border between civilization and the wilderness and championing the best qualities of both.[54] Embodied in the

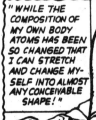

reluctant hero were the celebrated possibilities of American republican-
ism: virtuous citizens giving to the community without sacrificing their
freedom and individuality. The demands of World War II and the Cold
War had subverted whatever individuality superheroes like Superman
and Batman had once possessed for the sake of the national consensus.
Now the Fantastic Four opened the door for reluctant comic book
superheroes to pose an alternative to that consensus.

The Fantastic Four immediately became Marvel's top seller and
prompted an unprecedented barrage of fan mail. "It was one of the
most exciting things that ever happened to us," Lee recalled. "We found
out that there were actually real live readers out there . . . who took the
trouble to contact us . . . who wanted to talk to us about our characters,
about our stories." These readers showed enthusiasm for what Lee
called "realistic fantasy" stories about superheroes who performed impossible feats but evinced believable human qualities and failings. Significantly, the Marvel heroes resided in New York City rather than
mythical locales like Metropolis and Gotham City. If not quite "believable," these stories at least took place in a world more relevant to the audience.[55]

Lee and Kirby's next creation took the concept of the reluctant
superhero even further. A gentle, bespectacled atomic physicist named
Dr. Bruce Banner constructs a powerful new gamma bomb to be tested
at a U.S. Army base in New Mexico. The cigar-chomping General
"Thunderbolt" Ross barks at him to hurry up with the preparations,
but Banner warns that they are "tampering with powerful forces."
General Ross retorts, "Powerful forces! Bah! A bomb is a bomb! The
trouble with you is you're a milksop! You've got no guts!" Later, as the
explosion is imminent, Banner sees that a reckless teenager has wan-
dered onto the desert test site. He runs out to the site himself and leads
the youth to safety, but before Banner can protect himself, the bomb
explodes and bathes him in mysterious gamma radiation. Although he

From "The Fantastic Four Meet
the Skrulls from Outer Space, " *The
Fantastic Four* 2 (Marvel Comics,
January 1962). Marvel's Fantastic
Four introduced moral complexity
and emotional tension into
the vocabulary of the comic book
superhero and proved to be
the blueprint for a succession of
"flawed" superhero characters. The
central character of the group was
the Thing, who agonized over his
permanent transformation into an
orange rock-skinned monster.
Script by Stan Lee, art by Jack
Kirby.

survives the blast, he soon learns that the accident has changed him in incredible ways. When night falls, Banner grows and undergoes a Jekyll-Hyde transformation into a hulking gray man-monster with incalculable strength and an enraged personality. With the second issue, Lee and Kirby changed the character's color to green and the familiar Incredible Hulk was born.[56]

A most unlikely superhero, the Hulk's overriding desire is self-preservation and privacy. A hero by accident, he cares nothing for humankind but inevitably fights in its defense when a villain bent on world domination makes the mistake of attacking him. The fearful public, in turn, often regards him as a greater menace than the villains that he fights. The armed forces pursue him relentlessly. Only Banner's conscience working against the Hulk's bestial aggression keeps him from being the menace that people believe him to be. When one frightened woman asks the Hulk why he hates humanity so, he answers, "Why shouldn't I hate you? Why shouldn't I hate all mankind? Look what men have done to me! But they will hound me no longer! For now, the Hulk will fight back . . . on my own terms!"[57]

The Hulk was so offbeat that Lee and Kirby seemed unsure of what to do with him. After trying several different triggers for Banner's transformations into the Hulk, they finally settled upon the notion of an adrenaline surge sparked by anger or excitement. The character's personality and speech pattern also underwent periodic revision.[58] What remained consistent, however, was the Hulk's antagonistic relationship towards the forces of authority. He wished only to be left alone, but civilization would never let him be. His adventures read like an atomic-age Western outlaw tale. Roaming the lonely deserts of the Southwest, profoundly alienated from society, the Hulk stood as a creature of Cold War preoccupations and scientific progress gone horribly wrong. His very existence pointed to the failures of modern civilization, and so the Hulk proved intolerable to society's controlling forces.

From "The Coming of the Hulk," *The Incredible Hulk* 1 (Marvel Comics, May 1962). Stan Lee and Jack Kirby followed the success of the Fantastic Four with the even more offbeat Incredible Hulk. After Dr. Bruce Banner is accidentally exposed to a blast of radiation from an exploding "gamma bomb," he undergoes his first unexpected transformation into the Hulk. An update of Dr. Jekyll–Mr. Hyde and the Frankenstein monster for the atomic age, the Hulk was the most alienated superhero of all. Script by Stan Lee, art by Jack Kirby.

The Hulk eventually proved to be one of Marvel's most popular characters, but it was Lee's next creation that became the quintessential Marvel superhero. In a direct stab at the teenage market, Lee wanted to feature a superhero who was himself an adolescent—one who had to contend with his own insecurities and confusion even as he had to fight the bad guys. He would be a superhero who, as Lee explained, "would lose out as often as he'd win—in fact, more often." The premise was so unusual that Lee chose to debut the series tentatively in the last issue of a sci-fi title marked for cancellation.[59]

In retrospect, Lee had little cause for concern. Spider-Man was the most brilliant concept for a comic book superhero since Superman. Peter Parker furnished readers with an instant point of identification. All but the most emotionally secure adolescents could relate to Peter's self-absorbed obsessions with rejection, inadequacy, and loneliness. For young readers, Lee offered a reassuring narrative voice: "Alas, other teen-agers can sometimes, unwittingly, be so cruel to a shy young man. . . . Yes, for some, being a teen-ager has many heart-breaking moments." The bespectacled Peter escapes the taunts of his peers by losing himself in science. He attends a special exhibit on radioactivity where, unnoticed by anyone, a spider is caught in the radiation. The radioactive spider bites Peter and miraculously transfers its abilities to him. The startled teenager discovers that he now has the proportionate strength, speed, and agility of a spider, as well as the ability to cling to sheer surfaces and a mysterious "spider-sense" that warns him of danger. To make the most of his new abilities, the scientifically gifted student constructs a pair of web-shooting devices which he can wear on each wrist. Then, in keeping with the conventions of the genre, he designs a colorful red and blue costume and mask to conceal his identity and assumes the dramatic name *Spider-Man*.[60]

The adherence to convention ended there. Spider-Man makes no pledge to aid humanity. Why should he, after all? What had humanity ever done for him? The only people whom he cares for are his Aunt May and Uncle Ben, who have raised him as their own son since the death of his parents. "I'll see to it that they're always happy," he thinks. "But the rest of the world can go hang for all I care!" Under such fantastic circumstances, his was a remarkably human reaction. Initially, Spider-Man uses his extraordinary abilities for profit as an entertainer. He becomes so caught up in himself that he even refuses to help a police officer stop a thief who runs past him and escapes into an elevator. "What's with you mister?" snaps the officer. "All you hadda do was trip him, or hold him just for a minute!" Spider-Man coolly replies, "Sorry pal! That's your job! I'm through being pushed around—by anyone! From now on I just look out for number one—that means—me!"[61]

Some time later Peter returns home one evening and learns that a burglar has murdered his beloved Uncle Ben. As Spider-Man, he tracks down the killer and exacts vengeance with his powerful fists. He sees the man's face for the first time and discovers that it is the very fugitive that he had allowed to escape only days earlier. Startled and heartbroken, the teenager wanders off into the night, sobbing, "My fault—all my fault! If only I had stopped him when I could have! But I didn't—and now—Uncle Ben is dead!" In this instant Spider-Man becomes a true superhero. Tragedy has made Peter understand that "in this world, with great power there must also come—great responsibility." The closing sales pitch asked readers to "look for the further amazing exploits of America's most *different* new teen-age idol—Spider-Man!"[62]

When the sales reports and fan mail came in, Stan Lee knew that he had a winner and promptly issued a new series featuring the character. *The Amazing Spider-Man* became Marvel's best-selling title. Much of the credit for Spider-Man must also go to artist Steve Ditko. Lee had assigned the series to Ditko rather than Kirby because he appreciated Ditko's ability to emphasize the weakness and fragility of his characters. Kirby's superheroes were powerful and impressive, but that was not the image that Lee wanted for Spider-Man. Ditko effectively brought out the humanity of the teenage hero. Indeed, Ditko's own reputation within the field as a reclusive loner and a fierce individualist suggests that the artist put something of himself into this character.[63]

Lee and Ditko developed a cast of interesting supporting characters, supplied a series of mundane difficulties for the hero to contend with, and introduced numerous adolescent points of reference. Peter was always broke. When he tries to earn money by performing as Spider-Man, he finds that he cannot cash his paycheck because he has no identification in the name of Spider-Man. Later, Spider-Man applies for membership in the Fantastic Four, only to be rebuffed when Mr. Fantastic tells him that they pay no salaries. Peter lived at home with his Aunt May, whose doting was a source of constant inconvenience. He had to fabricate a variety of explanations for her when Spider-Man's lifestyle caused Peter Parker to stay out all night. Although Peter was a talented student, even he was prone to occasional inattentiveness in the classroom. He had trouble getting dates and keeping girlfriends. His chief nemesis was the high-school jock "Flash" Thompson, who was, ironically, also the president of the Spider-Man fan club.[64]

As an adolescent character, Peter underwent marked personal

growth. After a half-dozen issues, he stopped wearing glasses and shed much of his adolescent awkwardness in favor of a more mature outsider persona, coming to look and act more and more like a comic book version of James Dean. Comic book heroes rarely "aged," but Peter finished high school, went to college, and years later even went to graduate school. This unprecedented attention to subplots and character development made Peter Parker the first "average" comic book character who was as interesting as his costumed alter-ego. *The Amazing Spider-Man* became one of the first superhero soap operas, inviting readers to return each month to check in on the latest trials and tribulations of the hero and his supporting cast. It was all part of Lee's calculated marketing to teenagers. A typical closing sales pitch promised, "Next issue: More fascinating details about the life and adventures of the world's most amazing teen-ager—Spider-Man—the superhero who could be—you!"[65]

Spider-Man's plight was to be misunderstood and persecuted by the very public that he swore to protect. In the first issue of *The Amazing Spider-Man*, J. Jonah Jameson, publisher of the *Daily Bugle*, launches an editorial campaign against the "Spider-Man menace." The resulting negative publicity exacerbates popular suspicions about the mysterious Spider-Man and makes it impossible for him to earn any more money by performing. Eventually the bad press leads the authorities to brand him an outlaw. Ironically, Peter finally lands a job as a photographer working for Jameson's *Daily Bugle*.[66]

Even in the face of adversity, Spider-Man retained his youthful demeanor, irreverence, and self-deprecating sense of humor. He spouted off wisecracks while fighting middle-aged supervillains like the Vulture, Dr. Octopus, the Green Goblin, and Electro. At times Peter wondered if he enjoyed the thrill of his powers too much. Was the public correct to brand him a menace? This prompted some troubling introspection, as he asked himself, "Am I really some sort of a crack-pot, wasting my time seeking fame and glory? Am I more interested in the adventure of being Spider-Man than I am in helping people? Why do I do it? Why don't I give the whole thing up? And yet, I can't! I must have been given this great power for a reason! No matter how difficult it is, I must remain as Spider-Man! And I pray that some day the world will understand!"[67]

It is difficult to overstate the impact of these early Spider-Man comic books on the subsequent development of the industry. The young, flawed, and brooding antihero became the most widely imitated archetype in the superhero genre since the appearance of Superman.

While it took rival publishers years to successfully emulate the adolescent sensibilities embodied in Spider-Man, Stan Lee understood the
root of the character's appeal and wasted no time in following it up.
Superheroes with awesome powers and human shortcomings became
the defining feature of Marvel Comics.

Although none of Lee's subsequent creations equaled the conceptual or commercial success of Spider-Man, nearly all of them found a sizable and lasting audience. The first to follow was the mighty Thor— the Norse god of thunder, whose alter ego was the frail Dr. Donald Blake. An outsider in his own right, Thor is never completely at home with his fellow Norse gods of Asgard or with the mortals of his adopted world. His soap opera centers on his forbidden love with a mortal woman—a romance that his overbearing father Odin frowns upon. Thor's most obvious connection to youth culture, though, was unintentional: in a few years, his long hair would become a fashionable badge of rebellion among young men.[68]

Next came Marvel's most unusual superhero, the appropriately named Dr. Strange. A gifted but extremely selfish surgeon, Stephen Strange loses his ability to practice after suffering nerve damage in a car accident. Descending into alcoholism, Strange uses the last of his resources to travel to Tibet and seek a cure from the mysterious Ancient One. The elderly guru instead persuades Strange to forsake his selfish desires in the material world and undertake the study of the mystic arts. After having completed his spiritual tutelage under the Ancient One, Dr. Strange takes up residence at his sanctum sanctorum in New York's Greenwich Village and assumes his role as Earth's "Sorcerer Supreme." Though dedicated to protecting humanity from evil forces in this and other dimensions, Strange remains aloof from society—a mysterious outsider who emerges in times of crisis and withdraws into the shadows once his work is done.[69]

This series was indeed strange. Steve Ditko contributed some of his most surrealistic work to the comic book and gave it a disorienting, hallucinogenic quality. Dr. Strange's adventures take place in bizarre worlds and twisting dimensions that resembled Salvador Dali paintings. They involve mystical spells, trances, astral travel, and occult lore. Inspired by the pulp-fiction magicians of Stan Lee's childhood as well as by contemporary Beat culture, Dr. Strange remarkably predicted the youth counterculture's fascination with Eastern mysticism and psychedelia. Never among Marvel's most popular or accessible characters, Dr. Strange still found a niche among an audience seeking a challenging alternative to more conventional superhero fare.

WOULD YOU LIKE US TO HELP YOU CROSS THE STREET, SONNY? MEBBE WE COULD--

HMMPH! TOO BAD HE DOESN'T HAVE *COURAGE* TO MATCH!

YOU SAID IT, *LIZ*! COME ON, CHICK, LET'S *GO*! THIS COMPANY IS *BORIN'* ME!

HEY! WHAT GIVES? YOU OUGHTTA FEEL HIS ARM UNDER THIS JACKET, FLASH! PARKER'S GOT MUSCLES LIKE A WEIGHT LIFTER!

NOW EVEN *LIZ* THINKS I'M A *COWARD*! THAT SURE IS PRETTY HARD TO TAKE!

SO LONG, BRAIN WAVE! DON'T LET ANY KINDERGARTEN KIDS RUN AWAY WITH YOUR BOOKS!

THAT'S *ENOUGH*, FLASH! YOU NEEDN'T BE *THAT* CRUEL TO PETER!

WOMEN! I THOUGHT YOU WERE *MAD* AT 'IM!

LATER, WALKING HOME FROM SCHOOL, A THOUGHTFUL PETER PARKER OVERHEARS THE COMMENTS OF HIS NEIGHBORS...

WELL, I SEE THAT *SPIDER-MAN* CAPTURED THAT AWFUL *SANDMAN*!

ACCORDING TO THE EDITORIAL, *SPIDER-MAN* IS JUST AS BAD AS THE OTHER ONE!

JONAH JAMESON WRITES THAT *SPIDER-MAN* HAS NO BUSINESS TRYING TO CATCH CRIMINALS BY HIMSELF!

IF YOU ASK *ME*, THAT'S *RIGHT*! WHO KNOWS WHEN *SPIDER-MAN* MAY TURN *AGAINST* SOCIETY?!!

WHAT WOULD MAKE A GUY WEAR A GOOFY COSTUME AND RUN AROUND CHASIN' CROOKS?

I DUNNO! HE MUST BE A *NEUROTIC* OF SOME SORT! PROBABLY HAS DELUSIONS OF GRANDEUR!

DON'T YOU WISH *YOU* WERE *SPIDER-MAN*?

NAH! GIVE ME THE *HUMAN TORCH* ANY DAY!

FINALLY, ALONE IN HIS ROOM, THE AMAZING INDIVIDUAL CALLED *SPIDER-MAN* SEARCHES HIS SOUL, BEWILDERED, CONFUSED, AND BITTER!

CAN THEY BE *RIGHT*? AM I *REALLY* SOME SORT OF A CRACK-POT, WASTING MY TIME SEEKING FAME AND GLORY?? AM I MORE INTERESTED IN THE ADVENTURE OF BEING *SPIDER-MAN* THAN I AM IN HELPING PEOPLE?? WHY DO I DO IT? WHY DON'T I GIVE THE WHOLE THING UP?

AND YET, I *CAN'T*! I MUST HAVE BEEN GIVEN THIS GREAT POWER FOR A *REASON*! NO MATTER HOW DIFFICULT IT IS, I *MUST* REMAIN AS *SPIDER-MAN*! AND I PRAY THAT SOME DAY THE WORLD WILL UNDERSTAND!

ONE THING IS CERTAIN! THE WORLD WON'T HAVE LONG TO WAIT FOR *SPIDER-MAN'S* NEXT GREAT THRILLER! DUE TO YOUR EVER-INCREASING DEMAND, IT WILL BE ON SALE *SOON*! RESERVE YOUR COPY *NOW*!

21

For his next superhero, Lee turned to the military-industrial complex and the Cold War. When the famed American munitions industrialist Anthony Stark goes to South Vietnam to observe some of his military hardware in action, he is wounded by an enemy mine and taken prisoner by the Communists, who insist that he build a new weapon for them. To escape and keep his wounded heart beating, he secretly constructs a suit of transistor-powered armor that gives him great strength and destructive power. After having escaped the Communists, Stark launches a dual life as the superhero Iron Man, but the millionaire playboy is cursed to wear the iron chest plate in order to keep himself alive.[70]

Rounding out Marvel's core superheroes in the mid-1960s were the X-Men, a group of teenage mutants who hone their powers under the tutelage of the wheelchair-bound Professor Xavier; Daredevil, a blind attorney whose exposure to radiation has heightened his remaining senses; and the Avengers, a team of superheroes similar to DC's Justice League, except that the members of Marvel's team tended to bicker. Lee and Kirby also revived two of the publisher's most popular characters from the 1940s and recast them in the new Marvel style. Captain America returned as a World War II hero, literally revived out of suspended animation, haunted by past memories, and trying to adapt to 1960s society. The Sub-Mariner resumed his original incarnation as an antihero and waged a personal war against the surface world for destroying his kingdom of Atlantis with underwater atomic tests. They all joined in the ranks of what Stan Lee proudly hailed, with much justification, as the "Marvel Age of Comics."[71]

Marvel's introduction of ambiguity into the vocabulary of the comic book superhero fused the disorientation of adolescence and the anxieties of Cold War culture into a compelling narrative formula. The rejection of consensus and conformity found expression in super-

From "Nothing Can Stop the Sandman," *The Amazing Spider-Man* 4 (Marvel Comics, September 1963). Rejected by his classmates and distrusted by the public, the angstridden Spider-Man spoke directly to the confusion of adolescence. His heroic yet self-effacing qualities helped make him the most popular superhero in comic books. Script by Stan Lee, art by Steve Ditko.

REMEMBER THIS, MY SON-- HE IS LIKE NO FOE YOU HAVE EVER FOUGHT BEFORE! HIS POWER IS BEYOND DESCRIPTION--HIS WORLD IS FRAUGHT WITH STRANGE DANGERS--

IT IS TRULY SAID --IN ALL THE UNIVERSE, THERE IS NONE SO TO COMPARE TO THE DREAD DORMAMMU!

EVEN I, AT THE HEIGHT OF MY POWER, WAS UNABLE TO DEFEAT HIM! IF YOU SHOULD FAIL--THERE CAN BE NO HELP FOR YOU!!

I DARE NOT FAIL, MASTER!! TOO MUCH IS AT STAKE!!

SO BE IT, THEN!! BY THE SHADES OF THE SERAPHIM-- IN THE NAME OF THE ALL- SEEING AGAMOTTO--

--I DISPATCH THEE TO-- THE DOMAIN OF THE DREAD DORMAMMU!!!

IT IS DONE!! THERE CAN BE NO TURNING BACK!! I AM COMMITTED TO THE BATTLE OF MY LIFE!!

SLOWLY THE MISTS BEGIN TO CLEAR, AS A STRANGE, STARTLING WORLD TAKES FORM! A WORLD IN WHICH THE IMPOSSIBLE IS BELIEVABLE, AND THE INCREDIBLE IS COMMONPLACE -- THE WORLD OF THE DARK DOMAIN -- THE WORLD OF THE DREAD DORMAMMU!

THE JOURNEY IS OVER! BUT, JUDGING BY THE UNSPEAKABLE MENACE I SEE BEFORE ME, THE BATTLE IS JUST BEGUN!

3

heroes who were misunderstood by the public and persecuted by authorities. The dangers and uncertainties of the atomic age could be glimpsed in the fates of the Thing and Bruce Banner, both of whom had endured unwanted and irreversible mutations because they dared to tamper with unknown scientific forces. Banner's plight was especially poignant, having resulted from exposure to radioactive energy unleashed by a U.S. military test. Of course, the fact that supposedly lethal radiation also gave enviable superpowers to heroes like Spider-Man, Daredevil, and the X-Men may have caused some confusion among young readers. Nevertheless, the very notion of a troubled and brooding superhero who could not always accomplish what he set out to do betrayed the limited scope of his superpowers—and suggested perhaps the limitations confronting the American superpower as well.

Just as Marvel was launching many of its new superheroes in 1964, "Beatlemania" was sweeping the nation. More than just popular musicians, the Beatles won millions of young admirers with their charming irreverence, nonconformity, and self-deprecating humor. Marvel was not about to rival that kind of success, but Stan Lee recognized the wisdom of hip marketing. He cultivated an image of Marvel Comics as a maverick within the comic book field, much like the outsider superheroes themselves. His cover blurbs, house editorials, answers to reader letters, and script writing all established a distinctive "Marvel style." Willfully outrageous sales pitches ("One of the most eagerly-awaited action dramas of all time!"), self-deprecating humor, cross-references between titles, and recurring in-jokes all defined what it meant to be involved in this "hip happening" that was Marvel Comics.[72] Lee built affection for Marvel's characters while playfully acknowledging the absurdity of the whole enterprise. He introduced the start of one Hulk adventure, for instance, by posing the "burning question": "Can a man with green skin and a petulant personality find true happiness in today's status-seeking society?"[73] Lee also worked to generate reader intimacy

From "The Domain of the Dread Dormammu," *Strange Tales* 126 (Marvel Comics, November 1964). Among Marvel's most unusual superheroes, the appropriately named Dr. Strange used mystical spells, astral travel, and occult lore to combat bizarre extradimensional villains with names like the Dread Dormammu. Unintentionally predicting the 1960s fascination with psychedelia, artist Steve Ditko rendered Dr. Strange's adventures in a surrealistic Dali-like style. Script by Stan Lee, art by Steve Ditko.

with the Marvel staff, referring to it as the "Bullpen." He instituted a permanent space for creative credits—not only for the writer (most often himself) and principal artist but also for the inker and letterer. And he endowed the staff with affectionate nicknames like "Jolly" Jack Kirby, "Swinging" Steve Ditko, and "Smilin'" Stan Lee. Appearing in each title were Marvel editorials and house news items like "Stan's Soapbox" and "Bullpen Bulletins," all designed to impart that there was more to the Marvel experience then just reading a comic book and throwing it away.

Central to Lee's editorial strategy was his evolving concept of the "Marvel universe." Despite occasional lapses in consistency and continuity, the Marvel comic books all fit together as a collective narrative. Lee endeavored to weave his characters and plot references into a coherent modern mythology that invited an unusual degree of reader involvement. Storylines continued from one issue to the next, obliging readers to make repeated purchases of a title. Superheroes would show up in each others' titles, sometimes for only a cameo appearance, so that followers of one series ultimately met all of the Marvel stars. Lee hyped cross-promotional battles between the superheroes so that readers would take an interest in who might win in a fight between the Hulk and the Thing, Spider-Man and Daredevil, or the Fantastic Four and the X-Men.[74] Lee later explained that he "treated the whole thing as a gigantic advertising campaign. I wanted to give the product—which was Marvel Comics, and myself in a certain way—a certain personality . . . where the readers would identify with us and care about us." He wanted readers to feel part of "an 'in' thing that the outside world wasn't even aware of . . . sharing a big joke together and having a lot of fun with this crazy Marvel universe."[75]

Lee established a shrewd marketing strategy for comic books in the television age. The comic book industry would never again reach the almost universal young audience that it had enjoyed in previous decades, but a compelling product carefully grounded in adolescent sensibilities could still win a sizable audience in those looking for an alternative to the more homogenized offerings of mass culture.

The comics code still severely restricted the ability of comic book makers to fully explore audience concerns and interests. The code was not an insurmountable obstacle, however. Stan Lee had learned from the horror comics controversy of the 1950s that there was a great deal to lose by going too far in appealing to the subversive tendencies in youth culture. Outsiders though they might be, there was never a question as to the morality of the Marvel superheroes. They never hurt

innocent people, never killed anyone, and generally respected the law.
The U.S. Army might torment the Hulk, and the police might harass
Spider-Man, but superheroes and authority figures ultimately stood on
the same side. Likewise, while often insensitive and wrongheaded, respected authority never appeared corrupt or malicious. Hedging of this
sort allowed Marvel's quietly subversive overtures to slip past the censorship of the comics code to perceptive young readers.

Marvel managed to strike an antiestablishment pose without appearing political. For instance, Marvel's comic books at this time rarely
mention the civil rights movement, yet Marvel was the first publisher
to integrate African Americans into comic books. In 1966 Marvel debuted the first black superhero, a cosmopolitan African prince called
the Black Panther. Marvel's black superhero was apparently coinciden-
tal to the founding of the black militant group, but both clearly chose
the name because it evoked an image of black pride. Just as significant,
perhaps, was Marvel's gradual introduction of random African American citizens into common street scenes, in which they appeared as policemen, reporters, or mere passers-by. It was a belated but meaningful
comic book illustration of America as a multiracial society.[76]

Marvel attacked intolerance and bigotry without making explicit
reference to segregation or the struggles of African Americans. The
X-Men sometimes found themselves persecuted by bigots who were
opposed to mutants. A story appearing in the October 1965 issue of
The Avengers concerns an organization called the Sons of the Serpent,
which bore a close resemblance to the Ku Klux Klan and pledged to
rid America of "foreigners" and those of different "creeds" and "heritage." The Avengers expose the organization as a Communist front
working to instill hatred and disunity among Americans as a precursor
to foreign invasion. The argument for civil rights thus comes safely
couched in the incontrovertible language of anticommunism.[77]

Meanwhile, despite Lee's later claims to the contrary, Marvel's
comic books did little to advance feminism. Although each Marvel
superhero team had at least one integral female member, they were always subordinate to the male superheroes. While the men of the Fantastic Four did the hard fighting, the Invisible Girl tended to overexert
herself and faint often. The X-Men's Marvel Girl possessed the formidable power of telekinesis, but she too proved prone to fainting spells.
And both, of course, were women referred to as "girls," even though
teenage superheroes like Spider-Man and Ice Man were clearly not
"boys." A founding female member of the Avengers, the Wasp, was an
annoying airhead who spent most of her time panicking, fainting, and

worrying about smudging her makeup in the heat of battle.[78] Like his peers at DC, Stan Lee missed an opportunity to broaden the superhero audience across genders with appealing characters both powerful and feminine.

Marvel's comic books remained committed to the Cold War, despite the jarring character inconsistencies that anticommunism sometimes produced. The bestial Hulk, for instance, harbored a general hostility towards the human race, and his most determined nemesis was

From "The Fantastic Four Meet the Incredible Hulk," *The Fantastic Four* 12 (Marvel Comics, March 1963) and *The Amazing Spider-Man* 16 (Marvel Comics, September 1965). Marvel's super-antiheroes seemed to fight each other as often as they cooperated against the villains. Stan Lee used superhero encounters like these—between Spider-Man and Daredevil (*above,* art by Steve Ditko) and between the Fantastic Four and the Hulk (*facing page,* art by Jack Kirby)—to cross-promote the Marvel comic books and build the foundations for an increasingly complex "Marvel universe" of interrelated characters and stories. Of all the Marvel superhero battles, probably none generated more audience interest and speculation than the epic confrontations between the Hulk and the Thing.

the U.S. Army. An unlikely anticommunist crusader, he nevertheless turned his efforts against the Reds on several occasions.[79] Most of Marvel's comic book Communists were stock villains and only generic antagonists in the Cold War, but on rare occasions the Marvel superheroes ventured to Vietnam. A 1965 story found the mighty Thor in South Vietnam aiding the freedom-loving peasants in their fight against the merciless Viet Cong. He rescues a Vietnamese family from the Communists and vows, "I shall return, and when I do, the hammer of Thor shall be heard in every village—in every home—in every heart throughout this tortured land!" Alas, it was an empty gesture; the Thunder God never did return to Vietnam.[80]

The most political of Marvel's superheroes was Iron Man, a hero literally forged on the battlefields of Vietnam. In his first act as a superhero, he demolishes a Viet Cong military base and overthrows a sadistic Communist warlord. As Tony Stark, he serves a vital function in America's military-industrial complex, both as a weapons inventor and a defense contractor. As Iron Man, he foils Communist agents and battles Soviet supervillains in symbolic Cold War contests of power and will. When Iron Man receives a challenge from his Soviet counterpart, the Titanium Man, he must accept it as "a matter of national pride . . . of prestige." The Communists hope that by publicly defeating the armored champion of American capitalism they will score "a propaganda victory from which America will never recover." The mighty adversaries wage a fierce battle over the course of several issues until Iron Man inevitably emerges triumphant, exclaiming, "You picked the wrong enemy this time, mister! You made the worst mistake any Red can make . . . you challenged a foe who isn't afraid of you!" Iron Man's victory underscored America's determination to confront Communist aggression in whatever form it should take.[81]

The Iron Man series showed the extent to which Marvel endorsed Cold War assumptions. There was little room for dissent. As Iron Man once asserted, "No one has the right to defy the wishes of his government! Not even Iron Man!" The hawkish political tone established in the series, especially regarding the Vietnam War, became a source of some embarrassment to Stan Lee in later years. Writing in 1975, Lee explained that at the time these stories were written, "most of us genuinely felt that the conflict in that tortured land really was a simple matter of good versus evil." He hastened to add that "since that time, of course, we've all grown up a bit, we've realized that life isn't quite so simple, and we've been trying to extricate ourselves from the tragic entanglement of Indochina."[82]

Letters to the editor suggested that even as Iron Man and others fought the Communists, the Cold War consensus was cracking among Marvel's readers. One reader warned that Iron Man's brash assault on a Red Chinese air base in a recent issue seemed likely to provoke World War III. Another asked sarcastically if Marvel's membership in the John Birch Society had expired yet. Some letters urged Captain America to go to Vietnam, while others emphatically wanted him to stay out of the conflict. As the Vietnam War escalated and antiwar sentiment spread, Stan Lee gradually reduced the Cold War references in the comic books. Noting the deepening political divisions in the country and the increasing politicization of young people, he concluded by 1968 that Marvel's best policy was to hold the vital center and avoid political commentary of any kind, so as not to alienate either conservatives or liberals, hawks or doves.[83]

From 1962 to 1967, Marvel's average sales figures doubled while those of its competition remained steady or declined. By 1967 its total sales were a close second to DC's. More telling than raw sales, however, was the extent to which Lee's marketing had broadened Marvel's audience. The September 1966 issue of *Esquire* reported on the Marvel phenomenon at college campuses. "Bundles of mail" poured into Marvel's offices every day from more than 225 colleges. Some fifty thousand American college students had paid a dollar each to join Marvel's official fan club, the Merry Marvel Marching Society. Stan Lee himself became a much-requested speaker at colleges and universities like Columbia and New York University. The Princeton Debating Society invited him to speak in a lecture series that also included Senators Hubert Humphrey and Wayne Morse. At Bard College, Lee's lecture outdrew one by Dwight D. Eisenhower.[84]

Why were Marvel comic books so popular on campus? *Esquire* put the question to students around the country. A long-haired student at Southern Illinois University identified with the Hulk because "he's the outcast against the institution." A bearded Stanford University student cited Spider-Man as his favorite because the hero was "beset by woes, money problems, and the question of existence. In short, he is one of us." A 1965 college poll conducted by *Esquire* revealed that student radicals ranked Spider-Man and the Hulk alongside the likes of Bob Dylan and Che Guevara as their favorite revolutionary icons.[85] Stan Lee's enterprise had succeeded beyond even his initial hopes. The outsider hero had arrived as the most celebrated figure in youth culture, and Marvel had him.

Marvel's popularity among older readers also stemmed, at least in part, from revised assumptions about the virtues of popular culture in general. As pop artists like Andy Warhol and Roy Lichtenstein brought cartoons and comics into "serious" art, it became stylish for the young and college-educated to praise the virtues of popular culture products that elites held in contempt. A student could make a fashionable antiestablishment statement not only by reading a Marvel comic book on campus but also by proceeding to analyze it as if it were Sartre. Stan Lee even briefly made an overt and clumsy play for the Warhol audience by printing on all the Marvel covers a pretentious logo announcing "Marvel Pop Art Productions."

Marvel's success took its competitors, especially DC Comics, completely by surprise. DC initially reacted to Marvel's resurgence with bewilderment, disdain, and denial. Among the many clueless theories put forth by the editors was that the key to Marvel's success must have been its "bad art." Artist John Romita, who worked for DC and Marvel, recalled that DC "never knew what was going on. It never dawned on them that in the stories the [Marvel] characters were becoming human. And theirs weren't."[86]

Arnold Drake, who worked as a writer for DC, apparently understood better than his editors why Marvel was doing well. "The antihero was coming on the scene in general," Drake explained. "Marvel was not creating the antihero—the world was creating the antihero, by recognizing that things were not all that black and white—there were a lot of grays." The major difference between the competing publishers was that "Marvel occupied a secondary position and was willing to take chances that DC . . . was not willing to take." Drake recalled that senior DC editors thought that antiheroes were "uncommercial and bad for the house image." Editor Jack Schiff apparently resisted the introduction of moral complexity into superhero characters because he felt it was important to "keep things black and white for kids." Drake urged his supervisers to change direction, for fear the company would "eventually end up aping and mimicking Marvel."[87]

By 1967, DC had begun to do exactly that. DC Comics recruited Steve Ditko from Marvel to help create the Creeper and Hawk and Dove—offbeat superheroes derivative of the Marvel style. That same year, Drake created a series called "Deadman" about a self-absorbed circus performer who returns from the dead to hunt for his own killer. Featured in the title *Strange Adventures* and drawn in an impressively realistic style by a precocious young artist named Neal Adams, "Deadman" was DC's most ambitious attempt yet to appeal to mature readers.

It was evidently too much of a departure for the general market, however; DC discontinued it after less than a year.[88]

Yet even as publishers engaged in intensifying competition for the older market it had lost a decade earlier, television once again overwhelmed their efforts. The *Batman* television series with Adam West and Burt Ward was one of the most popular shows on the air during 1966 and 1967. Played strictly for camp, the show was a parody of comic book superheroes. It poked fun at every convention of superhero comics, from the sheer absurdity of the characters themselves to the goofy "sound effects" (Pow! Bam! Zap!). And, uncomfortably for comic book fans, it also seemed to be making fun of the people who read them. Television's *Batman* was so popular during these two years that it aired twice each week on prime time and boasted an impressive cast of television and film celebrities who lined up to appear on the program.

Although related to the spirit of pop art, the 1960s camp craze behind *Batman* implied a more derisive reading of popular culture and played upon the silliness of the subject at hand. DC Comics and, to a lesser extent, its competition benefited in the short term from the trendy preoccupation with superheroes that the show generated, but in the long run the show probably did more harm than good for the comic book industry. Watched by millions at the time, and millions more over subsequent years in syndication, the show reinforced in the public's mind the silliness and irrelevance of superheroes—and, by implication, comic books—in contemporary culture. With their over-the-top heroism and preposterous morality, these costumed relics seemed anachronistic in a self-consciously cynical time.

The show undermined much of what Stan Lee and Marvel had worked to accomplish. By revising superheros into more believable and appealing outsiders beset by the uncertainties of modern society, Lee had made such characters vital to a generation of adolescents and young adults. In so doing, Marvel had revitalized comic books. Yet if the industry was to thrive, comic book makers would have to demonstrate anew the relevance of their product within the rapidly changing world of their audience.

8

Questioning Authority

Comic Books
and Cultural Change,
1968–1979

The Green Lantern sees an assault in progress. A crowd of angry young men have surrounded a middle-aged gentleman in a business suit. Outraged by this disdain for law and order, the hero rescues the gentleman and teaches the young toughs "a little respect." Then another superhero, the bearded Green Arrow, emerges from the nearby tenements and tells Green Lantern that this affair is none of his business. Confused, the Green Lantern asks his costumed colleague why he is defending these "anarchists." Green Arrow asks him to look around. This is a slum, and the businessman whom Green Lantern has assisted is the "fat cat landlord who owns this dump . . . the creep who hasn't spent a cent for repairs in years" and now plans to evict the tenants so that he can convert their homes into a parking lot. Visibly shaken, Green Lantern defends his position. As an enforcer of law and order, he was only doing his duty. Green Arrow retorts, "Seems like I've heard that line before . . . at the Nazi war trials!" An elderly black man approaches Green Lantern and asks him why, in all of his efforts on behalf of governments and peoples of this and other worlds, he has never made an effort to help black people. Green Lantern has no answer and can only hang his head in shame.[1]

To appreciate the significance of this scene, one must first recall that the modern Green Lantern had begun his superhero crusade over

a decade earlier, at a time when DC's comic books projected a consensus of optimism and confidence in American progress. Green Lantern continued to champion this worldview even as events like the civil
rights struggle and the Vietnam War eroded the consensus. Not coincidentally, *Green Lantern*'s sales eroded at about the same rate. Towards
the end of 1969 editor Julius Schwartz hired writer Dennis O'Neil and
artist Neal Adams from the under-thirty generation, hoping that a
fresh creative perspective might revitalize the series. A politically interested writer with a background in journalism as well as fiction, O'Neil
had been deeply impressed with the work of authors like Norman
Mailer and Tom Wolfe. He wondered if something like their "New
Journalism" could be accomplished successfully in superhero comic
books. O'Neil later explained that while "enormously complex problems couldn't be dissected within a 25-page comic," he hoped that his
work "might awaken youngsters to the world's dilemmas, giving them
an early start so they might find solutions in their maturity." And in the
process, he and Adams hoped to advance the creative and commercial
potential of comic books.[2]

The *Green Lantern/Green Arrow* series immersed its superheroes in
the social and political issues of the times: racism, poverty, political
corruption, the "generation gap," the plight of Native Americans,
pollution, overpopulation, and religious cults. O'Neil cast the Green
Arrow as an impassioned leftist who engaged the moderate-conserva-
tive Green Lantern in one-sided debates laced with overstated rhetoric
about the widening gulf between American ideals and realities. Confronted with the sober realization that his Cold War assumptions have
been a lie, Green Lantern begins to understand that law and order are
less important than truth and justice.[3]

The series succeeded in many respects. Well-written by comic
book standards and beautifully illustrated, it garnered favorable notice
not only within the industry but in the mainstream media as well. The
New York Times, *Wall Street Journal*, and *Newsweek* all cited *Green Lantern* as evidence that comic books were "growing up" by tackling contemporary issues and concerns. *Green Lantern* failed, however, the most
crucial test—sales. For all their ambition and creative achievement,
O'Neil and Adams could not arrest the title's commercial slide.[4] They
wanted their work to reflect the culture of their times, and it did. The
Green Lantern/Green Arrow series sprang from the arching ideals and
hopes of the 1960s, but that idealism would not survive long into the
new decade.

EPILOGUE

GREEN LANTERN OF EARTH! HEED ME--HEED MY *ANGER!* YOU HAVE BEEN *INSUBORDINATE!* YOU DISOBEYED OUR ORDERS!

WE COMMANDED YOU TO REMAIN ON STATION UNTIL WE DECREED YOUR TASK *COMPLETED!*

I...I'M SORRY...

THAT'S RIGHT, *LANTERN...* APOLOGIZE! GROVEL IN FRONT OF THAT WALKING *MUMMY!*

YOU CALL YOURSELF A *HERO!* CHUM...YOU DON'T EVEN QUALIFY AS A *MAN!*

YOU'RE NO MORE THAN A *PUPPET*...AND THE *GUARDIANS* PULL YOUR STRINGS!

LISTEN...*FORGET* ABOUT CHASING AROUND THE *GALAXY!*...AND REMEMBER *AMERICA*...

...IT'S A *GOOD* COUNTRY...BEAUTIFUL ...FERTILE...AND TERRIBLY *SICK!*

THERE ARE CHILDREN DYING... HONEST PEOPLE COWERING IN FEAR...DISILLUSIONED KIDS RIPPING UP CAMPUSES...

ON THE STREETS OF *MEMPHIS* A GOOD *BLACK* MAN DIED...AND IN *LOS ANGELES,* A GOOD *WHITE* MAN FELL...

SOMETHING IS *WRONG!* SOMETHING IS *KILLING* US ALL...! SOME HIDEOUS MORAL CANCER IS ROTTING OUR *VERY SOULS!*

21

Comic Books and Youth Politics

Youth culture played a major part in reflecting and affecting the up-heavals of the 1960s. Young people waged the Vietnam War and pro-tested against it. At the vanguard of the movements for civil rights, black power, feminism, the New Left, and the counterculture were ide-alistic and angry young people determined to transform society by as-saulting "the establishment." While popular memory has tended to ex-aggerate the extent of the 1960s social revolt, it was nevertheless very real. Although only a minority of young people counted themselves as active members of social and political movements, many more came to view themselves as part of a generation that was morally and materially distinct from that of their parents. Indeed, much of the generation gap was actually personal and material, reflected more in lifestyle, fashion, and entertainment choices than in politics. Dustin Hoffman's character in the Oscar-winning movie *The Graduate* (1967) embodied the deep alienation that many young people felt towards traditional middle-class mores and aspirations.[5] The quest for an alternative led some into poli-tics but launched many more on a quest for personal fulfillment on their own terms. As the culture of subsequent decades would demon-strate, 1960s activism could not compete very long with the narcissistic forces liberated at the same historical moment.

Young people at that time certainly had the numbers to force sweeping cultural change. By the end of the 1960s, baby boomers in their teens and twenties constituted the largest market demographic in the nation, and protest and dissent became marketable commodities. Hollywood exploited the demand created by young people's dissatisfac-tion with remarkably successful films like *The Graduate* (1967), *Bonnie and Clyde* (1967), and *Easy Rider* (1969). But no enterprise understood and exploited youth preoccupations as well as the rock-and-roll music industry. The music itself had developed and matured a great deal since the beginning of the decade, encompassing a wide range of ambitious lyrical and musical ideas. Artists in folk-rock, psychedelic-rock, and soul music challenged their audiences to take the music as a call to

From "No Evil Shall Escape My Sight," *Green Lantern* 76 (DC Comics, April 1970). As a young and ambitious generation of comic book creators entered the field in the late 1960s, superheroes like DC's Green Lantern and Green Arrow spoke passionately to the political and social upheavals of the time. Script by Dennis O'Neil, art by Neal Adams.

social and political activism. Groups like the Doors and Jefferson Airplane fused rock music with radical politics and cultural revolution. Even pop artists like Elvis Presley, Bobby Darin, and Paul Revere and the Raiders recorded relevant "message" songs.[6] All the while, the music industry reaped a financial windfall by marketing rock-and-roll rebellion. As political upheaval met the consumer economy, youth dissention became increasingly commodified.

The comic book industry underwent some important changes of its own in the late 1960s. Both Marvel and DC became corporate properties. Martin Goodman sold Marvel to the Perfect Film and Chemical Corporation, later renamed Cadence Industries, and DC became the property of Warner Communications.[7] By 1968 Marvel's annual comic book sales of 55 million were enough to challenge DC for the industry's lead. Marvel ended its restrictive distribution deal with DC's Independent News Company and signed instead with the Curtis Circulation Company. Marvel's new sales clout and flexible distribution enabled it to expand and launch a number of new titles.[8] Still, Marvel overestimated the strength of the market. In 1969 comic book sales slumped throughout the industry. The superhero craze generated by the *Batman* television show had crested, and rising inflation in the war-heated economy compelled publishers to raise the price of comic books from twelve to fifteen cents each, further hurting sales.

Looking to boost sagging sales, Marvel and DC redoubled their efforts to interest young people in their products. Marvel's "antiestablishment" superheroes and company image gave it a decided advantage. While the publisher's ties to the counterculture were tenuous at best, Marvel still won a measure of hip credibility that eluded the more established DC. In 1968 a full-page advertisement appeared in Marvel comic books for an album by the underground rock band the Mothers of Invention; Peter Fonda's character in the counterculture film *Easy Rider* went by the name of Captain America; folk-singer Jerry Jeff Walker recorded a song called "Ballad of the Hulk" for his *Mr. Bojangles* album; and a full-color illustration of the Hulk, drawn by Marvel artist Herb Trimpe, adorned the 30 September 1971 issue of *Rolling Stone*. Although some of these appropriations were presumably meant to be ironic, they nevertheless betrayed a genuine affection for Marvel's super antiheroes.[9]

Marvel further exaggerated the disaffection of its superheroes by setting their adventures in the increasingly violent cultural upheavals of the late 1960s. Having long been hounded by the media and the police, Spider-Man reaches his breaking point in 1969. Clenching his

fist, he exclaims, "No matter what I do . . . nothing ever changes! The
more I try to help the law . . . the more they hunt me . . . the more they
hate me!" So he concludes, "I'm through being a public fall guy! From
now on . . . it's Spidey against the world! If they call me a menace . . .
and treat me like a menace . . . I might as well be a menace!" Similarly,
the Hulk's ongoing conflict with the U.S. Army intensified. The cover
of the October 1969 issue shows the Hulk under full-scale attack by
America's armed forces, with the Army commander shouting, "Kill
him! Kill the Hulk!" The dull-witted Hulk does not understand why
the authorities hate him, but he understands and prizes freedom. "Hulk
has been in chains before," he warns. "Before he is chained again . . . he
will destroy the army . . . the world!" Although driven to rage and even
violence by the harassment of authorities, the Marvel heroes maintain
their resolve to help society, remaining essentially idealistic figures.[10]

Perhaps the purest expression of this heroism in the face of adversity was Marvel's *Silver Surfer*. Created by Stan Lee and Jack Kirby in
1965, the Silver Surfer received his own title when Marvel expanded
its line in 1968. The notion of a shiny silver being from another planet
flying through the cosmos on a surfboard sounds ridiculous, but, in
fact, this was an unusually humorless series. The Silver Surfer first
comes to Earth as an advance scout for the planet-devouring entity
called Galactus. Having fallen under the spell of the Earth's beauty and
humanity's courage, the Surfer turns against Galactus and saves the
planet. As punishment for his insubordination, Galactus creates an energy barrier that prevents the Surfer from leaving Earth's atmosphere.
Now a prisoner on this alien world, the Surfer soon learns that there is
much about humanity that is not admirable. No matter where he goes
or what he does to aid human civilization, he is repaid with fear and
animosity. Yet, like a Christ figure sent to save the people of Earth, the
Surfer bears his cross and endures his lonely obligation.[11]

Stan Lee applied his most ambitious prose to the series and used
the Silver Surfer's existentialist observations to comment upon the
promise and tragedy of human civilization, raising consciousness about
racism, war, and environmental destruction along the way. Although
the series won a loyal following among older readers and became a
discussed topic on college radio stations, it was all probably too cerebral
for the core comic book audience. A twenty-five cent price tag did not
help. Marvel canceled the series after several years, and Lee noted its
premature end with great disappointment, citing *Silver Surfer* as one of
his favorites.[12]

Confronted with the undeniable success of Marvel's approach, DC

finally made a concerted effort to respond in kind. In 1969 the company ended its decentralized editorial department, united all of its titles under the direction of artist-editor Carmine Infantino, and charged him with revitalizing DC's line much like Lee had done for Marvel. Infantino brought in a new generation of creative talent and encouraged them to experiment with new ideas and twists for the DC characters. Most of these "new" ideas were actually clumsy imitations of the Marvel style. Dennis O'Neil and Neal Adams did the most innovative work at DC during this period, revitalizing *Green Lantern* and helping to restore *Batman*'s image. In a deliberate effort to separate the *Batman* comic books from the television show, they returned the character to his original incarnation as a grim avenger of the night. Although *Batman* remained among the company's best-sellers, its sales fell steadily along with most other DC titles. No longer the preeminent comic book publisher, DC now struggled to keep pace with Marvel, both creatively and commercially.[13]

Both publishers felt compelled to address the political and social concerns that seemed to interest young people. The 2 May 1971 issue of the *New York Times Magazine* ran a lengthy and favorable article on the comic book industry, explaining how comic books of recent years had matured. No longer a crude medium of childhood fantasies, the story went, comic books now featured more sophisticated themes and images, which readers of various ages could appreciate on different levels. They dealt with pressing issues like the Vietnam War, civil rights, feminism, and environmentalism. The *Wall Street Journal* and *Newsweek* also noted these developments, though with a measure of bemusement. The media catchword for the trend was *relevance*.[14] Relevance was hardly a new development in comic books, which had, of course, always related closely to the events and concerns of their times. What the media actually noticed as "relevance" was a proliferation of self-consciously leftist comic book explorations of political and social issues. Ironically, the last time that comic books had presented a social critique like this, public and official outrage had prompted the industry to censor itself. Times had changed to such an extent that comic books now garnered praise in the media for questioning old assumptions

Cover of *The Silver Surfer* 1 (Marvel Comics, August 1968). Confined to Earth after rescuing it from the planet-devouring entity called Galactus, Marvel's Christlike Silver Surfer bore his cross as a savior of mankind, even though people distrusted and persecuted him. As written by Stan Lee, the Surfer was prone to existentialist musings and outraged moralizing on such human maladies as war, environmental destruction, and famine. Art by John Buscema.

and challenging established authorities instead of endorsing traditional American values.

The relevance movement in comic books stemmed in part from the publishers' commercial imperative to innovate at a time of slumping sales. Taking their cue from recent trends of youth culture, comic book makers concluded that there was a sizable demand for entertainment that had something meaningful and political to say about the world. A number of young writers and artists also shared an earnest desire to reflect and affect issues that concerned them. The young individuals who entered the field after 1968 had been raised on a twin diet of 1960s idealism and Marvel comic books, a cultural pedigree that inspired them to challenge conventions. While most of their predecessors had approached comic book work as either a stepping-stone or a last resort, most of the new writers and artists entered the field as fans with career ambitions in the industry. Many had unprecedented artistic and literary aspirations for the medium. Not since the heyday of EC Comics had writers and artists felt so emboldened to push commercial comic books in so many new and challenging directions. Dennis O'Neil later recalled that during this period, "there was a feeling that we were taking an art form, a minor art form but an art form, and advancing it." They felt that they "were doing the best stuff that had been done . . . opening whole new vistas and . . . coming up with new ideas and new places to go and new things to try."[15] Some of these new ideas—like similar efforts undertaken in film and music—degenerated into overwrought and self-indulgent exercises of little artistic or commercial consequence, but others stood as a thoughtful and innovative body of work that advanced the creative possibilities of comic books and offered some illustrative documents of an American culture in crisis.

From his high-school beginnings to his entry into college life, Spider-Man remained the superhero most relevant to the world of young people. Fittingly then, his comic book also contained some of the earliest references to the politics of young people. In 1968, in the wake of actual militant student demonstrations at Columbia University, Peter Parker finds himself in the midst of similar unrest at his Empire State University. The students demonstrate against the university administration's decision to convert an empty building into an expensive hotel for visiting alumni instead of a low-rent dormitory for minority students. Peter has to reconcile his natural sympathy for the students with his assumed obligation to combat lawlessness as Spider-Man. As a law-upholding liberal, he finds himself caught between militant leftists and angry conservatives. Peter refuses to join the demonstration and wants to hear the dean's side of the story before he takes a stand himself. When radical students berate him for "chickening out" and not "getting involved," he retorts, "Anyone can paint a sign, mister! That doesn't make you right!" Yet as Peter leaves, he thinks to himself, "My sympathies are all with the kids." He simply does not want to be pushed around by anyone, no matter what their cause is. Ultimately, his moderate approach is vindicated when the administrators meet with the students and assure them that they had always intended to use the building for the benefit of low-income and minority students. The dean admits though that he was mistaken in thinking that "students should be seen and not heard." A young black student adds that he too has learned a valuable lesson. Acknowledging the dean's genuine concern for students, the young man realizes, "Sometimes it isn't easy to tell . . . who your real friends are."[16]

Superheroes like Spider-Man endorsed liberal solutions to social problems while rejecting the extreme and violent responses of both the left and the right—an ironic position to assume, since superheroes tacitly endorsed violent means to solve problems every time they slugged it out with the bad guys. Nevertheless, in an American society facing deepening political divisions, Marvel's superheroes worked to preserve what remained of the vital center.

DC's superheroes tended to take the same position. In one *Batman* story, a group of student leftists resembling the real-life radicals the Weathermen occupy an office building and threaten to blow it up unless the city converts it into low-rent housing. Batman stops them and explains that, while he sympathizes with the students' cause, he cannot condone their violent methods. When Batman's young partner Robin attends college, he too struggles to hold a moderate political course. While investigating the bombing of an ROTC building, Robin gets caught in the middle of a violent clash between the leftist Students for Democratic Action and right-wing fraternity jocks. He calls the groups "two of a kind," because they both use violence instead of civil dialogue to advance their views. Summing up the plight of a liberal superhero in these troubled times, Robin laments, "Politically both the radical left and the reactionary right consider me an enemy . . . while those in the middle and those who don't care . . . distrust me!" He meets a policeman who similarly explains, "To sick and fed-up students, I'm nothing more than a head-busting Establishment pig! To sick and fed-up townspeople, I'm too permissive in combating long-haired anarchist lawbreakers!" Robin sees the violence committed by both sides as "an easy

way out to the powerlessness that many people feel today," but he deplores it nonetheless as a "cancer" eating at society.[17]

Comic books advocated liberal solutions to racial issues as well. After years of relative silence on civil rights, comic books in the late 1960s began to address racial concerns with some regularity. Alienated superheroes like the Hulk and the Silver Surfer especially empathized with African Americans. The green Hulk befriends an impoverished black teenager and explains to him, "World hates us . . . both of us! . . . Because we're different!" Yet comic books also made it clear that militant black power was not the remedy for racial injustice. The leader of the aforementioned student demonstration at Peter Parker's university is a black student who justifies militancy, proclaiming, "We ain't never gonna get nowhere . . . until we kinda shake Whitey up a little!" Also participating in the demonstration is a young African American man named Randy Robertson, whose father happens to be the city editor of a leading New York newspaper. The elder Robertson sympathizes completely with the cause of the demonstrators but does not endorse their tactics. He wants to see young African Americans concentrate more on getting an education and fighting for civil rights reforms within the system. But his son explains, "I have to be tougher. . . . I have to be more militant . . . because of you! You've become part of the . . . White Man's establishment! I've gotta live that down!" Other demonstrators call the elder Robertson an "Uncle Tom," but his moderate approach ultimately proves to be the correct one.[18]

After having debuted the first African superhero several years earlier, in 1969 Marvel introduced the first African American superhero, the Falcon. Initially a supporting character in the *Captain America* series, the Falcon eventually became Captain America's full partner and shared billing with him. In his civilian identity, the Falcon is a Harlem social worker named Sam Wilson who endorses a liberal civil rights agenda but rejects black separatism. He encourages young people to

From "Crisis on Campus," *The Amazing Spider-Man* 68 (Marvel Comics, January 1969). Peter Parker occupied an uncomfortable place in the student revolts of the 1960s, as Marvel Comics struggled to stay hip to leftist trends in youth culture without alienating conservative readers. Parker rejected the extremism of the left and the right. Yet, however noncommittal he may have seemed, scenes like this indicated that his sympathies clearly rested with the advocates for social reform. Script by Stan Lee, art by John Romita and Jim Mooney.

stay in school and use their education as the best means to break out of the cycle of poverty. His girlfriend, on the other hand, is a black power militant who claims that "we don't need no more social workers to give our people pride!" Wilson counters that "it's a lot easier to get that pride when you've got a job—and you're savin' some bread!" Privately, Wilson admits, "I ain't sayin' we don't need to make it hot for the ones who been steppin' on us for years," but, he adds, "maybe it's just as important for some of us to cool things down—so we can protect the rights we been fightin' for!" Wilson's cautious position is shown to be the wise one, as his girlfriend's so-called black power organization later stands revealed as a bogus front for a criminal gang run by the Nazi Red Skull.[19]

In a 1970 *Daredevil* story, a gang similar to the Black Panthers accuses a black Vietnam veteran of waging a "white man's war." The veteran retorts, "I don't dig the war any more than the next brother . . . but I figure there's better ways to protest it than to join a hate-crew like you!" He adds that "nobody with half a brain is gonna fall for that 'white man's war' jazz you guys preach!" The gang then attacks the black veteran, calling him an Uncle Tom. The ironically named superhero Black Panther rescues the soldier and warns that, in these divisive times, it is important to recognize the difference between a dissenter and a criminal.[20]

While comic books were careful to sympathize with the cause, if not the means, of leftist groups, they simply vilified those on the right. A two-part Spider-Man story from 1970 introduced Sam Bullit, a former police officer campaigning for New York District Attorney on a law and order platform. Boasting that he "never had any time for liberals, or bleeding hearts, or big-talkin' long-haired do-gooders," he warns the silent majority of New York that "society today is at war . . . with the left-wing anarchists who are trying to destroy this great, proud nation of ours! We need strength . . . to punish those who mock the law!" Besides being an ugly and thoroughly despicable character, Bullit is also an outright crook with ties to organized crime. Spider-Man exposes him as such at the end of the story and gives the politician's disillusioned supporters cause to reflect upon the difference between "law and order" and justice.[21]

A 1970 story in *Daredevil*, appearing at the time of the Chicago Seven conspiracy trial, introduced a villain called the Tribune, a self-styled judge, jury, and executioner who preys upon antiwar demonstrators, draft-dodgers, and anyone else whom he judges to be a "Commie pinko." Almost simultaneously, DC's Green Lantern and Green Arrow

found themselves captured and put on trial by an alien kangaroo court
on trumped-up charges of conspiracy.[22] Such negative caricatures of
American authority figures had not been seen in comic books since
1954, before the comics code explicitly forbade such presentations.
Given these trends, conflict with the code authority was inevitable.

Unexpectedly, the pretext for revising the comics code came not
from the young liberals creating comic books but from the Nixon administration's Department of Health, Education, and Welfare. In 1970
the department sent Stan Lee a letter, asking him to incorporate an
antidrug message into one of Marvel's leading titles. Lee wove a cautionary message on the dangers of drug use into a three-part story appearing in its top-selling *The Amazing Spider-Man* title. In one of the
opening scenes, a young African American man who is "stoned right
out of his mind" walks off a rooftop believing that he can fly. Spider-
Man rescues the youth and leaves him in the care of sympathetic police
officers. As the hero departs, he thinks, "Any drug strong enough to
give you that kind of trip—can damage your brain—but bad!" Another
young black man who witnesses the scene clenches his fist and says,
"Man, this drug scene really bugs me! . . . Everyone figures it's the black
man's bag—but it ain't! We're the ones who hate it the most! It hurts
us more than anyone else," he explains, "'cause too many of us got no
hope—so we're easier pickins for the pushers! But it ain't just our problem," he says to the gathering crowd of white onlookers, "it's yours
too!"[23]

As the story develops, Peter Parker's best friend starts "popping
pills" in order to escape depression after being jilted by his girlfriend.
Then, in a memorable scene, Peter confronts the drug dealers supplying his friend and thrashes them without even bothering to change into
his Spider-Man costume. As the pushers drift into unconsciousness,
Peter warns them, "If I ever see you pushing that stuff—anywhere
again—you'll think this was just a playful picnic!"[24] The story presented a clear antidrug message, and it did so effectively in an exciting
adventure story without appearing preachy or judgmental. But the
comics code forbade any depiction or mention of drugs, so the code
office rejected it. Confident in the moral tone of the story and the sales
clout of Spider-Man, Lee issued the comic books anyway. They made
it to the newsstands as usual and sold well even without the seal of
approval. Rival publishers were upset by Lee's audacious move, but
many agreed that it was time to revise the code.[25]

Some of the younger comic book creators wanted to scrap the code
altogether, but in the end the publishers reached a compromise, agree-

ing to leave it in place and add liberalized provisions. These revisions emerged from a wrenching decade that had seen a highly controversial war, widespread demonstrations, racial conflict, assassinations, generation gaps, and political credibility gaps that made the feared horror comic books of the early 1950s seem rather quaint by comparison. Any adolescent exposed to the evening news knew of such things as the 1968 Chicago police riot, the My Lai massacre, the Kent State killings, and the Pentagon Papers. Readers could suspend disbelief in order to accept that a man could fly or stick to walls, but the code's persistence in the fiction that authority never erred was taking things too far, and it insulted the awareness of young people. So, the publishers amended the code to allow for the portrayal of corrupt police, judges, government officials, and similar "respected institutions." Other revisions permitted greater latitude in the presentation of moral ambiguity, drug and alcohol use, and dress. Even monsters were once again allowed in comic books, as long as they were presented in a tasteful manner.[26] In truth, the comics code henceforth permitted almost any situation that was not overly gruesome, offensive, or obscene. Creators still exercised restraint, but the liberalized code produced some immediate changes. In a not-very-subtle emulation of Marvel's antidrug stories, DC promptly issued a *Green Lantern* comic book with a cover depicting a superhero about to plunge a heroin needle into his arm.[27] Both major publishers also launched new horror and monster series. Yet none of these indulged in the gory excesses of their 1950s predecessors, and few sold well.

Comic Books and the Crisis of Authority

The revised code gave comic book makers the latitude to deal more honestly with controversial issues like the Vietnam War. As popular support for the war declined after 1968, comic books evinced a measure of qualified dissent. Some letters to the editor suggested that Peter Parker ought to enlist and go to Vietnam, but Stan Lee answered these by noting that Marvel had received fan mail "about equally divided" between those who loved and those who loathed Vietnam War stories. So Marvel made it a policy to generally avoid the war. Still, the issue was too large to ignore entirely. In a 1970 issue of *The Amazing Spider-Man*, Peter Parker's friend Flash Thompson leaves for a tour of duty in Vietnam. As Peter bids Flash farewell, he wonders to himself, "Which is worse? Staying behind while other guys are doing the fighting . . . or fighting in a war that nobody wants . . . against an enemy you don't even hate?" When Flash returns a few years later, he is morose and guilt-ridden over his part in a war that has caused so much suffering to innocent Vietnamese.[28]

Iron Man's background in the military-industrial complex made his series a most appropriate vehicle for commentary on the politics of the war and changing Cold War assumptions. Once a strident Cold Warrior, Iron Man underwent a dramatic political conversion after 1968. The symbolic Cold War confrontations that had dominated the series all but disappeared. Even when Soviet foes like the Crimson Dynamo returned to menace the hero, they did so only as deranged villains with no political agenda. Iron Man began to work less closely with the U.S. government and more for the American people. Instead of fighting Communists, he turned his attention towards social problems like racism, poverty, and pollution. As a liberal, he also resisted radical means to resolve these issues. The alternative philosophy is posed by Iron Man's foe, the Firebrand. Once an "all-American boy" who had demonstrated peacefully against injustice until he was "spat on by bigots" and "beat on by 'patriots,'" Firebrand now incites violent demonstrations on campus because, he concludes, "The only way to build anything decent is to tear down what's here and start over!"[29]

Political debate consumed the letters page in *Iron Man*. Some readers expressed more sympathy for the militant Firebrand than for the moderate Iron Man. One pointed out that "while Firebrand was marching, trying to bring about a more peaceful world, Stark Industries was probably building weapons for Vietnam where we 'destroyed a city in order to save it!'" Another reader warned that as a munitions manufacturer, Iron Man was "going to have to do some pretty big restructuring of his life to avoid being classified as an enemy of the people." One letter simply condemned the superhero as a "profiteering, capitalist, war-mongering pig." Many others concurred that Iron Man should at least stop manufacturing weapons of war. Published letters from liberals far outnumbered those from conservatives, who complained that the series had already moved too far to the left.[30]

Bowing to the liberal consensus, Iron Man spoke out more strongly against the right-wing establishment. In 1971 he argued with a conservative senator who condemns young demonstrators as a "new breed of people . . . who want to destroy the government that made America great!" The superhero who, several years earlier, had insisted that no one had the right to defy their government, now retorted that it is the American people and not the government that makes the country great. For that, the senator calls Iron Man an "anarchist." Later, rock-throwing student demonstrators picket Iron Man's munitions factory,

DOESN'T *SEEM* THAT LONG AGO--

--OR *DOES IT,* AVENGER?

A *LOT* HAS HAPPENED SINCE THEN... ONE *HECK* OF A *LOT!*

STARK INDUSTRIES, ONE OF THE WORLD'S *FOREMOST MUNITIONS* MANUFACTURERS, HAS GIVEN WAY TO *STARK INTERNATIONAL*--

--WHOSE BUSINESS IS *PEACE,* PURE AND SIMPLE, AND A *BETTER-MENT* OF MAN THROUGH *TECHNOLOGY!*

AND WHAT ABOUT *YOU,* TONY STARK? ONCE YOU WERE *DO OR DIE* FOR AMERICA AND *MOM'S APPLE PIE!* YOU DIDN'T DO MUCH *SOUL-SEARCHING* BACK THEN, DID YOU?

AS *IRON MAN* YOU BEAT THE *COMMIES* FOR DEMOCRACY WITHOUT EVER *QUESTIONING* JUST *WHOSE* DE-MOCRACY YOU WERE *SERVING*--

--OR JUST *WHAT* THOSE YOU SERVED INTENDED TO *DO* WITH THE WORLD ONCE YOU'D *SAVED IT* FOR THEM! *VIET NAM* RAISED *ALL* THOSE QUESTIONS, DIDN'T IT, TONY?

DIDN'T IT?

"LIKE: 'WHAT *RIGHT* HAD WE TO BE THERE IN THE *FIRST PLACE?'*

HEY YOU *MUD-HUGGERS!* LOOK!!

HOLY SPIT! IT'S *IRON MAN!*

WONDER WHAT *HE'S* DOIN' HERE?

"EVEN IF WE COULD'VE ANSWERED *THAT* QUESTION, I WAS STILL LEFT WITH SOME OF MY *OWN*...

2

and panicked security guards fire on them. Cries of "It's another Kent State!" erupt from the crowd. Iron Man intervenes to help the demonstrators but scolds them for "preaching peace while resorting to violence." The students insist that this is the only way that they can make the older generation hear them. Soon thereafter Iron Man turns completely against the Vietnam War and terminates his industry's weapons division, resolving to commit its resources to consumer goods and environmental protection instead.[31]

Iron Man began his superhero crusade as a self-assured champion of Communist containment, but it is a far more reflective and troubled superhero who ponders the meaning of Vietnam in 1975. The poignant story titled "Long Time Gone" opens with Iron Man sitting alone in his office, engaged in conversation with himself. He recalls how he "beat the Commies for democracy without ever questioning" the wisdom of his leaders. Now, thinking of Vietnam, he wonders, "what right had we to be there in the first place?" He flashes back to an incident in Vietnam, when he witnessed American weaponry of his own design lay waste to an entire village, killing enemy and innocent alike. Moved to tears by the carnage, Iron Man had buried the dead in a mass grave and marked it with the searching epitaph, "WHY?" Then, returning to the present, Iron Man strikes a dramatic pose and recommits himself to the role of hero, pledging to "avenge those whose lives have been lost through the ignorance of men like the man I once was!"[32]

As the upheavals of the 1960s weakened respect for traditional authorities and fostered national self-doubt, superheroes came to question their own authority and purpose. Story titles asked "Why must there be an Iron Man?" and even "Must there be a Superman?"[33] Speaking to the decline of traditional "heroes," writer Marv Wolfman created an intriguing villain called the Hangman in Marvel's *Werewolf by Night*. Conditioned as a child by John Wayne movies into seeing the

From "Long Time Gone," *Iron Man* 78 (Marvel Comics, September 1975). Once an ardent Cold Warrior, Iron Man's unquestioning support for U.S. anticommunist policies was shaken by the Vietnam War. The Vietnam experience—and a new generation of liberal comic book writers—also caused superheroes like Iron Man, Captain America, and Green Lantern to question their own moral authority and purpose. Script by Bill Mantlo, art by George Tuska and Vince Colletta.

world in terms of moral absolutes, the Hangman reacts to the "creeping permissiveness" of contemporary society by launching a personal vigilante crusade to root out and execute social deviants. Fancying himself a traditional hero in the John Wayne mold, he kidnaps independent-minded women and places them in bondage, believing that by doing so he is "protecting" them. The Hangman elicited a series of partisan letters from readers. One took exception to this "Eastern Liberal" portrayal of an all-American hero as a homicidal psychopath. Marvel defended their characterization, retorting that "the so-called all-American hero was, to our collective mind, a myth, a fabrication . . . and not a wholly civilized one at that." The Hangman was appropriately a villain because, as Marvel insisted, anyone who moved through society disguising their intolerance as morality was a far greater menace than the nonconformists whom he persecuted.[34] So complete was the cultural transformation of these years that a comic book could feature as its hero a werewolf with extremely antisocial tendencies while casting as its villain a professed champion of traditional moral values. The nation was indeed heading into some strange new cultural territory.

Perhaps more than any other superhero, Marvel's Captain America bore the burden of these political and cultural changes. As a sworn champion of patriotic values, Captain America had to determine what those values now meant. What was to be his role in the Vietnam era and beyond? Readers and creators alike recognized the symbolic significance of the question. As President Johnson sent U.S. troops to Vietnam in 1965, readers wrote to Marvel suggesting that Captain America ought to go as well. Others asked that he stay out. He stayed home, and the controversy over his meaning intensified in later years. While Captain America said little about Vietnam, the letters to the editor became a forum for prowar and antiwar readers to debate political issues having little or nothing to do with the stories in the comic books. Some readers called upon Captain America to abandon his allegiance to "the establishment." One argued that "it would fit the standards of today" if he was "more liberal." Another insisted that Captain America's blind patriotism was anachronistic. Stan Lee affirmed that the great majority of readers polled by Marvel wanted the hero to stay out of Vietnam. In 1971 he wrote that Captain America "simply doesn't lend himself to the John Wayne-type character he once was" and added that he could not "see any of our characters taking on a role of super-patriotism in the world as it is today."[35]

In the early 1970s Captain America reflected a nation weary of

Cold War adventures and consumed with social problems. Assisted by his African American superhero partner, the Falcon, Captain America waged a campaign against poverty, racism, pollution, and political corruption. In a multipart story written by Steve Englehart, Captain America took his crusade for justice all the way to the White House.[36] Running throughout 1973 and 1974, as the Watergate scandal unraveled, Englehart's multi-issue storyline made abundant and overt references to the Nixon administration. Captain America discovers that an organization called the Committee to Regain America's Principles (CRAP), led by a right-winger named Quentin Harderman (who bears a strong resemblance to H. R. Haldeman) is actually a front for the Secret Empire, a fascist organization bent upon taking control of the U.S. government. The hero follows a labyrinth of political conspiracies, assassinations, and cover-ups that ultimately leads him to the White House and the Oval Office itself. Although the lanky villain's face is obscured by shadows, there is little doubt as to his identity. Captain America gasps, "Good lord! You!" From the shadows, the villain answers, "Exactly! But high political office didn't satisfy me! My power was still too constrained by legalities!" Then, in what may have been a bit of wishful thinking on Englehart's part, the crook commits suicide, leaving Captain America in silent disillusionment. "This man trusted the country of his birth," reads the caption. Now, "Like millions of Americans each in his own way, he has seen his trust mocked! And this man is Captain America." For several issues thereafter, the hero dropped his patriotic name and called himself "Nomad, the man without a country." Yet after saying "nuts to the whole blamed Washington crew," he resumes his identity as Captain America and pledges to reclaim the ideals of America, which its leaders have trampled upon.[37]

Turning Inward and Reaching Out

By the middle of the 1970s readers and creators alike seemed to have concluded that crusades to bring about a more just society had taken superheroes too far from their basic appeal as escapist entertainment. Comic book makers interpreted declining sales as a signal that superheroes ought to spend less time proselytizing and more time punching. Some politically inclined writers like Steve Gerber, Steve Englehart, and Bill Mantlo did continue to address social issues in their comic books. Published from 1976 to 1979, Gerber's *Howard the Duck*, for instance, satirized political issues through the exploits of an extraterrestrial cigar-chomping duck and Gerber's own absurdist humor.[38] Aside

I'M LIKE A *DINOSAUR*--IN THE *CRO-MAGNON* AGE! AN *ANACHRONISM*--WHO'S *OUT LIVED* HIS TIME!

THIS IS THE DAY OF THE *ANTI-HERO*--THE AGE OF THE *REBEL*--AND THE *DISSENTER!*

IT ISN'T *HIP*--TO *DEFEND* THE *ESTABLISHMENT!*

--ONLY TO TEAR IT *DOWN!*

DRES

AND, IN A WORLD RIFE WITH *INJUSTICE*, *GREED*, AND *ENDLESS WAR*--

WHO'S TO SAY THE REBELS ARE *WRONG?*

BUT, I'VE NEVER LEARNED TO *PLAY* BY TODAY'S NEW RULES!

DRUGS

I'VE SPENT A *LIFETIME* DEFENDING THE FLAG--AND THE *LAW!*

PERHAPS--I SHOULD HAVE BATTLED *LESS*--AND *QUESTIONED* MORE!

3

CONTINUED AFTER NEXT PAGE

from these and other occasional exceptions, however, comic books of the later 1970s generally eschewed the self-conscious social commentary of their Vietnam-era predecessors.

Still, comic books clearly reflected deep cultural changes and a maturing audience. The writing and artwork became more sophisticated, as publishers took greater creative risks to interest discerning adolescent and adult readers, albeit with occasionally disastrous commercial consequences. Engaging, thoughtful, and highly literate series like Marvel's *Tomb of Dracula* and *Warlock* and DC's *Swamp Thing* found a devoted audience of older readers but failed to reach the kind of general market needed to make them profitable. Confronting an inflationary economy, choking distribution problems, and a shrinking audience, comic book makers spent most of the 1970s casting about for new ideas.

Publishers took some inspiration from the awakening of multiculturalism and the transformation of popular assumptions about race and gender. In 1972, on Stan Lee's initiative, Marvel took a chance with a new kind of black superhero. *Luke Cage, Hero for Hire* featured an African American superhero who had greater "street credibility" than his predecessors. While the Black Panther was a stately African prince and the Falcon was a middle-class social worker, Luke Cage was a lower-class black man from the ghetto. Inspired by recent "blaxploitation" films like *Shaft* (1971) and *Super Fly* (1972), Cage's adventures took place in an inner-city underworld of pimps, drug-dealers, poverty, and white harassment. Framed, sent to prison, and abused by sadistic white guards, Cage is subjected to a secret government chemical experiment that unexpectedly endows him with superhuman strength and invulnerability. He uses his new powers to break out of prison, clear his name, and begin a career as a "hero for hire," willing to work within or outside of the law for a price. A young African American artist named Billy Graham assisted with the illustration and occasionally the scripts, but white creators conceived and wrote the series. The earliest issues stayed with the morally ambivalent premise of the character, who harbored a well-founded suspicion of white society, but after a few years of sluggish sales Marvel renamed the series *Power Man* and recast the charac-

From "The Sting of the Scorpion," *Captain America* 122 (Marvel Comics, February 1970). The Vietnam War and social revolts of the 1960s led Captain America to reassess his meaning as a patriotic symbol. Script by Stan Lee, art by Gene Colan and Joe Sinnott.

ter as a more conventional superhero. Never among Marvel's better
selling titles, this initial effort at a leading African American superhero
still lasted into the 1980s.[39]

Other comic book efforts to introduce minority superheroes met
with moderate to minimal commercial results. Marvel's *Black Goliath*
debuted in 1975 and promptly went nowhere. DC's first African American superhero series, *Black Lightning*, did not debut until 1977, and it
lasted less than two years. That same year, Marvel introduced the
White Tiger, the first Hispanic superhero, but he remained only a limited supporting character in Spider-Man's comic books. Marvel's first
Native American superhero, Red Wolf, lasted only nine issues. While
Red Wolf's adventures were set in the Old West and transpired outside
the Marvel universe, the publisher's second Native American hero,
Thunderbird, was a founding member of the new X-Men. Cast as an
angry young man who was deeply hostile towards white society, Thunderbird fought constantly—even with his own white teammates. Then,
in a highly unusual move, the series' creators killed him off after only
three appearances. Capitalizing on the popular kung-fu craze, Marvel
then launched *Master of Kung Fu*, featuring a Chinese hero named
Shang-chi. Running from 1974 to 1983, this became the most successful of the titles featuring nonwhite heroes.[40]

None of these efforts achieved commercial results comparable to
similar titles featuring white superheroes, nor did any break completely
from racial stereotypes despite well-meaning intentions. Tony Isabella,
one of the few black writers working in the field at the time, explained
that even open-minded white writers found it difficult to portray minority characters in a way that was not offensive or patronizing. Meanwhile, Marvel writer-editor Roy Thomas believed that the problem had
more to do more with the market than the creators. He regretted that

Cover of *Luke Cage, Hero for Hire* 1 (Marvel Comics, June 1972). Marvel's efforts to introduce African American, Native American, Asian, and Latino superheroes during the 1970s yielded only marginal commercial results. Luke Cage was the first African American superhero to be featured in his own comic book, but he failed to attract the sizable audience enjoyed by his white superhero peers. Art by John Romita.

"you could get blacks to buy comics about whites, but it was hard to get whites to buy comics in which the main character was black."[41]

For decades comic book creators had presumed that the audience for superheroes was overwhelmingly male. There had been many female superheroes over the years, but most of these seemed targeted more at adolescent male lusts than at discerning female readers. And very few successful series featured women on their own. Acknowledging that most superheroes and most comic book readers were male, Stan Lee wondered, "do less females read comics because they seem to be aimed at a male audience, or are they aimed at a male audience because less females read them?"[42] Clearly uncomfortable writing for females, the men who created comic books simply had a greater feel for young male tastes. Nevertheless, with the increasing awareness of feminism in the 1970s, comic book makers tried some new ideas to attract young females.

Comic books portrayed the modern feminist movement with ambivalence. Although the number of female characters, both heroes and villains, multiplied in the early seventies, writers seemed to regard "women's lib" with the same bemusement and dismissiveness that others in the media did. Characters like Thundra and the Man-Killer were caricatures of feminists, who despised all men. Similarly, an Avengers story in which the male superheroes battle their female counterparts belittled feminism as a "battle of the sexes," in which the women call themselves the "Lady Liberators" and utter battle cries like "Up against the wall, Male Chauvinist Pig!" To make matters worse, the women superheroes later discover that they have been duped and manipulated by a villain posing as a female liberator.[43]

The feminist movement, which should have been a boon for DC's *Wonder Woman*, instead proved to be something of an ordeal. Women's activists like Gloria Steinem praised the character as a strong role model for girls, but Wonder Woman's response to the awakening of feminism was to lose her power, open up a fashion boutique, take up karate, and wear white jumpsuits. Even with the exposure of a popular prime-time television series in the mid-1970s, Wonder Woman remained only a mediocre seller for DC.[44]

In 1972 Marvel launched *Shanna the She-Devil*, *Night Nurse*, and *The Cat*. All featured female stars as well as the work of women writers and artists. *Shanna* was an ill-advised attempt to update the dreadful "jungle queen" genre. An unusual concept for comic books, *Night Nurse* focused on the adventures of working female nurses and, appar-

ently, found an audience of aspiring nurses who wrote to the editor
asking for career advice. Of these series, *The Cat* had the best chance
to succeed with both genders. With interesting powers and a well-
conceived origin story, the Cat conformed to Marvel's proven superhero formula. Yet her background as an attractive and intelligent young
woman who challenges sexism and gender discrimination also gave her
a compelling feminist edge.[45] Nevertheless, sales of all three titles were
abysmal, and none lasted beyond five issues.

The impoverished state of women in comic books was unintentionally illustrated in 1977 by Stan Lee's *The Superhero Women*, an anthol-
ogy devoted to showcasing Marvel's female superheroes. It featured ten
characters, five of whom were actually supporting characters in titles
dominated by male heroes. The other five starred in titles that had already been canceled or would be canceled in a few years. As difficult as
it was to get white readers to buy comic books about black characters,
explained Roy Thomas, "it was even harder to get boys to buy comics
about women."[46] And evidently, if white boys did not buy the comic
books, the comic books did not sell. Despite the inclusive efforts—
however flawed—of comic book makers in the 1970s, the female audience remained elusive.

Social Malaise and Fan Culture

While the youth culture of the 1960s involved audiences in the politics
of change, popular culture of the 1970s indulged young people in the
politics of the personal. Introspection, existentialism, and narcissism
became the marketable commodities in youth entertainment. Movies
like *Five Easy Pieces* (1970) and *Carnal Knowledge* (1971) emerged from
the hangover of 1960s idealism and explored the loneliness and spiritual desolation that remained. The rock-and-roll music industry produced sensitive singer-songwriters, self-indulgent "progressive" rock
acts, nihilistic punk rockers, and the epitome of the narcissistic lifestyle,
disco. In contrast to the political and socially conscious trends of the
1960s, these popular music styles all appealed to the politics of self-
discovery. Instead of asking what they could do for their country, millions of young people explored what they could do for themselves.[47]

Although it doomed the movement for "relevance" in comic books,
the political and spiritual drift that affected American culture after
Vietnam and Watergate proved to be a boon of sorts for the comic book
industry. The upheavals of the 1960s and early 1970s destroyed much
of the social and cultural framework upon which American assumptions had long rested. The Cold War consensus lay in tatters. Cynicism,

skepticism, and outright hostility towards authority of all kinds undermined respect for the government, corporations, and other centers of power. The feminist movement, the sexual revolution, and no-fault divorce laws challenged traditional concepts of gender and family. Stagflation and energy crises called into question the inevitability of American economic growth and material abundance. In short, young people growing up in the 1970s faced a world that was more confusing than ever before. A variety of cultural options existed for youngsters looking for meaning in a society seemingly devoid of it. Some turned to alcohol and drugs. Others looked to empathetic religious cults and therapeutic New Age philosophies. Most indulged in self-absorbing pursuits promising instant gratification. And, again, millions quietly lost themselves in the fantasy world of superhero comic books.

Communications professor John Fiske defines modern *fandom* as a subculture of postindustrial societies that "selects from the repertoire of mass-produced and mass-distributed entertainment certain performers, narratives, or genres" and reworks them into "an intensely pleasurable, intensely satisfying popular culture that is both similar to, yet significantly different from the culture of more 'normal' popular audiences." Fandom grows around "cultural forms that the dominant value system denigrates" and attracts individuals who are "disempowered by any combination of gender, age, class, and race."[48] Yet fandom also emerges from the historical conditions that leave individuals with the spiritual drift and disaffection that immersion in selected products of popular culture helps to ease.

There have long been comic book fans, fan clubs, and fan publications. Most of the early clubs and publications had been ephemeral, localized, or sponsored by the publishers as marketing devices.[49] During the 1970s, however, fan culture became a cottage industry in and of itself, complete with proprietary and factional divisions. Fans gathered at conventions or "ComicCons," often staged in conjunction with related Star Trek, sci-fi, and fantasy interests. They bought and sold old comic books and discussed creative and economic developments within the field. A lucky few developed contacts within the industry and went to work for their favorite publishers. Fan publications or "fanzines" like the *Comics Journal* and the *Comics Buyer's Guide* became profit-making ventures themselves. Sometimes these provided a forum for disgruntled fans to produce critical reviews and accuse the major publishers of selling out the mature tastes of discerning readers like themselves to pander to the "under-elevens, GIs, and morons" who comprised the mass comic book audience. Factions, sometimes quite hostile, developed between enthusiastic fans enamored with the sheer enjoyment of comic books and calculating fan-collectors more interested in their comic books' speculation value.[50]

As comic books lost much of their mass audience, they increasingly became the preserve of a fan subculture that viewed the mainstream with disdain. The disregard that much of the public held for comic books became, in this respect, the secret weapon that saved them from oblivion. For many fans, comic books offered more than a casual distraction. They opened up an absorbing alternative that helped disaffected young people carve out a sense of identity in a vapid consumer culture.

While hardcore fans constituted only a minority of the comic book audience, their loyalty and longevity (many remained avid consumers well into adulthood) made them a significant market. As publishers looked for a way out of their own financial malaise in the late 1970s, they came to appreciate more and more the wisdom of selling comic book fantasies directly to those who dreamed about them the most. Having entered the decade with superheroes on a crusade to change the world, comic book makers ended it with an imperative to change the world of superheroes. The industry was about to enter one of its most critical phases.

9

Direct to the Fans

The Comic Book Industry
since 1980

"Spider-Man is coming to Wall Street," proclaimed the *Wall Street Journal*. In the summer of 1991, Marvel Entertainment became the first comic book publisher listed on the New York Stock Exchange. Opening shares sold for $14 to $16. Within several months, their value increased over 300%. That same summer saw an issue of Marvel's *X-Men* sell a record 8.2 million copies. Marvel itself was no longer just a comic book publisher, it was a multimedia entertainment corporation with annual earnings in nine figures.[1] Comic books had finally emerged as a major force in the corporate entertainment world. Or so it seemed. Spider-Man really did come to Wall Street, in a sense at least. An actor clad in the familiar red and blue webbed costume accompanied Stan Lee to the floor of the New York Stock Exchange as a publicity stunt to advertise Marvel's shares. Yet, amidst all the enthusiasm, there was something vaguely unsettling about the superhero mingling with the suits and ties on Wall Street. Marvel may have arrived in the world of corporate entertainment, but Spider-Man looked rather out of place there. How much of the industry's growth was real, and how much was a comic book fantasy?

Comic Book Stagflation

The present structure of the comic book industry owes much to the reappraisal of comic books that began in the late 1960s. Stan Lee's edi-

torial and marketing strategies at Marvel Comics had broadened the
comic book audience to include older teenagers and young adults, some
of whom went on to create comic books themselves. While many comic
book makers entered the 1970s with aspirations to advance the literary
and artistic qualities of a medium long relegated to the gutter of American culture, enthusiasm turned to disillusion when their efforts garnered little commercial success. Part of the problem lay in the economic structure of the industry, which remained essentially unchanged from what it had been in the 1940s. Creators tended to be freelancers crafting work-for-hire products with no royalties, financial incentives, or collective bargaining agreement. Lack of respect was another part of the problem. Comic book makers had an enthusiastic and mature audience, but the mainstream still dismissed their products as cheap juvenile trash. That perception would not have been such a problem had it been confined to the general public, but distributors and retailers also had little respect for comic books. Increasingly, traditional comic book retail outlets like newsstands and mom-and-pop stores gave way to chain stores and shopping malls that stocked few or no comic books. This presented the industry with its most serious problem in decades. Resolving the crisis would require a major restructuring of the way in which comic books were created and sold.

Comic book makers, recognizing the need to generate more respect for their medium and profession, formed the Academy of Comic Book Arts (ACBA) in 1970, hoping, as Stan Lee put it, to "do for comics what the Academy of Motion Picture Arts and Sciences has done for films." The academy would sponsor comic-art exhibits, give awards for creative achievement, and generally promote popular appreciation for comic books.[2] Some members also hoped that the association would serve as a means for addressing concerns about industry working conditions.

The only previous attempt at an association or union of comic book creators had come in the early 1950s. At that time, an artist named Bernie Krigstein helped to form the Society of Comic Book Illustrators, which aimed to establish and enforce, through strike action if necessary, an industry-wide minimum pay rate for artists. Krigstein had hoped to end the "destructive competition between artists" and the publishers' "cynical use of inferior artists," which worked to lower rates and undermine the bargaining position of quality talent. The association failed, largely because creators felt too vulnerable and anxious about antagonizing their employers. It also suffered from a Cold War political culture that tended to equate unionism with Communism and organized crime. Indeed, Krigstein's efforts on behalf of artists hurt his own reputation with most publishers. The only one who would employ him at the time was William Gaines, who sympathized with the cause of comic book artists and paid them some of the highest rates in the field.[3]

Like its predecessor, the ACBA failed to achieve much for comic book professionals. It too suffered from a lack of unity and the reluctance of creators to take a stand against their employers. The most active member of the ACBA was Neal Adams, a young artist who had already developed a reputation as an advocate for "creators' rights" and a supporter of Jerry Siegel and Joe Shuster in their ongoing legal struggle to win compensation from DC for Superman. As the owner of his own successful commercial art studio, however, Adams had little to lose by upsetting publishers, and some of the more vulnerable creators viewed his leadership with suspicion. The ACBA did win a few concessions from publishers, like an insurance plan for freelancers, but it never developed into a real collective bargaining association.[4] Just as unsuccessful were the ACBA's efforts to garner popular respect for comic books, some of which degenerated into farce. In an attempt to emulate the motion-picture industry's Oscar awards, the ACBA gave "Shazam" awards to creators in recognition of their achievements. But the association was so impoverished that winners had to pay for their own award plaques, and many failed to do so. By 1975 the association had all but dissolved.[5]

Throughout the second half of the 1970s, comic book creators voiced their concerns and complaints about the industry through the fan press. Bemoaning low pay rates, job insecurity, and minimal benefits, some creators were more dissatisfied than others. Most shared general concerns about the economics of publishing, which rewarded quantity over quality and stifled innovation.[6] Some attributed their grievances to the chilly corporate atmosphere that the companies had assumed. As properties of Cadence Industries and Warner Communications, respectively, Marvel Comics and DC Comics were ultimately responsible to executives who cared only about the bottom line and nothing about the aesthetic or literary merit of comic books. Some at Marvel even despaired that the much-admired Stan Lee now seemed more interested in marketing established formulas than advancing creative progress.[7]

Financial incentives and creators' rights were the most contentious issues between creators and publishers. Since the beginning of the industry, publishers had employed creators on a work-for-hire basis. This

meant that any and all of the work done under contract became the
property of the publishers. In most instances, both parties had accepted
this arrangement. In the days when creators labored in anonymity and
obscurity, grinding out throwaway formula comics, few would have
benefited by owning the copyrights to their work. But those few who
did create characters of lasting popularity had no claim to royalties or
licensing revenue. Haunting ambitious creators was the tragic specter
of Jerry Siegel and Joe Shuster, who had sold Superman to DC for $130
and given up their claim to the millions of dollars that their creation
subsequently generated.

The young generation of creators in the 1970s had a greater sense
of entitlement than their predecessors, however, and they were well
aware that their counterparts in other entertainment industries enjoyed
royalties and creative incentives for their work. Some began to demand
similar rights from the publishers, arguing that these would benefit the
companies as well by resulting in more innovative and accomplished
comic books. Even Roy Thomas, a veteran writer and editor with
strong sympathies for the commercial interests of publishers, later admitted that he had consciously avoided creating characters for them
because, he "could not stand the idea of creating characters that" he
"didn't own a piece of."[8]

In 1978 a new federal copyright law went into effect, spelling out
more precisely exactly what rights a publisher purchased from a creator
in work-for-hire arrangements. The publishers promptly issued new
contracts to secure the rights to any work produced by their staff. Marvel's contract in particular stated that all work submitted by writers and
artists would be on a work-for-hire basis. Some creators, encouraged
by the new copyright law, called for negotiations to win greater creative
concessions. Again, Neal Adams took the lead and circulated a letter to
artists, urging them not to sign the new contracts. He also proposed
the formation of a guild to advance the bargaining rights of comic book
professionals.[9]

The Comics Guild was plagued from the start by a lack of common
purpose. Although most creators interviewed by the *Comics Journal*
seemed to be in favor of a guild, they failed to reach a consensus on
what to accomplish with it. Some of the more established writers like
Roy Thomas and Dennis O'Neil thought that the financial demands
being advanced by their younger peers were so unrealistic that the entire effort looked ridiculous. Although the guild was the most serious
attempt yet to establish a collective bargaining arrangement for comic
book professionals, it promptly dissolved as completely as its predeces-

sors. If the guild achieved anything, it was to further highlight the concerns of creators and their shared pessimism about the future of the industry.[10]

Those closer to the financial side of comic book publishing had their own complaints about some creators. They argued that the whole notion of creators' rights sprang from wrong-headed and self-important thinking about what comic books were supposed to be. Some pointed out that in their enthusiasm to expand the horizons of the art form, certain ambitious creators often neglected the basics of storytelling and the bottom line of commercial performance. Writers who appealed primarily to hardcore fans often alienated the mass of readers with their literary pretensions and convoluted plots. Talented artists sometimes took so much time completing their work that they caused costly delays and damaged relations with distributors.[11]

One matter upon which creators and publishers agreed was the problem of shrinking distribution and retail networks. Given a choice between allotting retail space to slick magazines with a $2 price tag or comic books that sold for thirty-five cents, retailers increasingly reduced or eliminated entirely their orders for the latter. Most of those who continued to stock comic books tended to retail only the couple dozen titles that could fit on a standard rotary comic book rack. This meant that much of the industry's output was not getting to consumers. Marvel and DC issued over fifty titles a month between the two of them. In 1975 Marvel alone had sixty-three titles on the market at one time. Some industry insiders warned that comic book publishing would cease to be profitable unless major changes were made in the distribution and retail systems.[12]

Compounding the industry's problems was the nation's general economic stagnation. Fuel and paper shortages coupled with inflation accelerated an alarming rate of comic book price increases.[13] Between 1935 and 1961 the standard price of a comic book stood at ten cents. In 1962 it increased to twelve cents, and in 1969 it became fifteen cents. It rose to twenty cents in 1972, twenty-five cents in 1974, thirty cents in 1976, thirty-five in 1977, forty in 1979, and fifty cents in 1981. This was substantial inflation for a core audience whose primary income may have been a weekly allowance of a dollar or two. With hikes like these, publishers threatened to price many of their young consumers out of the market.

Yet at the same time, price increases made comic books more attractive to distributors and retailers. Publishers also found it easier to defray the printing and distribution costs of an issue that retailed for a

higher price, even if it sold fewer copies than cheaper titles. With this
in mind, DC experimented for a time with thicker comic books that
carried a dollar price tag, Marvel issued a series of pricey black-and-
white comic magazines, and both published tabloid-size comic books
retailing between $1.50 and $2.50.[14]

Even with the shrinking comic book market, both Marvel and DC
remained profitable entities for their corporate parents, largely thanks
to revenue derived from foreign markets and licensing deals. The 1970s
brought an unprecedented increase in the variety and sales of superhero
merchandise, especially toys. The Mego toy company put out an extensive line of action figures and related playsets based on the Marvel
and DC superheroes. DC Comics enjoyed licensing profits and cross-
promotion from the Saturday-morning cartoons *Superfriends* and *Batman* and the live-action *Shazam* and prime time *Wonder Woman* television series. In 1978 Warner Brothers released the blockbuster movie
Superman, the first of several pictures starring Christopher Reeves in
the title role. Marvel's comic books outsold DC's, but Marvel had less
success licensing its characters. Still, Marvel enjoyed some valuable exposure and revenue from several prime time television series based on
its leading characters, the most successful being CBS's *The Incredible
Hulk.* Marvel also scored its own licensing coup when it won the rights
to print comic books adapted from the phenomenally popular *Star
Wars* movie.[15]

With licensing revenue far outpacing profits from comic book
sales, some corporate executives apparently questioned the need to
publish comic books at all. Most in the industry understood that the
popularity of licensed characters ultimately depended on the quality of
their comic books, however. So Cadence and Warner each brought
in new executive leadership to improve their respective comic book
divisions. In 1978 Marvel also appointed twenty-eight-year-old comic
book writer Jim Shooter to a position as editor-in-chief. Shooter endeavored to tighten up the editorial direction of Marvel's comic books
by reining in the self-indulgent excesses that he felt had marred many
of the stories in recent years. In the process, his heavy-handed approach
alienated a number of creators, who subsequently defected to the competition. An October 1979 article in the *New York Times* characterized
Marvel as a company wracked by "the sort of warring more commonly
reported at some of the mammoths of the corporate world." There was
talk "that the editor-in-chief is power-thirsty and that the top people
are more interested in coining money from licensing deals than they
are in the superheroes." Shooter and executives at Marvel disputed the

Times story, but interviews published in the fan press confirmed that a number of creators at the time did indeed feel disillusioned and betrayed by the company that they, as young fans, had once regarded with such affection.[16]

In 1976 DC Comics hired Jenette Kahn as its new publisher and gave her the formidable task of reversing the company's dramatic decline in the comic book market. As Marvel rode to the top of the industry on its image as a hip and exciting publisher, DC had become saddled with the unfavorable reputation of being, as one editor later put it, the *Wall Street Journal* of comic books. Upon arriving at the company, Kahn found "severe problems in both the editorial and business sides." Three of DC's editors were forty-eight, sixty, and sixty-five years old, and they seemed incapable of making the changes needed to bring the comic books more in step with current youth culture. Kahn worked to boost sales by revitalizing DC's reputation and enhancing the morale of its staff. She also undoubtedly had to overcome the skepticism of more than a few male creators who wondered what good a woman with no background in comic books could do for the ailing but still venerable comic book company.[17]

As the 1970s drew to a close, the industry once again found itself in a crisis. If comic books were to thrive and grow as a viable entertainment industry, a means would have to be found to bridge the interests of publishers, creators, and consumers. Fortunately for those concerned, such a means was already becoming apparent as the new decade dawned.

Direct Marketing

The industry's apparent savior was an alternative distribution and retailing network that became known as direct-market distribution. As traditional comic book retail outlets disappeared throughout the 1970s, new ones opened up. These were small shops devoted primarily or exclusively to the sale of comic books and commonly operated by proprietors who were also comic book fans. Many also stocked collectibles like baseball cards, movie posters, and assorted memorabilia. In 1974 comic book creator Mike Friedrich independently published *Star Reach*, an initial effort to combine the do-it-yourself approach of underground comics with the superhero stories of mainstream comic books. Distributed directly and exclusively to comic book stores, the first issue of *Star Reach* sold its entire print run of 14,000 copies. Subsequent issues sold as many as 30,000 copies exclusively through the direct market—small numbers compared to those commonly generated through traditional vendors but large enough for the major publishers to take notice. Marvel and DC steadily increased their shipments through the direct market. In 1976 Marvel's direct-market sales amounted to $1,500,000. In 1979 direct marketing earned Marvel over $3,500,000.[18]

Direct distribution held major advantages over standard magazine distribution for comic book publishers. Unlike most traditional vendors, comic book shop proprietors had a familiarity with the products and a good feel for the market. They also tended to order and stock all of the titles issued by the publishers. A few of these retailers started up distribution companies that served the direct market exclusively and provided the publishers with valuable market research in the process. Publishers and retailers enjoyed a mutually favorable arrangement, whereby specialty shops purchasing comic books enjoyed greater discounts than those given to other vendors in exchange for giving up the right to return unsold issues for a refund. Instead of returning issues to the publisher, the specialty retailer placed unsold comic books in plastic bags, boxed them, and retailed them—often with a higher price tag—as collectible back issues. This system gave publishers greater marketing flexibility and helped them to reduce costly refunds. Publishers had historically determined their profit margins on the basis of percentages of sales. In the boom years of the 1940s and 1950s titles had commonly sold in excess of 70 percent, but in recent years publishers had become accustomed to break-even sales of 30 to 40 percent. In effect, this meant that they printed about three copies of a comic book for every one they sold. Sales through direct distribution, on the other hand, were virtually 100 percent. At that rate, even small raw sales could translate into large profits. Direct marketing thus promised to offset much of the cost and waste associated with traditional distribution.[19]

The new importance of direct marketing had major ramifications for the creation as well as the distribution of comic books. Publishers recognized that fans, as opposed to casual buyers, accounted for most of the transactions conducted through comic book stores. Having graduated from a comic book fan to a writer and then to a position as manager of DC's business affairs all before he turned twenty-five years of age, Paul Levitz was uniquely qualified to proclaim in 1982 the "triumph of comics fandom." In an article published in a fan magazine, Levitz explained that "for better or worse, a majority of comics published today are produced for the entertainment of comics fans," and the major publishers were "consciously aiming their efforts directly at the fan market as their chief area of growth." This boded ill for publishers like Archie Comics, Gold Key Comics, and Charlton Publications, all of whom proved unable to build an audience of older fans. Archie maintained its perennial preadolescent readership, but its efforts to win a share of the direct market with its own superhero titles failed miserably. Unable to break into the direct market, Gold Key Comics and Charlton Publications discontinued their comic books altogether. With the largest fan base, Marvel benefited from the new marketing more than any other publisher, outselling DC by a two-to-one margin for much of the 1980s. New independent publishers started up to target the direct market, and most of these offered creative autonomy and generous royalties to lure talented creators away from the major publishers. Writers and artists with demonstrated popularity in the fan market now found their bargaining power substantially enhanced.[20]

DC and Marvel responded accordingly with concessions. Jenette Kahn worked to transform DC into a "creative rights company." In 1981 the company introduced a royalties plan for creators whose work sold over 100,000 copies per issue. Shortly thereafter, Marvel announced a similar plan of its own.[21] Creators welcomed the moves. Roy Thomas called DC's plan a "step in the right direction." By 1985 Dennis O'Neil noticed that the morale and enthusiasm of comic book professionals had improved markedly. Even Neal Adams applauded the publishers' concessions. Buoyed by rising pay rates, royalties plans, and other benefits, the average annual income for full-time creators rose to over $50,000 in 1985, and some earned six-figure incomes.[22]

Yet if creators' rights advocates had expected incentives to unleash a great flowering of literary and artistic advancement in comic books, they were mistaken. Comic books remained essentially the domain of superheroes and male adolescent fantasies. Even the new "independent" publishers like Eclipse Comics, First Comics, and Comico generally adhered to the superhero genre established by the major companies. If anything, in fact, the superhero genre became more entrenched than ever because the much-trumpeted creative incentives actually awarded commercial success, not necessarily innovation. Surveys of the direct market indicated that fans still wanted comic books about superheroes, albeit with more "realism." The institution of creators' rights, in effect, encouraged comic book makers to better accommodate the tastes of young people, for whom violence, cynicism, and moral ambiguity were the cultural commodities most in demand.

Costumed Vigilantes

The new emphasis on the direct market and the extension of creative incentives helped to create a comic book star system. Writers and art-

ists popular with fans commanded high salaries and won a measure of
creative autonomy. The biggest stars could boost the sales of titles by
their name recognition alone. Two of the first creators to benefit most
from the new system were writer Chris Claremont and writer-artist
John Byrne. Together they laid the creative foundations for one of the
most profitable comic book series in recent decades, *The X-Men*. Although Marvel's *X-Men* had been around since the early 1960s, the series had never sold particularly well, and by the early 1970s it consisted
wholly of reprints. In 1975 Marvel debuted a new team of mutant X-
Men and gave them a distinctive international and multicultural identity. They included: Nightcrawler, a German youth blessed with superhuman agility and the ability to teleport across space but cursed with
the terrifying appearance of a furry blue demon; Colossus, a steel-
skinned Russian with enormous physical strength; Storm, a beautiful
African princess with control over the weather; and Wolverine, a tem-
peramental Canadian armed with unbreakable steel claws, acute senses,
and the ferocious disposition of his namesake. Initially, the group also
had included an arrogant Japanese mutant named Sunfire and an angry
young Native American called Thunderbird, but the former left the
group after only a few issues and the latter was promptly killed off.
Leading the group were two holdovers from the original X-Men, Cy-
clops and the wheelchair-bound Professor Xavier.[23]

Chris Claremont assumed the writing of *The X-Men* after a few
issues and stayed with the series into the 1990s. Between 1977 and 1981
Claremont and artist John Byrne transformed it from a second-tier bimonthly series to the best-selling title in the industry. Its strength lay
in the characters developed by Claremont and Byrne. As outsiders who
were feared and hated by the society that they fought to defend, the X-
Men were well within the traditional Marvel formula. Claremont and
Byrne also added nuances to the interplay of the characters that made
for an especially compelling and absorbing narrative. Claremont created strong female characters who played more than the token supporting role traditionally allotted to women in comic books. He also
avoided the kind of ultrafeminist caricatures that had crept into comic
books during the early 1970s. Storm was later joined by Phoenix, Shad-
owcat, and Rogue to form a core of complex, assertive, and powerful
female X-Men. They helped to expand the title's appeal across the gender barrier, and *The X-Men* became one of the very few superhero titles
to win a significant female following.[24]

As the X-Men grew in popularity, fans inevitably developed a preference for individual characters in the group. Wolverine became the

clear favorite. When calm, Wolverine evinced the cold precision and ruthlessness of a government secret agent. Yet he also flew into fits of uncontrolled rage and savagery. His primary weapons were the steel claws embedded into his skeleton, and he did not shrink from using them, often drawing blood and sometimes even killing his enemies in the process. In 1984 Marvel featured Wolverine solo in a very popular four-part limited series, and in 1988 he won his own regular title. Wolverine was one of the many tough, right-wing antiheroes who emerged in popular culture to reflect the antigovernment attitudes generated by the Vietnam War, Watergate, and the reaction against the rights revolution of the 1960s. Unencumbered by bureaucratic technicalities or liberal sensibilities, Wolverine dispensed justice with righteous violence. John Byrne imagined him as "'Dirty Harry' with a Canadian accent."[25]

Byrne's own approach to comic books was well suited to the culture of the Reagan years. In a 1989 interview with the *New York Times*, Byrne explained that he had always tried to write with "a Middle America Bible Belt mentality." Byrne, who was born in England and grew up in Canada, felt that it was important to have his superheroes act on righteous motivations. In a 1980 interview, he expressed his intention to "get more fun back into comic books," insisting that "for too long a time in the late '60s and early '70s, comics became stories of doom, gloom, and that sort of thing. And who cares?" He felt that the best comic books were those that simply left readers feeling good. He also claimed to have no problem with the publishers' work-for-hire contracts and had refused to join the Comics Guild because it "stank of unions." Byrne was proud to be a "company man," but he also welcomed the royalties plans—especially since they had made him one of the highest paid creators in the industry.[26]

Owing to his work on *The X-Men*, Byrne developed a reputation as a rescuer of failing titles. He revitalized Marvel's slumping *Fantastic Four* in the early 1980s, and in 1986 DC contracted him to breathe new life into Superman. His formula was simple. He recalled what had made a popular series successful in the first place and then reworked these nostalgic qualities into a modern superhero narrative.[27] Byrne's back-

Cover of *The Uncanny X-Men* 126 (Marvel Comics, October 1979). The revamped X-Men became, along with Spider-Man and Batman, the most popular comic book superheroes of the 1980s and 1990s. The violent-tempered Wolverine (*lower left*) especially became a fan favorite, later winning his own solo comic book series. Art by Dave Cockrum and Terry Austin.

to-basics approach meshed nicely with the cultural politics of President Ronald Reagan and the ascendant New Right. According to the conservative worldview of the 1980s, the cultural upheavals of the 1960s and early 1970s were unfortunate developments that had hurt American morale, undermined patriotism, left society fragmented, and weakened the nation in the Cold War. The Reagan vision appealed to a nostalgic brand of patriotism that recalled the basic values that, proponents contended, had united Americans in the first place. Such a worldview reserved a powerful task for the president, to rescue the nation from the twin threats of international Communism and domestic malaise.

As long as this neoconservative vision held sway in mainstream American culture, Byrne's formula found success in the comic book market. But as the Reagan era passed, so apparently did Byrne's. In a 1990 interview Byrne expressed concern about the state of the comic book industry. He was especially critical of the current trends promoted by his creative peers, insisting that "there's been a distinct change in attitude among the people who are doing comics. The preservers are less in evidence and the destroyers are more in evidence." He bemoaned young creators who approached a series with the intent to deconstruct it and, in his view, take the fun out of superheroes.[28] Byrne's concerns were well-founded but belated. For even in the midst of the nostalgic and self-congratulatory Reagan years, the "destroyers" had been prominent all along.

While Byrne found success by appealing to the uplifting qualities of superheroes, other creators won critical acclaim and commercial fortune by exploring their characters' disturbing psychological motivations and cultural implications. Superheroes traditionally had stood as the champions of a good citizenry menaced by aberrant wrongdoers. In this cynical era, however, it was the superhero who was the aberration. Superheroes became a force for ruthless morality in a corrupt society that feared and despised them. Theirs was a seemingly impossible task that no sane individual would undertake, and, indeed, the sanity of superheroes did come into question. Once confident symbols of hope, superheroes now spoke to the paranoia and psychosis lurking behind the rosy veneer of Reagan's America.

The individual most closely identified with these creative trends was a young writer-artist named Frank Miller. No writer since Stan Lee has had a greater influence on American comic books. Miller characterized his childhood and adolescence in Vermont as "maladjusted" and "miserable"—conditions that led him naturally into the world of superhero comic books. In the late 1970s he moved to New York City and began work for Marvel Comics. Between 1979 and 1982 he and artist Klaus Janson helped transform Marvel's *Daredevil* into one of the most exciting and influential titles of its era. Preceding creators had already developed the blind superhero Daredevil, alias defense attorney Matt Murdock, into a brooding, isolated individual. Miller went even further in this direction, portraying him as a deeply tortured soul, torn apart by his own internal contradictions as a lawyer and an extralegal vigilante. His stories took place in the seedy underworld of a New York City run by corrupt politicians and gangsters posing as businessmen. Here, the law championed by Murdock was too often a commodity for sale to the highest bidder. Only the righteous justice enforced by Daredevil's fists stood a chance in this amoral urban hell.[29]

This compelling premise could have easily succumbed to clichés had it not been for the inspired contributions of its creators. Miller's plots were tight and absorbing, his scripts, terse and ironic. The art by Miller and Janson was stripped-down yet atmospheric, verging on a crude expressionism. Characters performed unbelievable physical acts but evinced believable human traits and motivations. Violence was a key feature. All superhero comic books portrayed some violence, but in *Daredevil* it was graphic and palpable. Fists broke jaws and cracked ribs. Crowbars crushed skulls. Knives ripped flesh. Yet, with few exceptions, Miller's work met the approval of the comics code, a testimony to its much liberalized standards and waning importance.[30]

Miller's work on *Daredevil* made him one of the industry's biggest stars. In 1983 DC contracted him to write a six-part limited series called *Ronin*, featuring characters created and owned by Miller. In 1986 he wrote another limited series for DC, this time featuring the company's most popular character. In *Batman: The Dark Knight Returns*, Miller recast the superhero as an older and slightly mad right-wing moralist in a dystopian Gotham City gutted by corruption and vice. The series sold out, and DC promptly issued it as a paperback "graphic novel" for sale in bookstores. In this format it became the first original superhero work to be reviewed seriously, and often favorably, in the mainstream press.[31] Moreover, *The Dark Knight Returns* sparked a major resurgence in Batman's popularity that peaked several years later with the release of Warner Brothers' enormously successful *Batman* movie, directed by Tim Burton and starring Michael Keaton and Jack Nicholson.

Frank Miller spearheaded a loose movement among comic book writers in the 1980s who worked to deconstruct superheroes while revitalizing them in the process. Whereas Miller envisioned the superhero

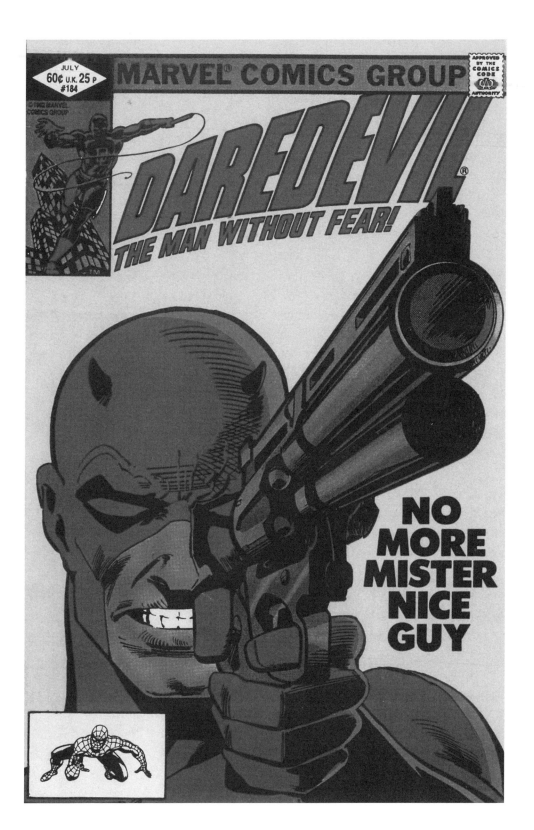

as a right-wing force fighting to preserve social order, another young writer-artist named Howard Chaykin examined social decay from a leftist perspective. In *American Flagg*, published by First Comics, Chaykin portrayed a twenty-first century consumed by rampant hedonism and conspicuous consumption incarnate. In this future, American political structures have been taken over by an omnipresent entertainment megacorporation called Plex-USA. The hero is Reuben Flagg, a former video star who serves as a Plexus Ranger—a sort of policeman for the corporation. Despite his ostensible duties as a defender of the establishment, Flagg is actually a cynical subversive who recognizes his nation for what it is—an obscene perversion of the American dream that, nevertheless, offers a lot of opportunities for fun. Flagg's world is a wild satirical caricature of 1980s America. Racial hatred and social tolerance are both prevalent. Alternative sexual lifestyles, gang violence, international terrorism, broken-down family structures, drug use, homelessness, "trickle-down economics," and corporate mergers are all exaggerated to an absurd degree. The series also boasted Chaykin's own political views. In a 1986 interview Chaykin admitted that he had "an intense aversion to the rich" and found conspicuous consumption "damning." Consumption was, in Chaykin's view, a means of false empowerment that enabled the financial elite to manipulate the poor and middle classes.[32]

A reviewer for *Atlantic* called Chaykin's *American Flagg* a "shallow parody of America," but added that "the shallowness is part of the point. It plays to our worst fears about our plastic, violent culture, with its philistine tastes and hunger for novelty."[33] Littered throughout the series were references to American junk culture: shopping malls, porn films, "B" movies, and, naturally, comic books. With his own affection for comic books, Chaykin tacitly acknowledged his complicity in the consumer culture. *American Flagg* thus implied there was hope that individuals in the consumer age could still find room for personal expression by appropriating the lowbrow castoffs of American popular culture and marshaling them into an absurdist resistance narrative. In this respect, the series brilliantly captured the essence of comic book fandom

Cover of *Daredevil* 184 (Marvel Comics, July 1982). Marvel's *Daredevil* does not use firearms, but this cover, obviously inspired by the *Dirty Harry* films, nicely captures the image of modern superheroes as ruthless vigilantes. Frank Miller's writing for *Daredevil* won him huge popularity among comic book fans, and he became one of the most influential creators in the field. Art by Frank Miller and Klaus Janson.

itself and predicted similar trends evinced in the postmodern or "alternative" youth culture of the late 1980s and 1990s.

Frank Miller and Howard Chaykin expanded the literary possibilities of the superhero genre, but it was an Englishman named Alan Moore who produced what was arguably the magnum opus of superhero comic books. By 1986 Moore had already established himself as a comic book writer of considerable talent and a fiercely independent nature. In 1985 Eclipse Comics published Moore's *Miracleman* series, which used a narrative style more akin to prose fiction than to comic books to explore what superheroes might be like if they really existed in the contemporary world.[34] In 1986 Moore took this proposition several steps further in a self-contained twelve-issue limited series published by DC. The series was called *The Watchmen*, and it was unlike anything the comic book industry had ever seen.

In collaboration with English artist Dave Gibbons, Moore conceived an alternate reality much like our own 1980s world, except that in this fictional "real" world, there are superheroes. Moore's superheroes immediately appeared different from other comic book superheroes. They talked and behaved like real people—or more appropriately, like real people who were strangely motivated to don colorful costumes and fight crime. Their intervention leads to such alternative historical developments as a U.S. victory in Vietnam and a multiple-term Nixon administration that continues into the 1980s. As these superheroes approach middle-age, however, society rejects them, and in 1977 the federal government passes an antivigilante act effectively outlawing all superheroes except for those few who agree to work for the government. Now, in the mid-1980s, the superheroes have re-emerged to head off an impending nuclear war between the United States and the Soviet Union.[35]

The Watchmen had the absorbing qualities of a tense thriller. Among the few comic book works to actually merit the pretentious label of

From *Batman: the Dark Knight Returns* (DC Comics, 1986). Frank Miller's radical reinterpretation of Batman as an aging crypto-fascist (accompanied by a female Robin) became the first superhero comic book, or "graphic novel," reviewed seriously by the mainstream press. Its success cemented Miller's reputation as an industry star and sparked a resurgence in Batman's popularity that culminated in a series of blockbuster Warners Brothers movies featuring the character. Art by Frank Miller and Klaus Janson.

graphic novel—which had come into wide use within the industry—it stood as the most complex and ambitious superhero series ever published. Like a good novel, its intricate plot defies easy summation, but Moore's central thesis was rather simple. *The Watchmen* was Moore's obituary for the concept of heroes in general and superheroes in particular. "I don't believe in heroes," he later confirmed. "A hero is somebody who has been set upon a pedestal above humanity," and "the belief in heroes . . . leads to people like Colonel Oliver North," who assume that the best interests of society are consistent with their own political views. Moore's superheroes reflected his ambivalence. However well-intentioned, they were prone to paranoid moral delusions and dangerous fascist tendencies. One character has to don his ridiculous Nite Owl costume to overcome his sexual impotence. Another is a brutally amoral government operative with a history of murder and rape. The only superhero in Moore's world who actually possesses superhuman power is the atomic-spawned Dr. Manhattan, who becomes so powerful that he loses touch with humanity and withdraws into isolation. One of the superheroes even turns out to be the primary villain—a handsome genius with the charisma of John F. Kennedy, who stages an elaborate and deadly hoax in order to restructure the world according to his own moral design.[36]

The most disturbing and, in some ways, the central character of the bunch was a masked vigilante called Rorschach. There had never been a "superhero" quite like him: born to an abusive prostitute mother and raised in a miserable slum, Rorschach is already prone to view mankind as innately evil, and he learns early in life to answer evil with ruthlessness. When a neighborhood bully harasses him as a child, he puts a lit cigarette into the boy's eye and bites his cheek off. He continues this approach as a grown superhero. In one especially horrific and pivotal episode, Rorschach tracks down the kidnapper of a six-year-old girl only to discover that the abductor has killed the child, cut her into pieces, and fed her to his dogs. Rorschach then burns the killer alive and watches him die in silent satisfaction.[37]

Rorschach views the world as a set of black-and-white values that take many shapes but never mix into shades of gray, similar to the ink blot tests of his namesake. Life itself is like a Rorschach test, he says. "Existence is random," and "has no pattern save what we imagine after staring at it for too long. No meaning save what we choose to impose." In this "rudderless world" there is no God, no fate, no vague metaphysical force that guides us. This leaves Rorschach free to "scrawl [his] own design" on a "morally blank world." His solemn undertaking is the task that an apathetic society has abdicated to him.[38]

Rorschach and his ilk were Moore's admonition to those who trusted in "heroes" and leaders to guard the world's fate.[39] To place faith in such icons, he argued, was to give up responsibility for our lives and future to the Reagans, Thatchers, and other "Watchmen" of the world who supposed to "rescue" us and perhaps lay waste to the planet in the process.

Lest Moore's work sink under the weight of its own pretensions, *The Watchmen* also benefited from a well-paced storyline, compelling script, attractive artwork, and a generous dose of graphic violence—qualities that made for a gripping and highly commercial comic book regardless of any deeper meanings embedded in the narrative. Published in the same year as Frank Miller's *Batman: The Dark Knight Returns*, *The Watchmen* helped DC briefly outsell Marvel in the direct-sales market. Moore followed *The Watchmen* with another graphic novel, this time featuring Batman. While not nearly as ambitious or accomplished as his earlier work, *Batman: The Killing Joke* was almost as violent and enjoyed even stronger sales, further cementing Moore's status as an industry star. Nevertheless Moore promptly turned his back on mainstream comic books and went on to pursue independent projects more suitable for his arching creative ambitions (such as graphic novels and other writing).[40]

Few superhero comic books approached the accomplished sophistication achieved by Frank Miller, Howard Chaykin, or Alan Moore, but many tried. Of the three, Miller remained the most enamored with superheroes, and so his work proved to be the most commercial and the most emulated. Beginning in the mid-1980s, the market became saturated with variations on Miller's brand of morally complex and ruthless superheroes. The most successful of these was the *Punisher*. Writer Gerry Conway had created the character for Marvel in 1974—the same year the vigilante film *Death Wish* was released—as a right-wing foil for the more liberal Spider-Man. In 1982 Frank Miller reintroduced the Punisher in *Daredevil* as a more extreme and unbalanced vigilante. A few years later, Marvel featured the character in his own title, and it promptly became one of the industry's top-sellers. Very much within the recent tradition of post-Vietnam antiheroes popularized in films like *Dirty Harry*, *Death Wish*, and *Rambo*, the Punisher bypassed ineffective and contemptible legal-bureaucratic agencies and waged an obsessive crusade for justice. A former U.S. Marine and Viet-

HEY, WAIT A MINUTE. THAT'S MINE!

WHAT *IS* THIS?

YOU'RE *GIVING* ME THIS? IS *THAT* IT?

LOOK, PLEASE, IF YOU'D JUST *SAY* SOME-THING...

HEY! HEY, ARE YOU *CRAZY*?

THAT'S *KEROSENE*!

YES.

NEVER MAKE IT IN TIME.

SHOULDN'T BOTHER TRYING TO SAW THROUGH HAND-CUFFS.

WHAT DO YOU *MEAN*? WHAT AM I SUPPOSED TO...

OH, GOD.

OH, JESUS, *NO*. YOU'RE *KIDDING*. YOU *HAVE* TO BE KIDDING.

EEEEAAAGH   Y!¡¡AAAGH

"STOOD IN STREET. WATCHED IT BURN.

"IMAGINED LIMBLESS FELT TORSOS INSIDE; BREASTS BLACKENING; BELLIES SMOLDERING; BURSTING INTO FLAME ONE BY ONE.

"WATCHED FOR AN HOUR."

NOBODY GOT OUT.

25

nam veteran who returns home to find his family murdered by gangsters, the Punisher assembles an arsenal of knives, guns, rifles, and assorted military hardware, dons a costume emblazoned with a skull and crossbones, and embarks on a solemn mission to rid the world of "filth" and "scum." The Punisher became so popular that Marvel used guest appearances by the character to boost the sales of other titles and launched a second title called *Punisher War Journal*. The editor and writer of the series, Mike Baron, who in a 1988 interview distanced himself from the Punisher's politics, attributed the character's popularity to "the average citizen's outrage at the failure of society to punish evil."[41]

Similar themes emerged in DC's *Green Arrow*. A character with an interesting history, Green Arrow was throughout the 1940s, 1950s, and most of the 1960s an undistinguished two-dimensional DC superhero who fought crime with a bow and trick arrows. In 1970 Dennis O'Neil and Neal Adams recast the character as a modern Robin Hood and a liberal social activist. Then after languishing for another decade and a half in relative commercial obscurity, Green Arrow reemerged in 1988, again as a latter-day Robin Hood. The new incarnation was a righteous defender of law-abiding citizens who were preyed upon by pimps, drug-dealers, and street gangs. Whereas the original Green Arrow had traditionally relied on nonlethal trick arrows to incapacitate his foes, he now employs regular sharp arrows to maim and kill his enemies. He disarms thugs by shooting arrows through their hands and stops fleeing crooks with arrows through their legs. The most depraved villains, murderers, and rapists could expect a fatal arrow through the chest, neck, or eye. Indicative of how such tactics had come to be expected from superheroes, writer Mike Grell did not portray the Green Arrow as a right-wing lunatic or even an obsessive loner like the Punisher. In his civilian identity he is a respected member of his middle-class Seattle community, enjoys a stable relationship with his female com-

From "The Abyss Gazes Also," *The Watchmen* 6 (DC Comics, February 1987). *The Watchmen* was one of the most ambitious mainstream comic book series ever published. And one of its central characters, Rorschach, was perhaps the most disturbing superhero ever created for comic books. His brutal perception of black-and-white morality reflected writer Alan Moore's critical deconstruction of the whole notion of heroes—a popular theme recurring in comic books since the 1980s. Script by Alan Moore, art by Dave Gibbons.

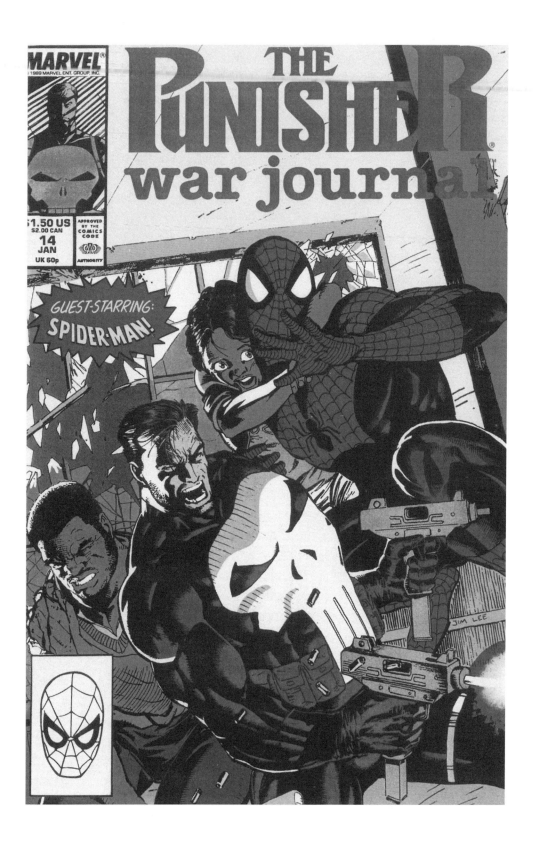

panion, and runs a flower shop. Green Arrow's justification for his crusade sounds reasonable enough, as he insists that "if the courts were more concerned with justicc than 'law,' there would be no need for men like me."[42]

By the end of the 1980s, brooding and ruthless vigilante superheroes like Wolverine, the Punisher, and Green Arrow had become a comic book cliché. Moreover, direct-market distribution permitted publishers to bypass the comics code entirely and indulge in the kind of graphic subject matter that had not been seen in comic books since the early 1950s. Even relatively mild and code-approved superheroes like Spider-Man now evinced occasional righteous streaks, as he found himself advocating brutal revenge as the sensible alternative to impotent courtroom law. Then, in 1990, Marvel revamped the Ghost Rider, a twisted variation on the classic "Shazam!" premise, wherein an adolescent boy gains the ability to summon forth his alter-ego, the Ghost Rider, at times "when innocent blood has been spilled." A terrifying character with demonic origins and a flaming skull for a head, the Ghost Rider is the hell-spawned spirit of vengeance personified. Eschewing altogether the principle of bureaucratic justice, he exacts fatal retribution on the wicked. The much-hyped series contained some of the most graphic and disturbing scenes ever to appear in a mainstream superhero comic book. Not coincidentally, several printings of the first issue sold out, and it became one of the industry's most popular titles of the early 1990s.[43]

The trend towards more graphic subject matter in comic books raised anew concerns about their effects on children. Yet while the issue of comic book violence garnered some high-profile attention in the media, most notably on CNN's *Larry King Live* and NBC's *Today* show, the debate failed to capture much public interest. This said more about American culture than about the comic books. By the late 1980s, comic books had only begun to catch up with trends towards greater violence and more explicit sex in the entertainment media. Those inclined to critique such developments overwhelmingly focused their attention on the more pervasive influences of movies, television, and rock and rap music. Nevertheless, some publishers, like DC Comics, adopted a loose

Cover of *Punisher War Journal* 14 (Marvel Comics, January 1990). The Punisher led the pack of thick-muscled and extremely violent vigilante superheroes who populated comic books during the late 1980s and 1990s. His hard-line approach to crime-fighting was often contrasted with that of more liberal superheroes like Spider-Man. Art by Jim Lee.

and rather cynical ratings system that labeled some comic books "For Mature Readers Only." This device, however, served mainly to enhance the appeal of the comic books to consumers of all ages, who naturally preferred the "mature" material.[44]

Crossovers and Collector's Items

The increasing sophistication and violent content of comic books helped to propel the industry's commercial expansion in the 1980s and early 1990s. Another marketing gimmick employed skillfully by comic book makers was the proliferation of "events" and "crossover" series. Inspired to some degree by the good-natured, yet calculating, huckster-ism used by Stan Lee in the 1960s, publishers hyped events like super-hero deaths, costume changes, and the work of star artists to heighten consumer anticipation and raise the speculation value of self-conscious comic book "collector's items." Oftentimes these comic book events took the form of sprawling crossover series that obliged loyal readers to purchase many issues of various titles in order to make sense of the convoluted story lines. Marvel inaugurated this trend in 1984 with its *Marvel Superheroes Secret Wars*, a twelve-issue limited series that featured most of the prominent characters in the Marvel universe and crossed over into dozens of superhero titles. The series itself sold an impressive average of 800,000 copies per issue. The following year Marvel published *Secret Wars II*, which did not sell as well but crossed over into even more issues and required even more purchases in order for readers to follow the plot. DC Comics followed suit with its derivative *Super-Powers* and *Crisis on Infinite Earths* limited series, the latter of which featured the death of Supergirl. Marvel's *Secret Wars* and DC's *Super-Powers* also tied in with an extensive line of licensed toy action figures. Subsequent crossover events persisted into the 1990s and grew increasingly unwieldy, inscrutable, and expensive. The expense, in fact, was another key to the industry's resurgence. With a loyal body of consumers through the direct market, publishers discovered to their delight that comic book price increases far surpassing the rate of inflation did not hurt sales.[45] By the early 1990s, most regular comic books retailed at $1.75, while special editions and graphic novels sold for anywhere from $2.50 to $25.00.

Publishers played heavily to the market for comic books as collectibles. They used the popularity of certain creators, usually artists, to hype the speculation value of particular issues. Comic book collectors and retailers colluded to some degree in this marketing by ascribing inflated prices to recent back issues. The best, or most notorious, ex-

ample of this was a new Spider-Man title launched by Marvel in 1990.
Marvel hyped this *Spider-Man* as the first series to be both written and
drawn entirely by a then very popular artist named Todd McFarlane.
The publisher printed multiple editions with several different covers
of the first issue, each of which was supposedly destined to become a
collector's item. That first issue sold well in excess of three million copies, a record at the time. Yet all that distinguished the issue and its mediocre story was McFarlane's distinctive artwork and marketable reputation. The following year, Marvel issued a similar "collectible" first issue
of a new X-Men title, which promptly sold over eight million copies.[46]

Publishers were well aware that their collectible *X-Men* issue did
not sell to eight million different consumers. Many were purchased by
speculators who bought multiple copies in order to hoard them for future sale at inflated prices in the collector's market. Of course, the fact
that publishers printed millions of these issues rendered any great future demand for them less likely. But speculation fever died hard. By
the 1990s, comic books had become the nation's third largest collectible
market, just after coins and stamps. Annual indices like the *Official
Overstreet Comic Book Price Guide* and periodicals like the *Comics Buyer's
Guide* and *Wizard* tracked the speculation value of comic books and
pointed readers to the "hottest" titles. Some fans bemoaned the importance that speculation had come to assume in comic book marketing and production. More than a few had watched in bemusement as
middle-aged men in business suits came into their local comic book
stores and picked through the shelves, leaving with hundreds of dollars
worth of comic books destined immediately for plastic bags to accrue
investment value. To encourage this kind of buying, publishers in the
1990s began to package some comic books in plastic bags ready-made
for speculators. Ideally, consumers would purchase at least two copies
of each issue, one to perhaps actually read and the other to preserve in
mint condition.[47]

The most valuable comic books from the 1930s and 1940s commanded prices in the five-figure range. While most collectors realized
that recent issues would never become so rare as to generate those kind
of prices, they were nevertheless beguiled by the occasional phenomenon epitomized by the *Teenage Mutant Ninja Turtles*. Initially a black-
and-white comic book published independently as a lark by two amateur cartoonists, the *Turtles* inexplicably proved to be one of the biggest
comic book successes of recent times, quickly graduating from comic
books into a megamerchandising bonanza. Those fortunate enough to
own one of the original three thousand copies of the 1984 comic book

could have sold it only seven years later for almost three hundred times its original value. Equally as unpredictable was the significance of a 1986 issue of *The Amazing Spider-Man*, which introduced a villain called Venom and was among the first to be drawn by Todd McFarlane. Within six years, the standard collector's price for the issue had increased 3,000 percent, and some dealers were asking as much as $100 for it. As long as the chance existed for such surprises, speculators would continue to purchase comic books as an investment, and publishers would gladly accommodate them.[48]

Publishers parlayed the fan and collector markets into spectacular growth. And, remarkably, they achieved this during a time when the size of the audience itself shrank to historically low levels. Surveys taken during the mid-1980s indicated that only about twenty million Americans, or 29 percent of the population between the ages of seven and twenty-four read comic books. Fewer people may have read comic books, but those who did consumed more issues and paid more for them than ever before. Surveys in the late 1980s revealed that the average consumer was a twenty-year-old male who spent about twenty dollars a month on comic books, and most of these transactions occurred through comic book stores. By facilitating the publishers' access to their niche audience, direct distribution had enabled the industry's sales to grow between 10 to 20 percent each year. By 1991 annual sales through comic book stores alone had reached $350 million. Moreover, newsstand circulation was improving as well. In 1993 industry-wide sales through all markets topped $1 billion. Chain stores like Waldenbooks had begun to stock comic books in the mid-1980s, thereby opening up all-important outlets in shopping malls. Increasing sales revenue allowed publishers to improve the physical quality and appearance of comic books by using sturdier paper and sharper color separation, and, as comic book sales increased along with the level of youth consumption in general, publishers finally began to attract more upscale advertising.[49] Replacing the old nickel-and-dime ads for X-ray Spex and plastic army-men were glossy advertisements for Hollywood films, video games, and fashionable clothing.

By the 1990s, the comic book industry had cause to congratulate itself. After decades in America's cultural gutter, comic books had finally emerged as a respectable and fantastically profitable entertainment industry worthy of a listing on the New York Stock Exchange. However, these impressive developments belied profound problems. The industry's audience remained precariously narrow, and comic books now had to compete with cable television, video games, and the

Internet for the increasing consumer dollars and shrinking attention spans of young people. The comic book industry had endured and overcome many challenges throughout its history, including public disdain, censorship efforts, shifting political culture, and changing youth tastes. Now, at the pinnacle of its earning power, the industry faced its greatest threat yet: disinterested young people.

Epilogue
The Death of Superman, or, Must There Be a Comic Book Industry?

In the fall of 1992 DC Comics announced that Superman would die. As expected, the event drew wide media coverage and editorial speculation on its cultural implications. A *New York Times* piece drew a convenient parallel to the recent electoral defeat of President George Bush and the failed Republican campaign of that year. Americans, according to the editorial, had rejected the Bush-Quayle version of "family values" for Bill Clinton, who, in spite of—or because of—his apparent personal failings, appealed to voters looking for new ideas, a younger vision, and a president more in touch with people like themselves. So, if Clinton was Spider-Man to Bush's Superman, how fitting then, that both of those respected, yet out-of-touch, heroes from the World War II generation should be retired in the same year. Of course, Superman did not really die. The event was only the latest in a series of concerted DC efforts to revive the Man of Steel's lackluster commercial performance. It worked, at least for a time; more than six million copies of the hyped "death issue" were sold and readers followed the drawn-out storyline culminating in the hero's inevitable reincarnation.[1]

A calculated stunt to be sure, the "Death of Superman" was nevertheless a powerful metaphor for American culture and the comic book industry in the post–Cold War era. The nation had changed tremendously since Superman first appeared in 1938. And if his time was passing, would Spider-Man's demise be far behind? Had popular culture's

landscape finally evolved beyond the capacity of the comic book industry to adapt? Was there still a meaningful place for comic books in
American culture and young lives?

The comic book industry suffered some shocks in the mid-1990s.
A fan backlash against artificial "collector's items" and one too many
confusing and expensive "crossover" series had cut deeply into Marvel's
and DC's sales. Industry sales had peaked at $1 billion in 1993 but fell
to $450 million by 1996.[2] Marvel bore much of the brunt. Under the
ownership of billionaire investor Ronald Perelman, Marvel Entertainment launched an aggressive licensing campaign in the early 1990s and
added two major sports trading card companies to its holdings. The
comic books themselves shrunk to only a small part of the corporation's
interests, as the percentage of Marvel's revenue earned from their sale
dropped from 88 percent in 1989 to only 17 percent in 1995. Plans for
Marvel theme parks, restaurants, and movies suggested that Perelman
had aspirations to become the next Walt Disney.[3]

A collapse in the trading card market following labor disputes in
professional baseball and hockey combined with a sharp fall-off in
comic book sales sent Marvel's stock plummeting. By December 1996
Marvel's debt had become so great that it filed for bankruptcy, and another billionaire investor, Carl Icahn, seized control of the company in
a high-level Wall Street power play. Marvel's comic book circulation
continued uninterrupted, but it was a humiliating spectacle for the
company and served to illustrate much of what had gone wrong in recent comic book publishing. Critics charged that overexpansion, inflation, and licensing ventures distracted from the quality of the comic
books, and readers had simply lost interest. A testament to their enduring popularity, Spider-Man and the X-Men were the only Marvel
superheroes whose comic books consistently sold well throughout the
crisis. In an effort to win back old fans and gain new ones, both major
publishers pared production, launched creative overhauls of their entire
lines, and capped rising comic book prices. Both had lost a percentage
of their sales to the small independent companies, which collectively
accounted for about a third of the contracted market.[4] In the late 1990s
Marvel launched an advertising campaign reemphasizing its roots as
the home of superheroes "willing to fight to protect our world, even
though we hate and fear them."[5]

The industry's troubles in recent years, however, run deeper than a
few misguided marketing and corporate strategies. The biggest problem is the transformation of American culture itself. The last decade of
the twentieth century saw a phenomenal expansion in the entertain-

ment choices available to young people and a glutted market for adolescent obsessions. Widely accessible cable television stations constantly air films, programs, and music videos directed at youth sensibilities. At least one station, the Sci-Fi Channel, is devoted exclusively to the kind of programming that overlaps with the fantasy appeal of comic books. Video and computer games have become one of the largest growth sectors of the entertainment industry by offering the kind of hands-on fantasy experience that comic books simply cannot match. And the Internet holds a potential for fantasy entertainment that is only beginning to be realized. Rather than simply reading about superheroes, interactive technology now makes it possible for young people to become virtual superheroes themselves. While comic book characters have successfully crossed over into all of these media, the consequences for the comic books themselves are less clear. Recognizing the significance of the new technology, Stan Lee, in his late seventies and serving as an honorary chairman of Marvel, launched a venture in 1999 to publish comic books exclusively over the Internet.[6] With so many appealing avenues for young people to indulge their angst and fantasies, the comic book industry has never faced more formidable competition.

There is yet another, more profound, transformation affecting American culture that raises problems for the comic book industry, and it is an ironic one. Comic books are losing their audience not because they have failed to keep up with changes in American culture but because American culture has finally caught up with them. Throughout their history, comic books thrived as a uniquely exaggerated and absurdist expression of adolescent concerns and sensibilities. But those qualities no longer make them unique. America at the turn of the twenty-first century has a pervasive consumer culture based largely on the perpetuation of adolescence. Young children acquire tastes in entertainment and fashion formerly reserved for their elder siblings, while middle-aged baby boomers go to rock concerts and buy designer athletic shoes once thought appropriate only for teenagers. In a media culture preoccupied with youth, commercials for investment firms look like music videos, televised sporting events look and sound like video games, and network political coverage can sound like the plot for an X-rated film. Is there a place for comic books in an America that has become a comic book parody of itself?

These are the challenges facing the comic book industry as it enters the new century. Its future may be in doubt. Yet, as recent outbreaks of violence at Columbine and other high schools have so horribly illustrated, young people continue to face a confusing, lonely, and sometimes frightening world that so often seems to spin out of control. For many, adolescence can be an age of intense pain and isolation, when emotional demons must be exorcised either through fantasy imitating life or by real action imitating fantasy. Should the former alternative be exhausted or denied, then some may choose the latter, possibly with tragic consequences. In these times it is as essential as ever to offer young people a wide choice for self-expression within a culture of empathy, compassion, and imagination. In this culture, comic books do have a place. And they will endure so long as they bring out the superhero in us all.

Notes

Introduction

1. John G. Cawelti, *Adventure, Mystery, and Romance* (Chicago: University of Chicago Press, 1976), 6.

2. William W. Savage Jr., *Comic Books and America, 1945–1954* (Norman: University of Oklahoma Press, 1990), xi.

1 Superheroes for the Common Man

1. "Superman," *Action Comics* 1 (DC Comics, June 1938).

2. John Kobler, "Up, Up, and Awa-a-y: The Rise of Superman, Inc.," *Saturday Evening Post*, 21 June 1941, 70; Mike Benton, *Superhero Comics of the Golden Age: The Illustrated History* (Dallas: Taylor Publishing Co., 1992), 9–12.

3. Lisa Yaszek, "'Them Damn Pictures': Americanization and the Comic Strip in the Progressive Era," *Journal of American Studies* 28 (April 1994): 23–28; "Funny Strips," *Literary Digest*, 12 December 1936, 18–19; Les Daniels, *Marvel: Five Fabulous Decades of the World's Greatest Comics* (New York: Harry N. Abrams, 1991), 14.

4. Daniels, *Marvel*, 15–21.

5. William H. Young Jr., "The Serious Funnies: Adventure Comics during the Depression, 1929–38," *Journal of Popular Culture* 3 (winter 1969): 404–27.

6. M. Thomas Inge, "A Chronology of the Development of the American Comic Book," in Robert M. Overstreet, ed., *The Official Overstreet Comic Book Price Guide*, no. 21 (New York: House of Collectibles, 1991), 71–72.

7. Ron Goulart, *Over Fifty Years of American Comic Books* (Lincolnwood, Ill.: Mallard Press, 1991), 18–19; Inge, "A Chronology," 72; Mike Benton, *The Comic Book in America: An Illustrated History* (Dallas: Taylor Publishing Co., 1989), 15–16.

8. Frank Jacobs, *The Mad World of William M. Gaines* (Secaucus, N.J.: Lyle Stuart, 1972), 54–55; Benton, *The Comic Book in America*, 17.

9. Ron Goulart, *The Comic Book Reader's Companion* (New York: Harper Collins, 1993), 60.

10. Jacobs, *Mad World*, 55–56.

11. Quoted in Les Daniels, *DC Comics: Sixty Years of the World's Favorite Comic Book Heroes* (Boston: Little, Brown, and Co., 1995), 15.

12. Goulart, *Over Fifty Years of American Comic Books*, 47; Bob Kane, "Bob Kane," interviewed by Dwight Jon Zimmerman, *Comics Interview* 31 (1986): 29; Barry Marx, ed., "Harry Donenfeld" and "Jack Liebowitz," *Fifty Who Made DC Great* (New York: DC Comics, 1985), 6–7, 12.

13. *Detective Comics* 1 (DC Comics, March 1937).

14. Daniels, *DC Comics*, 18.

15. Will Eisner, "Will Eisner: Reminiscences and Hortations," *Comics Journal* 89 (March 1984): 76.

16. Will Eisner, quoted in Steranko, *The Steranko History of Comics* (Reading, Pa.: Supergraphics, 1972), 2:112; Will Eisner, "Will Eisner Interview," interviewed by Cat Yronwode, *Comics Journal* 46 (May 1979): 34–49.

17. Joe Simon with Jim Simon, *The Comic Book Makers* (New York: Crestwood Publications, 1990), 41.

18. Will Eisner, "Getting the Last Laugh: My Life in Comics," *New York Times Book Review*, 14 January 1990, 26; Eisner, "Will Eisner: Reminiscences," 77.

19. Kobler, "Up, Up, and Awa-a-y," 73; "Slam Bradley," *Detective Comics* 1 (DC Comics, March 1937).

20. Marx, ed., "Harry Donenfeld" and "Sheldon Mayer," in *Fifty Who Made DC Great*, 6, 13.

21. Jerry Siegel, quoted in Kobler, "Up, Up, and Awa-a-y," 73.

22. Sheldon Mayer, quoted in Benton, *Superhero Comics*, 17; Sheldon Mayer quoted in Dennis O'Neil, ed., *Secret Origins of the Super DC Heroes* (New York: Warner Books, 1976), 13; Kobler, "Up, Up, and Awa-a-y," 73; *Action Comics* 1 (DC Comics, June 1938); Daniels, *DC Comics*, 22.

23. "Superman," *Action Comics* 1 (DC Comics, June 1938).

24. Richard Slotkin, *Gunfighter Nation: The Myth of the Frontier in Twentieth-Century America* (New York: Macmillan, 1992).

25. See Lawrence W. Levine, "American Culture and the Great Depression," *Yale Review* 74 (winter 1985): 196–218; Richard H. Pells, *Radical Visions and American Dreams: Culture and Social Thought in the Depression Years* (Middletown, Conn.: Wesleyan University Press, 1973).

26. Warren I. Susman, *Culture as History: The Transformation of American Society in the Twentieth Century* (New York: Pantheon Books, 1984), 184–210; Robert Sklar, *Movie-Made America: A Cultural History of American Movies* (New York: Random House, 1975), 175–214; Lary May, "Making the American Consensus: The Narrative of Conversion and Subversion in World War II Films," in Lewis A. Erenberg and Susan E. Hirsch, eds., *The War in American Culture: Society and Consciousness during World War II* (Chicago: University of Chicago Press, 1996), 79; David W. Stowe, *Swing Changes: Big-Band Jazz in New Deal America* (Cambridge: Harvard University Press, 1994), 13; Andrew Bergman, *We're in the Money: Depression America and Its Films* (New York: New York University Press, 1971), 167–68.

27. "Superman," *Action Comics* 1 (DC Comics, June 1938); Jules Feiffer, *The Great Comic Book Heroes* (New York: Dial Press, 1965), 17–18; "Revolution in San Monte," *Action Comics* 2 (DC Comics, July 1938).

28. "The Blakely Mine Disaster," *Action Comics* 3 (DC Comics, August 1938).

29. "The Economic Enemy," *Superman* 4 (DC Comics, spring 1940); see also "Luther's Incense Menace," *Superman* 5 (DC Comics, summer 1940), wherein American financiers and businessmen again conspire to lay off workers and plunge the nation into another depression. This time, however, the tycoons have been drugged and ordered to do so by the sinister Lex Luthor.

30. "Traffic Safety," *Action Comics* 12 (DC Comics, May 1939); "The Shoddy Subway Scheme," *Action Comics* 14 (DC Comics, July 1939); see also a similar story in which Superman brings to justice the crooked owner of a construction company who makes money by using dangerously cheap construction materials. "The Construction Racket," *Superman* 6 (DC Comics, October 1940).

31. "The Black Gold Oil Well," *Action Comics* 11 (DC Comics, April 1939).

32. "Gimpy the Fence," *Action Comics* 8 (DC Comics, January 1939); see also a

story in which Superman raises money for "Kid Town," a program that allows slum kids to spend time in a wholesome, rural environment. "Kid Town," *Action Comics* 15 (DC Comics, August 1939); for another example of poor urban juveniles being manipulated by adult racketeers, see "The Wonder Drug Racket," *Superman* 5 (DC Comics, summer 1940).

33. "Traffic Safety," *Action Comics* 12 (DC Comics, May 1939); "The Gambling Express," *Action Comics* 16 (DC Comics, September 1939).

34. Feiffer, *The Great Comic Book Heroes*, 18.

35. Kobler, "Up, Up, and Awa-a-y," 73.

36. Carmine Infantino and Sheldon Mayer, quoted in O'Neil, ed., *Secret Origins*, 14–15.

37. William W. Savage Jr., *Comic Books and America, 1945-1954* (Norman: University of Oklahoma Press, 1990), 7.

38. Kobler, "Up, Up, and Awa-a-y," 73–76.

39. "Escapist Paydirt," *Newsweek*, 27 December 1943, 55; Simon with Simon, *The Comic Book Makers*, 44.

40. Will Eisner quoted in Goulart, *Over Fifty Years of American Comic Books*, 85.

41. Simon with Simon, *The Comic Book Makers*, 40.

42. Bob Kane with Tom Andrae, *Batman and Me: An Autobiography of Bob Kane* (Forestville, Calif.: Eclipse Books, 1989), 35-43.

43. It would be easy to read too much into the psychological disposition of the comic book creators, but it may be worth noting that Bob Kane—unlike Jerry Siegel and Joe Shuster—was tall, handsome, and comfortable around women. Kane's own apparent self-confidence might explain his conception of a superhero who did not need superhuman powers. Jules Feiffer, a Superman fan, suspected "the Batman school of having healthier egos." Feiffer, *The Great Comic Book Heroes*, 27.

44. "The Case of the Chemical Syndicate," *Detective Comics* 27 (DC Comics, May 1939); "The Bat-Man Wars against the Dirigible of Doom," *Detective Comics* 33 (DC Comics, November 1939).

45. A frequent substitute, or "ghost artist," for Bob Kane, Jerry Robinson, cited *Citizen Kane* as a major influence on his own work and on that of his peers. Jerry Robinson, "Jerry Robinson," interviewed by Steve Ringgenberg, *Comics Interview* 57 (1988): 25.

46. "The Case of the City of Terror," *Detective Comics* 43 (DC Comics, September 1940).

47. For good examples, see "Batman vs. the Vampire," *Detective Comics* 32 (DC Comics, October 1939), featuring an eerie story set in the Balkans, complete with vampires and werewolves; see also "Professor Hugo Strange," *Detective Comics* 36 (DC Comics, February 1940); "The Screaming House," *Detective Comics* 37 (DC Comics, March 1940); and "The Horde of the Green Dragon," *Detective Comics* 39 (DC Comics, May 1940). This last story contains two bloody scenes in which men are killed with hatchets that are thrown into their skulls; Kane with Andrae, *Batman and Me*, 105–7; for examples of early Joker stories, see *Batman* 1 (DC Comics, spring 1940); and *The Greatest Joker Stories Ever Told* (New York: DC Comics, 1988), 11–36.

48. Kane with Andrae, *Batman and Me*, 46.

49. "The Human Torch" and "The Sub-Mariner," *Marvel Comics* 1 (Marvel Comics, November 1939).

50. "Capt. Marvel," *Whiz Comics* 2 (Fawcett Publications, February 1940).

51. "Doll Man," *Feature Comics* 27 (Quality Comics, December 1939); "Plastic Man," *Police Comics* 1 (Quality Comics, summer 1941); "The Spirit," *Police Comics* 11 (Quality Comics, September 1942); Eisner, "Will Eisner: Reminiscences," 80.

52. "The Flash" and "Hawkman," *Flash Comics* 1 (DC Comics, January 1940); "Dr. Fate," *More Fun Comics* 55 (DC Comics, May 1940); Gardner Fox to James Flanagan, 26 March 1979, reprinted in *Robin Snyder's History of the Comics* 2, no. 2 (February 1991), 14.

53. "The Spectre," *More Fun Comics* 52 (DC Comics, February 1940); "Dr. Mid-Nite," *All-American Comics* 24 (DC Comics, March 1941); "Hourman," *Adventure Comics* 48 (DC Comics, March 1940); "Introducing the Mighty Atom," *All-American Comics* 19 (DC Comics, October 1940).

54. "Wonder Woman," *Sensation Comics* 1 (DC Comics, January 1942); Gloria Steinem, "Introduction," *Wonder Woman* (New York: Holt, Rinehart, and Winston, 1972); Trina Robbins, *The Great Women Superheroes* (Northampton, Mass.: Kitchen Sink Press, 1996), 3–14; "The Milk Racket of Paula Von Gunther," *Sensation Comics* 7 (DC Comics, July 1942); in "Battle of the Bullfinch Store," *Sensation Comics* 8 (DC Comics, August 1942), Wonder Woman helps some young women improve working conditions in a department store.

55. "The Adventure of the Life Vitamin," *Wonder Woman* 7 (DC Comics, winter 1943).

56. For some of the more obvious bondage and domination images, see "The Slaves of the Evil Eye," *Wonder Woman* 10 (DC Comics, fall 1944), in which Diana Prince's boyfriend Steve Trevor is enslaved by a woman dressed in black and armed with a whip; and "The Treasonous Translator," *Sensation Comics* 13 (DC Comics, January 1943), in which Wonder Woman gets trapped in her own magic lasso (which happened a lot) and must obey a Nazi spy named Olga, whom she addresses as "Mistress"; William Moulton Marston, "Why 100,000,000 Americans Read the Comics," *American Scholar*, January 1944, 43.

57. Sheldon Mayer, quoted in Benton, *Superhero Comics*, 33.

58. Alan Brinkley, *The End of Reform: New Deal Liberalism in Recession and War* (New York: Alfred A. Knopf, 1995).

59. "The Tycoon's Legacy," *Green Lantern* 2 (DC Comics, winter 1941–42).

60. "The Slave Racket," *All-American Comics* 24 (DC Comics, March 1941).

61. "The Waterfront Mystery," *All-American Comics* 26 (DC Comics, May 1941); "The Taxi Cab Murder Plot," *Adventure Comics* 60 (DC Comics, March 1941); "The Minute Men of America," *Adventure Comics* 53 (DC Comics, August 1940).

62. "Smashing the Enemies of Free Speech," *National Comics* 2 (Quality Comics, August 1940).

63. "The Sign of the Green Lantern," *All-American Comics* 17 (DC Comics, August 1940); "The Adventure of the Underfed Orphans," *All-American Comics* 31 (DC Comics, October 1941).

64. "The Building Racket," *All-American Comics* 34 (DC Comics, January 1942); see also "Dr. Mid-Nite," *All-American Comics* 35 (DC Comics, February 1942), wherein Dr. Mid-Nite joins the Clean Government Society to fight corruption.

65. "Counterfeit Coal," *Adventure Comics* 66 (DC Comics, September 1941); see also "The Case of the City of Terror," *Detective Comics* 43 (DC Comics, September 1940), wherein Batman and Robin must free a town from the iron grip of a dictatorial political leader; "Bert Runyan's Campaign," *Superman* 7 (DC Comics, November–December 1940), in which Superman embarks on a campaign against "conniving public officeholders"; and "Campaign against the *Planet*," *Superman* 5 (DC Comics, summer 1940), in which a crooked grafting politician tries to buy the *Daily Planet* and use it for his own propaganda.

66. "Suicide Beat," *Batman* 6 (DC Comics, August–September 1941).

67. "A Buzz from the Green Hornet," *The Green Hornet* 2 (Helnit Publishing, March 1941).

68. William E. Leuchtenburg, *Franklin D. Roosevelt and the New Deal* (New York: Harper and Row, 1963), 107–8.

69. "The Taxi War," *All-American Comics* 33 (DC Comics, December 1941). See also "Bulldog Martin," *More Fun Comics* 52 (DC Comics, February 1940), in which a racketeer named Boss "Duke" Tweed gains control of the Barbers' Union, the Bartenders' Union, the Meat Cutters' Union, and the Teamsters' Union, before the hero and the police bring him to justice; see also "Terror in the Truckers' Union," *Superman* 4 (DC Comics, spring 1940); and "Trigger Daniel's Death Curse," *More Fun Comics* 63 (DC Comics, January 1941), both of which feature stories about racketeers who take over labor unions.

70. Grace Palladino, *Teenagers: An American History* (New York: Basic Books, 1996), 7–8; Richard A. Reiman, *The New Deal and American Youth: Ideas and Ideals in a Depression Decade* (Athens, Georgia: University of Georgia Press, 1992), 184–90.

71. Gary Cross, *Kid's Stuff: Toys and the Changing World of American Childhood* (Cambridge: Harvard University Press, 1997), 100–120.

72. Sterling North, "A National Disgrace," *Chicago Daily News*, 8 May 1940, reprinted in *Parents' Magazine*, March 1941, 26.

73. "Libraries to Arms," *Wilson Library Bulletin* 15 (April 1941): 670; Clara Savage Littledale, "What to Do about the 'Comics,'" *Parents' Magazine*, March 1941, 26–27, 93.

74. James Frank Vlamos, "The Sad Case of the Funnies," *American Mercury*, April 1941, 411–16.

75. Sklar, *Movie-Made America*, 195.

76. Slater Brown, "The Coming of Superman," *New Republic*, 2 September 1940, 301.

2 Race, Politics, and Propaganda

1. "Meet Captain America," *Captain America Comics* 1 (Marvel Comics, March 1941).

2. "The Comics and Their Audience," *Publishers Weekly*, 18 April 1942, 1479; "Superman Scores," *Business Week*, 18 April 1942, 54; "Escapist Paydirt," *Newsweek*, 27 December 1943, 55.

3. "Escapist Paydirt," 55; Michael C. C. Adams, *The Best War Ever: America and World War II* (Baltimore: Johns Hopkins University Press, 1993), 91; Lieutenant J.G., "Nudes Preferred," letter, *New York Times*, 2 August 1944; Theodore J. Harmatz, "Comics Have a Place," *New York Times*, 6 August 1944; Sanderson Vanderbilt, "The Comics," *Yank: The Army Weekly*, 23 November 1945.

4. "Escapist Paydirt," 55; *New York Times*, 16 May 1943, 39; William Woolfolk, "William Woolfolk," interviewed by Lou Mougin, *Comics Interview* 28 (1985): 33; Howard Nostrand, "The Mystery Artist," *Comics Journal* 96 (March 1985): 100; *New York Times*, 23 May 1945; *Captain Marvel Adventures* 41 (Fawcett Publications, November 1944).

5. Mike Benton, *Superhero Comics of the Golden Age: The Illustrated History* (Dallas: Taylor Publishing Co., 1992), 53–54; Woolfolk, "William Woolfolk," 33; Trina Robbins and Catherine Yronwode, *Women and the Comics* (Guerneville, Calif.: Eclipse Books, 1985), 50–52.

6. "A Message to Our Readers: Introducing the Editorial Advisory Board," *More Fun Comics* 72 (DC Comics, October 1941).

7. *Master Comics* 51 (Fawcett Publications, June 1944); *All-Hero Comics* 1 (Fawcett Publications, 17 March 1943); *Clue Comics* 4 (Hillman Periodicals, June 1943).

8. *Superman* 34 (DC Comics, May–June 1945); *Batman* 17 (DC Comics, June–July 1944); *Captain America Comics* 33 (Marvel Comics, December 1943); *Captain Marvel Adventures* 14 (Fawcett Publications, 21 August 1942); *Captain America Comics* 37 (Marvel Comics, April 1944); *All Star Comics* 12 (DC Comics, August–September 1942).

9. John Morton Blum, *V Was for Victory: Politics and American Culture During World War II* (New York: Harcourt Brace Jovanovich, 1976), 21–52; Clayton R. Koppes and Gregory D. Black, *Hollywood Goes to War: How Politics, Profits, and Propaganda Shaped World War II Movies* (New York: Free Press, 1987), 48–81.

10. Henry A. Wallace, "The Price of Free World Victory: The Century of the Common Man," *Vital Speeches of the Day* 7 (1942), 482–85; Richard Slotkin, *Gunfighter Nation: The Myth of the Frontier in Twentieth-Century America* (New York: Macmillan Publishing Company, 1992), 318–26; Lewis A. Erenberg and Susan E. Hirsch, "Introduction," in Erenberg and Hirsch, eds., *The War in American Culture: Society and Consciousness during World War II* (Chicago: University of Chicago Press, 1996), 1–13; Lary May, "Making the American Consensus: The Narrative of Conversion and Subversion in World War II Films," in Erenberg and Hirsch, eds., *The War in American Culture*, 78–96.

11. Jack Kirby, "Jack Kirby," interviewed by Gary Groth, *Comics Journal* 134 (February 1990): 62–66, 76; Benton, *Superhero Comics*, 50–51.

12. Joe Simon, interviewed by Carole Kalish, "The American Dream . . . Come True," *Comics Feature* 10 (July 1981): 26.

13. Les Daniels, *Marvel: Five Fabulous Decades of the World's Greatest Comics* (New York: Harry N. Abrams, 1990), 37–40.

14. "The Crocodiles of Death River," *Jungle Comics* 3 (Fiction House, March 1940); "The Return of Sam Broot," *Jungle Comics* 4 (Fiction House, April 1940); see also "The Pharaoh's Treasure," *Action Comics* 16 (DC Comics, September 1939), in which the hero exposes a white criminal who has duped some Arabs into believing that he is an Egyptian god, and "Gloria Desmond's Quest," *More Fun Comics* 59 (DC Comics, September 1940), wherein the hero fools his African captors into believing that he is a god.

15. "Sheena, Queen of the Jungle," *Jumbo Comics* 19 (Fiction House, September 1940).

16. "Zatara, Master Magician and the Zulu Diamond Mine," *Action Comics* 7 (DC Comics, December 1938); "The Arab Avalanche," *More Fun Comics* 64 (DC Comics, February 1941); "Captain Desmo," *Adventure Comics* 45 (DC Comics, December 1939); "Zara of the Jungle," *Mystic Comics* 2 (Marvel Comics, April 1940); "The War of the Green Gas," *Jumbo Comics* 11 (Fiction House, January 1940).

17. "Adventure in India," *More Fun Comics* 60 (DC Comics, October 1940); see also "Captain Desmo," *More Fun Comics* 63 (DC Comics, January 1941), wherein the captain foils an Axis agent who has enlisted the unwitting aid of Pacific Island natives in the war against the British; for an example of a hero defending the interests of the French Empire, see "The Coming of the Congo Lancers," *Jungle Comics* 1 (Fiction House, January 1940).

18. "Espionage," *Smash Comics* 1 (Quality Comics, August 1939).

19. "Espionage," *Smash Comics* 3 (Quality Comics, October 1939).

20. "Espionage," *Smash Comics* 5 (Quality Comics, December 1939); see also "The Atomic Bomb," *Target Comics* 11 (Novelty Publications, December 1940), in

which a belligerent foreign nation tries to frighten the United States into remaining neutral by producing an "atomic bomb." The bomb, naturally, turns out to be a hoax.

21. *Marvel Mystery Comics* 4 (Marvel Comics, February 1940); Harry B. Thomas and Gary M. Carter, "1941: Comic Books Go to War," in Robert M. Overstreet, ed., *The Official Overstreet Comic Book Price Guide*, no. 21 (New York: House of Collectibles, 1991), 81; Stan Lee, *Secrets behind the Comics* (New York: Famous Enterprises, 1947), 65.

22. "The Sub-Mariner Goes to War," *Marvel Mystery Comics* 4 (Marvel Comics, March 1940).

23. "The Human Torch," *The Human Torch* 3 (Marvel Comics, winter 1940–41); "Meet the Destroyer," *Mystic Comics* 6 (Marvel Comics, October 1941); "Blackhawk," *Military Comics* 1 (Quality Comics, August 1941); "Blitzkrieg of the Living Dead," *The Human Torch* 4 (Marvel Comics, summer 1941).

24. Ron Goulart, *The Comic Book Reader's Companion* (New York: Harper, 1993), 43; Dan Barry, "Dan Barry," interviewed by Rick Norwood and David Anthony Kraft, *Comics Interview* 82 (1992): 56; *Daredevil Battles Hitler* 1 (Your Guide Publications, July 1941).

25. "The Man of Hate: Adolf Hitler—Dictator of Germany," *Daredevil Battles Hitler* 1 (Your Guide Publications, July 1941).

26. "The Wizard," *Top-Notch Comics* 1 (MLJ Magazines, December 1939); "Anchors Aweigh," *Adventure Comics* 45 (DC Comics, December 1939); "Captain Battle, Savior of Chungking," *Captain Battle Comics* 1 (New Friday Publications, summer 1941); "The Bombing of Pearl Harbor," *National Comics* 18 (Quality Comics, December 1941); see also "The Floating Islands," *National Comics* 4 (Quality Comics, October 1940), wherein U.S. forces repel the invading force of "a small Asiatic power" near the Philippines, and "The Gruesome Secret of the Dragon of Death," *Captain America Comics* 5 (Marvel Comics, August 1941), which finds the Japanese plotting to attack Pearl Harbor.

27. "Uncle Sam," *National Comics* 1 (Quality Comics, July 1940); "Minute-Man," *Master Comics* 11 (Fawcett Publications, February 1941); "The Star-Spangled Kid," *Action Comics* 40 (DC Comics, September 1941); Thomas and Carter, "1941: Comic Books Go to War," 79–98.

28. "The True Story of Uncle Sam," *National Comics* 5 (Quality Comics, November 1940).

29. "The Justice Society of America," *All Star Comics* 11 (DC Comics, June–July 1942); "Green Lantern and Doiby Join the Army," *The Green Lantern* 4 (DC Comics, summer 1942); "Captain Marvel Joins the Army," *Captain Marvel Adventures* 12 (Fawcett Publications, June 1942).

30. "Superman," reprinted in Michael Uslan, ed., *America at War: The Best of DC War Comics* (New York: Simon and Schuster, 1979), 45.

31. "The Phony Pacifists," *Superman* 9 (DC Comics, March–April 1941); "Superman," *Action Comics* 36 (DC Comics, May 1941); "The American Crusader," *Thrilling Comics* 23 (Better Publications, December 1941).

32. "The House Where Time Stood Still," *Star Spangled Comics* 21 (DC Comics, June 1943).

33. "The Little Rebel," *Star Spangled Comics* 26 (DC Comics, November 1943).

34. "Red, White, and Blue," *All-American Comics* 31 (DC Comics, October 1941).

35. "Dr. Mid-Nite," *All-American Comics* 37 (DC Comics, April 1942); "The Black Widow," *Mystic Comics* 7 (Marvel Comics, December 1941); see also "Satan to

See You," *The Boy Commandos* 5 (DC Comics, winter 1943–44), in which Satan takes the form of a businessman and makes a deal with a Nazi for his soul, and "Catalyst for Catastrophe," *Star Spangled Comics* 29 (DC Comics, February 1944), wherein an industrialist accepts a defense contract from the government and then sabotages his own plant—it turns out he is a Nazi sympathizer and former member of the American Bund.

36. John W. Dower, *War without Mercy: Race and Power in the Pacific War* (New York: Pantheon Books, 1986), 9; for some transparently racist and hateful examples, see "The Terror of the Slimy Japs," *All Winners* 4 (Marvel Comics, spring 1942); "The Slant Eye of Satan," *Green Hornet Comics* 25 (Family Comics, July 1945); "Funeral for Yellow Dogs," *Green Hornet Comics* 22 (Family Comics, January 1945); "Terror in the Trees," *Star Spangled Comics* 39 (DC Comics, December 1944); "The Gruesome Secret of the Dragon of Death," *Captain America Comics* 5 (Marvel Comics, August 1941); "The Justice Society of America," *All Star Comics* 11 (DC Comics, June–July 1942); and "Airboy," *Air Fighters Comics* 2 (Hillman Periodicals, November 1942).

37. "The Justice Society of America," *All Star Comics* 12 (DC Comics, August–September 1942).

38. Ibid.; see also "Captain Marvel," *Captain Marvel Adventures* 8 (Fawcett Publications, March 1942), which portrays Japanese Americans working against the United States because the Japanese government has threatened to harm their families back in the home islands; in "The Atom," *All-American Comics* 41 (DC Comics, August 1942), a Japanese spy working in the United States escapes after F.B.I. agents start rounding up "all the Japanese aliens in this country."

39. For a few of the many examples of Hitler and the Nazis caricatured, see "Meet the Squiffles," *Superman* 22 (DC Comics, May–June 1943); "Castle of Doom," *Captain America Comics* 38 (Marvel Comics, May 1944); and "Daredevil Battles Hitler," *Daredevil Battles Hitler* 1 (Your Guide Publications, July 1941); Koppes and Black, *Hollywood Goes to War*, 281; two classic Nazi supervillains were Captain America's archenemy, the Red Skull, and Captain Marvel Jr.'s foe, Captain Nazi. See, respectively, "Meet Captain America," *Captain America Comics* 1 (Marvel Comics, March 1941); and "Captain Marvel, Jr." *Captain Marvel Jr.* 1 (Fawcett Publications, 18 November 1942).

40. Koppes and Black, *Hollywood Goes to War*, 281; "Skell the Ruthless," *Military Comics* 26 (Quality Comics, February 1944); "The Machine of Death," *Mystic Comics* 7 (Marvel Comics, December 1941); "The Biography of a Nazi," *Comic Cavalcade* 4 (DC Comics, fall 1943).

41. "Killers of the Bund," *Captain America Comics* 5 (Marvel Comics, August 1941); "Wings Wendall of the Military Intelligence," *Smash Comics* 7 (Quality Comics, February 1940).

42. "This Is Our Enemy," *All Star Comics* 24 (DC Comics, spring 1944).

43. "The Justice Society of America," *All Star Comics* 11 (DC Comics, June–July 1942).

44. For examples of American superheroes fighting alongside the Chinese, see "Commando Yank Defends the Great Wall of China," *Wow Comics* 16 (Fawcett Publications, August 1943); "Clip Carson," *More Fun Comics* 76 (DC Comics, February 1942); and "Dragons on the River," *Star Spangled Comics* 40 (DC Comics, January 1943); the specific reference to Chiang Kai-shek's regime appears in "Mother Wong," *Captain America Comics* 33 (Marvel Comics, December 1943).

45. "The Mallet Strikes," *Daredevil* 11 (Comic House, June 1942).

46. "The Lesson of the Lotus," *Boy Commandos* 12 (DC Comics, fall 1945).

47. "Mission to Finland," *Smash Comics* 10 (Quality Comics, May 1940).

48. "Kuzma, Russian Hero," *Heroic Comics* 26 (Eastern Color, September 1944); "The Siege of Krovka," *Detective Comics* 69 (DC Comics, November 1942); see also "Mary Marvel and the Anxious Auctioneer," *Wow Comics* 12 (Fawcett Publications, April 1943), in which Mary Marvel organizes an auction for Russian War Relief; Airboy is sent to Russia to help ensure the passage of lend-lease supplies in "Airboy," *Air Fighters Comics* 3 (Hillman Periodicals, December 1943).

49. "Green Lantern in South America," *Green Lantern* 1 (DC Comics, autumn 1941).

50. "The Steel Mask," *Captain America Comics* 35 (Marvel Comics, February 1944); "The Justice Society of America," *All Star Comics* 9 (DC Comics, February–March 1942); see also "Senorita Rio," *Fight Comics* 20 (Fiction House, August 1942), wherein Rio, a U.S. agent, helps the Argentine government combat the indigenous Condor Legion, described as the "vicious, black-shirted puppets of the Axis."

51. "South American Trap," *The Black Terror* 7 (Better Publications, August 1944); "The All-American Way," *Star Spangled Comics* 28 (DC Comics, January 1944).

52. "The Justice Society of America," *All Star Comics* 16 (DC Comics, February–March 1943).

53. "A Tale of a City," *Comic Cavalcade* 9 (DC Comics, winter 1944–45).

54. Examples of the latter could be found in virtually all jungle-adventure comic books; for examples of the former, see "Captain Marvel and the Copper Feud," *Captain Marvel Adventures* 11 (Fawcett Publications, May 1942). Billy Batson's valet, named "Steamboat" and portrayed in the style of a blackfaced minstrel performer with oversized white eyes and white-rimmed lips, was a comical supporting character in the series; see also the Spirit's "faithful servant" Ebony, another recurring sidekick caricature in "The Spirit," *Police Comics* 25 (Quality Comics, December 1943); see also Sunshine, a black youth with exaggerated lips who speaks in the semiliterate Southern vernacular commonly associated with these caricatures, in "Kid Patrol," *National Comics* 16 (Quality Comics, October 1941).

55. "Here Come the Indians," *Spy-Smasher* 1 (Fawcett Publications, fall 1941); see also "The Justice Society of America," *All Star Comics* 12 (DC Comics, August–September 1942), wherein Japanese agents incite Southwestern American Indians to attack a U.S. Army base, and "Empire of Exiles," *Green Lantern* 6 (DC Comics, winter 1942–43), in which various tribes throughout North and South America pledge to fight for their respective governments against the Axis. Unlike the stereotypes in the previous example, these Native Americans appear to be intelligent and cosmopolitan.

3 Confronting Success

1. "Captain Marvel and the American Century," *Captain Marvel Adventures* 110 (Fawcett Publications, July 1950).

2. *New York Times*, 25 June 1946.

3. Sanderson Vanderbilt, "The Comics," *Yank: The Army Weekly*, 23 November 1945.

4. "Cold Wave Permanent," advertisement, *Captain Marvel Jr.* 40 (Fawcett Publications, July 1946); "Do You Want Longer Hair?" advertisement, *Comic Land* 1 (Fact and Fiction Publications, March 1946); "Learning Radio," advertisement, *Firehair Comics* 1 (Fiction House, winter 1948).

5. Mike Benton, *The Comic Book in America* (Dallas: Taylor Publishing Co., 1989), 57.

6. Warren B. Kuhn, "Don't Laugh at the Comics," *Writer,* February 1951, 48.

7. James T. Patterson, *Grand Expectations: The United States, 1945–1974* (New York: Oxford University Press, 1996), 59–60.

8. For representative examples of the postwar Green Lantern, see "The Harlequin Haunts Green Lantern," *Green Lantern* 29 (DC Comics, December 1947–January 1948); and "The Impossible Mr. Paradox," *Green Lantern* 38 (DC Comics, May–June 1949); for examples of the postwar Batman see the stories reprinted in *Batman: From the 30s to the 70s* (New York: Bonanza Books, 1971), 88–230; see also *The Greatest Joker Stories Ever Told* (New York: DC Comics, 1988), 64–129; and *The Greatest 1950s Stories Ever Told* (New York: DC Comics, 1990).

9. For representative examples of postwar Superman stories, see those reprinted in *Superman: From the 30s to the 70s* (New York: Bonanza Books, 1971), 174–265.

10. "Supersuit," *Newsweek,* 14 April 1947, 65; "Superseding Superman," *Newsweek,* 19 July 1948, 51.

11. Longtime Superman artist Curt Swan and writer Alvin Schwartz both recalled that Weisinger insisted upon strict editorial control over all Superman stories. Weisinger, according to Swan and Schwartz, would either ignore or ridicule their suggestions for story ideas. See Curt Swan, "Curt Swan: An Interview with Superman's Main Artist," interviewed by Rich Morrisey, Dwight Decker, and Gary Groth, *Comics Journal* 73 (July 1982): 75; and Alvin Schwartz, "Alvin Schwartz," interview, *Comics Interview* 117 (1993): 25–28.

12. "Filipinos Are People," *Comic Cavalcade* 9 (DC Comics, winter 1944–45).

13. "Room for Improvement," *World's Finest Comics* 22 (DC Comics, July–August 1946).

14. Ibid.; in "Meet Charley Wing," *Comic Cavalcade* 12 (DC Comics, fall 1945), Johnny Everyman deplores the unfavorable stereotypes held about Asian Americans; and in "The American Dream," *World's Finest Comics* 22 (DC Comics, May–June 1946), Johnny urges children to recall that America is a land of diverse ethnic and racial heritage.

15. Marya Mannes, "Junior Has a Craving," *New Republic,* 17 February 1947, 23; "Talking Shop," *Wilson Library Bulletin* 23 (November 1948): 257.

16. Jack Schiff, "Public Service," *Robin Snyder's History of the Comics* 2, no. 7 (July 1991): 75; *New York Times,* 18 August 1949.

17. Schwartz, "Alvin Schwartz," 27.

18. "Know Your Country," *Mystery in Space* 2 (DC Comics, June–July 1951); "People Are People," *Mystery in Space* 13 (DC Comics, April–May 1952).

19. Ron Goulart, *The Comic Book Reader's Companion* (New York: Harper, 1993), 135.

20. Nazi war criminals are the preeminent international villains in "The Brand of the Swastika," *Master Comics* 63 (Fawcett Publications, September 1945); "Viper's Nest," *Master Comics* 67 (Fawcett Publications, April 1946); and "The Butcher," *Master Comics* 71 (Fawcett Publications, August 1946), which finds Radar pursuing Nazis who are hiding out in South America. Radar oversees U.S. and UN humanitarian relief to Europe in "Guest for Death," *Master Comics* 78 (Fawcett Publications, April 1947); "The Food Train," *Master Comics* 84 (Fawcett Publications, October 1947); and "Food for Thought," *Master Comics* 75 (Fawcett Publications, February 1947). See also "The International Bank Mystery," *Master Comics* 68 (Fawcett Publications, May 1946), which finds the profiteering fascist leader of a European nation hoarding the money loaned to his war-ravaged country by the UN's International Bank.

21. "Radar, the International Policeman," *Master Comics* 54 (Fawcett Publications, September 1944); "The Death-Dealing Playboy," *Master Comics* 79 (Fawcett Publications, May 1947); see also "The Sinister Smugglers," *Master Comics* 64 (Fawcett Publications, November–December 1945), in which an American businessman helps other American right-wingers smuggle Nazi war criminals into the United States in order to build an underground fascist army.

22. "The Cartels of Crime," *Master Comics* 62 (Fawcett Publications, July 1945); see also "The Red Cross Mystery," *Master Comics* 72 (Fawcett Publications, September 1946), wherein Radar brings to justice a foreign oil magnate and fascist named Francisco Perono, who has been using slave labor in his industry to help him undersell the international market.

23. "The Border Incident," *Master Comics* 77 (Fawcett Publications, March 1947).

24. "Arsenal of Hate," *Master Comics* 65 (Fawcett Publications, January 1946); "Mein Kampf—Post-War Version," *Master Comics* 68 (Fawcett Publications, May 1946).

25. "Captain Marvel and the Imperfect Perfection," *Captain Marvel Adventures* 113 (Fawcett Publications, October 1950).

26. "Captain Marvel: Citizen of the Universe," *Captain Marvel Adventures* 111 (Fawcett Publications, August 1950); see also "Captain Marvel and the United Worlds," *Captain Marvel Adventures* 97 (Fawcett Publications, June 1949).

27. "Atoman," *Atoman* 1 (Spark Publications, February 1946); Fawcett's Radar also endorsed international control of the atom bomb.

28. Ibid. In "Mission to Calcutta," *Master Comics* 80 (Fawcett Publications, June 1947), an Indian scientist invents a bomb even more powerful than the atom bomb and trusts Radar to deliver it safely to the UN for responsible international control.

29. "Captain Marvel and the World of Mr. Atom," *Captain Marvel Adventures* 90 (Fawcett Publications, November 1948); "Captain Marvel and the End of the World," *Captain Marvel Adventures* 71 (Fawcett Publications, April 1947).

30. "Captain Marvel and the Missing Atom," *Captain Marvel Adventures* 104 (Fawcett Publications, January 1950).

31. Charles Phillips, *Archie: His First Fifty Years* (New York: Abbeville Press, 1991); *Archie Americana Series: Best of the Fifties* (Mamaroneck, N.Y.: Archie Comic Publications, 1992); "The Old Home Town," *Archie Comics* 35 (Archie Comics, November–December 1948) explicitly underscores small town values; Archie affirms respect for parents and adult authority in "Pop's Tops!" *Archie Comics* 58 (Archie Comics, September–October 1951); and "There Oughta Be a Law," *Archie's Pals and Gals* 3 (Archie Comics, 1954–55); Betty and Veronica chase boys in almost every issue, but a good example of their self-assertion is "The Low-Down Highbrow," *Archie Comics* 58 (Archie Comics, September–October 1952), in which Veronica explicitly values intelligence over typical male buffoonery.

32. See the cover of *The Sub-Mariner* 24 (Marvel Comics, winter 1947–48); "Meet the Asbestos Lady," *Human Torch* 27 (Marvel Comics, summer 1947); "Golden Girl," *Captain America Comics* 66 (Marvel Comics, April 1948); see the cover of *Phantom Lady* 17 (Fox Features Syndicate, April 1948).

33. Trina Robbins and Catherine Yronwode, *Women and the Comics* (Guerneville, Calif.: Eclipse Books, 1985), 52–57. For a few of the many examples of sadomasochism, see the adventures of Tiger Girl, who ruled the jungles of India with a whip in "Tiger Girl," *Fight Comics* 53 (Fiction House, December 1947); in "Space Rangers," *Planet Comics* 40 (Fiction House, January 1946) a cruel alien woman keeps her slaves in line with a whip; in "Kayo Kirby," *Fight Comics* 49 (Fiction House, April

1947) a female villain binds a male victim with rope and places her high-heeled foot on his head.

34. See William W. Savage Jr., *Comic Books and America, 1945–1954* (Norman, University of Oklahoma Press, 1990), 75–77.

35. "Camilla," *Jungle Comics* 96 (Fiction House, December 1947); see also "Camilla," *Jungle Comics* 74 (Fiction House, February 1946), wherein Camilla must pacify a hostile native uprising so that the jungle can be cleared for white traders.

36. "Sheena, Queen of the Jungle," *Jumbo Comics* 104 (Fiction House, October 1947); "Sheena, Queen of the Jungle," *Jumbo Comics* 149 (Fiction House, July 1951).

37. Warren I. Susman with the assistance of Edward Griffin, "Did Success Spoil the United States?" in Lary May, ed, *Recasting America: Culture and Politics in the Age of Cold War* (Chicago: University of Chicago Press, 1989), 22–33.

38. Mike Benton, *Crime Comics: The Illustrated History* (Dallas: Taylor Publishing Co., 1993), 19–21.

39. Ibid., 33.

40. See for example, "Agency for Crimes," *Gang Busters* 1 (DC Comics, December 1947–January 1948); and "Warden of the Big House," *Gang Busters* 30 (DC Comics, October–November 1952), which undertook the formidable proposition of casting a prison warden as a hero.

41. "The Wild Spree of the Laughing Sadist—Herman Duker," *Crime Does Not Pay* 57 (Lev Gleason Publications, November 1947).

42. "Carlo Barrone, the Murderous Bully," *Crime Does Not Pay* 53 (Lev Gleason Publications, July 1947).

43. "The Woman Who Wouldn't Die," *Crime Does Not Pay* 52 (Lev Gleason Publications, June 1947); discussed with illustrations in Benton, *Crime Comics*, 50–51.

44. "Bullet Man of the Bowery," *Crime Must Pay the Penalty* 2 (Junior Books, June 1948); Benton, *Crime Comics*, 42. For an example of the crude style of Fox's crime comic books, see "James Wayburn Hall—the Arkansas Butcher," *Murder Incorporated* 5 (Fox Features Syndicate, September 1948); "Murder, Morphine, and Me," *True Crime Comics* 2 (Magazine Village, May 1947).

45. "Machine-Gun Kelly," *Crime Does Not Pay* 65 (Lev Gleason Publications, July 1948).

46. "The Short but Furious Crime Career of Irene Dague and Her Yes-Man Husband," *Crime Does Not Pay* 57 (Lev Gleason Publications, November 1947); "Mike Alex," *Crime Does Not Pay* 67 (Lev Gleason Publications, September 1948); "Bonnie Parker," *Crime Does Not Pay* 57 (Lev Gleason Publications, November 1947). See also "Adam and Eve—Crime Incorporated," *Lawbreakers Always Lose* 1 (Marvel Comics, spring 1948); and "The Cleveland Vulture," *Crime Must Pay the Penalty* 7 (Junior Books, April 1949), wherein a domineering woman goads a small-time burglar into committing more ambitious crimes for her.

47. "Mike Alex," *Crime Does Not Pay* 67 (Lev Gleason Publications, September 1948); "Albert Judson," *Crime Does Not Pay* 65 (Lev Gleason Publications, July 1948).

48. "New Hope for Bad Skin Sufferers," advertisement in *Crime and Punishment* 31 (Lev Gleason Publications, October 1950); "Redoos-U-Suit," advertisement in *Crime and Punishment* 36 (Lev Gleason Publications, March 1951); "Kitchen Knives" and "Mutual Hospitalization Insurance," advertisements in *Crime and Punishment* 35 (Lev Gleason Publications, February 1951); and "Sportsman Knives" and "Dick Tracy Tommy-Gun," advertisements in *Crime Does Not Pay* 53 (Lev Gleason Publications, July 1947).

4 Youth Crisis

1. *New York Times*, 11 December 1948; *New York Times*, 23 December 1948; "Fighting Gunfire with Fire," *Newsweek*, 20 December 1948, 54.

2. Thomas Doherty, *Teenagers and Teenpics: The Juvenilization of American Movies in the 1950s* (Boston: Unwin Hyman, 1988), 44–46; Grace Palladino, *Teenagers: An American History* (New York: Basic Books, 1996), 97–115; James Gilbert, *A Cycle of Outrage: America's Reaction to the Juvenile Delinquent in the 1950s* (New York: Oxford University Press, 1986), 26–41.

3. "540 Million Comics Published during 1946," *Publishers Weekly*, 6 September 1947, 1030; J. Donald Adams, "Speaking of Books," *New York Times Book Review*, 16 December 1945, 2.

4. Reita I. Bean, "The Comics Bogey," *American Home*, November 1945, 29.

5. Benjamin Spock, *The Common Sense Book of Baby and Child Care* (New York: Duell, Sloan, and Pearce, 1946), 320–21.

6. *New York Times*, 12 August 1947, 20; *New York Times*, 12 September 1947; *New York Times*, 21 January 1948.

7. Quoted in Judith Crist, "Horror in the Nursery," *Collier's*, 27 March 1948, 22.

8. *New York Times*, 15 September 1947; *New York Times*, 22 May 1948; *New York Times*, 19 August 1948.

9. Marya Mannes, "Junior Has a Craving," *New Republic*, 17 February 1947, 20–23.

10. Ibid.

11. Gershon Legman, *Love and Death: A Study in Censorship* (New York: Breaking Point, 1949); Malcolm Cowley, "Sex, Censorship and Superman," *New Republic*, 10 October 1949, 18–19.

12. Legman, *Love and Death*, 39–42; Cowley, "Sex, Censorship and Superman," 19.

13. Legman, *Love and Death*, 41–50

14. Gilbert, *A Cycle of Outrage*, 94–95; "Psychiatry in Harlem," *Time*, 1 December 1947, 50–52.

15. Gilbert, *A Cycle of Outrage*, 96; Fredric Wertham, "The Dreams That Heal," *New Republic*, 3 November 1947, 25–27.

16. Crist, "Horror in the Nursery," 22–23, 96–97.

17. Gilbert, *A Cycle of Outrage*, 98.

18. "Puddles of Blood," *Time*, 29 March 1948, 66–68; Fredric Wertham, "The Comics . . . Very Funny!" *Saturday Review of Literature*, 29 May 1948, 29.

19. Fredric Wertham, quoted in Crist, "Horror in the Nursery," 22.

20. Ibid., 22–23.

21. Ibid., 23.

22. Ibid.

23. Fredric Wertham, "The Comics . . . Very Funny!" 6–7.

24. Ibid., 7.

25. Ibid., 27–29.

26. David Pace Wigransky, "Cain before Comics," letter, *Saturday Review of Literature*, 24 July 1948, 19; M. P. Keeley, letter, *Saturday Review of Literature*, 25 September 1948, 22.

27. *New York Times*, 4 September 1948; Gilbert, *A Cycle of Outrage*, 106.

28. Gilbert, *A Cycle of Outrage*, 106; *New York Times*, 23 April 1949.

29. *New York Times*, 25 May 1948; *New York Times*, 29 June 1948; *New York Times*, 11 November 1948; *New York Times*, 25 November 1948; *New York Times*, 30 November 1948.

30. *New York Times*, 5 October 1948; *New York Times*, 4 October 1948; the Los Angeles County ordinance is reprinted in Charles S. Rhyne, *Comic Books—Municipal Control of Sale and Distribution—A Preliminary Study* (Washington, D.C.: National Institute of Municipal Law Officers, 1948), 12–13.

31. "Fighting Gunfire with Fire," 56; Rhyne, *Comic Books*, 13–16; *New York Times*, 16 December 1948; *New York Times*, 27 January 1949; *New York Times*, 23 December 1948.

32. Dorothy Barclay, "Army to Limit the Sale of Comics," *New York Times*, 18 January 1949.

33. Rhyne, *Comic Books*, 6–12.

34. *Winters v. New York*, 333 US 507 (1948).

35. Rhyne, *Comic Books*, 5–6; Charles S. Rhyne, "Municipal Control of Comic Books," *American City*, December 1948, 153.

36. "Threat to International Culture Relations," *School and Society*, 26 March 1949, 220; Joseph A. Barry, "Juvenile Books and French Politics," *New York Times Book Review*, 13 February 1949, 25; Barry Marx, ed., "Emile Keirstilk" and "Bernard Trout," in *Fifty Who Made DC Great* (New York: DC Comics, 1985), 18, 28.

37. "Canada's Comics Ban," *Newsweek*, 14 November 1949, 62; *New York Times*, 8 December 1949; "Outlawed," *Time*, 19 December 1949, 34; Martin Barker, *A Haunt of Fears: The Strange History of the British Horror Comics Campaign* (London: Pluto Press, 1984).

38. *New York Times*, 6 November 1948; Francis J. Bassett, "Comic Books for Germany," letter, *New York Times*, 11 November 1948.

39. *New York Times*, 13 November 1948; "ECA Denies Granting Credits for 'Comics' in Germany," *Publishers Weekly*, 11 December 1948, 2346.

40. *New York Times*, 14 December 1950.

41. *New York Times*, 16 October 1949; *New York Times*, 20 December 1949.

42. "A Note from the Editors of Marvel Comics Group," *Lawbreakers Always Lose* 5 (Marvel Comics, December 1948).

43. "This Is Our Testimony," *Crime Does Not Pay* 56 (Lev Gleason Publications, October 1947); Felix L. Lynch, "Don't Let Reformers Kid You," *Crime and Punishment* 16 (Lev Gleason Publications, July 1949); *Crime Does Not Pay* 81 (Lev Gleason Publications, November 1949).

44. Leverett S. Gleason, "Comics Censorship Opposed," letter, *New York Times*, 5 February 1949.

45. *New York Times*, 2 July 1948; "Purified Comics," *Newsweek*, 12 July 1948, 56; *Code of the Association of Comics Magazine Publishers, 1948*, reprinted in U.S. Senate Committee on the Judiciary, *Comic Books and Juvenile Delinquency, Interim Report*, 84th Cong., 1st sess., 1955, 35.

46. U.S. Senate Committee on the Judiciary, *Comic Books and Juvenile Delinquency*, 30.

47. Ibid.; "New York Officials Recommend Code for Comics Publishers," *Publishers Weekly*, 19 February 1949, 978; "Fighting Gunfire with Fire," 56–57.

48. See for example, "Out to Murder," *Crime Does Not Pay* 80 (Lev Gleason Publications, October 1949), which relates how a police detective courageously brings a gang of criminals to justice, and "Our Police Hall of Fame," *Crime Does Not Pay* 81 (Lev Gleason Publications, November 1949); by contrast the code-approved story "The Smell of Death," *Crime Does Not Pay* 100 (Lev Gleason Publications, July 1951) concerns a woman who plots to kill her own father, and the police are nowhere to be seen.

49. "New York Officials Recommend Code for Comics Publishers," 977; Bar-

clay, "Army to Limit Sale of Comics," 26; Bess Furman, "Comic Books Debated as Good or Evil," *New York Times*, 30 October 1948; "Fighting Gunfire with Fire," 56–57.

50. Henry E. Schultz, "The Comics as Whipping Boy," *Recreation*, August 1949, 239; Henry E. Schultz, "Censorship or Self-Regulation?" *Journal of Educational Sociology* 23 (December 1949): 215–24.

51. U.S. Senate Committee on the Judiciary, *Comic Books and Juvenile Delinquency*, 31.

52. *New York Times*, 14 January 1949.

53. *New York Times*, 11 March 1949; "State Laws to Censor Comics Protested by Publishers," *Publishers Weekly*, 12 March 1949, 1244; "Comic Book Censorship," editorial, *New York Times*, 25 February 1949.

54. "Comics Censorship Bill Passes New York Senate," *Publishers Weekly*, 5 March 1949, 1160.

55. "Comics Censorship Bills Killed in Two States," *Publishers Weekly*, 30 April 1949, 1805; *New York Times*, 29 December 1949.

56. *New York Times*, 20 February 1949; *New York Times*, 6 May 1949; Richard B. Gehman, "Deadwood Dick to Superman," *Science Digest*, June 1949, 57.

57. Catherine Mackenzie, "Comics to Undergo Scrutiny at N.Y.U.," *New York Times*, 22 September 1947; *New York Times*, 16 November 1949; Harvey W. Zorbaugh, editorial, *Journal of Educational Sociology* 23 (December 1949): 193.

58. Josette Frank, "Some Questions and Answers for Teachers and Parents," *Journal of Educational Sociology* 23 (December 1949): 206–14; Henry E. Schultz, "Censorship or Self-Regulation?," ibid., 215–24; Harvey Zorbaugh, "What Adults Think of Comics as Reading for Children," ibid., 226–33; *New York Times*, 24 January 1950.

59. Madeleine Loeb, "Anti-Comics Drive Reported Waning," *New York Times*, 21 January 1950.

60. Jesse L. Murrell, "Cincinnati Rates the Comic Books," *Parents' Magazine*, February 1950, 38; Jesse L. Murrell, "Cincinnati Again Rates the Comics," *Parents' Magazine*, October 1950, 120.

61. "Personal and Otherwise," *Harper's*, July 1951, 8; Fredric Wertham, "Wham! Socko! Pow!," *Harper's*, September 1951, 16.

62. Gilbert, *A Cycle of Outrage*, 98.

5 Reds, Romance, and Renegades

1. "Backyard Battleground," *Daring Confessions* 5 (Youthful Magazines, January 1953).

2. Ibid.

3. In "Blackhawk," *Blackhawk* 25 (Quality Comics, June 1949), the Blackhawks defeat a European "Peoples' Dictatorship."

4. "Captain Marvel, Jr., Battles the Mad Mongol Monster," *Captain Marvel, Jr.* 115 (Fawcett Publications, November 1952); "Capt. Marvel, Jr., Battles Vampira, Queen of Terror," *Captain Marvel, Jr.* 116 (Fawcett Publications, December 1952); the elder Captain Marvel goes to Korea and helps U.S. troops against another ridiculous Communist villain called the Red Crusher in "Captain Marvel Battles the Red Crusher," *Captain Marvel* 139 (Fawcett Publications, December 1952).

5. "Captain Marvel, Jr., and the Hammer of Hate," *Captain Marvel, Jr.* 118 (Fawcett Publications, April 1953); "The Regiment That Was Afraid to Fight," *Captain Marvel, Jr.* 119 (Fawcett Publications, June 1953).

6. "Link-Up in Korea," *John Wayne Adventure Comics* 12 (Toby Press, December 1951).

7. In "Thick of Combat," *Battle* 24 (Marvel Comics, December 1953) Red Chinese troops charge shouting "Banzai!" See the covers of *G.I. Joe* 22 (Ziff-Davis, June 1953), *G.I. Joe* 8 (Ziff-Davis, February 1952), and *G.I. Joe* 9 (Ziff-Davis, March 1952) for examples of smiling American soldiers killing ugly North Koreans and Chinese; for an example of the "gung-ho" tone of these stories, see "23 Notches for Zeb," *G.I. Joe* 6 (Ziff-Davis, December 1951), which tells the story of a fun-loving Kentuckian who enjoys fighting Communists so much that he keeps a score of his kills.

8. "Revenge," *Spy Cases* 13 (Marvel Comics, October 1952).

9. See William W. Savage Jr., *Comic Books and America, 1945–1954* (Norman: University of Oklahoma Press, 1990), 51–59 for his discussion of Korean War comic books.

10. "Do or Die" and "The Last Patrol," *Fighting Fronts* 1 (Harvey Publications, August 1952).

11. "Fear," *Battle* 9 (Marvel Comics, June 1952).

12. "The Road Back," *Battle* 9 (Marvel Comics, June 1952).

13. See "With Bayonet in Hand," *Battle Action* 4 (Marvel Comics, August 1952); and "Blood and Steel," *The Fighting Man* 4 (Farrell, February 1953) for good examples of vicious close-quarters combat with knives and bayonets.

14. "The Kidnapping of General Syin," *Spy Cases* 13 (Marvel Comics, October 1952); "Decoy for Death," *U.S. Tank Commandos* 2 (Avon Periodicals, August 1952); "Dead End River," *U.S. Marines in Action* 3 (Avon Periodicals, December 1952).

15. "Operation Havoc," *Fighting Undersea Commandos* 2 (Avon Periodicals, August 1952).

16. "Destruction at Kumjom," *U.S. Paratroops* 5 (Avon Periodicals, October 1952); see also "Airborne Assault on Gensan," *U.S. Paratroops* 4 (Avon Periodicals, August 1952), in which Communists use peace negotiations as a cover to build up their strength for a surprise offensive.

17. "Ransom," *U.S. Marines in Action* 3 (Avon Periodicals, December 1952); a South Korean policeman kills his own brother after learning that he is a Communist traitor in "Guerrilla Hell-Hole," *Battle* 24 (Marvel Comics, December 1953).

18. For the initial response to the bomb by scientists and the public, see Paul Boyer, *By the Bomb's Early Light: American Thought and Culture at the Dawn of the Atomic Age* (New York: Pantheon Books, 1985), 27–106.

19. "Mission Demolition" and "The Ice-Box Invasion," *Atomic War* 2 (Junior Books, December 1952).

20. "Operation Vengeance," *Atomic War* 2 (Junior Books, December 1952).

21. "The Secret Tunnel," *The Sub-Mariner* 40 (Marvel Comics, June 1955).

22. "The Betrayers," *Young Men* 24 (Marvel Comics, December 1953).

23. "Black Cobra Crashes the Ring of Red Death," *Black Cobra* 1 (Excellent Publications, October–November 1954); "The Fog Robbers," *The Avenger* 1 (Magazine Enterprises, February–March 1955); Les Daniels, *Marvel: Five Fabulous Decades of the World's Greatest Comics* (New York: Harry N. Abrams, 1991), 70–71; "First Assignment," *Fighting American* 1 (Headline Publications, April–May 1954).

24. See Savage, *Comic Books and America.* Savage's central thesis is that comic books of the postwar decade mirrored a society that demanded less escapism and more political and social relevance from popular culture.

25. "Condemned to Death," *Kent Blake of the Secret Service* 5 (Marvel Comics, January 1952).

26. "Bloody Oil," *John Wayne Adventure Comics* 21 (Toby Press, July 1953).

27. "Trouble's Double," *T-Man* 3 (Quality Comics, January 1952); see also "Assassins of Baghdad," *T-Man* 9 (Quality Comics, January 1953) and "The Killers of

the Nile," *T-Man* 18 (Quality Comics, October 1954), in which Trask exposes Soviet intrigue in Iraq and Egypt, respectively. In the latter story, the Soviets fabricate an ultranationalist "Anubis Party," apparently inspired by Gamal Abdel Nasser's pan-Arabism.

28. "Red Cargo for Destruction" and "Master of Destruction," *T-Man* 26 (Quality Comics, June 1955); "Final Decision," *Kent Blake of the Secret Service* 5 (Marvel Comics, January 1952).

29. "Hop on the Welfare Wagon," *Mystery in Space* 8 (DC Comics, June–July 1952); "Be Sure of Your Facts," *The House of Mystery* 3 (DC Comics, May 1952).

30. "Duel of the Planets," *Mystery in Space* 3 (DC Comics, August–September 1951).

31. "The Race to Peril Point," *Tomahawk* 11 (DC Comics, May–June 1952).

32. Elaine Tyler May, "Explosive Issues: Sex, Women, and the Bomb," in Lary May, ed., *Recasting America: Culture and Politics in the Age of Cold War* (Chicago: University of Chicago Press, 1989), 154–70; Wini Breines, *Young, White, and Miserable: Growing Up Female in the Fifties* (Boston: Beacon Press, 1992), 33.

33. *Young Romance* 1 (Feature Publications, September 1947).

34. Mike Benton, *The Comic Book in America* (Dallas: Taylor Publishing Co., 1989), 167–69; "Love on a Dime," *Time*, 22 August 1949, 41.

35. "The Farmer's Wife," *Young Romance* 1 (Feature Publications, September 1947).

36. "My Perfect Man," *Lovelorn* 25 (American Comics Group, May 1952); "Buy Me That Man," *Young Romance* 24 (Feature Publications, August 1950).

37. "Danger, Man-Trap," *Young Romance* 24 (Feature Publications, August 1950).

38. "I Tried to Buy Love with Kisses," *Teen-Age Romances* 16 (St. John Publishing, June 1951); "Questions and Answers about That Kiss," *Young Romance* 33 (Feature Publications, May 1951); see also "My Dates Were Phony," *Teen-Age Romances* 17 (St. John Publishing, August 1951).

39. "Back Door Love," *Young Romance* 15 (Feature Publications, November 1949); the same lesson applied to women who were attracted to wealthy men. In romance comics, women who married average, middle-class men were inevitably more happy than those who chased after wealth and excitement. See "I Could Have Married a Millionaire," *Real Love* 32 (A. A. Wyn, June–July 1950); and "Nancy Hale's Problem Clinic," *Young Romance* 24 (Feature Publications, August 1950).

40. "I Ran Away with a Truck Driver," *Teen-Age Romances* 23 (St. John Publishing, August 1952); see also "I Thought It Was Love," *My Past* 7 (Fox Features, August 1949); and "My Heart Was a Flame," *My Own Romance* 13 (Red Circle Magazines, October 1950) for other examples of women who look for excitement, meet with unhappiness, and ultimately embrace stability.

41. "Homecoming," *Teen-Age Brides* 5 (Home Comics, April 1954).

42. "Dark Delusion," *Romantic Secrets* 23 (Fawcett Publications, October 1951).

43. "Lady, I'll Break You," *Young Romance* 15 (Feature Publications, November 1949).

44. "The Honeymoon Is Over," *Romantic Love* 11 (Realistic Comics, May 1952).

45. "I Hate Men," *Darling Love* 11 (Archie Comics, 1952); groundless jealousy on the part of women also jeopardizes secure relationships in "Second Fiddle Wife," *Darling Love* 4 (Archie Comics, April 1950); "Savage Love," *First Love Illustrated* 19 (Harvey Publications, July 1952); and "Jealousy," *Teen-Age Brides* 5 (Home Comics, April 1954).

46. "I Married You, Didn't I?" *Romantic Love* 11 (Realistic Comics, May 1952); in "With This Ring," *Love Romances* 26 (Marvel Comics, January 1952), the widow of a deceased war veteran champions his name and the cause he died for; "I Was Scarred by Love," *Teen-Age Romances* 16 (St. John Publishing, June 1951), suggested that wartime service made men more mature and better husbands.

47. "Lovelife of an Army Nurse," *Wartime Romances* 1 (St. John Publishing, July 1951); "Our Love Was Battle-Scarred," *Realistic Romances* 8 (Avon Periodicals, November 1952).

48. Jesse L. Murrell, "How Good Are the Comic Books?" *Parents' Magazine*, November 1951, 32–33, 134; Jesse L. Murrell, "Annual Rating of Comic Magazines," *Parents' Magazine*, November 1952, 132–35; Jesse L. Murrell, "Annual Rating of Comic Magazines," *Parents' Magazine*, October 1953, 54–55, 101–5; Murrell, "Annual Rating of Comic Magazines," *Parents' Magazine*, August 1954, 48–49, 111–14.

49. Jesse L. Murrell, "Annual Rating of Comic Magazines," *Parents' Magazine*, November 1952, 134; *G.I. Joe* earned a "B" grade in each of the four annual surveys cited.

50. Frank Jacobs, *The Mad World of William M. Gaines* (Secaucus, N.J.: Lyle Stuart, 1972), 59–64; William M. Gaines, "An Interview with William M. Gaines," interviewed by Dwight R. Decker and Gary Groth, *Comics Journal* 81 (May 1983): 55–56; John Benson, ed., "The Transcripts: 1972 EC Convention," *Squa Tront* 8 (1978): 25.

51. Benson, "The Transcripts," 23.

52. Ibid., 37.

53. Gaines, "An Interview," 83; the marginalization of social criticism in the entertainment industries is discussed in Stephen J. Whitfield, *The Culture of the Cold War* (Baltimore: Johns Hopkins University Press, 1991); and Peter Biskind, *Seeing Is Believing: How Hollywood Taught Us to Stop Worrying and Love the Fifties* (New York: Pantheon Books, 1983).

54. Joe Orlando, "The Many Worlds of Joe Orlando," interviewed by Paul Levitz, *Amazing World of DC Comics*, May 1975, 4; Bernie Krigstein, "Bernie Krigstein," *Squa Tront* 6 (1975), 22; William M. Gaines and Al Feldstein, "Bill Gaines and Al Feldstein . . . an Interview," *Monster Times*, 31 May 1972, 18; Gaines, "An Interview," 66.

55. Benson, "The Transcripts," 22.

56. "The Guilty," *Shock SuspenStories* 3 (EC Comics, June–July 1952).

57. "In Gratitude," *Shock SuspenStories* 11 (EC Comics, October–November 1953).

58. "Shock Talk," *Shock SuspenStories* 13 (EC Comics, February–March 1954).

59. "Shock Talk," *Shock SuspenStories* 16 (EC Comics, August–September 1954).

60. "Judgment Day," *Weird Fantasy* 18 (EC Comics, March–April 1952).

61. "The Whipping," *Shock SuspenStories* 14 (EC Comics, April–May 1954); see also "Hate," *Shock SuspenStories* 5 (EC Comics, October–November 1952), which attacks anti-Semitism.

62. "The Patriots," *Shock SuspenStories* 2 (EC Comics, April–May 1952); "Shock Talk," *Shock SuspenStories* 3 (EC Comics, June–July 1952); see also, "The Hazing," *Shock SuspenStories* 16 (EC Comics, August–September 1954), in which redbaiting college students falsely accuse a hated professor of being a Communist, thereby destroying his reputation and his career.

63. "Confession," *Shock SuspenStories* 4 (EC Comics, August–September 1952); "A Kind of Justice," *Shock SuspenStories* 16 (EC Comics, August–September 1954);

see also "The Squealer," *Crime SuspenStories* 25 (EC Comics, October–November 1954), for another example of a police officer beating a confession out of an innocent man.

64. Harvey Kurtzman, "An Interview with the Man Who Brought Truth to the Comics: Harvey Kurtzman," interviewed by Kim Thompson and Gary Groth, *Comics Journal* 67 (October 1981): 69–71; Harvey Kurtzman, interview, *Two-Fisted Tales* (West Plains, Mo.: Russ Cochran, 1980), vol. 1; Benson, "The Transcripts," 30.

65. "Kill," *Two-Fisted Tales* 23 (EC Comics, September–October 1951); see also, "The Big If," *Frontline Combat* 5 (EC Comics, March–April 1952), which typified Kurtzman's musings on the randomness of death in war.

66. Al Feldstein, interview, *The Haunt of Fear* (West Plains, Mo.: Russ Cochran, 1985), vol. 2.

67. "The 10th at Noon," *Weird Fantasy* 11 (EC Comics, January–February 1952); see also "And Then There Were Two," *Weird Fantasy* 6 (EC Comics, March–April 1951), a dystopian tale about the annihilation of human beings by nuclear warfare.

68. "The Last Man," *Weird Science* 12 (EC Comics, March–April 1952).

69. "Custer's Last Stand," *Two-Fisted Tales* 27 (EC Comics, May–June 1952); see also "Washington," *Two-Fisted Tales* 29 (EC Comics, September–October 1952), in which George Washington appears exasperated nearly to the point of insanity by his inability to control the panicking militia under his command.

70. "Caesar," *Frontline Combat* 8 (EC Comics, September–October 1952); Harvey Kurtzman, untitled interview, *Frontline Combat* (West Plains, Mo.: Russ Cochran, 1982), vol. 2.

71. Benson, "The Transcripts," 32–35; Kurtzman, interview, *Frontline Combat*, vol. 2.

72. Harvey Kurtzman, interview, *Mad* (West Plains, Mo.: Russ Cochran, 1986), vol. 1; Harvey Kurtzman, interview, *Mad* (West Plains, Mo.: Russ Cochran, 1986), vol. 2; Harvey Kurtzman, interview, *Mad* (West Plains, Mo.: Russ Cochran, 1987), vol. 4; "Black and Blue Hawks," *Mad* 5 (EC Comics, June–July 1953); "Starchie," *Mad* 12 (EC Comics, June 1954); "Superduper Man," *Mad* 4 (EC Comics, April–May 1953); see also "Bat Boy and Rubin," *Mad* 8 (EC Comics, December–January 1953–54); and "Mickey Rodent," *Mad* 19 (EC Comics, January 1955).

73. "What's My Shine?" *Mad* 17 (EC Comics, November 1954).

74. Harvey Kurtzman and William M. Gaines, "A Conversation with Harvey Kurtzman and Bill Gaines," interviewed by John Benson, reprinted in *Mad*, vol. 2.

75. Harvey Kurtzman and William M. Gaines, interview, *Mad*, vol. 1.

76. "Who's Next?" *Crime SuspenStories* 16 (EC Comics, May–June 1953).

77. "Beauty and the Beach," *Shock SuspenStories* 7 (EC Comics, February–March 1953).

78. "The Neat Job," *Shock SuspenStories* 1 (EC Comics, February–March 1952).

79. "Horror in the School Room," *The Haunt of Fear* 7 (EC Comics, May–June 1951); see also "Let's Play Poison," *Vault of Horror* 29 (EC Comics, February–March 1953), adapted from a Ray Bradbury tale in which schoolchildren kill their cruel teacher by burying him alive.

80. "Grounds . . . for Horror," *Tales from the Crypt* 29 (EC Comics, April–May 1952); see also "Daddy Lost His Head," *Vault of Horror* 19 (EC Comics, June–July 1951), wherein a sweet eight-year-old girl takes a bite out of a gingerbread man given to her by a friendly witch and thereby decapitates her wicked stepfather; and "Shoe-Button Eyes," *Vault of Horror* 35 (EC Comics, February–March 1954), in which another wicked stepfather gets his fatal comeuppance.

81. "The Small Assassin," *Shock SuspenStories* 7 (EC Comics, February–March 1953).

82. "The Orphan," *Shock SuspenStories* 14 (EC Comics, April–May 1954).

83. Benson, "The Transcripts," 24.

84. "The Living Death," *Tales from the Crypt* 24 (EC Comics, June–July 1951).

85. "What's Cookin'?," *The Haunt of Fear* 12 (EC Comics, March–April 1952); "Out of His Head," *Vault of Horror* 32 (EC Comics, August–September 1953); "Foul Play," *The Haunt of Fear* 19 (EC Comics, May–June 1953).

86. Al Feldstein, interview, *The Vault of Horror* (West Plains, Mo.: Russ Cochran, 1982), vol. 3. Readers may recognize the ghoulish Crypt Keeper, and many of the EC stories themselves, from the more recent television series *Tales from the Crypt*, which has aired on HBO and FOX.

87. Benson, "The Transcripts," 23; Johnny Craig, "Johnny Craig," *Squa Tront* 4 (1970); Gaines, "An Interview," 70, 78; Kurtzman, "Harvey Kurtzman," 81; Harvey Kurtzman, interview, *Frontline Combat* (West Plains, Mo.: Russ Cochran, 1982), vol. 1.

6 Turning Point

1. *New York Times*, 28 December 1953.

2. U.S. Senate Committee on the Judiciary, *Comic Books and Juvenile Delinquency, Interim Report: Comic Books and Juvenile Delinquency*, 84th Cong., 1st sess., 1955, 3; "The Hundred Million Dollar Market for Comics," *Publishers Weekly*, 1 May 1954), 1906; Edward L. Feder, "Comic Book Regulation," *Legislative Problems* (Berkeley: Bureau of Public Administration, University of California, 1955), 2; *New York Times*, 3 September 1953; *New York Times*, 24 April 1953.

3. Jesse L. Murrell, "Cincinnati Again Rates the Comics," *Parents Magazine*, October 1950, 44, 120–24; Jesse L. Murrell, "How Good Are the Comic Books?" *Parents Magazine*, November 1951, 32–33, 134–35; Jesse L. Murrell, "Annual Rating of Comic Magazines," *Parents' Magazine*, November 1952, 132–35; Jesse L. Murrell, "Annual Rating of Comic Magazines," *Parents' Magazine*, October 1953, 54–55, 101–5.

4. "Captain Marvel and the Death Horror," *Whiz Comics* 153 (Fawcett Publications, January 1953); "Captain Marvel Battles the Legend Horror," *Whiz Comics* 155 (Fawcett Publications, June 1953); Stan Lee, quoted in Les Daniels, *Marvel: Five Fabulous Decades of the World's Greatest Comics* (New York: Harry N. Abrams, 1991), 68; "The Vault-Keeper's Corner," *The Vault of Horror* 22 (EC Comics, December–January, 1951–52).

5. H. H. Wubben, "American Prisoners of War in Korea: A Second Look at the 'Something New in History' Theme," in Randy Roberts and James S. Olson, eds., *American Experiences: Readings in American History, vol. 2* (New York: Harper Collins, 1994), 264–73.

6. U.S. Senate, Special Committee to Investigate Organized Crime in Interstate Commerce, *Juvenile Delinquency*, 81st Cong., 2d sess., 1950, 6; *New York Times*, 12 November 1950.

7. *New York Times*, 4 December 1951; *New York Times*, 15 April 1952.

8. Fredric Wertham, *Seduction of the Innocent* (New York: Rinehart, 1954). Subsequent page numbers in text refer to this book.

9. Fredric Wertham, "Comic Books—Blueprints for Delinquency," *Reader's Digest*, May 1954, 24–29; Fredric Wertham, "What Parents Don't Know about Comic Books," *Ladies' Home Journal*, November 1953, 50–53, 214–20; "Readers Write," *Ladies' Home Journal*, February 1954, 4–6; James B. Gilbert, *A Cycle of Outrage: America's*

Reaction to the Juvenile Delinquent in the 1950s (New York: Oxford University Press, 1986), 104.

10. Harold C. Gardiner, "Comic Books: Moral Threat?" *America*, 24 April 1954, 340–42; John B. Sheerin, "Crime Comics Must Go!" *Catholic World*, June 1954, 162; Wolcott Gibbs, "Keep Those Paws to Yourself, Space-Rat!" *New Yorker*, 8 May 1954, 137; C. Wright Mills, "Nothing to Laugh At," *New York Times Book Review*, 25 April 1954, 20.

11. Reuel Denney, "The Dark Fantastic," *New Republic*, 3 May 1954, 18–19.

12. Bruce Gorman, *Kefauver: A Political Biography* (New York: Oxford University Press, 1971), 68–74; William Howard Moore, *The Kefauver Committee and the Politics of Crime* (Columbia, Mo.: University of Missouri Press, 1974); Gilbert, *A Cycle of Outrage*, 143–49.

13. U.S. Senate, Committee on the Judiciary, *Hearings Before the Subcommittee to Investigate Juvenile Delinquency (Comic Books)*, 83d Cong., 2d sess., 21 April 1954, 5–6. Subsequent page numbers in text refer to these hearings.

14. William M. Gaines, "An Interview with William M. Gaines," interviewed by Dwight R. Decker and Gary Groth, *Comics Journal* 81 (May 1983): 74.

15. Ibid., 74–75.

16. Ibid., 73.

17. Ibid., 76.

18. Ibid., 73–76.

19. *New York Times*, 22 April 1954; "Horror Comics," *Time*, 31 May 1954, 78; Sheerin, "Crime Comics Must Go!" 162; T. E. Murphy, "The Face of Violence," *Reader's Digest*, November 1954, 56; Ruth A. Inglis, "The Comic Book Problem," *American Mercury*, August 1955, 119.

20. U.S. Senate, Committee on the Judiciary, *Hearings Before the Subcommittee to Investigate Juvenile Delinquency (Comic Books)*, 83rd Cong., 2d sess., 4 June 1954.

21. Nora Brown, "Reform of Comic Books Is Spurred by Hearings," *New York Times*, 13 June 1954; *New York Times*, 29 June 1954.

22. *New York Times*, 8 September 1954; Emma Harrison, "Magistrate Is Made Comics 'Czar,'" *New York Times*, 17 September 1954.

23. *Code of the Comics Magazine Association of America* (New York: Comics Magazine Association of America, 26 October 1954); reprinted in Amy Kiste Nyberg, *Seal of Approval: The History of the Comics Code* (Jackson: University Press of Mississippi, 1998), 166–69.

24. Comics Magazine Association of America, *Facts about the Comics Code* (New York: Comics Magazine Association of America, 1956), 9–20.

25. Harrison, "Magistrate Is Made Comics 'Czar,'" 1, 25; CMAA, *Facts About the Comics Code*, 9.

26. *New York Times*, 27 September 1954; Mort Weisinger, "How They're Cleaning Up the Comics," *Better Homes and Gardens*, March 1955, 60; CMAA, *Facts about the Comics Code*, 13–14; *New York Times*, 23 September 1954.

27. Dorothy Barclay, "New Comic Books to Be Out in Week," *New York Times*, 29 December 1954; Weisinger, "How They're Cleaning Up the Comics," 59–60, 263.

28. "Progress on Comic Book Cleanup," editorial, *America*, 30 October 1954, 114; *New York Times*, 25 November 1954; *New York Times*, 12 November 1954.

29. U.S. Senate Committee on the Judiciary, *Comic Books and Juvenile Delinquency, Interim Report*, 17–33; *New York Times*, 19 February 1955.

30. Emma Harrison, "Whip Knife Shown as 'Comics' Lures," *New York Times*, 5 February 1955; *New York Times*, 12 February 1955; *New York Times*, 22 March 1955.

31. *New York Times,* 3 May 1955; *New York Times,* 30 March 1955; *New York Times,* 9 May 1955; *New York Times,* 14 May 1955.

32. *New York Times,* 11 July 1955.

33. "A Special Editorial: This Is an Appeal for Action," *Shock SuspenStories* 18 (EC Comics, December–January 1954–55); John Benson, ed., "The Transcripts: 1972 EC Convention," *Squa Tront* 8 (1978), 23.

34. "A Special Editorial," *Shock SuspenStories* 18 (EC Comics, December–January 1954–55).

35. Lyle Stuart, "Don't Get Even, Get *Mad*," *Publishers Weekly,* 10 January 1986, 80; Weisinger, "How They're Cleaning Up the Comics," 59–60.

36. *New York Times,* 19 September 1954; "Horror on the Newsstands," *Time,* 27 September 1954, 77; "In Memorium: Tales from the Crypt," *Tales from the Crypt* 46 (EC Comics, February–March 1955).

37. Gaines, "An Interview," 78; Benson, "The Transcripts," 41.

38. Gaines, "An Interview," 78.

39. *New York Times,* 12 November 1955; T. E. Murphy, "Progress in Cleaning Up the Comics," *Reader's Digest,* February 1956, 105–8; "Comic-Book Czar Resigns," editorial, *America,* 23 June 1956, 295–96.

40. Fredric Wertham, interviewed by Ed Summer, 12 June 1974, *Inside Comics* 4 (winter 1974–75): 17–19; Stan Lee, "Stan the Man Raps with Marvel Maniacs at James Madison University," *Comics Journal* 42 (October 1978): 49.

41. Wertham, interview, 17–19; Alan Hewetson and Fredric Wertham, "Censorship Is Not the Answer; It Is Not Even the Question," *Comics Journal* 133 (December 1989): 84; Gilbert, *A Cycle of Outrage,* 217; Les Daniels, *Comix: A History of Comic Books in America* (New York: Outerbridge and Dienstfrey, 1971), 83–89; Benson, "The Transcripts," 38.

7 Great Power and Great Responsibility

1. "Spider-Man," *Amazing Fantasy* 15 (Marvel Comics, August 1962).

2. Amy Kiste Nyberg, *Seal of Approval: The History of the Comics Code* (Jackson: University Press of Mississippi, 1998), 125–26.

3. J. Ronald Oakley, *God's Country: America in the Fifties* (New York: Dembner Books, 1986), 110.

4. David P. Szatmary, *Rockin' in Time: A Social History of Rock-and-Roll* (Upper Saddle River, N.J.: Prentice Hall, 1996), 44–47.

5. Thomas Doherty, *Teenagers and Teenpics: The Juvenilization of American Movies in the 1950s* (Boston: Unwin Hyman, 1988).

6. Howard Nostrand, "Nostrand by Nostrand," *Comics Journal* 95 (February 1985): 86; Les Daniels, *Marvel: Five Fabulous Decades of the World's Greatest Comics* (New York: Harry N. Abrams, 1991), 80, 130; Peter Bart, "Advertising: Superman Faces New Hurdles," *New York Times,* 23 September 1962.

7. *Archie Americana Series: Best of the Fifties* (Mamaroneck, N.Y.: Archie Comic Publications, 1992).

8. Bart, "Advertising: Superman Faces New Hurdles."

9. "Mystery of the Human Thunderbolt," *Showcase* 4 (DC Comics, October 1956).

10. "S.O.S. Green Lantern," *Showcase* 22 (DC Comics, October 1959).

11. "Creature of a Thousand Shapes," *The Brave and the Bold* 34 (DC Comics, March 1961); "Birth of the Atom," *Showcase* 34 (DC Comics, October 1961).

12. *The Justice League of America* 1 (DC Comics, October–November 1960).

13. James T. Patterson, *Grand Expectations: The United States, 1945–1974* (New York: Oxford University Press, 1996), 407–9.

14. In "The Day Superman Broke the Law," *Superman* 153 (DC Comics, May 1962), Superman is arrested after he has rescued a child from an escaped elephant and violates a hospital quiet zone in the process.

15. Trina Robbins, *The Great Women Superheroes* (Northampton, Mass.: Kitchen Sink Press, 1996), 104–8).

16. "The Man Who Stole Central City," *The Flash* 116 (DC Comics, November 1960); "King of the Beatniks," *The Flash* 114 (DC Comics, August 1960); "Menace of the Runaway Missile," *Showcase* 22 (DC Comics, October 1959).

17. Julius Schwartz, "Interview with JLA Editor Julius Schwartz," *Amazing World of DC Comics*, March 1977, 34.

18. Julius Schwartz, "Julius Schwartz," interviewed by Renee Witterstaetter, *Comics Interview* 88 (1990): 41; Adam Strange first appeared in "Secret of the Eternal City," *Showcase* 17 (DC Comics, December 1958). "The World at My Doorstep," *Strange Adventures* 95 (DC Comics, August 1958); "War of the Jovian Bubble-Men," *Strange Adventures* 107 (DC Comics, August 1959).

19. "The Man Who Weighed 100 Tons," *Strange Adventures* 109 (DC Comics, October 1959); "The Man with the Head of Saturn," *Strange Adventures* 156 (DC Comics, September 1963).

20. "The Rise of the Atomic Knights," *Strange Adventures* 117 (DC Comics, June 1960).

21. Ibid.; "Threat of the Witch-Woman," *Strange Adventures* 156 (DC Comics, September 1963); "When the Earth Blacked Out," *Strange Adventures* 144 (DC Comics, September 1962).

22. "Censored Barks Pages See Print," *Comics Journal* 54 (March 1980): 26; Gaylord Dubois, "Gaylord Dubois," interviewed by Lou Mougin, *Comics Interview* 17 (November 1984): 13.

23. *N. W. Ayer and Son's Directory of Newspapers and Periodicals, 1961* (Philadelphia: N. W. Ayer and Son, 1961), 1388; *N. W. Ayer and Son's Directory of Newspapers and Periodicals, 1964* (Philadelphia: N. W. Ayer and Son, 1964), 1406; Mike Benton, *The Comic Book in America* (Dallas: Taylor Publishing Co., 1989), 109–19.

24. "Day of Reckoning," *Jungle War Stories* 2 (Dell Comics, January–March 1963).

25. "Requiem for a Red," *Jungle War Stories* 1 (Dell Comics, July–September 1962).

26. "A Walk in the Sun," *Jungle War Stories* 2 (Dell Comics, January–March 1963).

27. "The Year of the Cat," *Jungle War Stories* 4 (Dell Comics, July–September 1963); "The Enemy in Vietnam," *Jungle War Stories* 2 (Dell Comics, January–March 1963); "Deadly Masquerade," *Jungle War Stories* 7 (Dell Comics, April–June 1964); "Surprise Party," *Jungle War Stories* 8 (Dell Comics, July–September 1964); "The Big Blow-Up," *Jungle War Stories* 11 (Dell Comics, April–June 1965); "The Enemy Has Many Faces," *Jungle War Stories* 9 (Dell Comics, October–December 1964).

28. "Pinch the Devil," *Jungle War Stories* 8 (Dell Comics, July–September 1964).

29. "Frontal Assault," *Guerrilla War* 12 (Dell Comics, July–September 1965).

30. "A Letter from Vietnam" and "Face of the Enemy," *Jungle War Stories* 11 (Dell Comics, April–June 1965).

31. *Tales of the Green Beret* 1 (Dell Comics, January 1967); "Captain Hunter,"

Our Fighting Forces 102 (DC Comics, August 1966); *Super Green Beret* 1 (Milson Publishing Co., April 1967); "Pop Goes the War," *Newsweek*, 12 September 1966, 66.

32. Benton, *The Comic Book in America*, 98–99.

33. "The American Way," *Romantic Secrets* 46 (Charlton Publications, September 1963); "Your Role in the Cold War: Are You Physically Fit?" *Battlefield Action* 48 (Charlton Publications, September 1962); "Your Role in the Cold War: God Is Never out of Style," *Fightin' Army* 50 (Charlton Publications, January 1963).

34. "The Enemy Demands," *Fightin' Army* 51 (Charlton Publications, March 1963) and "Enemy Zone," *Fightin' Marines* 42 (Charlton Publications, July 1961) concern Communist intrigue in Europe; "The Last Barrier," *Fightin' Air Force* 39 (Charlton Publications, July 1963), and "Operation Missile," *Fightin' Army* 54 (Charlton Publications, September 1963), both concern the conflict between the United States and Cuba. The latter finds U.S. Army agents covertly sabotaging a Cuban missile base with the assistance of Cuban freedom fighters; in "Terror over Taiwan," *Fightin' Air Force* 38 (Charlton Publications, May 1963), a U.S. pilot assists Chiang Kai-shek's forces in defense of Taiwan; "High Cost of Living," *Fightin' Air Force* 43 (Charlton Publications, March 1964), explicitly warns against cutting the U.S. defense budget.

35. George C. Herring, *America's Longest War: The United States and Vietnam, 1950–1975*, 3d ed. (New York: McGraw-Hill, 1996), 159.

36. "The Man in the Green Beret," *Army War Heroes* 8 (Charlton Publications, May 1965); "Jungle Jump," *Battlefield Action* 47 (Charlton Publications, May 1963).

37. "A Tough War," *Fightin' Army* 74 (Charlton Publications, June 1967).

38. "Executioners from Hanoi," *Fightin' Marines* 68 (Charlton Publications, March–April 1966).

39. "Hidden Eyes," *Fightin' Marines* 67 (Charlton Publications, January 1966).

40. Eugene Gilbert, *Advertising and Marketing to Young People* (Pleasantville, N.Y.: Printers' Ink Books, 1957); Grace Palladino, *Teenagers: An American History* (New York: Basic Books, 1996), 195; James M. Gilbert, *A Cycle of Outrage: America's Reaction to the Juvenile Delinquent in the 1950s* (New York: Oxford University Press, 1986), 196–211.

41. S. N. Eisenstadt, *From Generation to Generation: Age Groups and Social Structure* (Glencoe, Ill.: Free Press, 1956); Paul Goodman, *Growing Up Absurd: Problems of Youth in the Organized System* (New York: Random House, 1960); Edgar Z. Friedenberg, *The Vanishing Adolescent* (Boston: Beacon Press, 1959), 63.

42. Daniels, *Marvel*, 78–81.

43. Ibid.

44. Will Jacobs and Gerard Jones, *The Comic Book Heroes* (New York: Crown Publishers, 1985), 62.

45. Daniels, *Marvel*, 81. Examples of this style are numerous, but see "The Escape of Monsteroso," *Amazing Adventures* 5 (Marvel Comics, October 1961), and "'X,' the Thing That Lived," *Tales to Astonish* 20 (Marvel Comics, June 1961). In "The Scarecrow Walks," *Strange Tales* 81 (Marvel Comics, February 1961), an inanimate scarecrow is transformed by an atomic blast into a giant rampaging monster; in "Fin Fang Foom," *Strange Tales* 89 (Marvel Comics, October 1961), and "Grogg," *Strange Tales* 83 (Marvel Comics, April 1961), monsters wreak havoc on the Red Chinese and the Soviets, respectively.

46. "The Last Man on Earth," *Amazing Adult Fantasy* 7 (Marvel Comics, December 1961); see also "The Man in the Iron Box," *Strange Tales* 69 (Marvel Comics, June 1959), based on a very similar premise.

47. See also "For Whom the Drum Beats," *Tales to Astonish* 22 (Marvel Comics,

August 1961), and "When the Totem Walks," *Strange Tales* 74 (Marvel Comics, July 1960).

48. Tom Englehardt, *The End of Victory Culture: Cold War America and the Disillusioning of a Generation* (New York: Basic Books, 1995), 153.

49. *Amazing Adult Fantasy* 7 (Marvel Comics, December 1961). Circulation figures culled from the Statements of Ownership, Management, and Circulation in *Strange Tales* 83 (Marvel Comics, April 1961) and *Tales to Astonish* 18 (Marvel Comics, April 1961); Stan Lee, *Origins of Marvel Comics* (New York: Simon and Schuster, 1974), 16.

50. Lee, *Origins of Marvel Comics*, 16–17; Stan Lee, *The Fantastic Four* (New York: Pocket Books, 1977), 5–6.

51. "The Fantastic Four," *The Fantastic Four* 1 (Marvel Comics, November 1961).

52. Ibid.; "The Fantastic Four Meet the Skrulls from Outer Space," *The Fantastic Four* 2 (Marvel Comics, January 1962); "The Menace of the Miracle Man," *The Fantastic Four* 3 (Marvel Comics, March 1962); "The Coming of the Sub-Mariner," *The Fantastic Four* 4 (Marvel Comics, May 1962); "Prisoners of Doctor Doom," *The Fantastic Four* 5 (Marvel Comics, July 1962); "Captives of the Deadly Duo," *The Fantastic Four* 6 (Marvel Comics, September 1962).

53. "The Fantastic Four Meet the Skrulls from Outer Space," *The Fantastic Four* 2 (Marvel Comics, January 1962); Lee, *Origins of Marvel Comics*, 75.

54. See Robert B. Ray, *A Certain Tendency of the Hollywood Cinema, 1930–1980* (Princeton: Princeton University Press, 1985); and Richard Slotkin, *Gunfighter Nation: The Myth of the Frontier in Twentieth-Century America* (New York: Atheneum, 1992).

55. Lee, *The Fantastic Four*, 5–6; Lee, *Origins of Marvel Comics*, 73.

56. "The Coming of the Hulk," *The Incredible Hulk* 1 (Marvel Comics, May 1962); Lee, *Origins of Marvel Comics*, 76.

57. "The Terror of the Toad Men," *The Incredible Hulk* 2 (Marvel Comics, July 1962).

58. As noted earlier, initially Banner had transformed into the Hulk when night fell. The adrenaline surge became Banner's principal means of transformation, beginning in "The Incredible Hulk," *Tales to Astonish* 60 (Marvel Comics, October 1964).

59. Lee, *Origins of Marvel Comics*, 133.

60. "Spider-Man," *Amazing Fantasy* 15 (Marvel Comics, August 1962).

61. Ibid.

62. Ibid.

63. Flo Steinberg, "Flo Steinberg," interviewed by Jim Salicrup and Dwight Jon Zimmerman, *Comics Interview* 17 (November 1984): 61; Lee, *Origins of Marvel Comics*, 134–36; Jacobs and Jones, *The Comic Book Heroes*, 62; Ditko has rarely given interviews concerning his *Spider-Man* work or any other topic. In his public statements and writings, Ditko emphasizes the primacy of individualism and often invokes the arguments of archconservative Ayn Rand. See Ditko's commentary in *The Masters of Comic Book Art*, produced and directed by Ken Viola (Ken Viola Productions), 1987; Steve Ditko, "The Sore Spot Cause and Crusade," *Robin Snyder's History of the Comics* 4, no. 1 (January 1993): 9–11.

64. See "Spider-Man" and "Spider-Man vs. the Chameleon," *The Amazing Spider-Man* 1 (Marvel Comics, March 1963); "Duel to the Death with the Vulture," *The Amazing Spider-Man* 2 (Marvel Comics, May 1963); "Spider-Man versus Doctor Octopus," *The Amazing Spider-Man* 3 (Marvel Comics, July 1963); "Nothing Can

Stop the Sandman," *The Amazing Spider-Man* 4 (Marvel Comics, September 1963); "Marked for Destruction by Dr. Doom," *The Amazing Spider-Man* 5 (Marvel Comics, October 1963); "Face to Face with . . . the Lizard," *The Amazing Spider-Man* 6 (Marvel Comics, November 1963); "The Return of the Vulture," *The Amazing Spider-Man* 7 (Marvel Comics, December 1963).

65. "The Terrible Threat of the Living Brain," *The Amazing Spider-Man* 8 (Marvel Comics, January 1964); "The Man Called Electro," *The Amazing Spider-Man* 9 (Marvel Comics, February 1964).

66. "Spider-Man," *The Amazing Spider-Man* 1 (Marvel Comics, March 1963); "Duel to the Death with the Vulture," *The Amazing Spider-Man* 2 (Marvel Comics, May 1963).

67. "Nothing Can Stop the Sandman," *The Amazing Spider-Man* 4 (Marvel Comics, September 1963).

68. "Thor the Mighty and the Stone Men from Saturn," *Journey into Mystery* 83 (Marvel Comics, August 1962); "The Return of Zarrko the Tomorrow Man," *Journey into Mystery* 97 (Marvel Comics, October 1963).

69. "The Origin of Dr. Strange," *Strange Tales* 115 (Marvel Comics, December 1963); "Dr. Strange, Master of Black Magic," *Strange Tales* 110 (Marvel Comics, July 1963.

70. "Iron Man Is Born," *Tales of Suspense* 39 (Marvel Comics, March 1963); Stan Lee, *Son of Origins of Marvel Comics* (New York: Simon and Schuster, 1975), 43–45.

71. "X-Men," *The X-Men* 1 (Marvel Comics, September 1963); "The Origin of Daredevil," *Daredevil* 1 (Marvel Comics, April 1964); "The Coming of the Avengers," *The Avengers* 1 (Marvel Comics, September 1963); "Captain America Joins . . . the Avengers," *The Avengers* 4 (Marvel Comics, March 1964); "The Coming of the Sub-Mariner," *The Fantastic Four* 4 (Marvel Comics, May 1962); "The Castle of Nefaria," *The Avengers* 13 (Marvel Comics, February 1965).

72. "Spidey Strikes Back," *The Amazing Spider-Man* 19 (Marvel Comics, December 1964); Daniels, *Marvel*, 105.

73. "The Incredible Hulk," *Tales to Astonish* 60 (Marvel Comics, October 1964).

74. "The Hulk vs. the Thing," *The Fantastic Four* 25 (Marvel Comics, April 1964); "Duel with Daredevil," *The Amazing Spider-Man* 16 (Marvel Comics, September 1964); "We Have to Fight the X-Men," *The Fantastic Four* 28 (Marvel Comics, July 1964).

75. Stan Lee, "Stan Lee," interviewed by Jim Salicrup, David Anthony Kraft, and Dan Hagen, *Comics Interview* 5 (July 1983): 57; Stan Lee, quoted in Daniels, *Marvel*, 105.

76. The Black Panther actually debuted in *The Fantastic Four* 52 (Marvel Comics, July 1966), but he did not become an established character until he joined the Avengers in "Death Calls for the Arch-Heroes," *The Avengers* 52 (Marvel Comics, May 1967); random black bystanders, college students, and policemen can be seen for the first time in the 1965 issues of *The Amazing Spider-Man*. See "Never Step on a Scorpion," *The Amazing Spider-Man* 29 (Marvel Comics, October 1965); and "The Claws of the Cat," *The Amazing Spider-Man* 30 (Marvel Comics, November 1965). The first major African American supporting character in Marvel Comics was the *Daily Bugle*'s city editor Joe Robertson, who debuted in "The Tentacles and the Trap," *The Amazing Spider-Man* 52 (Marvel Comics, September 1967).

77. "Unus the Untouchable," *The X-Men* 8 (Marvel Comics, November 1964); "To Smash a Serpent," *The Avengers* 33 (Marvel Comics, October 1965).

78. "The Hulk vs. the Thing," *The Fantastic Four* 25 (Marvel Comics, April 1964); "The Invasion of the Lava Men," *The Avengers* 5 (Marvel Comics, May 1964).

79. "The Gladiator from Outer Space," *The Incredible Hulk* 4 (Marvel Comics, November 1962); "The Hordes of General Fang," *The Incredible Hulk* 5 (Marvel Comics, January 1963); "On the Rampage against the Reds," *Tales to Astonish* 65 (Marvel Comics, March 1965).

80. "Into the Blaze of Battle," *Journey into Mystery* 117 (Marvel Comics, June 1965).

81. "Iron Man Is Born," *Tales of Suspense* 39 (Marvel Comics, March 1963); "Trapped by the Red Barbarian," *Tales of Suspense* 42 (Marvel Comics, June 1963); "Iron Man Faces the Crimson Dynamo," *Tales of Suspense* 46 (Marvel Comics, October 1963); "If I Must Die, Let It Be with Honor," *Tales of Suspense* 69 (Marvel Comics, September 1965); "Fight On! For a World Is Watching," *Tales of Suspense* 70 (Marvel Comics, October 1965); and "What Price Victory?" *Tales of Suspense* 71 (Marvel Comics, November 1965).

82. "The Return of the Titanium Man," *Tales of Suspense* 81 (Marvel Comics, September 1966); Lee, *Son of Origins of Marvel Comics*, 45.

83. "Mails of Suspense," *Tales of Suspense* 81 (Marvel Comics, September 1966); "Mails of Suspense," *Tales of Suspense* 77 (Marvel Comics, May 1966); "Mails of Suspense," *Tales of Suspense* 72 (Marvel Comics, June 1965); "Mails of Suspense," *Tales of Suspense* 71 (Marvel Comics, November 1965); Stan Lee, "Stan's Soapbox," *Daredevil* 44 (Marvel Comics, September 1968). Captain America makes a rare trip to Vietnam in "The Strength of the Sumo," *Tales of Suspense* 61 (Marvel Comics, January 1965). For more on Marvel Comics and the Vietnam War see Bradford Wright, "Vietnam in the Comic Books," in James S. Olson, ed., *The Vietnam War: Handbook of the Literature and Research* (Westport, Conn.: Greenwood Press, 1993), 439–47.

84. See the relative circulation figures in *N. W. Ayer and Son's Directory of Newspapers and Periodicals, 1962* (Philadelphia: N. W. Ayer and Son, 1962), 1390; and *N. W. Ayer and Son's Directory of Newspapers and Periodicals, 1967* (Philadelphia: N. W. Ayer and Son, 1967), 1442; "O.K., You Passed the 2-S Test—Now You're Smart Enough for Comic Books," *Esquire*, September 1966, 115.

85. "As Barry Jenkins, Ohio '69, Says: 'A Person Has to Have Intelligence to Read Them,'" *Esquire*, September 1966, 117; *Esquire*, September 1965, 97.

86. John Romita, "John Romita," interviewed by Jim Salicrup, *Comics Interview* 89 (1990): 37; Roy Thomas, "Roy Thomas," interviewed by Lou Mougin, *Comics Interview* 66 (1989): 15.

87. Arnold Drake, "Arnold Drake," interviewed by Lou Mougin, *Comics Interview* 16 (October 1984): 6–7. Gil Kane, a highly respected artist who worked for both companies during the 1960s, later credited Marvel for its creativity and blasted DC for being "restrained [and] conservative to the point of sterility." Gil Kane, "An Interview with Gil Kane," interviewed by Gary Groth, *Comics Journal* 38 (February 1978): 36.

88. "The Coming of the Creeper," *Showcase* 73 (DC Comics, April 1968); "Hawk and Dove," *Showcase* 75 (DC Comics, June 1968); Drake, "Arnold Drake," 11; "Who Has Been Lying in My Grave?" *Strange Adventures* 205 (DC Comics, October 1967); "Deadman's Chest," *Strange Adventures* 214 (DC Comics, September–October 1968).

8 Questioning Authority

1. "No Evil Shall Escape My Sight," *Green Lantern* 76 (DC Comics, April 1970).

2. Neal Adams, "An Interview with Neal Adams," interviewed by Gary Groth, *Comics Journal* 43 (December 1978): 50; Dennis O'Neil, "Green Thoughts," *Hard-*

Traveling Heroes: The Green Lantern/Green Arrow Collection (New York: DC Comics, 1992), vol. 1; Barry Marx, ed., "Denny O'Neil," *Fifty Who Made DC Great* (New York: DC Comics, 1985).

3. "No Evil Shall Escape My Sight," *Green Lantern* 76 (DC Comics, April 1970); "Journey to Desolation," *Green Lantern* 77 (DC Comics, June 1970); "A Kind of Loving, a Way of Death," *Green Lantern* 78 (DC Comics, July 1970); "Ulysses Star Is Still Alive," *Green Lantern* 79 (DC Comics, September 1970).

4. Saul Braun, "Shazam! Here Comes Captain Relevant," *New York Times Magazine*, 2 May 1971, 32–55; Richard J. Howe, "Updating Superman: Comic Book Heroes Are Being Modernized," *Wall Street Journal*, 15 April 1970; "Comic Realities," *Newsweek*, 23 November 1970, 98; O'Neil, "Green Thoughts."

5. James T. Patterson, *Grand Expectations: The United States, 1945–1974* (New York: Oxford University Press, 1996), 671–72.

6. See George Lipsitz, "Who'll Stop the Rain: Youth Culture and Social Crises," in David Farber, ed., *The Sixties: From Memory to History* (Chapel Hill: University of North Carolina Press, 1994), 206–34; Presley recorded "In the Ghetto," Darin wrote and recorded the antiwar "Simple Song of Freedom," and Paul Revere and the Raiders had a hit with the socially conscious "Indian Reservation"; see also John Sinclair, "Rock and Roll Is a Weapon of Cultural Revolution," reprinted in Alexander Bloom with Wini Breines, eds., *Takin' It to the Streets: A Sixties Reader* (New York: Oxford University Press, 1995), 301.

7. *Wall Street Journal*, 25 August 1967; Les Daniels, *Marvel: Five Fabulous Decades of the World's Greatest Comics* (New York: Harry N. Abrams, 1991), 139–40.

8. Daniels, *Marvel*, 139.

9. Frank Zappa and the Mothers of Invention, *We're Only in It for the Money*, advertisement in *Marvel Tales* 13 (Marvel Comics, March 1968); *Rolling Stone*, 30 September 1971.

10. "Point of No Return," *The Amazing Spider-Man* 69 (Marvel Comics, February 1969); "Spider-Man Wanted," *The Amazing Spider-Man* 70 (Marvel Comics, March 1969); "On the Side of . . . the Evil Inhumans," *The Incredible Hulk* 120 (Marvel Comics, October 1969).

11. "The Origin of the Silver Surfer," *The Silver Surfer* 1 (Marvel Comics, August 1968).

12. Stan Lee, "Stan's Soapbox," *The Fantastic Four* 107 (Marvel Comics, February 1971); Stan Lee, "Stan Lee," interviewed by Darrel L. Boatz, *Comics Interview* 64 (1988): 8.

13. Will Jacobs and Gerard Jones, *The Comic Book Heroes: From the Silver Age to the Present* (New York: Crown Publishers, 1985), 151–54; O'Neil, "Green Thoughts"; Jennete Kahn, "In Tribute to the Publication of a Rare Masterpiece," *Super Friends* 5 (DC Comics, June 1977); "Carnival of the Cursed," *Batman* 224 (DC Comics, August 1970); "The Demon of Gothos Mansion," *Batman* 228 (DC Comics, December 1970).

14. Braun, "Shazam," 32–55; Howe, "Updating Superman," 1; "Comic Realities," 98.

15. Dennis O'Neil, "War and Peace with Denny O'Neil," interviewed by Gary Groth, *Comics Journal* 66 (September 1981): 57; Roy Thomas, "Roy Thomas," interviewed by Lou Mougin, *Comics Interview* 66 (1989): 5–32; Steve Gerber, "An Interview with Steve Gerber," interviewed by Gary Groth, *Comics Journal* 41 (August 1978): 31–32; Don McGregor, "The Gene Colan Interview," *Comics Scene* 4 (July 1982): 42.

16. "Crisis on Campus," *The Amazing Spider-Man* 68 (Marvel Comics, January

1969); "Mission: Crush the Kingpin," *The Amazing Spider-Man* 69 (Marvel Comics, February 1969); "Spider-Man Wanted," *The Amazing Spider-Man* 70 (Marvel Comics, March 1969).

17. "Take-Over of Paradise," and "Danger Comes A-Looking," *Batman* 230 (DC Comics, March 1971); "Grounded," *Batman* 231 (DC Comics, May 1971); "Vengeance for a Cop," *Batman* 234 (DC Comics, August 1971).

18. "And Who Shall Mourn for Him?" *The Silver Surfer* 5 (Marvel Comics, April 1969); "A Titan Stalks the Tenements," *The Incredible Hulk* 131 (Marvel Comics, September 1970); "Crisis on Campus," *The Amazing Spider-Man* 68 (Marvel Comics, January 1969); "Spider-Man Wanted," *The Amazing Spider-Man* 70 (Marvel Comics, March 1969).

19. "The Coming of . . . the Falcon," *Captain America* 117 (Marvel Comics, September 1969); "The Badge and the Betrayal," *Captain America* 139 (Marvel Comics, July 1971); "Power to the People," *Captain America* 143 (Marvel Comics, November 1971).

20. "A Life on the Line," *Daredevil* 69 (Marvel Comics, October 1970); see also "Pursue the Panther," *The Avengers* 74 (Marvel Comics, March 1970), in which a hate group called the Sons of the Serpent try to incite a race war between African Americans and white people.

21. "To Smash the Spider," *The Amazing Spider-Man* 91 (Marvel Comics, December 1970); "When Iceman Attacks," *The Amazing Spider-Man* 92 (Marvel Comics, January 1971).

22. "The Tribune," *Daredevil* 70 (Marvel Comics, November 1970); "Even an Immortal Can Die," *Green Lantern* 80 (DC Comics, October 1970).

23. Stan Lee, *The Amazing Spider-Man* (New York: Simon and Schuster, 1979), 9; "And Now the Goblin," *The Amazing Spider-Man* 96 (Marvel Comics, May 1971).

24. "And Now the Goblin," *The Amazing Spider-Man* 96 (Marvel Comics, May 1971); "In the Grip of the Goblin," *The Amazing Spider-Man* 97 (Marvel Comics, June 1971); "The Goblin's Last Gasp," *The Amazing Spider-Man* 98 (Marvel Comics, July 1971).

25. Braun, "Shazam," 46.

26. Ed Summer, "The Comics Code, 20 Years of Self-Strangulation?" *Inside Comics* 3 (Fall 1974): 25; Roy Thomas, "Waiter, There's a Werewolf in My Soup," *Giant-Size Werewolf by Night* 1 (Marvel Comics, July 1974); Lee, "Stan Lee," 18; Comics Magazine Association of America, *Code of the Comics Magazine Association of America* (New York: Comics Magazine Association of America, 1971), reprinted in Amy Kiste Nyberg, *Seal of Approval: The History of the Comics Code* (Jackson: University Press of Mississippi, 1998), 170–74; Nyberg, *Seal of Approval*, 140–43.

27. "Snowbirds Don't Fly," *Green Lantern* 85 (DC Comics, August–September 1971).

28. "The Spider's Web," *The Amazing Spider-Man* 70 (Marvel Comics, March 1969); "The Schemer," *The Amazing Spider-Man* 83 (Marvel Comics, April 1970); "Vengeance from Viet Nam," *The Amazing Spider-Man* 108 (Marvel Comics, May 1972).

29. "From the Conflict . . . Death," *Iron Man* 22 (Marvel Comics, February 1970); "This Doomed Land, This Doomed Sea," *Iron Man* 23 (Marvel Comics, March 1970); "The Fury of the Firebrand," *Iron Man* 25 (Marvel Comics, May 1970).

30. "Sock It to Shell-Head," *Iron Man* 31 (Marvel Comics, November 1970); "Sock It to Shell-Head," *Iron Man* 33 (Marvel Comics, January 1971); "Sock It to Shell-Head," *Iron Man* 35 (Marvel Comics, March 1971); "Sock It to Shell-Head," *Iron Man* 38 (Marvel Comics, June 1971).

31. "When Demons Wail," *Iron Man* 42 (Marvel Comics, October 1971); "Menace at Large," *Iron Man* 46 (Marvel Comics, May 1972); "Why Must There Be an Iron Man?" *Iron Man* 47 (Marvel Comics, June 1972); "Deathplay," *Iron Man* 50 (Marvel Comics, September 1972).

32. "Long Time Gone," *Iron Man* 78 (Marvel Comics, September 1975).

33. "Why Must There Be an Iron Man?" *Iron Man* 47 (Marvel Comics, June 1972); "Must There Be a Superman?" *Superman* 247 (DC Comics, February 1972).

34. "Comes the Hangman," *Werewolf by Night* 11 (Marvel Comics, November 1973); "Weremail by Night," *Werewolf by Night* 14 (Marvel Comics, February 1974); "Weremail by Night," *Werewolf by Night* 15 (Marvel Comics, March 1974); a deranged right-wing crusader also appears as a villain in "The Crusader Syndrome," *The Fantastic Four* 164 (Marvel Comics, November 1975).

35. "Mails of Suspense," *Tales of Suspense* 71 (Marvel Comics, November 1965); "Let's Rap with Cap," *Captain America* 110 (Marvel Comics, February 1969); "Let's Rap with Cap," *Captain America* 113 (Marvel Comics, May 1969); "Let's Rap with Cap," *Captain America* 116 (Marvel Comics, August 1969); "Let's Rap with Cap," *Captain America* 142 (Marvel Comics, October 1971).

36. Steve Englehart, "Steve Englehart in Transition: An Interview with Steve Englehart," interviewed by Ralph Macchio, *Comics Journal* 63 (May 1981): 281; Ronald Levitt Lanyi, "Comic Books and Authority: An Interview with 'Stainless Steve' Englehart," *Journal of Popular Culture* 18 (fall 1984): 144.

37. "When a Legend Dies," *Captain America* 169 (Marvel Comics, January 1974); "Before the Dawn," *Captain America* 175 (Marvel Comics, July 1974); "Captain America Must Die," *Captain America* 176 (Marvel Comics, August 1974); "The Coming of the Nomad," *Captain America* 180 (Marvel Comics, December 1974); "Nomad: No More," *Captain America* 183 (Marvel Comics, March 1975).

38. "Sock It to Shell-Head," *Iron Man* 36 (Marvel Comics, April 1971); Stan Lee, "Stan Lee's Soapbox," *Iron Man* 36 (Marvel Comics, April 1971); Dick Giordano, "Brushes and Blue Pencils: An Interview with Dick Giordano," interviewed by Gary Groth, *Comics Journal* 62 (March 1981): 64. For examples of Gerber's satirical style, see "World Gone Sane," *The Defenders Annual* 1 (Marvel Comics, 1976); and "Open Season," *Howard the Duck* 8 (Marvel Comics, January 1977); for examples of Mantlo's social commentary, see "Like a Tiger in the Night," *The Spectacular Spider-Man* 9 (Marvel Comics, August 1977), and "Brother Power, Sister Sun," *The Spectacular Spider-Man* 12 (Marvel Comics, November 1977).

39. Daniels, *Marvel*, 158; "Out of Hell—a Hero," *Luke Cage, Hero for Hire* 1 (Marvel Comics, June 1972); Jacobs and Jones, *The Comic Book Heroes*, 166.

40. *Black Goliath* 1 (Marvel Comics, February 1976); *Black Lightning* 1 (DC Comics, April 1977); "Like a Tiger in the Night," *The Spectacular Spider-Man* 9 (Marvel Comics, August 1977); *Red Wolf* 1 (Marvel Comics, May 1972); "Second Genesis," *Giant-Size X-Men* 1 (Marvel Comics, summer 1975); "War Hunt," *The X-Men* 95 (Marvel Comics, October 1975); *Master of Kung Fu* 17 (Marvel Comics, April 1974).

41. Dwight Decker, "Doc's Bookshelf," *Comics Journal* 37 (December 1977): 57; Roy Thomas, quoted in Daniels, *Marvel*, 161.

42. Stan Lee, *The Superhero Women* (New York: Simon and Schuster, 1977), 7.

43. "Thundra and Lightning," *The Fantastic Four* 151 (Marvel Comics, October 1974); "The Man-Killer," *Marvel Team-Up* 8 (Marvel Comics, April 1973); "Come on in, the Revolution's Fine," *The Avengers* 83 (Marvel Comics, December 1970).

44. Gloria Steinem, introduction, *Wonder Woman* (New York: Holt, Rinehart, and Winston, 1972); Trina Robbins, *The Great Women Superheroes* (Northampton,

Mass.: Kitchen Sink Press, 1996), 118–19; Jacobs and Jones, *The Comic Book Heroes*, 138; *New York Times*, 19 October 1972.

45. "Marvel Bullpen Bulletins," *Werewolf by Night* 2 (Marvel Comics, November 1972); "The Sahara Connection," *Shanna the She-Devil* 1 (Marvel Comics, December 1972); "The Secret of Sea-Cliff Manor," *Night Nurse* 4 (Marvel Comics, May 1973), "Beware the Claws of the Cat," *The Cat* 1 (Marvel Comics, November 1972).

46. Lee, *Superhero Women*; Roy Thomas, quoted in Daniels, *Marvel*, 161.

47. See David P. Szatmary, *Rockin' in Time: A Social History of Rock-and-Roll* (Upper Saddle River, N.J.: Prentice Hall, 1996), 192–220; and Christopher Lasch, *The Culture of Narcissism: American Life in an Age of Diminishing Expectations* (New York: W. W. Norton, 1978).

48. John Fiske, "The Cultural Capital of Fandom," in Lisa A. Lewis, ed., *The Adoring Audience: Fan Culture and Popular Media* (London: Routledge, 1992), 30; Jeffrey A. Brown, "Comic Book Fandom and Cultural Capital," *Journal of Popular Culture* 30, no. 4 (spring 1997): 13–31.

49. Thomas, "Roy Thomas," 9; Roy Thomas, "Fifteen Years at Marvel: Interview with Roy Thomas," interviewed by Rob Gustaveson, *Comics Journal* 61 (January 1981), 76–79; Jacobs and Jones, *The Comic Book Heroes*, 140–41; Matthew Pustz, *Comic Book Culture: Fanboys and True Believers* (Jackson: University Press of Mississippi, 1999).

50. "ComicCon," *New Yorker*, 21 August 1965, 23–24; Dwight Decker, "Dilemma of the Adult Fan," *Comics Journal* 32 (January 1977): 11; Gary Groth, "Editorial," *Nostalgia Journal* 27 (August 1976): 2–6; Gary Groth, "Punch Drunk Pap," *Comics Journal* 39 (April 1978): 46; Kim Thompson, "Spider-Woman: Incest in the Marvel Family," *Comics Journal* 39 (April 1978): 51–52; Thomas, "Fifteen Years at Marvel," 76; "International Fandom Inflation Control Club," *Nostalgia Journal* 30 (November 1976): 18.

9 Direct to the Fans

1. *Wall Street Journal*, 13 June 1991; Randall Smith, "Can Perelman's Future IPOs Be as Good as Marvel's?" *Wall Street Journal*, 24 October 1991.

2. Stan Lee, "Stan's Soapbox," *Daredevil* 69 (Marvel Comics, October 1970).

3. Bernie Krigstein, "Bernie Krigstein," interview, *Squa Tront* 6 (1975): 22; Jack Kirby, "Jack Kirby," interviewed by Gary Groth, *Comics Journal* 134 (February 1990): 78.

4. Doug Murray, "Flacks and Hacks at ACBA," *Inside Comics* 1 (spring 1974): 26–28; Gary Groth, "The Comics Guild," *Comics Journal* 42 (October 1978): 17; Neal Adams, "Neal Adams," interviewed by Paul Power, *Comics Interview* 91 (1991): 39.

5. Murray, "Flacks and Hacks at ACBA," 26–28.

6. Doug Murray, "The Dirty Dozen," *Inside Comics* 3 (fall 1974), 10–13; Marshall Rogers, "From Detective to Detectives Inc.: An Interview with Marshall Rogers," interviewed by Gary Groth, *Comics Journal* 54 (March 1980): 62–67; Marv Wolfman, "Marv Wolfman," interviewed by Heidi MacDonald, *Comics Journal* 100 (July 1985): 171; Groth, "The Comics Guild," 17–18.

7. Rogers, "An Interview," 68; Steve Gerber, "An Interview with Steve Gerber," interviewed by Gary Groth, *Comics Journal* 41 (August 1978): 32–41; Neal Adams, "An Interview with Neal Adams," interviewed by Gary Groth, *Comics Journal* 43 (December 1978): 45; Ronald Levitt Lanyi, "Comic Books and Authority: An Interview with 'Stainless Steve' Englehart," *Journal of Popular Culture* 18 (fall 1984): 146.

8. Groth, "The Comics Guild," 15; Roy Thomas, "Roy Thomas at Creation," interviewed by Adam Malin, *Comics Journal* 71 (March 1982): 94.

9. Groth, "The Comics Guild," 15.

10. Ibid., 17–32; Gary Groth, ed., "Birth of the Guild, May 7, 1978," *Comics Journal* 42 (October 1978): 22–26.

11. Roy Thomas, "Thomas on ERB and *The Journal*," *Comics Journal* 40 (June 1978): 16; Marv Wolfman, "An Interview with Marv Wolfman," interviewed by Kim Thompson, *Comics Journal* 44 (January 1979): 41; "The Ever-Rising Cost of Comics," *Comics Journal* 38 (February 1978): 10; Les Daniels, *Marvel: Five Fabulous Decades of the World's Greatest Comics* (New York: Harry N. Abrams, 1991), 173; Dick Giordano, "An Interview with Dick Giordano," interviewed by Gary Groth, *Comics Journal* 62 (March 1981): 63; Richard Greenberger, "Marvel Turns 20," *Comics Scene* 1 (January 1982): 15.

12. Jenette Kahn, "Whatever Happened to . . . ?" *The Metal Men* 54 (DC Comics, November 1977); Daniels, *Marvel*, 173; "The DC Implosion," *Comics Journal* 41 (August 1978): 5; Murray, "The Dirty Dozen," 10; "Newswatch," *Comics Journal* 38 (February 1978): 5.

13. Stan Lee, "Stan's Soapbox," *The Amazing Spider-Man* 75 (Marvel Comics, August 1969); "The Spider's Web," *The Amazing Spider-Man* 133 (Marvel Comics, June 1974); "Marvel Bullpen Bulletins," *Iron Man* 91 (Marvel Comics, October 1976).

14. "The Ever-Rising Cost of Comics," 9; "Newswatch," *Comics Journal* 38 (February 1978): 8–9; "The DC Implosion," 5; Paul Levitz, "An Interview with DC's Boy Wonder Paul Levitz," interviewed by Jay Zilber, *Comics Journal* 39 (April 1978): 28–31; Daniels, *Marvel*, 154; Stan Lee, "Stan the Man Raps with Marvel Maniacs at James Madison University," *Comics Journal* 42 (October 1978): 55; "Newswatch," *Comics Journal* 36 (August 1977): 5; "KISS Scores, Beatles Bomb," *Comics Journal* 45 (March 1979): 15.

15. Jeffrey H. Wasserman, "Funnybook Finances," *Comics Journal* 41 (August 1978): 49; Susan Magolis, "Marvel Comics Is About to Let Loose Its Whole Menagerie of Superheroes and Villains on British Soil," *Wall Street Journal*, 30 July 1973; "Marvel U.K. Puts Fans in Charge," *Comics Journal* 44 (January 1979): 12; Barry Marx, ed., "The Licensing Company of America," *Fifty Who Made DC Great* (New York: DC Comics, 1985), 36; Dick Giordano, "An Interview," 48; Mike Gold, "Attack and Counter-Attack," *Comics Journal* 39 (April 1978): 18–19; Daniels, *Marvel*, 181.

16. Daniels, *Marvel*, 173–77; Jim Shooter, "An Interview with Jim Shooter," interviewed by Gary Groth, *Comics Journal* 60 (November 1980), 56–83; N. R. Kleinfield, "Superheroes' Creators Wrangle," *New York Times*, 3 October 1979, 25–26; "Magazine Line Reorganized; New Editor Hired," *Comics Journal* 50 (October 1979): 9; Kim Thompson, "Roy Thomas Leaves Marvel," *Comics Journal* 56 (June 1980): 9–12; Roy Thomas, "Fifteen Years at Marvel: Interview with Roy Thomas," interviewed by Rob Gustaveson, *Comics Journal* 61 (January 1981): 85–98; Gene Colan, "Gene Colan," interviewed by Lou Mougin, *Comics Interview* 59 (1988): 29.

17. Philip S. Gutis, "The Real Wonder Woman," *San Francisco Chronicle*, 25 January 1985, 30–31; Jenette Kahn, "Jenette Kahn," interviewed by Stan Timmons, *Comics Journal* 37 (December 1977): 54; Susan K. Reed, "Zap! Pow! Shazam!" *Savvy*, January 1984, 70–73; Gil Kane, "An Interview with Gil Kane," interviewed by Gary Groth, *Comics Journal* 38 (February 1978): 36.

18. Marx, ed., "Phil Seuling" and "Bud Plant," *Fifty Who Made DC Great* (New

York: DC Comics, 1985), 46–47; Mike Friedrich, "Reaching for the Stars with Mike Friedrich," interviewed by Kim Thompson, *Comics Journal* 71 (March 1982): 85; "The Direct Sales Boom," *Comics Journal* 64 (July 1981): 7.

19. Mike Friedrich, "And Now the Good News: Mass-Market Comics Stores," *Comics Journal* 132 (November 1989): 119; Milton Griepp, "Milton Griepp," interviewed by Mark Borax, *Comics Interview* 43 (1987): 43–51; Roy Furchgott, "A Mild-Mannered Ex-Postman by Day," *Business Week*, 8 September 1997, 92–94; "Comic Books Regain Their Readership—and Outlets," *Publishers Weekly*, 6 December 1985, 34.

20. "The Direct Sales Boom," *Comics Journal* 64 (July 1981): 7; "Marvel Focuses on Direct Sales," *Comics Journal* 59 (October 1980): 11; Paul Levitz, "The Triumph of Comics Fandom," *Comics Scene* 1 (January 1982): 63–65; "Archie Comics Cuts Back, Revamps Line," *Comics Journal* 71 (March 1982): 13; "Gold Key Comics Line Discontinued," *Comics Journal* 53 (winter 1980): 17; "Charlton Goes Down for the Count," *Comics Journal* 103 (November 1985): 10–11; Frank Miller, "The Price," *Comics Scene* 3 (May 1982): 40; Mark Evanier, "This Business of Comics: An Interview with Mark Evanier," interviewed by Ken Jones, *Comics Journal* 113 (December 1986): 87; Gary Groth, "Editorial," *Comics Journal* 83 (August 1983): 6.

21. Kahn, "Jenette Kahn," 54; Gutis, "The Real Wonder Woman," 31; "DC Creates New Royalties System for Freelancers," *Comics Journal* 69 (December 1981): 16–17; "Marvel Announces Royalties Program," *Comics Journal* 70 (January 1982): 10–11; Jim Galton, "Jim Galton," interviewed by David Anthony Kraft, *Comics Interview* 1 (February 1983): 60–61.

22. "Comics Contracts: What the Various Companies Offer," *Comics Journal* 113 (December 1986): 19–23; "New Contracts at DC," *Comics Journal* 125 (October 1988): 11–13; Miller, "The Price," 40; Thomas, "Roy Thomas at Creation," 94; Dennis O'Neil, "Denny O'Neil," interviewed by Lee Wochner, *Comics Journal* 100 (July 1985): 124; Neal Adams, "Neal Adams," interviewed by Gary Groth, *Comics Journal* 100 (July 1985): 78; Steve Englehart, "Steve Englehart," interviewed by Peter Sanderson, *Comics Journal* 100 (July 1985): 90; Steve Gerber, "Steve Gerber," interview, *Comics Interview* 1 (February 1983): 25; "Shooter Speaks Out on Kirby's Art," *Comics Journal* 104 (January 1986): 9.

23. Daniels, *Marvel*, 168; "Second Genesis," *Giant-Size X-Men* 1 (Marvel Comics, summer 1975).

24. Chris Claremont, "Chris Claremont," interviewed by Margaret O'Connel and Gary Groth, *Comics Journal* 50 (October 1979): 57; Chris Claremont, "All They Have to Lose Is a Cog in the Wheel," interviewed by Kim Thompson, *Comics Journal* 152 (August 1992): 84; most of the *X-Men* issues published between 1975 and 1981 are serialized in *The Essential X-Men* (New York: Marvel Entertainment, 1996) and *The Uncanny X-Men* (New York: Marvel Comics, 1984).

25. Peter Sanderson, "Wolverine: the Evolution of a Character," *The Incredible Hulk and Wolverine* 1 (Marvel Comics, October 1986); *Wolverine* (New York: Marvel Comics Group, 1984); *The Essential Wolverine*, vol. 1 (New York: Marvel Entertainment, 1996); John Byrne, "John Byrne," interviewed by Mitch Itkowitz, J. Michael Catron, Peter Sanderson, and Ed Via, *Comics Journal* 57 (summer 1980): 68.

26. Lili Wright, "The Man Who Energizes the Hulk," *New York Times*, 7 May 1989; Byrne, "John Byrne," 63–82; John Byrne, "On Creators' Rights," *Comics Scene* 2 (March 1982): 57; John Byrne, "John Byrne," interviewed by Jim Salicrup, *Comics Interview* 25 (August 1985): 93; "Shooter Speaks Out on Kirby's Art," 9.

27. Wright, "The Man Who Energizes the Hulk"; *Man of Steel* (New York: DC Comics, 1987).

28. John Byrne, "John Byrne," interviewed by Patrick Daniel O'Neill, *Comics Interview* 86 (1990): 7.

29. Frank Miller, "Frank Miller: A Talk with the Writer-Artist of Daredevil," interviewed by Dwight R. Decker, *Comics Journal* 70 (January 1982): 69–88; some of Miller's early work on *Daredevil* is reprinted in *Daredevil: The Elektra Saga* (New York: Marvel Comics, 1989).

30. See for examples, *Daredevil: The Elektra Saga;* "Last Hand," *Daredevil* 181 (Marvel Comics, April 1982); Daniels, *Marvel,* 188–89; and "Good Guys Wear Red," *Daredevil* 184 (Marvel Comics, July 1982); Miller's popular 1985–86 work on *Daredevil* is reprinted in *Daredevil: Born Again* (New York: Marvel Entertainment, 1989); "Comics Code Rejects Daredevil Story," *Comics Journal* 57 (summer 1980); Miller, "Frank Miller," 88.

31. *Ronin* (New York: DC Comics, 1987); *Batman: The Dark Knight Returns* (New York: DC Comics, 1986); Frank Miller, "Frank Miller: Return of the Dark Knight," interviewed by Kim Thompson, *Comics Journal* 101 (August 1985); Lloyd Rose, "Comic Books for Grown-Ups," *Atlantic,* August 1986, 78; Mikail Gilmore, "Comic Genius: Frank Miller's *The Dark Knight Returns,*" *Rolling Stone,* 27 March 1986, 56–58.

32. "State of the Union, Part One," *American Flagg* 7 (First Comics, April 1984); "State of the Union, Part Two," *American Flagg* 8 (First Comics, May 1984); Will Jacobs and Gerard Jones, *The Comic Book Heroes: From the Silver Age to the Present* (New York: Crown Publishers, 1985), 277–79; Howard Chaykin, "I Have a Hard Time with Vigilantes: An Interview with Howard Chaykin," interviewed by Marilyn Bethke, *Comics Journal* 109 (July 1986): 84.

33. Rose, "Comic Books for Grown-Ups," 80.

34. Alan Moore, "Watchmen Round Table: Moore and Gibbons," interviewed by Martin Skidmore, *Comics Interview* 65 (1988): 17; "A Dream of Flying," *Miracleman* 1 (Eclipse Comics, August 1985); "Dragons," *Miracleman* 2 (Eclipse Comics, October 1985).

35. *The Watchmen* (New York: DC Comics, 1987).

36. Ibid.; Alan Moore, interviewed in Ingio Silva, prod., Alejandro Vallyo, dir., *The History of the Comics* (Ingio Silva Productions), vol. 4, 1987; *The Watchmen.*

37. "The Abyss Gazes Also," *The Watchmen* 6 (DC Comics, February 1987).

38. Ibid.

39. Moore, "Watchmen Round Table," 7.

40. *Batman: The Killing Joke* (New York: DC Comics, 1988); Moore, "Watchmen Round Table," 19; "DC Ranks #1 in Direct Sales Comic Market Share," *DC News,* 20 August 1987; Alan Moore, "Mainstream Comics Have at Best, Tenuous Virtues," interviewed by Gary Groth, *Comics Journal* 152 (August 1992): 89–100.

41. "The Punisher Strikes Twice," *The Amazing Spider-Man* 129 (Marvel Comics, February 1974); "Child's Play," *Daredevil* 183 (Marvel Comics, June 1982); "Good Guys Wear Red," *Daredevil* 184 (Marvel Comics, July 1982); *The Punisher* (New York: Marvel Entertainment, 1988); Mike Baron, "Mike Baron," interview, *Comics Interview* (1988): 6.

42. *Green Arrow: The Longbow Hunters* (New York: DC Comics, 1989); "Hunter's Moon," *Green Arrow* 1 (DC Comics, February 1988); "The Trial of Oliver Queen," *Green Arrow* 20 (DC Comics, July 1989).

43. "Original Sin," *The Spectacular Spider-Man* 107 (Marvel Comics, October 1985); "Life's Blood," *Ghost Rider* 1 (Marvel Comics, May 1990).

44. "Excerpts from the Report on Violence in Comics of the National Coali-

tion on Television Violence," *Comics Journal* 133 (December 1989): 67–73; Dick Giordano, "Dick Giordano," interviewed by Gary Groth, *Comics Journal* 119 (January 1988): 71.

45. *Marvel Super Heroes Secret Wars* 1–12 (Marvel Comics, May 1984–April 1985); *Secret Wars II* 1–9 (Marvel Comics, July 1985–March 1986); *Super Powers* 1–6 (DC Comics, July 1984–February 1986); *Crisis on Infinite Earths* 1–12 (DC Comics, April 1985–March 1986); Furchgott, "A Mild-Mannered Ex-Postman," 94; Floyd Norris, "Boom in Comic Books Lifts New Marvel Stock Offering," *New York Times*, 15 July 1991.

46. "The Marvel Guide to Collecting Comics," insert in *The Amazing Spider-Man* 234 (Marvel Comics, November 1982); Len Wein, "Len Wein," interviewed by Robert Greenberger, *Comics Journal* 100 (July 1985): 163; Milton Griepp and John Davis, "Speculating in New Issues," *Retailers "How-to . . ." Manual* (New York: DC Comics, 1985); "Torment, Part One," *Spider-Man* 1 (Marvel Comics, August 1990); Smith, "Can Perelman's Future IPOs Be as Good," 2.

47. Kim Howard Johnson, "Crisis of Infinite Comics," *Comics Scene* 46 (July 1993): 10–14, 66; Gary Groth, "Comics: The New Culture of Illiteracy," *Comics Journal* 152 (August 1992): 3–6; Lisa Towle, "Zap! Pow! Profit from Appreciating Comics," *Money*, July 1988, 28.

48. For the most comprehensive list of comic book values see annual editions of Robert M. Overstreet, *Official Overstreet Comic Book Price Guide* (New York: House of Collectibles). Comic book values cited here are based on figures in the 1991 edition; Douglas C. McGile, "Turning Teenage Mutant Ninja Turtles into a Monster Hit," *New York Times*, 25 December 1988.

49. "Comic Books Regain Their Readership—and Outlets," 34–37; Lisa Towle, "What's New in the Comic Book Business," *New York Times*, 31 January 1988; Douglas Martin, "Can Superman Be Superseded by a Capeless Wonder?" *New York Times*, 12 January 1997, sec. 1, 36; "DC Raises Prices to 75 cents, Goes to Mondo Paper," *Comics Journal* 82 (July 1983): 11; Michael Lev, "Reaching beyond the Ghouls and Gore for Major Payoffs," *New York Times*, 17 February 1991.

Epilogue

1. Frank Rich, "Term Limit for the Man of Steel: Yes, It's Time for Him to Go," *New York Times*, 22 November 1992; "The State of the Industry 1992–93," *Comics Journal* 156 (February 1993): 10.

2. Deborah Shapley, "Creating Parallel Universes for Profit," *New York Times*, 30 September 1996; Douglas Martin, "Can Superman Be Superseded by a Capeless Wonder?" *New York Times*, 12 January 1997.

3. "Marvel Sells Stock, Breaks Sales Records," *Comics Journal* 143 (July 1991): 9–10; "Marvel 1991: The Biggest Gets Bigger," *Comics Journal* 147 (December 1991): 13–15; Floyd Norris, "Boom in Comic Books Lifts New Marvel Stock Offering," *New York Times*, 15 July 1991; *Wall Street Journal*, 22 April 1993; Jeffrey A. Trachtenberg, "Fleer Executives Get a Hefty Dowry in Marvel Nuptials," *Wall Street Journal*, 29 July 1992; David Leonhardt, "What Evil Lurks in the Heart of Ron?" *Business Week*, 20 January 1997, 44.

4. Jeffrey A. Trachtenberg, "Marvel Says Net in '94 to be Lower Than Expected," *Wall Street Journal*, 21 December 1994; *Wall Street Journal*, 17 August 1994; Shapley, "Creating Parallel Universes for Profit," 9; Leonhardt, "What Evil Lurks," 44; Laura Jereski and John Lippman, "Marvel Plans Expansion Despite Filing for Chapter 11, Perelman-Icahn Battle," *Wall Street Journal*, 30 December 1996; Andrew

E. Serwer, "The Dustup over Marvel," *Fortune*, 13 January 1997, 22; John Lippman, "Bam! Perelman Cedes Control of Marvel to Dissident Bondholders Led by Icahn," *Wall Street Journal*, 10 March 1997.

5. Advertisement for Marvel Comics in *Rolling Stone*, 5 March 1998.

6. "Stan Lee Media, Inc.," www.stanleemedia.com, 1999

Notes on Sources

Anyone interested in researching comic books is in for a lot of fun and a lot of headaches. The greatest obstacle is the dearth of substantial archival collections. With some notable exceptions, most university libraries have not seen fit to establish holdings in comic books. This, as William W. Savage Jr. noted in his bibliographic essay in *Comic Books and America, 1945–1954*, "suggests the low esteem in which most libraries have held comic books, despite the extremes to which they might be willing to go in order to preserve other significant but somehow more dignified ephemeral literature." Because the best and most complete collections are in private hands and generally inaccessible to researchers, Savage warned that "anyone interested in the study of comic books had best be prepared to become a collector; and . . . be prepared for inordinate expenditures of time and money." Fortunately, things are no longer quite so bleak as they were when Savage's book appeared in 1990. While it certainly helps to have one's own collection, it is quite possible to pursue extensive research into comic books within archives open to the public. As popular culture studies in general have become more "respectable," the sources available to researchers have become more accessible. A couple dozen university libraries now hold collections of comic books, several of which are very substantial, with holdings in excess of 10,000 issues.

Towering above all of these is the Comic Art Collection at Michigan State University. With a collection of more than 100,000 comic books, copies of virtually every book ever published about comic books, and a wide variety of clippings files, fan magazines, and other related items, it is the foremost archive for comic book research. Virtually every comic book cited in this study is held there. Especially indispensable among the Michigan State holdings is the Jerry Bails Microfilm Library of Comic Art, which contains more than 3,000 extremely rare comic books from the 1930s to the 1950s. Anyone interested in comic book studies is advised to begin by consulting the comprehensive Internet website for the Comic Art Collection's reading room index (www.lib.msu.edu/comics/rri/index.htm).

Should one wish to acquire a personal collection, the best place to start is the local comic book store. Besides their common display of current issues, most comic book stores have boxes of back issues for sale. While few of these contain very many copies predating 1970, comic books published since the early 1970s are often surprisingly affordable, especially if they are in poor physical condition. Robert M. Overstreet's *Official Overstreet Comic Book Price Guide* (New York: House of Collectibles) provides a comprehensive annual listing of virtually every comic book ever published with recommended prices for dealers and collectors.

Often it is possible to track down an older comic book story that has been reprinted in a more recent and far more affordable edition. The two largest current publishers, Marvel Comics and DC Comics, have published many volumes of reprints. Original Marvel comic books from the 1960s are anthologized in *Origins of Marvel Comics* (New York: Simon and Schuster, 1974), *Son of Origins of Marvel Comics* (New York: Simon and Schuster, 1975), *Bring on the Bad Guys* (New York: Simon and Schuster, 1975), and *The Superhero Women* (New York: Simon and Schuster, 1977), each of which includes commentary by Stan Lee. The multiple volumes in Marvel's *Essential* series reprint comprehensive black-and-white collections of early issues of its most popular comic books in an inexpensive and easily available format. A good place to start is with *The Essential Spider-Man* (New York: Marvel Comics, 1996). DC Comics has reprinted popular superhero stories from the 1930s to the 1990s in its *Greatest Stories Ever Told* series. The best of these are *The Greatest Superman Stories Ever Told* (New York: DC Comics, 1987), *The Greatest Batman Stories Ever Told* (New York: DC Comics, 1997), and *The Greatest Golden Age Stories Ever Told* (New York: DC Comics, 1990). Dennis O'Neil, ed., *Secret Origins of the Super DC Heroes* (New York: Warner Books, 1976) reprints the origin stories of DC's most popular heroes with commentary. Jules Feiffer, *The Great Comic Book Heroes* (New York: Dial Press, 1965) reprints a collection of stories from the 1930s and early 1940s with insightful and witty introductions by the author, a noted cartoonist. The original EC Comics have been reprinted for sale by Russ Cochran Publications both as standard retailing issues and in comprehensive hardcover collections.

Researchers ought to approach periodicals devoted to comic books with caution. Many of the articles in them are written by fans who either want to promote the products of major publishers or have a critical ax to grind. In any case, most of the material is preoccupied with current comic books and the collector's market. Sometimes, however, the fan magazines publish useful interviews with individuals associated with the comic book industry. The best of the fan magazines, because of their published interviews, are *Comics Journal* and *Comics Interview*. The former featured a wealth of revealing interviews in the late 1970s and 1980s, although its primary interest since the early 1990s has been with "alternative" comic books outside of the industry mainstream. A sporadically published fan magazine called *Squa Tront* was devoted entirely to an appreciation of EC Comics and provides interviews with creators who worked for the company. These and many other such periodicals are held in the Comic Art Collection at Michigan State University.

Scholars, and historians especially, will find much of the published work on comic books frustrating. Few books on the subject can truly claim to be scholarly, and fewer still pay much attention to historical context. Those interested in such context should begin with William W. Savage Jr., *Comic Books and America, 1945–1954* (Norman: University of Oklahoma Press, 1990), Martin Barker, *A Haunt of Fears: The Strange History of the British Horror Comics Campaign* (London: Pluto Press, 1984), and my essay, "The Vietnam War and Comic Books," in James S. Olson, ed., *The Vietnam War: Handbook of the Literature and Research* (Westport, Conn.: Greenwood Press, 1993). All three consider comic books within the broad political-cultural context that informed them.

For serious, although not historical, analyses of comic books as an art form, see Scott McCloud, *Understanding Comics* (Northampton, Mass.: Kitchen Sink Press, 1993), Robert C. Harvey, *The Art of the Comic Book: An Aesthetic History* (Jackson: University Press of Mississippi, 1996), and Joseph Witek, *Comic Books as History: The Narrative Art of Jack Jackson, Art Spiegelman, and Harvey Pekar* (Jackson: University Press of Mississippi, 1989). McCloud's book is the best study of the aesthetic vocabulary that comprises comic art. Harvey's work is exactly what the title implies, and Witek's study is a literary analysis of the work of several independent cartoonists working outside of the industry mainstream.

The best study of Fredric Wertham and juvenile delinquency in the 1950s is James B. Gilbert, *A Cycle of Outrage: America's Reaction to the Juvenile Delinquent in the 1950s* (New York: Oxford University Press, 1986). Although, by neglecting to consider the comic books themselves, Gilbert gives an incomplete analysis of the controversy. While it lacks important consideration of historical context, Amy Kiste Nyberg, *Seal of Approval: The History of the Comics Code* (Jackson: University Press of Mississippi, 1998) is a good survey of the efforts to control and censor comic books and the decisions that went into the institution and shaping of the Comics Code. Bruce Gorman, *Kefauver: A Political Biography* (New York: Oxford University Press, 1971) and William Howard Moore, *The Kefauver Committee and the Politics of Crime* (Columbia: University of Missouri Press, 1974) give some background on the government's investigations into juvenile delinquency that came to encompass the investigation of the comic book industry. For perspectives from critics of comic books, see Fredric Wertham, *Seduction of the Innocent* (New York: Rinehart, 1954) and Gershon Legman, *Love and Death: A Study in Censorship* (New York: Breaking Point, 1949).

Most of the books published on comic books are nonscholarly works written by fans and collectors or authors contracted by the comic book publishers. Scholars in all disciplines will be put off by the "gosh-wow!" style of these books, and many will find their general lack of footnotes or other documentary evidence exasperating. Sometimes these works make intriguing assertions but offer no evidence for scholars to trace. Nevertheless, a number of them are valuable for their encyclopedic information and, especially, for their generous amount of illustrations. The best of these are Mike Benton, *The Comic Book in America* (Dallas: Taylor Publishing, 1993), Mike Benton, *Superhero Comics of the Golden Age: The Illustrated History* (Dallas: Taylor Publishing, 1992), Les Daniels, *Marvel: Five Fabulous Decades of the World's Greatest Comics* (New York: Harry N. Abrams, 1991), Les Daniels, *DC Comics: Sixty Years of the World's Favorite Comic Book Heroes* (Boston: Little, Brown, and Co., 1995), Ron Goulart, *Over Fifty Years of American Comic Books* (Lincolnwood, Ill.: Mallard Press, 1991), Ron Goulart, *The Comic Book Reader's Companion* (New York: Harper Collins, 1993), Charles Phillips, *Archie: His First Fifty Years* (New York: Abbeville Press, 1991), and Will Jacobs and Gerard Jones, *The Comic Book Heroes* (New York: Crown Publishers, 1985). For a survey of women cartoonists and female superheroes, see Trina Robbins and Catherine Yronwode, *Women and the Comics* (Guerneville, Calif.: Eclipse Books, 1985) and Trina Robbins, *The Great Women Superheroes* (Northampton, Mass.: Kitchen Sink Press, 1996).

There are only a handful of biographies on comic book creators. The best of these are Frank Jacobs, *The Mad World of William M. Gaines* (Secaucus, N.J.: Lyle Stuart, 1972), Bob Kane with Tom Andrae, *Batman and Me: An Autobiography of Bob Kane* (Forestville, California:

Eclipse Books, 1989), and Joe Simon with Jim Simon, *The Comic Book Makers* (New York: Crestwood Publications, 1990). All contain interesting firsthand information and anecdotes about the first generation of comic book creators and their favorite superheroes and titles, but none, surprisingly, offer much insight into the creative process behind the stories themselves.

My analytic approach to popular culture borrowed from ideas in Robert Sklar, *Movie-Made America: A Cultural History of American Movies* (New York: Random House, 1975), John G. Cawelti, *Adventure, Mystery, and Romance* (Chicago: University of Chicago Press, 1976), Robert B. Ray, *A Certain Tendency of the Hollywood Cinema, 1930–1980* (Princeton: Princeton University Press, 1985), Richard Slotkin, *Gunfighter Nation: The Myth of the Frontier in Twentieth-Century America* (New York: Macmillan Publishing, 1992), John Fiske, *Understanding Popular Culture* (London: Routledge, 1991), Lawrence W. Levine, "The Folklore of Industrial Society: Popular Culture and Its Audiences," *American Historical Review* 99 (December 1992): 1369–99, George Lipsitz, *Time Passages: Collective Memory and American Popular Culture* (Minneapolis: University of Minnesota Press, 1990), and Michael Kammen, *American Culture, American Tastes: Social Change and the Twentieth Century* (New York: Alfred A. Knopf, 1999).

As an entertainment product marketed to young people, comic books must properly be considered within the broader context of youthful tastes and consumer culture. For insights into this context, see Matthew Pustz, *Comic Book Culture: Fanboys and True Believers* (Jackson: University Press of Mississippi, 1999), Grace Palladino, *Teenagers: An American History* (New York: Basic Books, 1996), Tom Englehardt, *The End of Victory Culture: Cold War America and the Disillusioning of a Generation* (New York: Harper Collins, 1995), Joe Austin and Michael Nevi Willard, eds., *Generations of Youth: Youth Cultures and History in Twentieth-Century America* (New York: New York University Press, 1998), Wini Breines, *Young, White, and Miserable: Growing Up Female in the Fifties* (Boston: Alfred A. Knopf, 1995), Gary Cross, *Kid's Stuff: Toys and the Changing World of American Childhood* (Cambridge: Harvard University Press, 1997), and Lisa A. Lewis, ed., *The Adoring Audience: Fan Culture and Popular Media* (London: Routledge, 1992).

For a good overview of the major developments in rock-and-roll music, see Charlie Gillett, *The Sound of the City: The Rise of Rock and Roll* (New York: Da Capo Press, 1996), David P. Szatmary, *Rockin' in Time: A Social History of Rock-and-Roll* (Upper Saddle River, N.J.: Prentice Hall, 1996) and Michael Erlewine, Vladimir Bogdanov, and Chris Woodstra, ed., *All Music Guide to Rock* (San Francisco: Miller Freeman Books, 1995). The latter, although a reference work, is also the most comprehensive and informative critical work on rock-and-roll. For contemporary perspectives on the critical transformation of youth culture in the late 1950s, see Eugene Gilbert, *Advertising and Marketing to Young People* (Pleasantville, N.Y.: Printers' Ink Books, 1957), Edgar Z. Friedenberg, *The Vanishing Adolescent* (New York: Dell Publishing, 1959), and Paul Goodman, *Growing Up Absurd: Problems of Youth in the Organized System* (New York: Random House, 1960).

Insights into the historical context of comic books came from many books and articles as well as from immersion into the popular films, television, and music of the periods under consideration. The most helpful books on the Great Depression and New Deal include Warren I. Susman, *Culture as History: The Transformation of American Society in the Twentieth Century* (New York: Pantheon Books, 1984), Alan Brinkley, *The End of Reform: New Deal Liberalism in Recession and War* (New York: Alfred A. Knopf, 1995), Richard A. Reiman, *The New Deal and American Youth: Ideas and Ideals in a Depression Decade* (Athens: University of Georgia Press, 1992), David W. Stowe, *Swing Changes: Big-Band Jazz in New Deal America* (Cambridge: Harvard University Press, 1994), and Lawrence W. Levine, "American Culture and the Great Depression," in *Yale Review* 74 (winter 1985): 196–223.

For the culture of World War II, see Lewis Erenberg and Susan E. Hirsch, eds., *The War in American Culture: Society and Consciousness during World War II* (Chicago: University of Chicago Press, 1996), John W. Dower, *War without Mercy: Race and Power in the Pacific War* (New York: Pantheon Books, 1986), William M. Tuttle, *Daddy's Gone to War: The Second World War in the Lives of America's Children* (New York: Oxford University Press, 1993), Clayton R. Koppes and Gregory D. Black, *Hollywood Goes to War: How Politics, Profits, and Propaganda Shaped World War II Movies* (New York: Free Press, 1987), and Michael C. C. Adams, *The Best War Ever: America and World War II* (Baltimore: Johns Hopkins University Press, 1994). Although the comic books of World War II support key arguments advanced in all of these books, the only author to make reference to them is Tuttle, who mentions them briefly.

For key insights into the culture of the postwar years and the 1950s, see David Halberstam, *The Fifties* (New York: Villard Press, 1993), Paul Boyer, *By the Bomb's Early Light: American Thought and Culture at the Dawn of the Atomic Age* (New York: Pantheon Books, 1985), Peter Biskind, *Seeing Is Believing: How Hollywood Taught Us to Stop Worrying and Love the Fifties* (New York: Pantheon Books, 1983), James T. Patterson, *Grand Expectations: The United States, 1945–1974* (New York: Oxford University Press, 1996), Stephen J. Whitfield, *The Culture of the Cold War*, 2d ed. (Baltimore: Johns Hopkins University Press, 1996), and Lary May, ed., *Recasting America: Culture and Politics in the Age of Cold War* (Chicago: University of Chicago Press, 1989). None of these works discusses comic books, although the article by Warren I. Susman with the assistance of Edward Griffin, "Did Success Spoil the United States," in *Recasting America* appropriately groups the crime comics of the postwar decade in amongst film noir and other representations of American cultural tension.

The interaction of youth culture, liberal politics, and social change in the 1960s is discussed at length in articles published in David Farber, ed., *The Sixties: From Memory to History* (Chapel Hill: University of North Carolina Press, 1994), especially George Lipsitz's "Who'll Stop the Rain: Youth Culture and Social Crises," Todd Gitlin, *The Sixties: Years of Hope, Days of Rage* (New York: Bantam Books, 1987), and Douglas T. Miller, *On Our Own: Americans in the Sixties* (Lexington, Mass.: D. C. Heath). The decline of political consciousness in post-1960s popular culture is explored in Christopher Lasch, *The Culture of Narcissism: American Life in an Age of Diminishing Expectations* (New York: W. W. Norton and Co., 1978), Edwin Shur, *The Awareness Trap: Self-Absorption Instead of Social Change* (New York: Quadrangle, 1976), and Daniel Yankelovich, *New Rules: Search for Self-Fulfillment in a World Turned Upside Down* (New York: Random House, 1981).

One final thought that researchers may or may not wish to consider is the matter of ambience. While scholarly writing is often done in silence or perhaps with classical or jazz music playing softly in the background, this work was most often prepared to a backing soundtrack of rock-and-roll from the 1950s to the 1990s, often of the trashiest and most nonsensical sort. While this may have distracted more than it helped, it did, I believe, set a mood appropriate for the consideration of an adolescent entertainment form. Such immersion into the guilty pleasures of popular culture may remind scholars in this field that in analyzing the creation of fun, we need not neglect the fun in what we study.

Index

Boldface numerals designate illustrations.